New Canadian Readings

# CITIES AND URBANIZATION

*Canadian Historical Perspectives*

3?7.? STE

New Canadian Readings

# CITIES AND URBANIZATION

## *Canadian Historical Perspectives*

Edited by
Gilbert A. Stelter

Copp Clark Pitman Ltd.
A Longman Company
Toronto

© Copp Clark Pitman Ltd., 1990

All rights reserved. No part of this work covered by the copyrights hereon may be reproduced or used in any forms or by any means—graphic, electronic, or mechanical—without the prior written permission of the publisher.

Any request for photocopying, recording, or taping, or for storing on information storage and retrieval systems of any part of this book shall be directed in writing to the Canadian Reprography Collective, 379 Adelaide Street West, Suite M1, Toronto, Ontario M5V 1S5.

**ISBN** 0-7730-4764-6

Editing: Melanie Sherwood

Cover: Toronto, Court and Church Streets, about 1950. From a sketch by the late Gordon Couling, OCA. Private collection, with the permission of the Couling estate. Effectively captured are the different scales of nineteenth and twentieth century city building.

Typesetting: Barbara G. Cholewa

Printing and binding: Alger Press Limited

**Canadian Cataloguing in Publication Data**

Main entry under title:

Cities and urbanization

Includes bibliographical references.

ISBN 0-7730-4764-6

1.Cities and towns—Canada—History.

2.Urbanization—Canada—History. 3.Sociology, Urban—Canada. I.Stelter, Gilbert A., 1933– .

HT127.C58 1990 307.76′0971 C90-093035-7

Copp Clark Pitman
2775 Matheson Blvd. East
Mississauga, Ontario
L4W 4P7

Associated Companies:
Longman Group Ltd., London
Longman Group Inc., New York
Longman Cheshire Pty., Melbourne
Longman Paul Pty., Auckland

Printed and bound in Canada

# FOREWORD

*New Canadian Readings* is an on-going series of inexpensive books intended to bring some of the best recent work by this country's scholars to the attention of students of Canada. Each volume consists of ten or more articles or book sections, carefully selected to present a fully formed thesis about some critical aspect of Canadian development. Where useful, public documents or even private letters and statistical materials may be used as well to convey a different and fresh perspective.

The authors of the readings selected for inclusion in this volume (and all the others in the series) are all first-rank scholars, those who are doing the hard research that is rapidly changing our understanding of this country. Quite deliberately, the references for each selection have been retained, thus making additional research as easy as possible.

Like the authors of the individual articles, the editors of each volume are also scholars of note, completely up-to-date in their areas of specialization and, as the introductions demonstrate, fully aware of the changing nature of the debates within their professions and genres of research. The list of additional readings provided by the editor of each volume will steer readers to materials that could not be included because of space limitations.

This series will continue into the foreseeable future, and the General Editor is pleased to invite suggestions for additional topics.

J.L. Granatstein
General Editor

# Contents

# INTRODUCTION

> A profound change in the character of Canadian society, and more important, in the lives of individual Canadians, is expressed in the cold statistics of city growth.[1]

The big city made a major impression on the consciousness of Canadians early in the twentieth century, but the source of this "profound change" remained, and remains, a rather vague process in most accounts. Urban growth and urbanization are said to have transformed society, but a good deal of confusion exists, even among those who specialize in urban studies, about how this growth and urbanization are related. Are they synonymous? And what about industrialization? We often mention it in the same breath to explain late nineteenth century economic development and social change. Do industrialization and urbanization depend on each other, or are they separate phenomena, capable of happening separately?

For the past two decades, scholars from a variety of disciplines have been fascinated with the "urban" dimension of life in Canada.[2] The result has been a virtual outpouring of publications, most of them dedicated to the kind of approach proposed by Oscar Handlin in 1963:

> However useful a general theory of the city may be, only the detailed tracing of an immense range of variables, in context, will illuminate the dynamics of the processes here outlined. We can readily enough associate such gross phenomena as the growth of population and the rise of the centralized state, as technological change and the development of modern industry, as the disruption of the traditional household and the decline of corporate life. But how these developments unfolded, what was the causal nexus among them, we shall only learn when we make out the interplay among them by focussing upon a city specifically in all its uniqueness.[3]

Handlin's position, and others like it, formed the basis for the development of the subfield of urban history in Canada. The city, not urbanization, was the principal subject of study. That this is still the case is illustrated by a recent editorial in the *Urban History Review*, the major Canadian publication in the field. The editor concluded that the articles in the journal exemplified "the belief that urbanization is merely an abstraction and that people make and remake cities."[4] It is not surprising, therefore, that the most popular form of urban history has been the city biography, in which the author can focus upon "a city specifically in all its uniqueness."

Whether this specific emphasis will ever illuminate the dynamics of the larger processes, as Handlin expected, is extremely doubtful, however. The study of individual urban places has simply not thrown much light on the large questions raised earlier, which is not to suggest that Canadian scholars are particularly dense or stubborn about these matters. Rather, the problem is more general and the solutions not obvious, for models and middle-level generalizations that might prove useful in integrating the myriad details about cities into some comprehensive pattern are "not yet up to the task," in the words of one observer.[5] In some respects the problem parallels the current concern of theoretical physicists who are trying to integrate macro-level theory (relativity) with the micro-level (quantum physics).[6]

If we propose to attempt to go beyond "what might be called the urban aspect of local history," as H.J. Dyos put it, "to an investigation of altogether broader historical processes and trends that completely transcend the life cycle and range of experience of particular communities,"[7] what are our options? We could begin, perhaps, with a clear idea of what it is we wish to understand and explain. We have a fairly clear idea of what happened, for instance. On an international scale, population has concentrated in a growing number of increasingly larger urban places until this urban population has become the majority of society's total population. We also have some good suggestions as to how this happened. In the modern era this process has been closely related to industrial technology and more general economic development. The mechanism for the process has usually been rural to urban migration or migration from abroad. We are less clear, however, about what it all means. Is it possible to show that changes in the quantity and scale of human settlements affected the nature of life in these places?

We may have to explore the immense body of theoretical literature on urbanization if we wish to make some sense out of the complexity of the process. This effort may not be for those who become faint of heart at the sight of sociological jargon or whose breath is taken away by vast, unsubstantiated generalizations.[8] But a growing body of theoretical and empirical work on European urbanization does offer some valuable indications on how we might proceed through this maze.[9] It has become obvious to most observers that the traditional definitions of urbanization have focussed too narrowly on only one aspect, the demographic, with its emphasis on population concentration and on an increase in the urban proportion of the population. Most scholars who begin with demographic concentration now also include a concern for the physical environments created by the process, the built city. A more suitable term for this aspect of urbanization, therefore, would be demographic/ecological, reflecting current thinking on the strong connection between population and environment.

Equally important is structural urbanization, which refers to the redistribution of population and functions among cities and towns in a developing urban system. A third aspect is closely related to the other two and involves the effects that urbanization has on the behaviour of people, hence, behavioural urbanization.

This three-headed definition attests to the complexity of the process, but it should enable us to be more precise in our discussions about the nature of urbanization. In the following pages, each of these aspects will be described in more detail, based on the theoretical literature. As well, these aspects will be related to the essays which have been reprinted in this volume in an effort to demonstrate how these can be read in the light of these large scale trends.

## Demographic/Ecological Urbanization

Much of the early work on the concept of urbanization emphasized the demographic aspects only. That is, authors thought about the process of population concentration resulting in an increase in the urban proportion of the population during the nineteenth century and about the deconcentration characteristic of suburbanization during the twentieth century. Critics who looked for "a picture of urbanization in which not only people, but also towns occupied a central place," suggested a broadened concept in which population would still be central.[10] Both a theoretical and empirical picture was provided by Eric Lampard who proposed a broadened definition of urbanization which went beyond population to include the environment, and the mediating factors of technology and social organization.[11] Lampard's approach encompasses not only concentrating population, but also the role of industrialization in this concentration, the city-building process in the technological sense (everything from transportation to buildings), and the deconcentration of population in the move to suburbanization. Each of these aspects of demographic/ecological urbanization deserves further elaboration.

The story of population concentration is a familiar one. Those scholars who begin with the origins of cities in the ancient world refer to "genuine urbanization" as something that happened only in the nineteenth and twentieth centuries. Thus, in 1800, about 3 per cent of the world's population lived in places of 5000 or more; by 1900, the proportion had risen to 13.6 per cent. This concentration into urban places took place on a massive scale first in the Netherlands and Great Britain, and later in the United States, Prussia, and Australasia. By 1921, it had reached about 80 per cent in Britain, a sort of top limit which signalled the virtual end of the concentration phase.[12] While Canada lagged behind Britain and the United States, it clearly had a level of urbanization higher than the world average as early as the mid-nineteenth century. Canada experienced a sharp "take-off" toward a higher level of urbanization in the 1870s and 1880s; by 1921, fully one-half of the population was considered by the Census Bureau to be living in urban places.[13]

A second element of demographic/ecological urbanization is clearly spelled out by Lampard: the concentration of population was closely associated "in time and place with industrialization of productive activities."[14] Certainly most informed observers in the nineteenth century "took it for granted that the unprecedented growth of towns was intimately bound up with the expansion of industry."[15] The Canadian experience seems to confirm this. For example, the establishment of new industrial towns in Nova Scotia was an example of this correlation, as L.D. McCann's article in this volume illustrates. Unfortunately the connection continued to hold true after the collapse of the manufacturing base in the 1920s, for industrial and population decline were virtually synonymous in places like New Glasgow and Trenton.

The transition from commercial to industrial city has been well documented in studies of Toronto, for example. Population concentration was at least partially due to the centralization and concentration of industrial capital which transformed the organization of production and the nature of work. In Toronto, for example, workers began to be gathered together into larger production units from the 1850s, as handicraft shops were consolidated in small manufactories, with increasing division of labour, and eventually into modern factories. Gregory Kealey has described how this shift took place in four areas—cabinetmaking, metallurgy, shoe manufacturing, and tobacco manufacturing. The modern technology of steam was introduced very unevenly; it was heavily used in machinery, foundries, and metalworking, but much less so in the clothing and shoe industries.[16] The centralization and concentration process was also apparent at a regional level as industrial production was increasingly located in Toronto at the expense of smaller manufacturing towns in Toronto's vicinity. This centrifugal pull of the major regional city was enhanced by an improved regional transportation system focussed on Toronto.[17]

Closely associated with industrialization is a third element of demographic/ecological urbanization—the city-building process. Cities as physical entities reflected this concentration of people and activities. The form and structure of these growing entities was determined by large-scale economic, political and social forces as well as by thousands of individual, community, institutional and corporate decisions.[18] The activity of city-building itself became one of society's most powerful engines of economic growth, as an increasing proportion of total national investment went into planning and development, building houses, public institutions, transportation infrastructures, and public utilities. The building of housing has not been studied extensively in Canada, but recent research by Michael Doucet and John Weaver suggests that residential building accounted for 50 to 65 per cent of total expenditures in construction in most years in the nineteenth and twentieth centuries.[19] In their article in this volume, Doucet and Weaver outline the activities of one real estate company in order to explain some of the major features of the building industry—the source of finance, building practices, land development, the source of designs, and sales and rental practices. These authors realize that their findings are localized, reflecting the character of the building industry, and that conclusions about the typicality of their data must await similar work on other places.

A fourth element of demographic/ecological urbanization involves a dissociation of the process from industrialization in the Western World in the twentieth century, leading to a new phenomenon—deconcentration of population. The strictly demographic trends of deconcentration become apparent on a large-scale in Canada soon after World War I, about the time that the Census Bureau described a majority of the country's population as urban. Since then the peripheries of cities have grown faster than the central cores.[20] The result has been a new metropolitan form, one that is increasingly diffuse and structurally complex, more multi-centred in terms of organization, with a larger spatial scale and considerably lower average population densities.[21] This demographic decentralization has not had the dramatic negative consequences so apparent in the United States, where depopulation and decaying inner cities have become common. The reasons for some of these differences have been attributed in a provocative study by John Mercer and Michael Goldberg, to differences in cultural values.[22]

The term we usually use for the deconcentration of cities—suburbanization—seems particularly appropriate for describing modern city-building activities. The expansion of cities beyond their central cores is a process as old as cities themselves, however. David Hanna's essay on Montreal's suburban expansion in the mid-nineteenth century is an example of this feature of urban growth prior to industrialization. As in later decades, this outward thrust reflected the desire of the "better classes" to move from the constricted, noisy, even dangerous older city to a more desirable location. The relationship between this early suburbanization and the massive movement of the twentieth century is ably outlined by Paul-André Linteau's general survey in this volume. Linteau's article is a useful reminder of the value of maintaining a balanced perspective on the process which relates the large-scale, international trends and the activities of thousands of individual actors in a particular time and place.

## Structural Urbanization

Some of the most important new work on the history of urbanization stresses the evolution of urban systems and changes in the structure of these systems. This aspect of urbanization is obviously closely related to demographic and ecological aspects, but it does incorporate several characteristics which tend to be overlooked in the approaches described previously. In general, an emphasis on structural urbanization recognizes the concentration of activities and organizations as well as that of population, and looks for patterns in the way urban places (as nodes of activities) are related to each other in hierarchic systems.[23] This involves the complex interplay between power and decision making, on the one hand, and the "timing of space," the temporal and spatial dimensions of this power, on the other hand. Charles Tilly has related this aspect of urbanization to the appearance and expansion of large-scale co-ordinated activities in a society, especially the operation of a centralized state, the rise of organized religion with a professional priesthood, factory production in an industrial system, and the supervision of long range marketing organizations.[24]

Several of the co-ordinated activities mentioned by Tilly occur long before the industrial and technological revolutions of the past two hundred years, suggesting that urbanization as a process can predate industrialization. Much of the scholarship on pre-modern societies supports this suggestion. Those who study the origins of urbanism (an urban way of life) in the ancient world have concluded that early cities were key elements of a major social transformation—from egalitarian, ascriptive, kin-structured societies to those which were socially stratified, politically organized, and territorially based.[25] For example, recent work on Mayan society now recognizes some system of formalized territorial organization based on a confederation of related cities. A hierarchical relationship within this confederation was publicly acknowledged and demonstrated by "emblem glyphs"—hieroglyphic symbols denoting the major city—which appeared on monuments in the smaller, subject places.[26]

The same kind of symbolic representation of a hierarchic urban structure appeared in late medieval Italy, where city-states such as Venice and Florence successfully dominated smaller rivals in their vicinity. In the case of the Venetian-dominated towns of Vicenza and Verona, for example, the Venetian emblem of St. Mark's lion was prominently displayed in their central squares. That these pre-modern urban hierarchies really amounted to urban systems has been effectively argued by Gilbert Rozman in his work on urban networks in China, Japan, and Russia. Rozman goes even further and suggests that mature urban networks were a necessary prerequisite for industrialization.[27] As a result of these new perspectives on urbanization, we are now in a position to see the process at full stretch, rather than just as a modern phenomenon. It therefore becomes possible to explore the changing significance of cities in society, from pre-modern times when they were the loci of political and religious power, to having become, in modern times, society itself.

The structural dimensions of urbanization can be related to Canadian history more clearly by discussing several levels of urban systems, including the early European system, the Canadian nation-state as a system, regions within the nation-state, and the lowest level, the city-centered region.[28] Each of these levels is intimately related to every other level, and changes in one affect the activity of others. The changing nature of the early European system is effectively described and analysed in Jan de Vries, *European Urbanization 1500–1800*. His concern is to understand the organizational innovations that increased the range of urban activities and thereby increased the need for new methods of co-ordination and communication.

The creation of Europe's modern urban system, as de Vries shows, was reflected less in the size of the urban population than in the redistribution of population among cities in the system. This redistribution took place in the context of the development of nation-states, the control of new empires, the integration of regional marketing systems, and the systematization of a dispersed approach to industrial production.

The significance of these changes in the European urban system for the establishment of early Canadian urban places is described in the first essay in this volume. The imperial administrative centres such as London and Paris which headed the emerging European system, depended on government and overseas trade for their power and growth. At the bottom of the urban hierarchy were the innumerable new towns, some created to consolidate the expanding frontiers of European states such as France under Louis XIV, and others, planted overseas, became direct agencies of imperial expansion in the New World. Because so much of town building in North America took place in the context of a world wide struggle between France and Britain, early Canadian places were usually military in their orientation; that is, their location, their shape, their functions, and even their population were determined by the priorities of imperial strategy.

The emergence of an early national urban system is outlined in Peter Goheen's essay in this volume. By an analysis of communications among cities based on the economic content of newspapers, Goheen found that by the mid-nineteenth century, cities still continued to rely most heavily on their international or imperial connections; their success at developing effective regional and local systems has to be placed within this larger context. When a national system did develop, it continued to be markedly open to international influences, and the power structure of the national system resembled the old imperial-colonial relationship. J.M.S. Careless has graphically depicted the "feudal-like chain of vassalage" among cities, with Winnipeg, for example, tributary to Montreal and later Toronto, while serving as a submetropolis of its own empire in the prairie West.[29] The result, at a national level, has been a core–periphery pattern of regional power; the cities of the core are concentrations not only of large populations but of capital, technology and entrepreneurial direction, and the cities of the peripheral regions specialize in the processing and distribution of raw materials produced in their regions.[30]

Below the national level, urban systems can also be seen as a sort of skeleton or framework for regions such as Atlantic Canada and the West, or of particular provinces, for political boundaries can have a major impact on the spatial and hierarchical patterns of settlement. At this level, several studies of Canadian regions have emphasized the place of a local urban system as the co-ordinating structure of socio-economic activities. Notable are Raoul Blanchard's pathbreaking volumes, including *L'Est du Canada français*, and Jacob Spelt's *Urban Development in South-Central Ontario*. In the literature on the relationship between cities and regions, at least two perspectives have emerged. J.M.S. Careless views regional cities as windows on a larger world, serving as agencies of national, standardizing trends. In his words, "regions generally centre on metropolitan communities, which largely organize them, focus their views and deal with the outside metropolitan forces on their behalf."[31] Alan Artibise, in the essay on the West reprinted here, recognizes the impact that Central Canada has had on the West and its cities, but he is also sensitive to the way in which a particular region has shaped the character of its cities.[32]

While the study of an individual city has been the most popular form of urban history in Canada, less attention has been devoted to placing a city in its regional setting. An early study by Donald C. Masters, *The Rise of Toronto, 1850–1890* analysed Toronto's domination over most of Ontario and its competition with Montreal for national hegemony. Other studies include L.D. McCann's examination of Halifax's place in the Maritime region and Robert McDonald's look at Vancouver and Victoria in the west coast region.[33] The way in which a smaller regional centre emerged at the head of a local system is traced by Fred Dahms in his article on Guelph in this volume. The methodology outlined by Dahms is suggestive of ways in which many smaller places could be studied in the future; he proposes integrating the analyses of systems (as described above) with the central place theories of Walter Christaller into a evolutionary approach which would accommodate both large-scale factors and the actions of individuals and groups. As in other work which emphasizes structural urbanization, Dahms deals with urban functions as well as population in defining the process of urban concentration.

## Behavioural Urbanization

The preceding outline of two aspects of urbanization should provide us with some idea of what the process is and how it works. What still needs to be described, however, is what this process has done to people and activities in cities, and also to society in general. In other words, how did the urbanization process affect the behaviour, the modes of thought, and the types of activities of people who lived in urban places, and what was the affect of this process on society as a whole? These aspects of the process are usually referred to as behavioural urbanization, but obviously are closely related to the characteristics already described.

The classic statement on these issues was made by Louis Wirth in an article entitled "Urbanism as a Way of Life," published in 1938.[34] Because Wirth's definitions have permeated the conceptions of everyone in urban studies, they merit a brief description. To Wirth, a city was defined as "a relatively large, dense and permanent settlement of socially heterogeneous individuals." In contrast to town or rural life, in which primary-group relationships dominated, the urban context led to relationships which were impersonal, superficial and often predatory. Urban life therefore was anonymous, isolated, secular, and sophisticated. For people to exist in this social environment, they were forced to combine with others in a number of collective activities involving associations, government and impersonal mass media communication. With hindsight, we can now see to what extent Wirth's definitions were time and culture bound—they were actually fairly useful descriptions of American inner cities during the industrial era. But his suggestions still point the way to some of the questions we need to pose and answer.

Some of the clearest thinking about these questions has been done by Theodore Hershberg as an aspect of his large-scale project on Philadelphia's society. Simply put, he is concerned about "how the urban environment, at one point in time or over time, affected things that occurred in it."[35] Hershberg isolates work and residence as the basic building blocks of an urban environment and suggests that major changes in these blocks occur when their environments change. For example, changes in the modes and means of productive activity affect both the setting in which work takes place (the artisan's shop or the factory) and the content of that work. During the transition from a mid-nineteenth century commercial phase of urban development to an industrialized late nineteenth century phase, work and residence became separated, productive tasks became specialized, and work was reorganized hierarchically. This transformation of the urban context, Hershberg argues, "gradually affected identity, roles, values and expectations, social networks, class consciousness, and so on through an almost endless list of human experience."[36]

Bettina Bradbury's essay on Montreal in this volume examines these aspects of social change during the transition from a commercial to an industrial orientation in the city. She does not use the term "urbanization," but her discussion of larger forces which reshaped the geography of the city, the organization of production, and the nature of work is very much relevant here. As has been demonstrated for other Canadian cities during this era of industrialization, Montreal's social landscape was increasingly differentiated by function and by class, with the growth of distinctive industrial areas and working class suburbs.[37] The scale and mechanization of industrial enterprises increased, but many establishments remained small and continued to operate with older methods. The nature of Montreal's production directly affected the character of the workforce—almost 42 per cent were women and children. The author's analysis of the resulting family economy and household structure has important implications for research on the society of other Canadian cites. She clearly shows that the particular character of the community's economy had a direct bearing on the behaviour of individuals, families and groups who lived there.

Another dimension of the impact of urbanization on urban dwellers goes beyond features which are quantifiable and therefore measurable in a demographic sense: this involves attempts to read the city in terms of psychological perceptions. An example is Robert Harney's discussion of ethnicity and neighbourhoods in Toronto, which is also a call to interpret more subtlely the views of the immigrants themselves "as serious actors in the city's history." This study of *mentalités*, as Harney suggests, looks at the neighbourhood as a psychic world. The physical and psychic space created by these immigrants—these ethnic "nooks and crannies"—did not correspond entirely either to those of the host society or to that of the country of origin.

The consequences of the process of urbanization for urban dwellers are paralleled in some respects by the spread of an "urban way of life" beyond the boundaries of the city. The extent and potency of this aspect of urbanization appears to differ greatly over time. For example, cities in the ancient world were usually the location of a society's political and religious power, but urbanism hardly penetrated the bulk of the population which was overwhelmingly rural. Even by the early modern era, the diffusion of an urban way of life was subject to severe limitations, and in smaller places rural influences were still very strong. The urbanization of society itself became more apparent during the nineteenth century, although this phenomenon has received relatively little scholarly attention. Some Canadian examples include David Gagan's study of the town of Brampton and rural Peel County. Gagan contrasts urban and rural characteristics by analysing fertility ratios, age-at-marriage, and occupational structures; by 1870, after two decades of separate development, the town had acted as an instrument of change in areas of conventional wisdom, tastes, attitudes, modes of production, and forms of social organization.[38]

That smaller towns and villages have undergone a general process of urbanization during the past century is argued by geographer Fred Dahms. His basic conclusion in several regional studies in Ontario is that the small agricultural service centres have taken on one or two specialized urban roles such as tourism, wholesaling, or crop processing.[39] What this means in social and psychological terms is effectively captured in a novel by Fred Jacob, *Day Before Yesterday*, published in 1925. Jacob recalled the spirit of the decade of his childhood, the 1880s—when "the older towns of Ontario were self-contained social entities, loosely connected with the world outside their walls." By the 1920s, in contrast, town life had been "ironed out, and standardized, and knit more closely together town to town."[40]

If we wish to look at the process of urbanization "at full stretch," we must include the sprawling urban areas typical of developments since World War II. Our language about the urban phenomenon is still based on nineteenth-century concepts, however, and may not be adequate for defining what "city" and "urban" mean in the modern world. In other words, our idea of city is tied to place in a specific time period; to large, dense, heterogeneous population concentrations in particular locations. But we appear to be moving towards a new kind of settlement pattern where an urban way of life is no longer the exclusive property of those who live in large cities. With communications and information processing technology breaking down the traditional distinction between urban and rural, our notion of urbanism may become associated with a state of mind rather than with a sense of place.[41]

## Conclusion

This survey of approaches to the nature of the process of urbanization should clarify some of the basic issues which were raised earlier, such as, that of the relationship of cities to urbanization, or urbanization to industrialization, and of urbanization to social change. Several aspects of these issues alluded to earlier can be made more explicit.

First, some of the new concepts about the nature of urban systems correspond to some of the most advanced scientific thinking about the interconnectedness and interdependence of all phenomena. A good deal of Social Science thinking still depends, however, on Cartesian reductionism—the notion that complex phenomena can be understood if broken down to their basic components; and on a Newtonian universe of predictable, mechanical forces which can be reduced to mathematical certainty.[42] But urban systems, like social systems in general, are open, not closed universes, in the sense that they are imbedded in total society and linked to it by very dense "feedback loops." A holistic rather than a reductionist approach is necessary to appreciate the complete picture. And the patterns we find may be untidy and imprecise, requiring a more humanistic touch than has generally been the case in urban studies in the past.

A second issue involves the role of the urban place in the larger society. Two seemingly contradictory concepts underlie most of the discussions about urban development, and depend to a certain extent on what it is the observer is trying to understand. One regards the urban place simply as a passive location. The essential aspects of this view are social processes such as class relations; urban places are the loci of these interactions between contending forces.[43] An example is the approach of Donald Davis who argues that "ambitions, like dominance and power, are attributes of élites not cities. Nor do cities exercise control; entrepreneurs and business corporations do."[44] On the other hand, those who make the urban place itself the unit of study emphasize the dynamism inherent in some concentrations of people in particular places. What seems obvious to some observers is the creative strength of collective activity whereby cities seem to "make themselves," influencing life within and around them. This urban consciousness appears to transcend the interests of particular individuals, groups, or classes.[45] At first glance these two opposing views seem mutually exclusive, yet it should be obvious that each conveys a significant dimension of the urban phenomena. To use a theatrical metaphor, "the city has been at once a social and psychological landscape, both producing and reflecting the modern consciousness. It is an arena of action that in the modernist period often seems to usurp the center stage."[46]

A third issue involves the re-emphasis of time in defining the relationship between cities and urbanization. This may seem to be carrying coals to Newcastle in a volume emphasizing the historical approach, but so-called universal principles in urban studies have turned out to be time and culture bound, usually relevant only to the modern era. For example, urbanization was a significant process in society long before its close association with industrialization in the nineteenth century. And it has continued, in a different guise, in the modern, post-industrial era. In this respect, Jan de Vries suggests that "each epoch of urbanization can be thought of as having distinct demographic behavioural and structural dimensions."[47] This implies the necessity of some sort of periodization, of defining stages in the process. Some attempts at outlining these stages have emphasized technological change focussing on energy and construction materials.[48] Some rely on the traditional periodization of the history of the western world: ancient, medieval, early modern, modern.[49] Those who have worked out schemes for the United states and Canada tend to emphasize the changing functions of urban places: mercantile, commercial, industrial. A periodization like this is legitimate if one wishes to study cities and urbanization in their own right. If we wish to go further, however, and integrate these phenomena into Canadian history more generally, we will have to devise a scheme that also incorporates other facets of societal change.

# Notes

1. Robert Craig Brown and Ramsay Cook, *Canada, 1896–1921, A Nation Transformed* (Toronto: McClelland and Stewart, 1974), 98.
2. For an assessment of this Canadian literature, see Alan F.J. Artibise and Paul-André Linteau, *The Evolution of Urban Canada: An Analysis of Approaches and Interpretations,* Report No. 4 (Winnipeg: Institute of Urban Studies, 1984); and Chad Gaffield, "Social Structure and the Urbanization Process: Perspectives on Nineteenth-Century Research," in *The Canadian City: Essays in Urban and Social History,* ed. Gilbert A. Stelter and Alan F.J. Artibise (Ottawa: Carleton University Press, 1984), 262–81.
3. "The Modern City as a Field of Historical Study," in *The Historian and the City,* ed. Oscar Handlin and John Burchart (Cambridge, Mass.: M.I.T. Press, 1963), 26.
4. John C. Weaver, "Editorial," *Urban History Review* 17 (June, 1988): 3.
5. Jan de Vries, *European Urbanization 1500–1800* (Cambridge, Mass.: Harvard University Press, 1984), 343, note 23.
6. See, for example, the provocative account by Stephen Hawking, *A Brief History of Time* (New York: Bantam, 1988).
7. "Agenda for Urban History," in *The Study of Urban History,* ed. Dyos (New York: St. Martin's Press, 1968), 7.
8. A recent survey of various approaches to urbanization is provided in S.N. Eisenstadt and A. Schachar, *Society, Culture and Urbanization* (Beverly Hills: Sage Publications, 1987), Part I.
9. These include Jan de Vries, *European Urbanization,* cited earlier; H. Schmal, ed., *Patterns of European Urbanization Since 1500* (London: Croom Helm, 1981); Paul Hohenberg and Lynn H. Lees, *The Making of Urban Europe, 1000–1950* (Cambridge, Mass.: Harvard University Press, 1985).

10. P. Kooij, "Urbanization. What's in a name," in *Patterns of European Urbanisation Since 1500*, ed. Schmal, 56.

11. Lampard's theoretical proposals were outlined in "American Historians and the Study of Urbanization," *American Historical Review* 67 (October, 1961): 49–61. A lengthy and substantial empirical study showing how these ideas could be applied is his "The Nature of Urbanization," in *The Pursuit of Urban History,* ed. Derek Fraser and Anthony Sutcliffe (London: Edward Arnold, 1983), 3–53. Lampard has incorporated the city-building process with his conceptualization of urbanization in his "City Making and Mending in the United States: On Capitalizing a Social Environment," in *Urbanization in the Americas: The Background in Historical Perspective*, ed. Woodrow Borah, Jorge Hardoy and Gilbert A. Stelter (Ottawa: National Museum of Man, 1980), 105–118. For the direct application of Lampard's proposals to the Canadian scene, see J.M.S. Careless, "Some aspects of Urbanization in Nineteenth-Century Ontario," in *Aspects of Nineteenth-Century Ontario,* ed. F.H. Armstrong, H.A. Stevenson, and J.D. Wilson (Toronto: University of Toronto Press, 1974), 65–79.

12. The pioneering study of this concentration was Adna F. Weber, *The Growth of Cities in the Nineteenth Century: a Study in Statistics* (Ithaca: Cornell University Press, 1966 reprint of 1899 edition). The term "genuine urbanization" is from Kingsley Davis, "The Origin and Growth of Urbanization in the World," *American Journal of Sociology* 60 (March, 1955): 429–37. These statistics, particularly the 3 per cent urban proportion, are sharply questioned by Jan de Vries, *Urbanization in Europe*, 348–49, who argues that recent scholarship indicates a proportion of more than double these early estimates.

13. The major demographic study is Leroy O. Stone, *Urban Development in Canada, An Introduction to the Demographic Aspects* (Ottawa: Dominion Bureau of Statistics, 1967).

14. Lampard, "The Nature of Urbanization," in *The Pursuit of Urban History*, ed. Fraser and Sutcliffe, 4.

15. Ibid., A good survey of the extensive Canadian experience of communities including industrial location and expansion is Elizabeth Bloomfield, "Community, Ethos and the Local Initiative in Urban Economic Growth: Review of a Theme in Canadian History," *Urban History Yearbook* (1983), 53–72.

16. For good accounts of the process of industrialization in Toronto, see Gregory S. Kealey, *Toronto Workers Respond to Industrial Capitalism, 1867–1892* (Toronto: University of Toronto Press, 1980), chap. 2; and J.M.S. Careless, *Toronto: An Illustrated History* (Toronto: Lorimer, 1984), chap. 4. For Montreal, see the article by Bettina Bradbury reprinted in this volume, and Joanne Burgess, "L'industrie de la chaussure à Montréal: 1840–1870—Le passage de l'artisant à la fabrique," *Revue d'Histoire de l'Amérique Française* 31 (September, 1977): 187–210.

17. Warren R. Bland, "The Changing Location of Metal Fabricating and Clothing Industries in Southern Ontario, 1881–1932," *Ontario Geography* 9 (1975): 35–57.

18. The theoretical basis for studying this process is well established in Roy Lubove, "The Urbanization Process: An Approach to Historical Research," *Journal of the American Institute of Planners* 33 (January, 1967): 33–39. For a general application to Canadian history, see Gilbert A. Stelter, "The City-Building Process in Canada," in *Shaping the Urban Landscape: Aspects of the Canadian City-Building Process*, ed. G.A. Stelter and Alan F.J. Artibise, (Ottawa: Carleton University Press, 1982), 1–29.

19. Michael Doucet and John Weaver, "Material Culture and the North American House: The Era of the Common Man, 1870–1920," *Journal of American History* 72

(1985): 560–87. A good introduction to the subject and sources is Richard Harris, "Housing in Canadian Cities: An Agenda and Review of Sources," *Urban History Review* 14 (February, 1986): 259–66.

20. Stone, chap. 8; Leo F. Schnore and Gene P. Petersen, "Urban and Metropolitan Development in the United States and Canada," *Annals of the American Academy of Political and Social Sciences* 316 (March, 1958): table 3.

21. Larry S. Bourne, "Urban Canada in Transition: Recent Patterns of Social and Demographic Change," *Zeitschrift der Gesellschaft für Kanada—Studien* 7 (1984): 65–84.

22. John Mercer and Michael Goldberg, "Value Differences and Their Meaning for Urban Development in Canada and the United States," in *Power and Place: Canadian Urban Development in the North American Context,* ed. Gilbert A. Stelter and Alan F.J. Artibise (Vancouver: University of British Columbia Press, 1986), 343–95.

23. The literature on urban systems is vast. Much of the earlier work is cited in Fred Dahms, "The Evolution of Settlement Systems," reprinted in this volume. See also, L.S. Bourne and J.W. Simmons, eds., *Systems of Cities: Readings on Structure, Growth, and Policy* (New York: Oxford, 1978).

24. For a brief, but valuable discussion of "The Idea of Urbanization," see Charles Tilly, *The Vendée* (London: Edward Arnold, 1964), 16–20.

25. Among the best works on urbanism in the ancient world is Robert Adams, *The Evolution of Urban Society* (Chicago: Aldine, 1966), and Paul Wheatley, *The Pivot of the Four Quarters* (Chicago: Aldine, 1971).

26. Charles Gallenkamp, *Maya, The Riddle and Rediscovery of a Lost Civilization* (New York: Viking, 1985), 118–20.

27. For an introduction to Rozman's immense scholarly output, see his "Urban Networks and Historical Stages," *Journal of Interdisciplinary History* 9 (1978): 65–91.

28. For a more detailed discussion of levels of urban systems, see Gilbert A. Stelter, "A Regional Framework for Urban History," *Urban History Review* 13 (February, 1985): 193–206.

29. Careless, "Frontierism, Metropolitanism and Canadian History," *Canadian Historical Review* 35 (1954): 1–21.

30. For fuller explanations of the core-periphery character of the national urban system, see James Simmons, "The Impact of the Public Sector on the Canadian Urban System," in *Power and Place* ed. Stelter and Artibise, 21–50; and L.D. McCann, ed., *Heartland and Hinterland, A Geography of Canada* 2d ed. (Scarborough: Prentice-Hall, 1987).

31. Careless, "Aspects of Metropolitanism in Atlantic Canada," in *Regionalism in the Canadian Community, 1867–1967*, ed. Mason Wade, (Toronto: University of Toronto Press, 1969), 117.

32. One of the most compelling examples of this approach is David Goldfield, "The Urban South; A Regional Framework," *American Historical Review* 86 (1981): 1009–1034. For an important analysis of Southern Ontario as a region, see John U. Marshall and W.R. Smith, "The Dynamics of Growth in a Regional Urban System: Southern Ontario, 1851–1971," *Canadian Geographer* 22 (1978): 22–40.

33. L.D. McCann, "Staples and the New Industrialism in the Growth of Post Confederation Halifax," *Acadiensis* 8 (1979): 47–79; Robert McDonald, "Victoria, Vancouver and the Evolution of British Columbia's Economic System, 1888–1914," in *Town and City: Aspects of Western Canadian Urban Development,* ed. Alan F.J. Artibise (Regina: Canadian Plains Research Centre, 1981), 31–58.

34. Wirth, "Urbanism as a Way of Life," *American Journal of Sociology* 44 (1938): 1–24.
35. Hershberg, "The New Urban History; Toward an Interdisciplinary History of the City," *Journal of Urban History* 5 (1978): 3–40.
36. Ibid.
37. Among the most useful studies in this regard are Peter Goheen, *Victorian Toronto, 1850–1900: Pattern and Process of Growth* (Chicago: University of Chicago Press, 1970); Alan Artibise, *Winnipeg: A Social History of Urban Growth, 1874–1914* (Montreal: McGill-Queen's University Press, 1975); and Michael Katz, *The People of Hamilton, Canada West: Family and Class in a Mid-Nineteenth Century City* (Cambridge, Mass.: Harvard University Press, 1975).
38. David Gagan, *Hopeful Travellers: Families, Land, and Social Change in Mid-Victorian Peel County, Canada West* (Toronto: University of Toronto Press, 1981).
39. For an example, see Dahms, "The Process of 'Urbanization' in the Countryside: A Study of Huron and Bruce Counties, Ontario, 1891–1981," *Urban History Review* 12 (February, 1984): 1–18.
40. Fred Jacob, *Day Before Yesterday* (Toronto: Macmillan, 1925), 319.
41. William Sharp and Leonard Wallock, "From 'Great Town' to 'Nonplace Urban Realm': Reading the Modern City," in *Visions of the Modern City*, ed. Sharpe and Wallock (New York: Columbia University, 1983), 7–46.
42. Among the most readable explanations of new scientific thinking are Fritjof Capra, *The Turning Point* (New York: Bantam Books, 1983), and Ilya Prigogine and Isabelle Stengers, *Order Out of Chaos, Man's New Dialogue with Nature* (New York: Bantam Books, 1984).
43. See, for example, Philip Abrams, "Towns and Economic Growth: Some Theories and Problems," in *Towns in Societies, Essays in Economic History and Historical Sociology*, ed. Abrams and E.A. Wrigley (Cambridge: Cambridge University Press, 1979), 9–34.
44. Davis, " 'The Metropolitan Thesis' and the Writing of Canadian Urban History," *Urban History Review* 14 (October, 1985): 108.
45. See the article by Alan Artibise in this volume for a further elaboration.
46. Sharpe and Wallock, "From 'Great Town'," 13.
47. *European Urbanization*, 13.
48. A good outline of the ideas of Patrick Geddes, whose scheme underlies the work of Lewis Mumford, is presented in Mumford, *The Culture of Cities* (New York: Harcourt Brace Jovanovich, [1938], 1970), 495–96.
49. This is the scheme used by de Vries and other European historians.

# THE CHANGING IMPERIAL CONTEXT OF EARLY CANADIAN URBAN DEVELOPMENT*

GILBERT A. STELTER

Early Canadian history makes very little sense if one assumes that it begins with the founding of Quebec City in 1608. Early settlement patterns, and the use of towns in the settlement process, were imposed from Europe by imperial officials or private individuals, representatives of commercial ventures. The methods used in imposing particular settlement patterns on a portion of the New World had been developed earlier in Europe for the purpose of consolidating or extending national boundaries. Two traditions of European town building appear to have become combined in the minds of those making decisions about colonial towns—the medieval bastide and the ideal towns of the Italian theorists and practitioners.

In some respects, towns and cities are definable entities, urban places which are distinct from what is not urban. For example, Fernand Braudel has effectively argued that towns share some common characteristics wherever they are located in time and place. These characteristics include a concentration of population, a division of labour, and a collective self-consciousness—a desire to be distinguished from other concentrations of population.[1] If, however, we are to develop explanations of more than local relevance, it will be necessary to reunite the urban place with its larger social environment. In other words, towns and cities are and were subsystems within larger political, economic, and social systems and can only be fully understood from the perspective of these larger systems.[2]

Two elements of this larger approach require some additional comments. The first is that the urban dimension of society is inextricably linked with the totality of a particular culture. Culture here is defined as a mental system

*This is a revised version of a paper presented at the annual meeting of the Canadian Studies Association, McMaster University, May 1986. I am grateful for the constructive comments at the time by James Sturgis of the University of London and Pierre Guillaume of the Université de Bordeaux.

which includes ideas about political economy, about the nature of society and even about how the settlement process should work. Some of the most successful efforts to relate culture to urban places are Carl Schorske's *Fin-de-Siècle Vienna* and Sharpe and Wallock, *Visions of the Modern City.*[3] Different periods of time within the same society often represent distinctive conceptions of what is socially desirable and aesthetically pleasing. The significance of this for the shape of cities was well summarized by Lewis Mumford: "The dome and the spire, the open avenue and the closed court, tell the story, not merely of different physical accommodations, but of essentially different conceptions of man's destiny."[4] The point here is simply that it is extremely relevant that early French-Canadian society was created in the French world of the Counter-Reformation and absolutism, and that British Canada was spawned during the neo-classical spirit of the Age of Enlightenment.

The use of culture in this sense may seem to suggest the approach of the old, idealist historians such as Burckhardt and Huizinga. In some respects one can appreciate their notion of a definable spirit of an age, or as Carlo Ginzburg puts it, distinguishing "the mental coordinates of an entire age."[5] But this amounts to more than the high culture of the dominant classes imposed upon the subordinate classes in society. In terms of urban development, the question involves, for example, the "modernist" Renaissance styles of architecture and town planning in relation to the "medieval" vernacular style. In European urban places, a sort of "circularity" seemed to apply; reciprocal influences travelled both ways between the ruling and subordinate classes as it did in other aspects of culture.[6]

A second element in redefining the place of towns and cities in the larger society concerns the nature of the process of urbanization. The most widely used conception, that of demographic urbanization, hardly applies for much of the early modern period in Europe. Between 1500 and 1700 the urban proportion of the total population actually dropped, only to rise again slightly in the eighteenth century.[7] But major changes were taking place in the structural dimensions of the European urban system, changes which led to significant redistributions of population among cities in the system and, hence, in the hierarchy of cities. This kind of urbanization was the product of decision making of various kinds, such as that of the controllers of capital about their investments, or, what is particularly significant, that of the state about political issues. The thrust of these political decisions in Europe was towards growth of the nation-state and control of new empires. The implications for the developing urban system were threefold: first, larger cities grew enormously if they were the main administrative centres—Paris, London, Madrid. Second, those places which were ports serving the colonies became more important within the national system. At the same time, hundreds of smaller European places declined, for other factors of growth were weak. Inland trading centres, ecclesiastical centres, and manufacturing centres did not cash in on the boom created by government and overseas trade. Third, hundreds of new towns were established in Europe to consolidate frontiers, and many more were created overseas, as agencies of imperial expansion.[8]

An important element of the state's role in the structural aspects of urbanization was the use of the military in determining the pattern of settlement. Decision makers in Western Europe were well aware of this tradition in the histories of their countries, for the physical evidence still surrounded them in many communities. For example, the Roman army had created many of the existing towns and cities. Some had originally been colonies of discharged veterans, and were designed to be showcases of Roman urban life—civilized life—as at Colchester in England, Lyon in France, and Merida in Spain. Or they began as legionary fortresses, such as Chester and York in England, and Strasbourg, Bonn and Cologne in the Rhineland. This military tradition in town building was maintained through the medieval period and into the early modern era in France and England.[9]

And this military tradition had a major bearing on the nature of early Canadian settlement. While Canadians like to picture themselves as a peaceful people and their country as the product of gradual evolution rather than of violent revolution,[10] much of the structure of the modern urban system was created in what could be called the Second Hundred Years War between France and England in the seventeenth and eighteenth centuries. Decisions about where a town would be located, what its function would be, how it would be shaped, and what kind of people would live in it were often made in the context of military considerations. The decision makers were usually military officers and surveyors, and commercial and colonization potentials were regarded as an adjunct, albeit an important adjunct, of an empire's strategic needs.

## Outline of Stages in European/Canadian Urban Development

The use of towns as agencies of imperial expansion is a process almost as old as civilization itself. Urbanism had been imposed on Europe as the result of the extension of empire, for Europe was not one of the seven areas of the world where a primary generation of urban forms took place.[11] Even "colonial" towns in frontier regions shared characteristics of urban places throughout the world in that they were not only "an aggregation of population of critical size and density but also an organizing principle, an agent of regional integration, in short, a creator of effective space."[12] As portions of northwestern Europe matured, these incipient states also began to use towns to consolidate their territories and to extend their frontiers. The nature of these colonial towns changed as the culture of these expanding societies evolved and changed. The same principle applied to the colonial towns of the New World, for they reflected particular stages of European development. Our concern will be primarily with the French and British cases, and with the consequences for what became British North America in 1763.

## The Medieval Heritage

The general urban revival dating from about the eleventh century produced two clusters of cities, a southern region centring in Northern Italy, and a northern region, focussing on the Low Countries, with Paris and London as important satellites. By the year 1400, Paris had emerged as the largest city in Europe with a population of 275 000; it was disproportionately large for its region, typical of areas or countries which were not highly urbanized.[13]

As in Spain, where the medieval struggle to win the country from the Moors led to the founding of strong urban enclaves which then provided the model for settling the New World,[14] the French colonial practice was established by centuries of experience of consolidating the nation-state. In some respects the old Gallo-Roman system continued to be the basis for town life in the medieval period, for Gaul had been the most urbanized of Rome's provinces. Early medieval *civitates* and *burgi* like Limoges, Tours, and Dijon, evolved around a nucleus of church and castle or with competing nuclei, eventually surrounded by a common wall. By the eleventh and twelvth centuries, *villes neuves* were used by lords and bishops to open new territory and extend settlement. Places like Saint-Denis remained unfortified for a time and emphasized their functions as markets. The form was a simple agglomeration with two streets informally focussing on the abbey's precincts.[15]

The most significant models for New World expansion—the bastides of the twelfth and thirteenth centuries—combined the notion of compact settlements and fortifications. The term bastide is the Gascon word for a planted town, derived from the verb meaning "to build"; the builders of new towns thus were bastidors.[16] These plantation towns were common throughout Europe, as lords, kings, and emperors sought to expand or retain their territory, from the Spanish Christian princes' use of them in the reconquest, to frontier expansion in Eastern Europe and the defensive functions in Eastern Russia or China. Several characteristics of these places in France are particularly relevant for later overseas colonial use. The political function was crucial. In Southern France where most were built, they were used in the territorial struggle between the king and the counts of Toulouse. The lord was responsible for the walls which were built through the labour of the residents of the town and area. These towns usually were not feudal, but their purposes were political and territorial. The settlers were freemen, attracted to the place by promises of land, building materials, and especially exemption from feudal obligations. Directly related to the political function was the agricultural function, for these were to be protected places making agricultural expansion possible.

The plans of these bastides were generally more regular than those of most medieval towns, where houses, not streets, were the primary elements of composition. In fact, plans became more stereotyped as the thirteenth century progressed, with rectangular grids becoming the norm (Fig. 1). The plans reflected the functions directly. Designed from periphery to interior, the walls first determined the shape. The gates in the walls determined the basic layout of the principal streets; the streets then became the organizing features, not the houses. The extent to which the fortifications determined the physical internal layout was the basis of many ideas about town planning during the Renaissance and Baroque periods.[17]

The English medieval tradition of new town building included some dramatic examples of schemes which combined the fortress and market functions, so that these towns became central points of settlement. The greatest royal bastidor was Edward I, who planted a large number of new towns in the last three decades of the thirteenth century. More than 70 bastides were built in Gascony, which he held as Duke of Aquitaine. These were not usually fortified places, but small market centres designed to meet the English demand for the regional wine. The ten bastides he built in Wales, on the other hand, clearly had a military function. The soaring castles connected to each town, as in Caernavon and Conwy, were meant to awe the Welsh in the same way that the market in one of their small squares was meant to entice them into commercial relationships. In order to attract English settlers to these towns, promises of land were offered to each family. Land was divided into three zones: the town itself, with lots of equal size; a larger garden lot outside the town, and a farm lot beyond the garden lots. This combination of urban and rural activity must have worked out fairly well in practice because it was to have a long life as the settlement pattern of the New World.[18]

## The Mercantile Era (1500–1800)

The use of the term "mercantile" to identify this period reflects a need to recognize a distinctive phase of European development which existed between what are conventionally called the pre-industrial and industrial stages.[19] The era was characterized by the growth of a centralized state in which the monarch sometimes achieved absolute power. Imperial ambitions and mercantilist policies can be set within the context of an Atlantic-oriented economy. In other respects, it was an age of "proto-industrial production," of widespread manufacturing growth, which preceded factory-scale production by several centuries.[20] And it was the era of the "ville classique," a time of great cultural brilliance for some cities, when Renaissance and Baroque urbanism transformed medieval towns.[21]

For at least the first two centuries of this era, the proportion of the population that was urban actually declined in several parts of Europe. The city states on the southern end of the "dorsal spine of Europe" lost their primacy of place to the new nation-states of the northwest—France, Holland, and England.[22] By 1700, London, population 550 000, had slightly surpassed Paris, population 530 000, as the largest city in the northwest, and Amsterdam followed at 172 000.[23] Within the most rapidly expanding nation-states, a certain amount of functional differentiation characterized urban growth, especially in the case of administrative centres, fortress cities, naval ports, and some manufacturing centres. The most successful of these were the court and port cities, which acted as physical symbols of mercantilism.

Within the structure of changes described above are several more stages in the evolution of European culture. Each of these stages represents a distinctive change in the shape of European towns and cities and in a most direct fashion, reflects the creation of colonial towns.

## The Renaissance and Reformation Periods

The Roman principles of symmetry, regularity, and organized composition had not totally died out during medieval times. While the medieval city was typically irregular, "medieval man could conceive the ideal city as perfectly geometrical," as Alberto Perez-Gomez argues, "and indeed implemented this geometry both in the cathedral and in the transformation of public spaces into stage-sets for mystery plays."[24] The Renaissance town planner, on the other hand, thought of order that was totally human, and yet represented the "immutable order of the cosmic creation."[25]

In practice, Renaissance town planning usually amounted to the creation of order and regularity in small portions of existing towns and cities. In Paris, François I strengthened the nexus of city and monarchy by building the new Louvre, and Henry IV later stimulated Renaissance-style development in Paris with the creation of the Place Royale (Fig. 2). Some new town development also took place. The first of these ideal towns in France were military establishments designed to fortify France's eastern boundaries. François I chose a leading Italian architect, Girolamo Marini, to supervise the design of places like Vitry-le-Françoise, which guarded an important passage against the Holy Roman Emperor, Charles V. The basic shape of the town was a square, and the surrounding fortifications were designed using the latest Italian concepts, for medieval-type fortresses had proved unable to withstand artillery using gun powder. In the new plan, each projecting bastion was defended by other bastions. A large central *place d'armes* dominated the interior space, with streets either radiating to the walls or intersecting in grid fashion.[26]

France's slight interest in the New World was partly a response to the growing colonial empires of the Spanish and Portuguese. In 1534 the king commissioned Jacques Cartier of St. Malo to explore the area north of Spanish territory, to find a passage to Asia and to discover gold as the Spanish had in Mexico. His voyages failed to establish a colony, and interest in the area was maintained only by the fishermen from French ports who also became involved in trading furs with the natives. But Cartier's voyage did lead to the discovery of the two most eligible sites for European urban settlement in what would become New France, the Indian villages of Stadacona (Quebec City), and Hochelaga (Montreal). In the case of Hochelaga, an Italian engraver produced a town plan based on Cartier's account of his 1535 voyage, which could be considered to be the first published plan of a North American town. The circular form with fortifications, the well arranged grid, and huge central "piazza" reflected the European view of an ideal New World town[27] (Fig. 3).

Attempts at colonization were not to begin until the early seventeenth century, after the devastating religious wars in Europe. The initiative was largely private and commercial. The new monarch, Henry IV, appointed Pierre de Gua, Sieur de Monts, as lieutenant-general of the vast and vaguely known regions of Acadia and the St. Lawrence, and granted him a ten year monopoly of the fur trade. This led to his association with a lieutenant destined to become the first colonizer and town planner in Canada, Samuel de Champlain. Trained as a painter and draftsman, Champlain had served in Henry IV's army as a quartermaster, where he appears to have participated in sieges and attacks on various French towns when Henry was still the leader of the dissident Protestants, the Huguenots. Champlain had also travelled to the Spanish West Indies as a navigator, and would have been familiar with that empire's approach to colonization through town-building. In 1603 he helped choose the site for the first settlement in Acadia, a small island in the Ste. Croix River, and then designed around a central square what vaguely resembled a Spanish town. This site was abandoned the following year because of its exposed location, and a new site was chosen across the Bay of Fundy at Port Royal. In contrast to the open character of Ste. Croix, the new plan chosen was that of a compact trading post-fortress which resembled the layout of a medieval, fortified abbey.

In 1608, after withdrawing from Acadia because they lost their fur trade monopoly, de Monts and Champlain turned their attention to the St. Lawrence area. The primary motive for founding a new place was not settlement, despite Champlain's use of the term. The approximate site of what would be Quebec was Stadacona, the Indian village where Cartier had wintered in 1535. Here the St. Lawrence narrowed sufficiently for cannon to command the river. A great cliff dominates the river at this point, making it one of the best natural strongholds on the continent. Whoever controlled this spot controlled river access to the interior of a potentially vast empire. Champlain's first building, a "habitation," was located on a narrow strand, a low-lying bank at the base of the great cliff (Fig. 4). The habitation was a more elaborate version of that at

Port Royal, and incorporated three two-storey buildings—a residence, and mercantile and supply stores. The defensive features resembled those of a late medieval castle with a fifteen foot moat and a surrounding stockade.[28]

The state's eventual involvement in the feeble colony combined military control with that of the zealous, Counter-Reformation religion of Cardinal Richelieu. In 1629 Richelieu reduced La Rochelle, the Huguenot centre, as part of his move against the 150 Huguenot strongholds which he felt comprised a state within a state. Paris, with its great many new convents and churches became a second Rome, a vanguard of the Counter-Reformation. In New France, Richelieu established a new company more interested than Champlain in populating the region, and he appointed officials who created a radial plan for the extension of Quebec to above the cliff. Several religious institutions dominated the expanded settlement. Religious enthusiasm and missionary zeal also led, in 1641, to the founding of a small mission post in west Montreal.[29]

Although Champlain had usually sailed from Honfleur, a little fishing village in Normandy, the colony's main connection was with Rouen, Normandy's major city. Rouen's commercial vitality as a port seemed tenuous, for it was located over forty miles from the Atlantic on the Seine, but its merchants traded extensively with the English and with the new colony. The medieval character of Rouen's townscape was only mildly affected by the new Renaissance styles. The impressive cathedral and the Palais de Justice had both been built in flamboyant Gothic style and the shops and houses of the main commercial street, the rue du Gros-Horloge, were built in half-timbered medieval style, even during the sixteenth and seventeenth centuries.[30] It is therefore not surprising that the original townscapes of Quebec and Montreal resembled medieval Norman towns[31] (Fig. 5).

By the seventeenth century, the number of people in England who lived in towns (about 20 per cent) was considerably less than in Holland (59 per cent) and slightly higher than in France (16 per cent). A modest rise in the urban portion of the population was accompanied by far-reaching changes in the urban hierarchy. London's growth was the most striking urban phenomenon in Western Europe, making it the centre of the English economy. Also growing were provincial towns such as Bristol, York, Norwich, Exeter, and Newcastle, usually ports depending on the new emphasis on foreign trade and colonial expansion. There were also a significant number of new towns with highly specialized roles: industrial towns like Halifax and Manchester, fortified dockyard towns like Chatham and Portsmouth, and spas such as Bath and Tunbridge Wells.[32]

Two types of imperial activity were characteristic of English expansion abroad in the early seventeenth century. One was a Roman-like system with central control of the colony, and responsibility for introducing English settlers into the indigenous population. For example, a relatively undeveloped part of Ireland, Ulster, provided an outlet for the aspirations of both state and mercantile interests when the long-standing struggle between the English and the Gallic Irish led to the "Flight of the Earls" and the forfeiture of their lands in 1607. Government officials quickly proposed a plan of regional settlement through a series of planted towns, but laid the burden of implementing the scheme on the City of London, whose Common Council set up a prototype of a development corporation. Derry and Coleraine were among the sixteen new towns that eventually were established. They were both fortified bastides with rectangular street arrangements and central squares. The population was usually about one-third English or Scottish and two thirds native Irish. By 1641 a "new urban network or system had been created and was the direct outcome of a political strategy."[33]

In the New World, the English adopted something similar to the Greek system, in which, like cells dividing, groups of settlers from the metropolis simply set up shop in some new location. The population was thus essentially the same as that of the metropolis, and the indigenous population was pushed back beyond the boundaries of the colony or destroyed. As in early New France, colonization in English American territories like Virginia was originally directed by chartered companies interested in exploiting natural resources. Although resistance to central English government control was particularly obvious in the case of the Puritan colonies in New England, English medieval villages with surrounding farm land were established. The most northern American territory, Newfoundland, varied from this type, for English authorities refused to recognize it as a colony, even though it had claimed this status since John Cabot had entered St. John's harbour in 1497. As a result of the power in parliament of English West Coast fishing interests, the island was regarded as only a convenience for migratory summer fishing fleets, and settlement was prohibited. The rude community which grew to be St. John's existed, therefore, in spite of official policy.[34]

## Seventeenth Century Baroque

The term "baroque" is used here not only to describe art or architecture but in the sense Lewis Mumford suggested, to designate profound political and economic transformations occurring during the later seventeenth century.[35] A "cult of power" was apparent especially in France, where the state increased its control of the economy, the military expanded its role in the state's political economy, and new or transformed cities became showcases of the central state's new position in society. All of these elements were directly reflected in the way imperial officials perceived the colonies.

The new age in town planning and building in France and the French colonies was ushered in when the young Louis XIV took the reins of government in the 1660s. His chief minister, Colbert, reorganized the economy to reflect France's stature as an empire, and used military power to achieve wealth. To Colbert, "trade was perpetual combat," and the achievement of mercantilist objectives meant in practice constant military initiatives against the Dutch and English. It also required the colonies become an integral part of the mercantile system by providing raw materials and a market for French manufactured products.[36] The symbol of the new dispensation was Versailles, the quintessential combination of baroque power and urban design. Versailles was the absolute unity of city, palace, and park, all laid out symmetrically along a central axis so that the entire scheme focussed on the residence of the Sun King. Although Louis distrusted Parisians, their city was partially modernized in an effort to create a French national style distinct from the Italian baroque. Some of the major projects included additions to the Louvre, and a new avenue, the Champs-Elysées. And in sharp contrast to capitals elsewhere on the continent, the city's walls were torn down.

This dramatic gesture of opening the city was only possible because Louis had thoroughly established his control inside France, secured the frontiers with armies, and fortified frontier towns with the help of the great military engineer, Vauban. A series of concentric rings, ever widening, illustrate how Vauban's fortified towns expanded to the northern, eastern and southwestern frontiers. Much has been made of Vauban's so-called fortifications systems, but he seems to have adopted three solutions to the problem of relating fortifications and communities. The first and most common was the construction of a citadel next to an existing town of considerable size, as in the cases of the inland towns of Lille, Arras, and Besancon. Because loyalties in these places were questionable, the purpose of the citadel was to intimidate the town as well as protect it. Another type of fortification designed and built by Vauban involved the construction of fortifications around an existing town, as at the port La Rochelle, which had become the major port for trade and communications with New France.

Vauban's third type was a new town built primarily for defensive purposes. These often resembled the proposals of Renaissance theoreticians in which the town's shape was subjugated to the requirements of the peripheral walls. For his new towns at Hunique, Saar-Louis, Longwy, and especially at Neuf-Brisach, his last and most highly regarded work, he used an orthogonal interior design, with rectangular or square blocks. At Neuf-Brisach, the military equipment and barracks were placed next to the walls, freeing the interior of the town for civilian purposes[37] (Fig. 6).

The moves to centralize royal authority during Louis XIV's reign had their effect on the colony of New France, where royal control replaced company jurisdiction. A rudimentary urban system was established along the St. Lawrence River, with Quebec as the administrative, religious, military, and cultural centre of the colony. Under government control, Quebec grew more quickly; the 547 in 1666 became 2000 by 1700. Together with Montreal, about half as large, the two towns represented about 20 per cent of the colony's population. In spite of the distance from France, the colonial towns physically resembled French provincial towns. The domestic architecture was basically medieval, as was the informal relationship of buildings on the streets. Some of the institutional architecture, on the other hand, according to Alan Gowans, uniquely combined medieval and baroque styles. While the ruling class was familiar with the fashionable baroque, the artisans and craftsmen still clung to the medieval tradition. The results in many churches and in the great buildings of the Jesuits were plain medieval exterior designs and elaborate, ornamented baroque interiors[38] (Fig. 7).

Colonial officials consulted directly with Vauban about defences at the existing towns. The royal engineer for the colony, de Nere, had been with Vauban in several seiges. The problem was not only the English to the south, but the powerful Iroquois Confederacy of five Indian nations which had successfully assaulted smaller frontier villages. The larger cities of Quebec and Montreal were not effectively fortified during the seventeenth century, but smaller places, such as Trois-Rivières, were surrounded with a bastioned wall. Vauban's principles seem to have been applied to some of the far flung western outposts, such as Cadillac's settlement at Detroit in 1701. Like the earlier builders of bastides in his native Gascony, Cadillac claimed his settlement would have military, commercial, and agricultural functions, for it would hold the territory for France by restraining the Iroquois; by preventing further English expansion, it would attract French traders and farmers to the interior of the continent.[39]

The term baroque does not seem to be as suitable a label for Restoration England as it is for Louis XIV's France, particularly in reference to the authority of the monarchy. Charles II attempted to impose baroque plans, such as those of Christopher Wren and John Evelyn, on London after the Great Fire, but with a notable lack of success. London had become the metropolis of mercantilism, the seat of the great merchants, and a separate entity from Westminster, the seat of the Court. The overall character of the city was shaped by the land speculators and builders rather than by a monarch's assertion of taste. But "modernist" continental styles, the Italian piazza and the residential square, and great baroque buildings such as Wren's St. Paul's were slowly introduced into the largely medieval urban fabric.[40]

The characteristics described above were also present in designs for English colonies in America. William Penn's scheme for Pennsylvania included his 1683 plan for Philadelphia which was a huge grid similar to several of the proposals for rebuilding London. Resembling the traditional bastide, two major streets intersected at a large, central square. The ideas of Wren were even more directly applied by colonial administrator Francis Nicholson in the early 1690s when he designed Annapolis on a rather grand scale with two great circles and several radiating streets. Later, as Governor of Virginia, he was involved in laying out the new capital city of Williamsburg along grandiose lines which featured a wide street as a principal axis and buildings terminating the vistas at either end. Significantly, however, the attempts by the Crown to direct the settlement process through a network of planned towns in Maryland and Virginia were nullified by the opposition of the local planters.[41]

## Eighteenth Century Classicism

In the years between 1700 and 1763, the English (now the British) emerged as the dominant economic and naval power in the Atlantic world. A Greco-Roman classicism set the trend in the cultural life of the fashionable British, and this in turn influenced the shape of towns and cities. This late-blooming Renaissance reintroduced the principles of classical proportion—rationality, harmony, and measure—as an aesthetic ideal. This ideal was based on the assumption that humans could control their world. Therefore, the location and form of urban places could be planned rationally rather than merely allowing them to evolve spontaneously. The hearth of these changes was London; it and other spectacular examples such as Bath and Edinburgh were, however, only "the tip of the iceberg," for the faces of many British towns were affected. In new town building, a sort of prototype developed which could be termed the "Georgian New Town" (Fig. 8). Whether it appeared in Scotland, Ireland, or America, this new town usually took the form of a bounded grid with symmetrically arranged, balanced series of streets of varying widths focussed on a central square. This Georgian form maintained older English traditions, but the regular features of the bastide type were accentuated and formalized on neo-classical principles.[42]

In France, the last decades of the *ancien régime* witnessed an economic upswing and the cultural flowering of the Enlightenment. A remarkable amount of private building took place in Paris, notably the *hôtels particulars*, in a more restrained classical style than that of the preceding baroque era. Outside Paris, the port of Bordeaux typified the changes taking place, for its older medieval townscape was redone with the latest Parisian classical flourishes. Bordeaux's prosperity was based on its regional position, but especially on its function as a link between northwestern Europe and the New World; its exports, except wine, were primarily re-exports. Another example of changes in urban settings was the inland, eastern city of Nancy, the seat of the Dukes of Lorraine. Here particularly the exuberance of eighteenth century classicism left its mark, in the organization of ceremonial space, a *place royale*, and in the ornamentation employed on buildings, fountains, and screens.[43]

The early part of the eighteenth century witnessed a great intensification of town building in North America by France. New frontier towns such as St. Louis and New Orleans were founded on the Mississippi. The fortifications of Quebec and Montreal became more sophisticated, and these towns evolved into major urban centres. But the epitome of French colonial towns was Louisbourg, planned in 1713 as a major Atlantic fortress. Royal engineers who were disciples of Vauban built a massive fortification which dictated the town's internal organization (Fig. 9). As in some Vauban projects, the king's bastion at Louisbourg was designed to protect imperial officials from the townspeople as well as from any British imperial threat. In terms of economic function, Louisbourg played an effective role as a commercial centre of the north Atlantic cod fishery and of the trade between Canada (Quebec) and the French West Indies.

The British countered with a settlement scheme that bore a remarkable resemblance to the earlier Ulster plantations. Although France had ceded Nova Scotia to the English, the Acadian French occupied the best agricultural land. This population was scattered throughout the colony in little rural hamlets of several farmsteads each. After lengthy discussions between British and American officials, a plan by Governor Shirley of Massachusetts succeeded: a number of "Protestant" towns, designated on a map by little grids, would be planted in the midst of the hostile Acadian population. When, in 1749, ships bearing over 2500 settlers arrived, the weather forced the commanding officer to drop them all off at one place on the Atlantic side. This was Halifax, destined to become Britain's Gibralter in North America (Fig. 10). The rest of the scheme was abandoned but the Acadians' expulsion in the 1750s opened the way for several "planter's towns," composed of migrants from New England.[44]

The struggle between France and England during the Seven Year's War (or French and Indian War) had disastrous consequences for France's settlements. The British had concentrated their military expenditures on their navy in order to control certain waterways, and thus defend their colonies and colonial trade. Their towns, except minor palisades like Halifax, were not usually heavily fortified. The French could only send out squadrons each year. Their defensive efforts, therefore, went into fortifying ports, such as Louisbourg, according to Vauban's principles. But Louisbourg was an excellent example of what John McNeill called a "product of metropolitan logic and decisions imperfectly inflicted on people and places poorly understood by the metropolitans."[45] Vauban's continental fortresses were designed to be relieved by supporting armies after several weeks of seige. No such possibility existed in the case of Louisbourg. It fell twice, and the second time in 1758, its walls were dynamited and its population dispersed. The military situation also doomed the rest of the colony. Quebec fell in 1759 after a lengthy siege and bombardment which destroyed one of the finest cities on the continent. Montreal surrendered the following year. The future of these communities was to be played out under the flag of the old enemy. Ironically, Quebec would soon emerge as Britain's military bulwark against its former colonies to the south.

In summary, three themes can be reiterated. First, there are several successive Europes, and it is essential to know which we are talking about when trying to estimate the degree to which European modes of urban development were transmitted to the New World.

Second, we should recognize that early Canadian places were elements, albeit minor and peripheral elements, of a European urban system that was undergoing massive structural changes in the early modern era. Although much of the writing about European urban history ignores or plays down the significance of the towns of the New World, these outposts of a European system were factors in determining which European places succeeded or failed within that system.

And third, we should recognize the role of the state in the creation of these early urban systems. Much of the state's colonial town planning and building had a military function, since this territory lay between two aggressive empires. This tradition of town building during war or the threat of war continued well into the nineteenth century, as the United States replaced France as the external threat.

The interpretation presented here has emphasized the European conception of how to settle the New World. It is only one side of the story, of course, for little space has been given to the application of these ideas. It is important to recognize the unsuitability of these conceptions in practice, and how geography, new conditions, and local decision making affected subsequent development, as these colonial places became dynamic centres of a world less directly controlled by Europe.

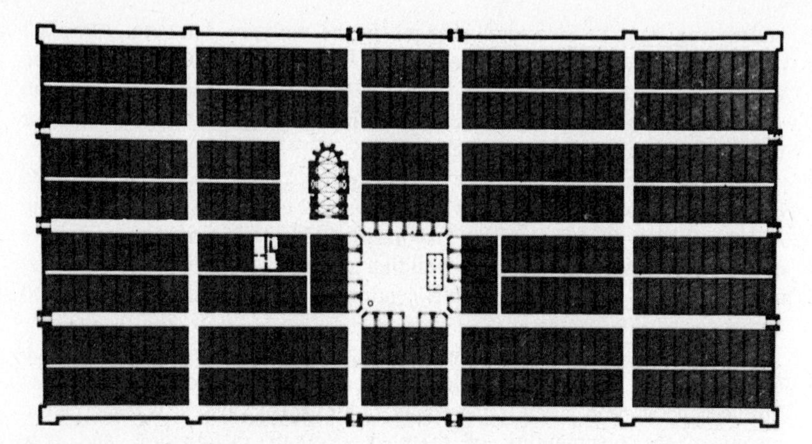

**FIG. 1** *The Formally Planned Medieval Bastide: Monpazier, France, 1284*
SOURCE: Victor Ainé, *Annales Archiologiques* 12 (Paris, 1852).

More regular than earlier bastides, Monpazier reflected a concern for spatial order which later became commonplace in the planning of colonial towns in the New World.

**FIG. 2** *French Renaissance Urbanism: Place Royale, Paris*

This residential square, designed in 1608, illustrates Renaissance conceptions of architecture and planning in the French capital.

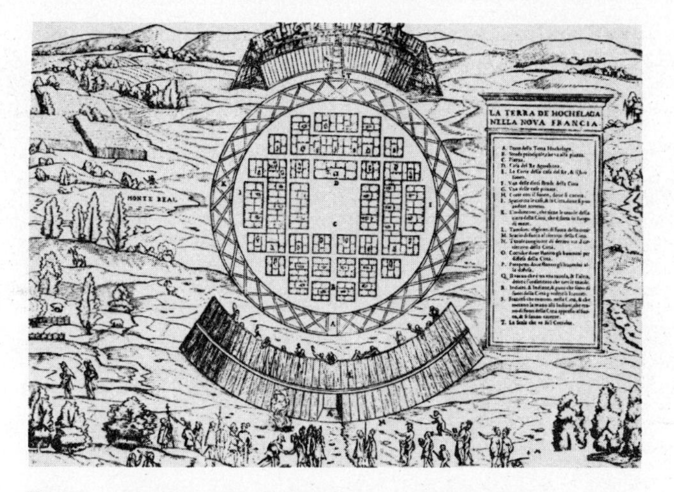


**FIG. 3** *A Canadian Indian Village Depicted as an Italian Ideal Town*
SOURCE: Ramusio's *Navigationi et viaggi* 3, 1565, National Map Collection, PAC.

An Italian version of Hochelaga, the Indian village near what became Montreal, based on Jacques Cartier's descriptions of his second voyage of 1535.

**FIG. 4** *A Medieval Fortification in New France: Champlain's Habitation at Quebec*
SOURCE: C.H. Laverdière, ed., *Oeuvres de Champlain* (Quebec, 1870).

Like the Spanish "factories" in Latin America, Champlain's habitation, built in 1608, combined the functions of residence, trading post and defensible fortress.

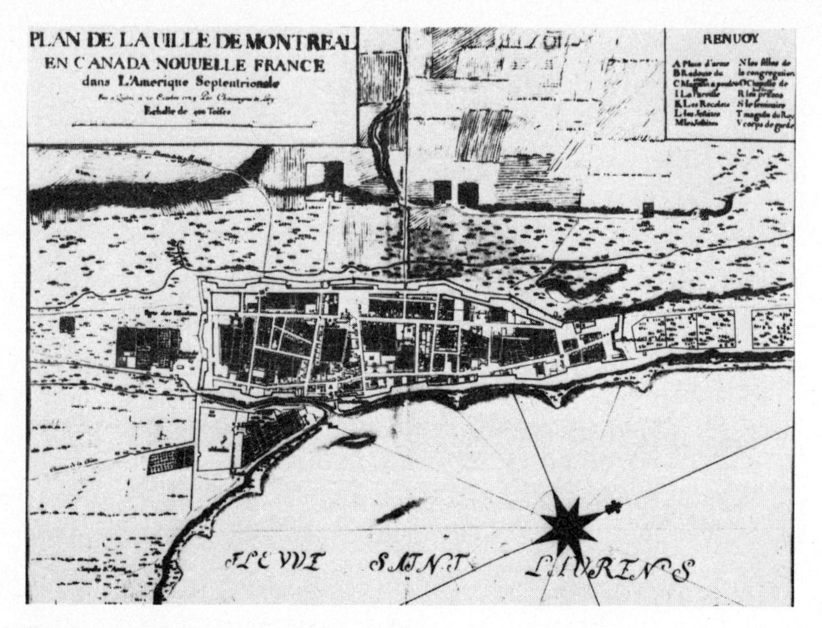


**FIG. 5** *A Bastide in New France: Montreal in 1724*
SOURCE: Chassegros de Lery, *L'Amérique Septentrionale*, 1724, National Map Collection, PAC.

This plan emphasises the semi-rural character of the space within the walls, the extensive system of gardens, as well as the agricultural activity in the earliest suburbs.

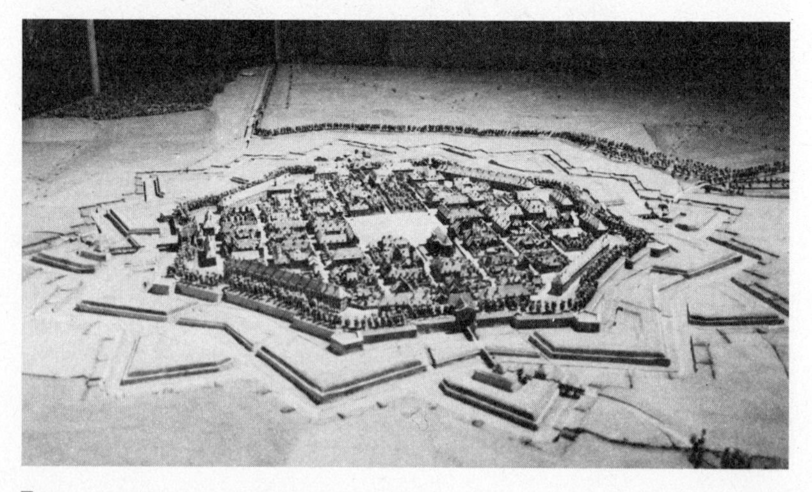

**FIG. 6** *An Ideal French Fortified Town: Neuf-Brisach*
SOURCE: Photo of wooden model in Musée du Plans-Reliefs, Army Museum, Hôtel des Invalides, Paris.

Designed in the late 17th century by the great military engineer Sebastian Vauban, this town's primary function was the defense of France's Rhine River frontier.

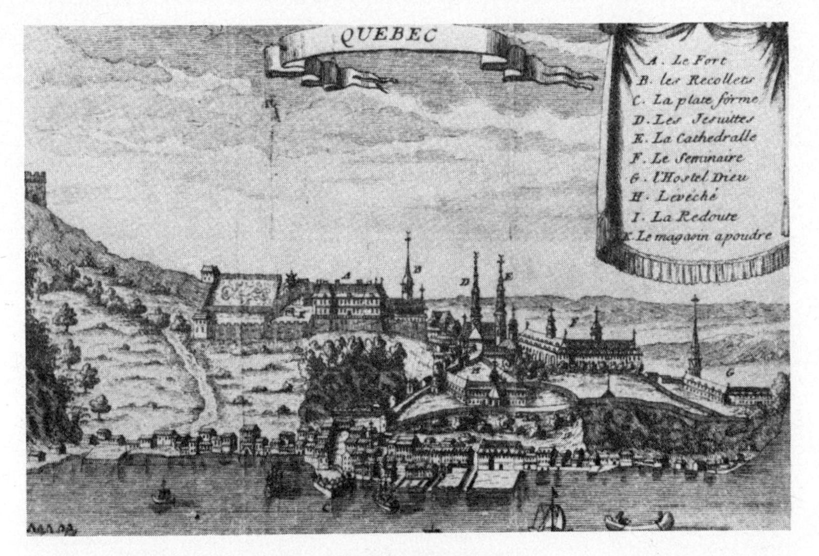


**FIG. 7** *A Baroque Town in the New World: Quebec City 1722*
SOURCE: Bacqueville de la Pothrie, *Histoire de l'Amérique Septentrionale*, 1722, National Map Collection, PAC.

In the two-part city, commerce and residences were located in Lower Town, at the river, and great religious institutions and government buildings above the cliff in Upper Town.

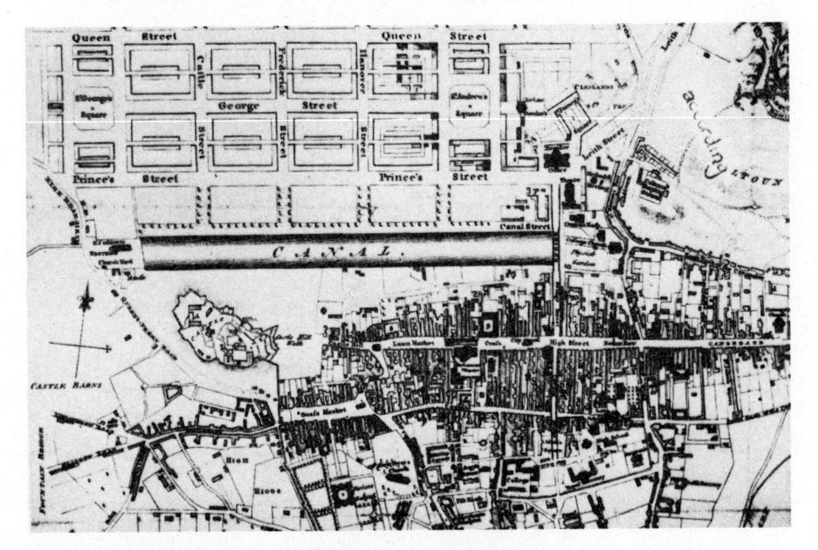


**FIG. 8** *Georgian New Town Planning: Edinburgh in the 1770s*
SOURCE: Scottish Record Office, Edinburgh

The Georgian new town built north of the crowded medieval city was characterized by a spacious grid focussed on two squares.

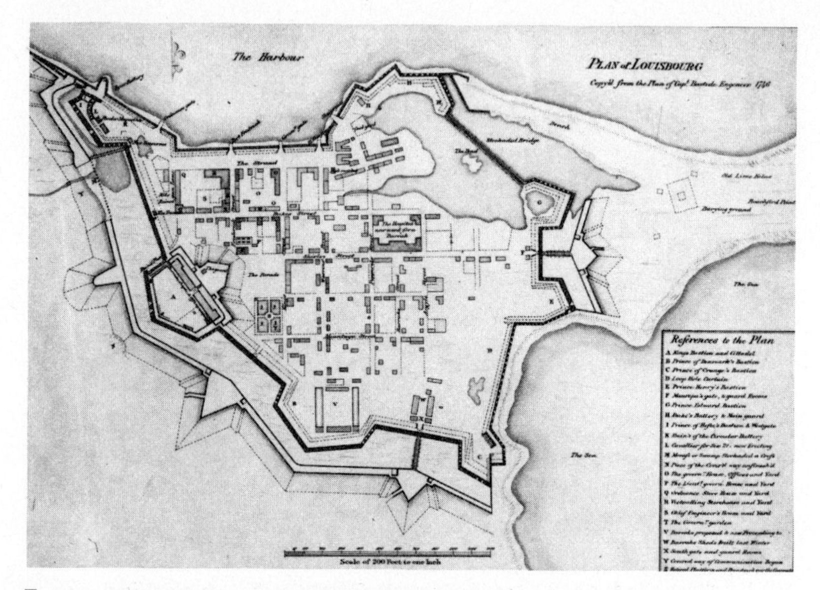


**FIG. 9** *The French Gibraltar in North America: Louisbourg, 1746*
SOURCE: 1912 copy of plan drawn by Captain John Bastide, National Map Collection, PAC.

Designed by military engineers working in the Vauban tradition, Louisbourg was dominated by massive works on its landward side.

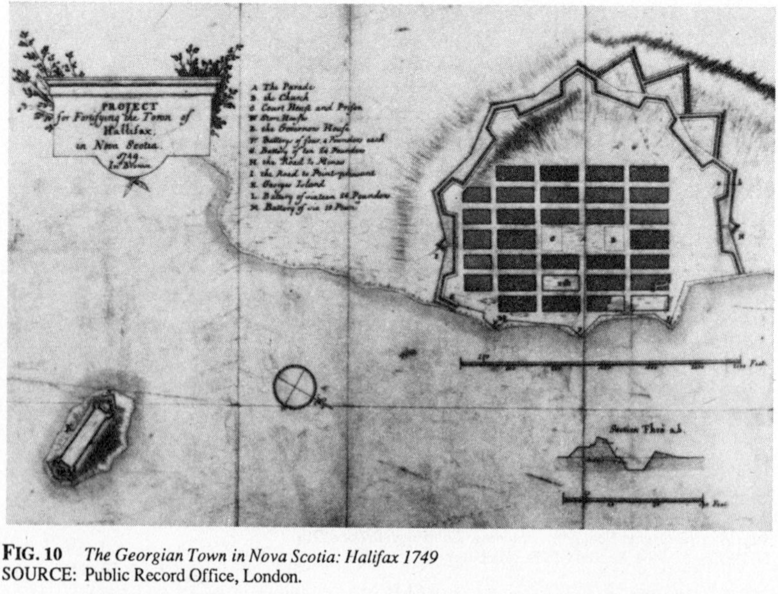

**FIG. 10** *The Georgian Town in Nova Scotia: Halifax 1749*
SOURCE: Public Record Office, London.

The Georgian grid focussed on a central parade was designed by John Brewse, who also proposed impressive walls which were never built. His plan shows British and French officials thought similarly about the relation between community and defense.

# Notes

1. *The Structures of Everyday Life* (New York: Fontana [1979], 1985), 481–83.
2. For an elaboration of this idea, see Jan de Vries, "The Problem of the City in Early Modern Europe," chap. 1 of his *European Urbanization, 1500–1800* (Cambridge, Mass.: Harvard University Press, 1984). See also Paul Wheatly, "European Urbanization: Origins and Consummation," *Journal of Interdisciplinary History* 17 (Autumn 1986): 415–30.
3. Car Schorske, *Fin-de Siècle Vienna, Politics and Culture* (New York: Knopf, 1980); William Sharpe and Leonard Wallock, eds, *Visions of the Modern City: Essays in History, Art, and Literature* (New York: Columbia University, 1983).
4. *The Culture of Cities* (New York: Harvest Books [1938], 1970), 5.
5. *The Cheese and the Worms* (Baltimore: John Hopkins Press, [1976] 1980), xxiii.
6. The concept of circularity stems from Mikhail Bakhtin's, *Rabelais and His World* (Cambridge, Mass.: Harvard University Press, 1968), 144–45, as applied to popular and élite culture.
7. Paul Bairoch, "Population urbaine et taille des villes en Europe de 1600 à 1970: Présentation de séries statistiques," in *Démographie urbaine, XVe–XXe siècle* (Lyon: Centre d'Histoire Economique et Sociale de la Région Lyonnaise, 1977), 1–42.
8. This is the perspective of Jan de Vries, *European Urbanization.* Similar in conception is the best recent overview of European history, Paul Hohenberg and Lynn H. Lees, *The Making of Urban Europe, 1000–1950* (Cambridge, Mass.: Harvard University Press, 1985).
9. Thomas H. Watkins, "Roman Legionary Fortresses and the Cities of Modern Europe," *Military Affairs, The Journal of Military History* 47 (February, 1983): 15–24; and Roger Kain and Heather Norris, "Military Influence on European Town Planning," *History Today* 32 (April, 1982): 10–15.
10. For example, Northrup Frye suggests that the Canadian tradition "might well be called a quest for the peaceable kingdom" and historian William Kilbourn used this concept as the title of his guide to the history and culture of the country: *Canada, A Guide to the Peaceable Kingdom* (Toronto: Macmillan, 1970), especially xvii–xviii.
11. The terminology here is from Paul Wheatley, *The Pivot of the Four Quarters, A Preliminary Enquiry into the Origins and Character of the Ancient Chinese City* (Chicago: Aldine Publishing, 1971), a brilliant comparison of the nature of "urbanism" in the various part of the ancient world. Also useful is Paul Bairoch, *De Jéricho à Mexico, Villes et économie dans l'histoire* (Paris: Gallimard, 1985), translated as *Cities and Economic Development, From the Dawn of History to the Present* (Chicago: University of Chicago, 1988), which effectively places the European experience within a larger context.
12. Paul Wheatley and Thomas See, "Defining the Urban Entity," in their *From Court to Capital, A Tentative Interpretation of the Origins of the Japanese Urban Tradition* (Chicago: University of Chicago, 1978), 7. A similar approach to urban places and their role in the organization of space is Robert McC. Adams, "The Natural History of Urbanism," in *Ancient Cities of the Indus*, ed. G.L. Possehl (New Delhi: Vikas, 1979), 18–26.
13. Hohenberg and Lees, 11, 59–73.

14. Jorge Hardoy, "European Urban Forms in the Fifteenth to Seventeenth Centuries and Their Utilization in Latin America," in *Urbanization in the Americas from its Beginnings to the Present*, ed. R.P. Schaedel, J.E. Hardoy, and N.S. Kinzer (The Hague: Mouton, 1978), 215–48.

15. E.A. Gutkind, *Urban Development in Western Europe: France and Belgium*, Vol. 5 of *International History of City Development* (New York, Free Press, 1980), 11–45.

16. Maurice Beresford, *New Towns of the Middle Ages* (London: Butterworths, 1967), 8–9.

17. Ibid., 45–74; James Vance, *This Scene of Man: The Role and Structure of the City in the Geography of Western Civilization* (New York: Harper's College Press, 1977), 167–200; André Cherville, Jacques Le Goff, and Jacques Rossiaud, *La ville medievale*, Vol. 2 of *Histoire de la France urbaine* (Paris, Éditions du Seuil, 1980), 303–22; Jacques Le Goff, "The Town as an Agent of Civilization, c. 1200 – c.1500," in *The Fontana Economic History of Europe*, ed. C.M. Cipolla (London: Fontana, 1972), I: 71–106.

18. Caroline Shillaber, "Edward I, Builder of Towns," *Speculum* 22 (July, 1947): 297–309.

19. Perhaps the best example of the old dichotomy is Gideon Sjoberg, *The Preindustrial City* (New York: Free Press, 1960).

20. The era is characterized as "proto-industrial" by Hohenberg and Lees, 101–105.

21. Emmanuel Le Roy Ladurie, ed., *La ville classique*, Vol. 3 of *Histoire de la France urbaine* (Paris: Éditions du Seuil, 1981).

22. Immanuel Wallerstein, "Failed Transitions or Inevitable Decline of the Leader? The Workings of the Capitalist World-Economy," in *Failed Transitions to Modern Industrial Society: Renaissance Italy and Seventeenth Century Holland*, ed. F. Krantz and Paul Hohenberg (Montreal: Interuniversity Centre for European Studies, 1974), 78.

23. Hohenberg and Lees, 11.

24. "The City as a Paradigm of Symbolic Order" (Paper presented to the Symposium on Urban History and Architecture, Carleton University, November, 1985), 7.

25. Ibid.

26. Horst De La Croix, "Military Architecture and the Radial City Plan in Sixteenth Century Italy," *Art Bulletin* 42, 4 (1960): 275–76, plate 15. E.A. Gutkind, 103–94. David Thomson, *Renaissance Paris, Architecture and Growth, 1475–1600* (Berkeley: University of California Press, 1984).

27. G.B. Ramusio's plan of Hochelaga, 1556 edition, reprinted in 1565. National Map Collection (NMC)—No. 1908. Some historians of New France tend to regard this plan as largely imaginary. Marcel Trudel, *Histoire de la Nouvelle-France*, Vol. 1: *Les vaines tentatives, 1524–1603* (Montreal: Les Éditions Fides, 1963).

28. Marcel Trudel, "Samuel de Champlain," *Dictionary of Canadian Biography*, Vol. I (Toronto: University of Toronto Press, 1968), 186–89. H.P. Biggar, *The Works of Samuel de Champlain* (Toronto: Champlain Society, 1922), 1: 91–202, 274; 2: 24–56, 332–36.

29. K. Bussman, *Paris and the Ile de France* (Paris: Dumont, 1984), 146–48, 185–88; Father Lejeune, 1636, in R.G. Thwaites, ed., *Jesuit Relations*, Vol. 9 (New York: Pageant [1896–1901], 1959): 132; André Charbonneau, Yvon Desloges, and Marc Lafrance, *Québec. The Fortified City: From the 17th to the 19th Century* (Ottawa: Parks Canada, 1982), 331–34; Gustave Lanctôt, *Montreal Under Maissoneuve* (Toronto: Clarke Irwin, 1969).

30. J. Levainville, *Rouen: Étude d'une Agglomeration Urbaine* (Paris: Libraire Armand Colin, 1913).

31. Alan Gowans, "The Earliest Church Architecture of New France from the Foundation to 1665," *Journal of the Royal Architectural Institute of Canada* 26 (1949): 291–98.

32. Peter Clark and Paul Slack, *English Towns in Transition, 1500–1700* (London: Oxford University Press, 1976). Penelope Corfield, "Urban Development in England and Wales in the Sixteenth and Seventeenth Centuries," in *Trade, Government and Economy in Pre-Industrial England*, ed. D.C. Coleman and A.H. John (London: Weidenfeld and Nicolson, 1976), 214–47. F.J. Fisher, "London as an 'Engine of Economic Growth'," in *The Early Modern Town, A Reader*, ed. Peter Clark (London: Longman, 1976), 205–15.

33. R.S. Butlin, "Irish Towns in the Sixteenth and Seventeenth Centuries," in *The Development of the Irish Town*, ed. Butlin (London: Croom Helm, 1977), 87; Gilbert Camblin, *The Town in Ulster* (Belfast: Mullan, 1951).

34. A useful overview is John Reps, *Town Planning in Frontier America* (Princeton: Princeton University Press, 1969). An important analysis of the European background to New England settlement practices is Anthony Garvan, *Architecture and Town Planning in Colonial Connecticut* (New Haven: Yale University Press, 1951); For a description of "town-making fever" in one American region, see James T. Lemon, *The Best Poor Man's Country* (Baltimore: John Hopkins Press, 1972), chap. 5.

35. Lewis Mumford, *The City in History* (New York: Harcourt, Brace and World, 1961), chap. 12.

36. Herbert Priestly, *France Overseas through the Old Régime, A Study of European Expansion* (New York: Appleton-Century, 1959), 146–57. Raymond Betts, *Europe Overseas, Phases of Imperialism* (New York: Basic Books, 1968).

37. Reginald Blomfield, *Sébastien le Prestre de Vauban, 1633–1707* (New York: Methuen, 1938); Bruce W. Fry, *'An Appearance of Strength', The Fortifications of Louisbourg*, Vol. I (Ottawa: Parks Canada, 1984): 37–45; Gutkind, 5, 200–201; Charbonneau, Desloges, Lafrance, chaps. 10 and 11; Alphonse Halter, Roger Herscher, and Jules Roth, *Neuf-Brisach* (Colmar-Ingersheim: SAEP, 1972). Alberto Perez-Gomez, *Architecture and the Crisis of Modern Science* (Cambridge, Mass., M.I.T. Press, 1983), chap. 6. My description of Vauban's fortified towns also depends on my study of the models of these places which were made in the late seventeenth and early eighteenth centuries and are housed in the Musée de Plans–Reliefs, part of the Army Museum at the Hôtel des Invalides in Paris; and on-site visits in May, 1985.

38. Alan Gowans, *Building Canada, An Architectural History of Canadian Life* (Toronto: Oxford University Press, 1966), 12–38.

39. Memorandum from Governor Denonville to Vauban; Vauban to Marepas, 7 January 1699, Archives Nationales (AN), Paris, Colonies C11A, 5: 365v, in *La correspondence de Vauban relative au Canada*, ed. Louise Dechêne (Quebec, 1968), 26–28, 37–45; Lavasseur de Neré to Minister, 18 October 1705, AN, Colonies, C11A, 22:348.; Lavasseur de Neré, 15 November 1705, concerning Trois-Rivières, AN, Section Outre-Mer, Dépôt des fortifications des Colonies, Amérique septentrionale, no. d'ordre 460.

40. Among the best literature on London during this period is the early portion of John Summerson's *Georgian London* (New York: Charles Scribners, 1946). For Wren, see Geoffrey Beard, *The Work of Christopher Wren* (Edinburgh: John Bartholomew, 1982).

41. Reps, 129–44.

42. Peter Borsay, "Culture, Status, and the English Urban Landscape," *History* 67 (February, 1982): 1–12. Gilbert Stelter, "The Classical Ideal: Cultural and Urban Form in Eighteenth Century Britain and America," *Journal of Urban History* 10 (August, 1984): 351–82. D.G. Lockhart, "Planned Village Development in Scotland and Ireland, 1700–1850," in *Ireland and Scotland, 1600–1850: Parallels and Contrasts in Economic and Social Development*, ed. T.M. Devine and D. Dickson (Edinburgh: Scottish Universities' Press, 1983), 12–29.

43. Hohenberg and Lees, 139–145; Roger Kain, "Classical Urban Design in France, The Transformation of Nancy in the Eighteenth Century," *The Connaisseur* 26 (November, 1979): 190–97.

44. Gilbert Stelter, "The English New Town Tradition in the Settling of Mid-Eighteenth Century Nova Scotia" (Paper presented at Eastern Historical Geography Association, Castine, Maine, September, 1985).

45. *Atlantic Empires of France and Spain, Louisbourg and Havana, 1700–1763* (Chapel Hill: University of North Carolina Press, 1985), xvi.

# CREATION OF AN EARLY VICTORIAN SUBURB IN MONTREAL*

DAVID B. HANNA

Mount Royal stands out in singular splendour as a solid chunk of rock over the largely sedimentary and uniformly flat Saint Lawrence plain, rising 759 feet above the St. Lawrence River. During the seventeenth and eighteenth centuries, the southern slope of Mount Royal was a part of Montreal's agricultural hinterland. Little is known of the agricultural activity during this period except that the mountain slope formed a part of the cadastral block known as "la côte Saint-Antoine" with access provided by the road of the same name. By the beginning of the nineteenth century some elements of change were evident in the rural landscape. The staple fur trade of the previous century had done little to advance settlement or income distribution in the colony, but it had made a handful of men extremely rich and these fur traders became Montreal's first resident merchant élite. Fur barons such as James McGill, Joseph Frobisher, Simon McTavish and William McGillivray realized the status potential of large summer homes on the mountain slope. One by one they purchased a farm or two in "côte Saint-Antoine," transforming them into estates made up of a country house and ornamental gardens with the remainder of the lot continuing as farmland, probably by lease or by hire. House sites were invariably chosen to take full advantage of the sweeping view of Montreal, the St. Lawrence River and the plain beyond. A fundamental condition for creating a prestige neighbourhood had been acknowledged by these first 'urban' owners.

By 1825, the fur traders had for the most part either departed from Montreal or died and the bucolic scene they left behind would not remain intact much longer. Beginning in 1839, Montreal's export trade, with Upper Canadian wheat in the lead, was booming and would continue to surge upwards throughout the early 1840s. The importing field, the real source of Montreal's

* *Urban History Review/Revue d'histoire urbaine* IX, 2 (October/octobre 1980): 38–64.

wealth due to the high value of the merchandise, grew rapidly immediately after 1838, no doubt because of the period of privation during the Canadian rebellions and economic depression (Fig. 1). As always, inland farmers could only indulge in the wide range of imported goods offered by Montreal if staple exports, on which their income depended, were in demand. Consequently, the unprecedented boom in staple products in 1841 gave rise to the equally amazing leap in import sales the following year. This fact is reflected in Montreal's urban development, 1842 being the year the first major subdivision plans for the Mount Royal plateau were drawn up and presumably the year importers gained enough surplus cash to entertain the idea of speculative building. The year 1843 was a setback in both exporting and importing, but in 1844 the boom returned. The passage of the Canada Corn Act in 1843, granting Canadian wheat almost duty-free access to the British market, sent exports to new heights, in turn fostering further import sales. The renewed high import profits of 1844 coupled with the confidence gained from the Canada Corn Act appear to have provided the means as well as a psychological boost to importers interested in speculative building, as construction of the first terraces on the plateau was undertaken that year, almost all by major Montreal wholesalers and retailers.

The opening of housing construction near Mount Royal was only a fringe manifestation of a true building boom which evidenced itself throughout the city in early 1840s. Although any formal census collection of housing stock is lacking for the years between 1831 and 1842, the overall pace of cumulative growth was obviously slow, a mere 600 units or so having been added during that period (Fig. 2). The addition of nearly 2000 houses to the net stock within a short space of two years (1842–1844) shows clearly that a real estate boom of unprecedented proportions occurred, and it is in this light that rapid subdivision of the southern slope of Mount Royal should be viewed.

In the space of four years, a new generation of landowners on the southern slope of Mount Royal subdivided vast portions of their properties, effectively paving the way for large scale urban development on the plateau. The first of these was John Redpath, an extremely versatile and successful man in contemporary business terms. Long before establishing the important sugar company bearing his name, he was one of the most successful contractors in the country, having supervised the building of a vast array of Montreal mansions, commercial and institutional buildings during the 1820s and 1830s, including the Montreal Water Works, Montreal General Hospital, military barracks on St. Helen's Island, and Notre Dame Church.[1] He also participated in the construction of Rideau Canal along with several partners. Having made his fortune by the age of forty, Redpath began to invest in real estate. For £10 000 Redpath purchased the huge 235 acre Desrivières estate from the owner's heirs in November, 1836. He established a large mansion known as "Terrace Bank" much in the manner of the fur barons, high up the slope of the mountain at the foot of a cliff. Yet, unlike the fur barons, this new generation Scotsman wasted little time in seeking a return on his land

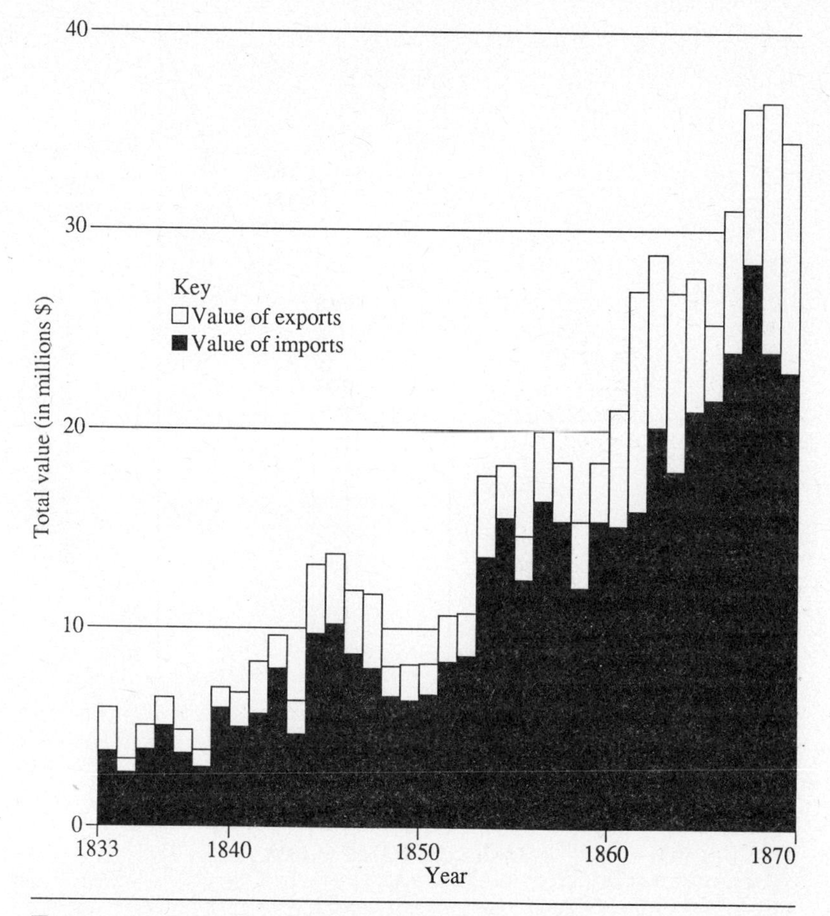


**FIG. 1** *Montreal Import–Export Trade 1833–1869*

SOURCE: Semi-Centennial Report of the Montreal Board of Trade (1893)

investment. In 1842 he opened Drummond Street, named after his wife Jane Drummond. Presumably at the same time he extended rue de la Montagne (by now referred to as Mountain Street by the Anglo-Saxon element) north of Dorchester Street and extended Ste Catherine and Sherbrooke streets through his property. Significantly, anticipating a special class of clientele, he subdivided the land not into ordinary house lots but into much larger mansion lots or "villa lots" in Victorian parlance (Map 1). The principle at work here was the same that had brought Redpath to the mountain slope, and the fur barons before him—that a panoramic view was highly desirable and therefore would attract a special clientele.

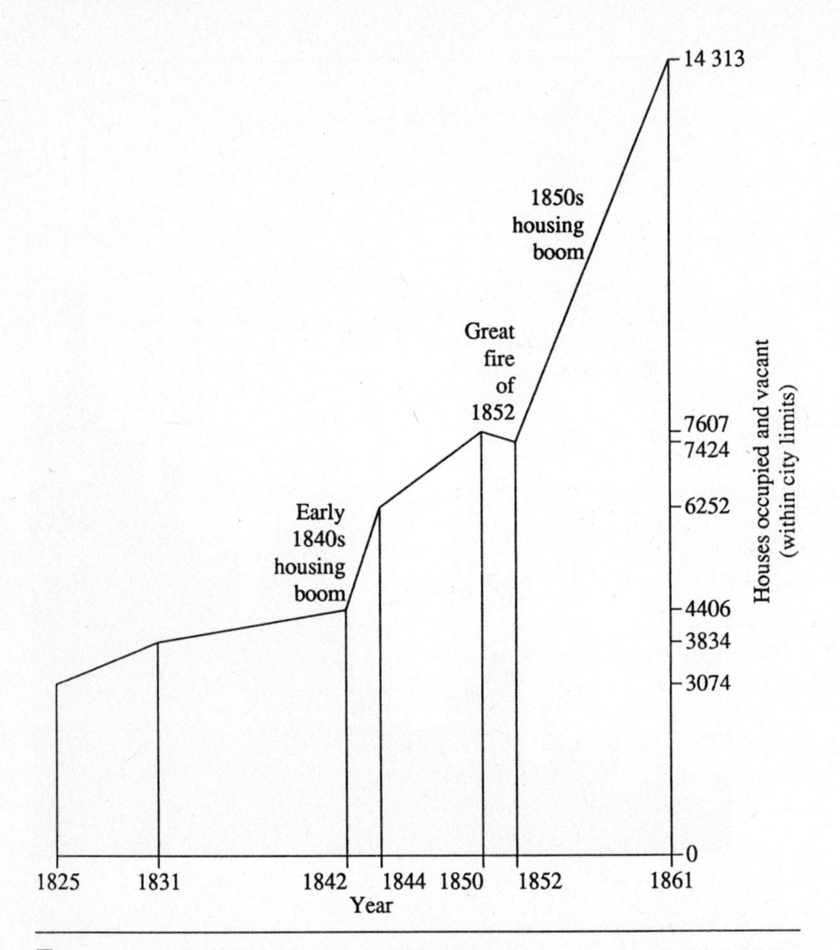


FIG. 2 *Montreal Housing Stock 1825–1861*

The Redpath subdivision had a profound influence on the shape of things to come. Boldly established in relative isolation on the plateau area, its design was also visionary. Planting the firm imprint of a grid pattern on the mountain slope, its scale set new standards for Montreal's urban development. The streets imparted a sense of grandeur because of their greater width, while the huge blocks provided ample space for long street vistas, generous backyards and housing setbacks. The element of spaciousness in John Redpath's plan is perhaps best explained by concurrent events at City Hall and Redpath's involvement in them. During 1840 and 1841, John Ostell, the City Surveyor (between 1840 and 1845) and coincidentally an architect by profession, was busily engaged in the preparation of Montreal's first comprehensive city plan.

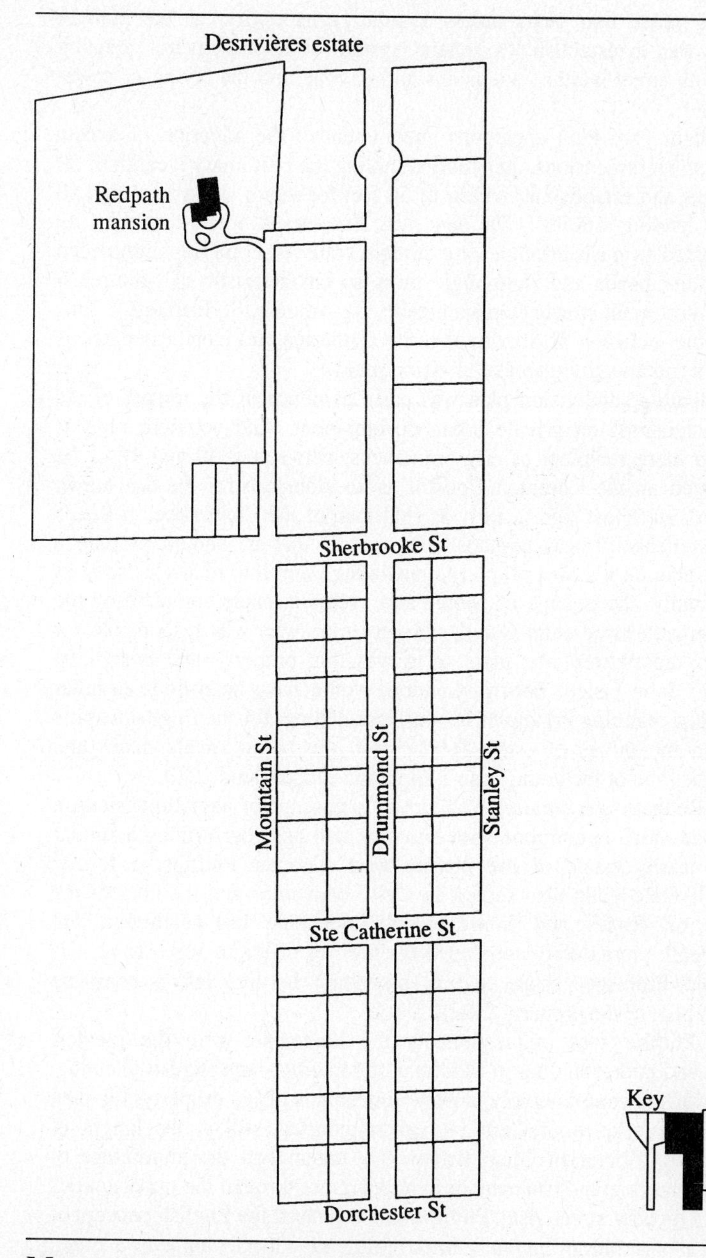


**MAP 1** *Redpath Subdivision Plan*

SOURCE: 1846 Map of Montreal, J. Cane

The city's Committee on Roads and Improvements continually deferred road work during those two years unless absolutely necessary, as the plan in preparation was to establish "a general system of improvement," dealing primarily with street widths, extensions and paving, and the laying of sewer lines.

The resultant City Plan apparently recommended the adoption of a new standard of street dimensions, generally doubling the customary breadth of 30 feet to 60 feet and establishing widths of 50 feet for minor side streets and 80 feet for outstanding arteries.[2] The new plan also served notice that the City was determined to push through long straight transverse arteries unimpeded by the constant bends and right-angle turns so characteristic of Montreal's older East-West main streets (Lagauchetiere, St. Antoine, St. Paul, etc.). This resulted in the inclusion of Sherbrooke, Ste Catherine and Dorchester streets in Redpath's and all subsequent subdivision plans.

John Redpath's subdivision plan was early evidence of the impact of the new street standards on private urban development. And yet Redpath was more than a mere recipient of city ordinances; between 1840 and 1843, he himself served on the Common Council as an alderman for the downtown Centre Ward, and most significantly as chairman of the Committee on Roads and Improvements. It was perhaps only natural that he should prepare a subdivision plan on his own property, translating them into reality as soon as possible. Finally, the linkage of people and events is made complete by the fact that Redpath hired John Ostell, the very man who was responsible for drawing up the master city plan, to survey his property and design its subdivision.[3] John Ostell, born in London, would have been quite familiar with the urban planning principles he was formulating, for the English capital had been in the throes of estate subdivision into broad streets, lanes and squares at the time of the young man's apprenticeship around 1830.

As John Redpath was creating a suburban townscape of new dimensions, a man who had much in common with him was also busy performing a similar task in a nearby estate of the plateau area. Thomas Phillips, a former contractor like Redpath, also served as a city councillor and member of the Committee on Roads and Improvements alongside his neighbour, but Phillips's death prematurely concluded his term of office in June, 1842. His was the old Frobisher estate and at his death he had left a complete subdivision plan of the property (Map 2).

Thomas Phillips was unquestionably the landowner with the greatest knowledge and understanding in Montreal of contemporary English planning, for in spite of the comparatively narrow dimensions of his property, his plan followed the true spirit of Georgian urban planning still at the height of fashion in early Victorian Great Britain. He understood the importance of stimulating a more grandiose manner in architecture through the opportunities created by a broader street vista. Phillips also espoused the English concept of the square, a large plot of greenery interrupting the normal course of a street,

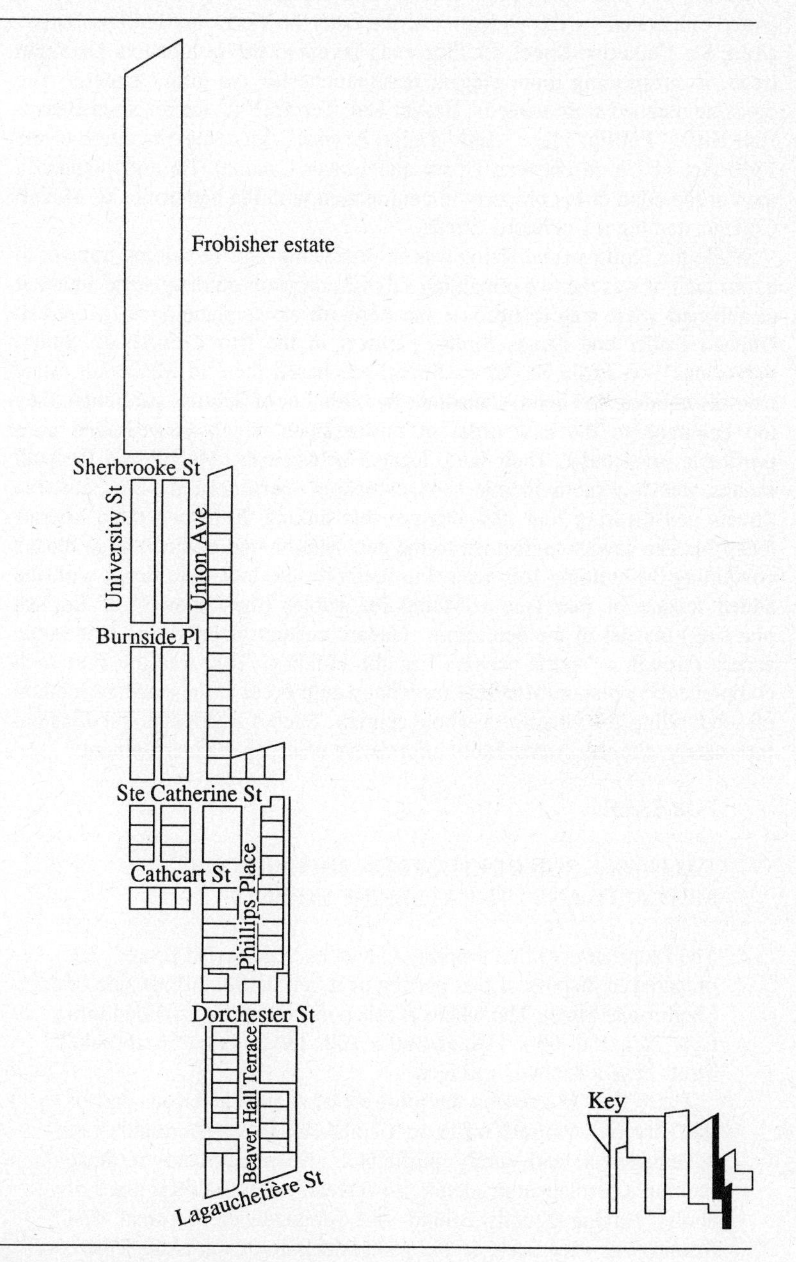


**MAP 2** *Phillips Subdivision Plan*

SOURCE: 1846 Map of Montreal, J. Cane

by laying out two in his plan: Beaver Hall Square along Dorchester Street (since obliterated by the widening of the latter in 1955) and Phillips Square along Ste Catherine Street. Phillips even favoured the fashionable Georgian trend of substituting more elegant designations for the term "street." The roads he planned were named "Beaver Hall Terrace" (since renamed Beaver Hall Hill), "Phillips Place" and "Union Avenue" (in commemoration of the 1840 Act of Union between Upper and Lower Canada). He also planned a road at the edge of his property in conjunction with the authorities of McGill College, naming it University Street.

While the Phillips subdivision was an interesting case of cultural transfer to a new land, it was the two remaining subdivision plans on the plateau area that established what was to become the norm in street planning in Montreal. Duncan Fisher and James Smith, partners in the firm "Fisher & Smith, Advocates" on Little St. James Street, purchased the Old McTavish estate from its uninterested heirs. Canadians by birth, but of Scottish parentage, they too belonged to the new order of businessmen which viewed land as a profitable investment. Their land, located between the McGill and Redpath estates, was duly subdivided in 1845, extending Sherbrooke and Ste Catherine Streets and creating four new cross-streets linking those two main arteries (Map 3). The streets conformed to the new breadth and outlined huge blocks containing 36 building lots each. Furthermore, the lots were deep, with the added feature of rear lane servicing for stables (the "mews" of English planning) instead of the heretofore standard custom of providing rear stable access through a "porte-cochère" in the building. This was the first such comprehensive plan in Montreal for what would become the standard method of subdividing for virtually a whole century. Such a significant subdivision, fortunately, elicited a remarkably informative newspaper advertisement:

> FOR SALE
>
> VALUABLE BUILDING LOTS ON SHERBROOKE, METCALFE AND STE CATHERINE STREETS.
>
> The Proprietors of that property known as "McTavish Estate" are prepared to dispose of that portion of it, on the South-East side of Sherbrooke Street. The whole of this portion has been divided into Lots 72 x 150, 60 x 118, and 60 x 100. The Lots on Sherbrooke Street have a depth of 150 feet.
>
> These lots, situated on the most elevated and salubrious part of the City of Montreal, offer to Capitalists, rare opportunities of advantageous, and surely profitable, investment; and to those seeking a permanent residence, an agreeable and healthful place of abode. Having directly behind—the Mountain of Montreal, and forming the very back, of the gentle declivity towards the Town, they must ever command delightful views, and the purest air.

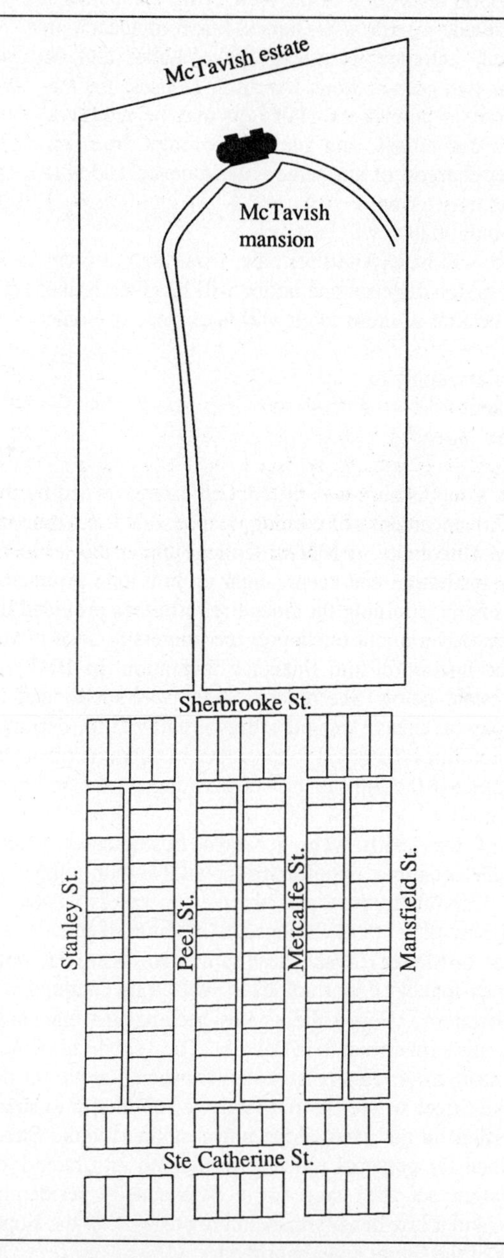


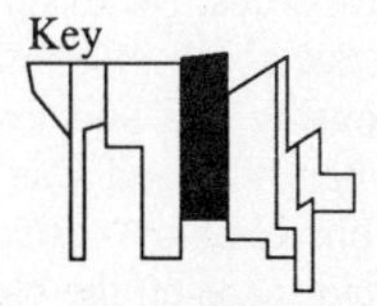


**Map 3** *Fisher and Smith Subdivision Plan*

SOURCE: 1846 Map of Montreal, J. Cane

It will be observed, on inspection of the Plan, lying at the office of Mr. J. Wells, Architect, 47, Little St. James' Street, that each of the lots, has a back entrance by means of a Lane, and is sufficiently large for two commodious Dwelling Houses; for the convenience, therefore, of purchasers, Half Lots may be acquired.

This property is commuted, and for ever exempt from all Seigneurial and other charges, of any nature, whatsoever, and will be sold on liberal and easy terms.

Titles, of validity indubitable, will be given.

A few of these lots will be exposed for Sale, from time to time, at public auction, of which disposal due notice will be given in the City Newspapers. The first of these sales, will take place on some early day in May.

For further particulars, apply to
John Wells, Architect
47, Little St. James' Street[4]

Adjacent to the Phillips's subdivision was the McGill estate, owned by the Royal Institution for the Advancement of Learning, responsible for setting up a university known as the University of McGill College under the terms of James McGill's will. The Institution had been caught up in a long protracted legal battle with McGill's heirs, straining the financial resources provided by his will. The refusal of the Government to support the university once it was set up further plunged the institution into financial destitution. In 1845 the southern portion of the estate below Sherbrooke Street was subdivided in order to raise revenue to pay off debts. This plan, drawn up by H.M. Perrault, John Ostell's associate, was almost identical to the adjacent subdivision of the McTavish estate and completed the bulk of the subdividing on the southern slope of Mount Royal (Map 4).

The new landowners of the 1840s were generally businessmen whose wealth was derived from the economic opportunities available within the city. These men were the new élite of Montreal and like the fur traders wished to enjoy their wealth and display their status through the medium of prestigious estates located on the slope of Mount Royal. These same men, however, were not insensitive to the money-making opportunities of real estate dealings in a rapidly expanding local economy. Hence the estates became just one more link in their chains of lucrative investments in the city. They subdivided their properties, each implementing a conscious distinction between that part of the estate south of Sherbrooke Street where the flat land was divided into small housing lots and that portion on the steep slope north of Sherbrooke Street where the land was retained for personal use or else divided into huge lots. This clear-cut differentiation set the stage for a high-density residential townscape on the plateau, and a low-density mansion townscape on the slope, the two basic components of the future neighbourhood.

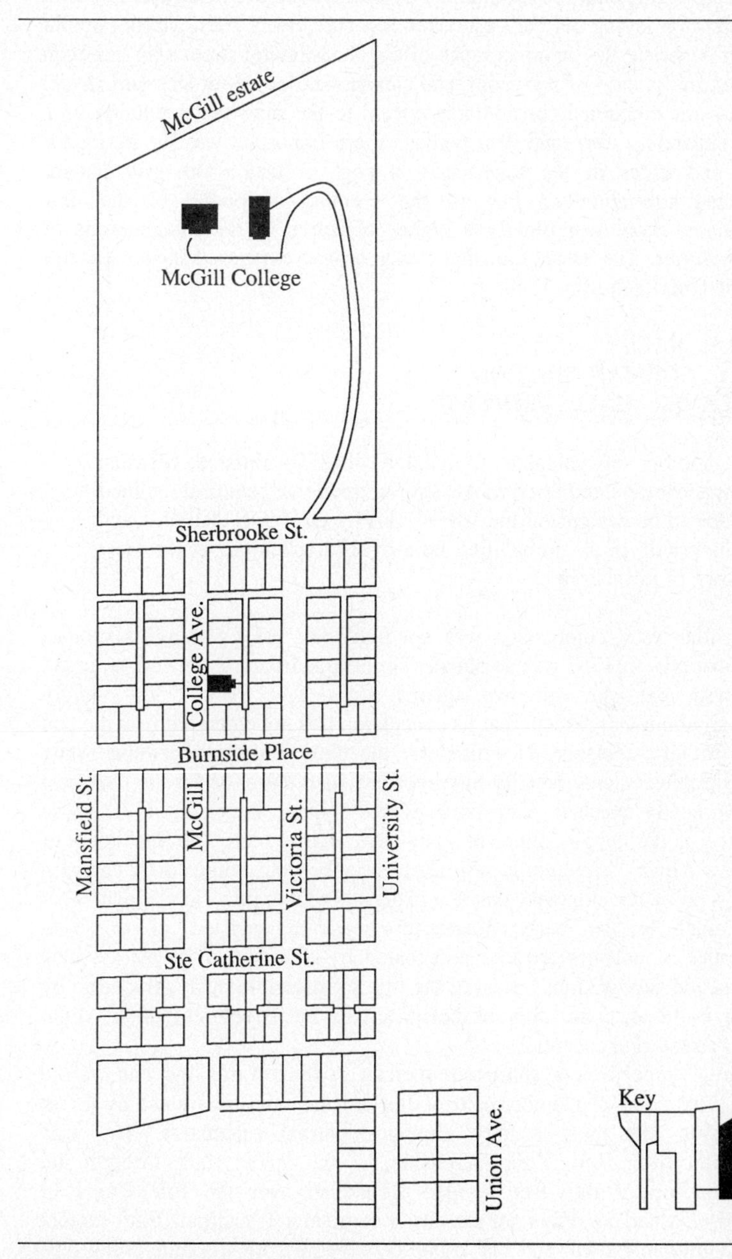


**Map 4** *McGill Subdivision Plan*

SOURCE: 1846 Map of Montreal, J. Cane

It is noteworthy that the mountain side subdividers chose the quadrilateral grid pattern on laying out their estates in lots and streets. Particularly popular in North America, the preponderance of the quadrilateral street plan has been explained by its ease of surveying and standardization of lot size and shape. Both features contained considerable appeal to the merchant mentality of a rapidly expanding new land. But perhaps more important was the desire for system and order in the townscape, a goal to which the grid pattern contributed substantially.[5] For all the seeming simplicity of the new subdivisions, there was clearly a higher objective in the imaginations of contemporaries. The essence of that image is best expressed in this excerpt from The *Gazette*, 8 May 1844:

> FOR SALE
> BY NORMAN BETHUNE
> BEAVER HALL PROPERTY
>
> A number of valuable BUILDING LOTS, situated between Lagauchetière and Sherbrooke Streets; upon that beautiful inclined plane to be designated the 'NEW TOWN OF MONTREAL,' and which will, in all probability, be a rival in splendour of the New Town of Edinburgh.

The enthusiastic comparison was not ludicrous, for Edinburgh's famous New Town plan of 1767 was an equally simple quadrilateral network of broad streets with rear lanes and two squares. Montreal's "New Town" hardly offered anything less, except that its conception had not emerged from the pen of one solitary designer. Nevertheless, the close linkages between estate owners, architects, and the City Surveyor provided the basis for the next best thing—a neatly meshed plan born of the mutual interests of all those concerned, under the guidelines of a new civic master plan. The fulfillment of the "New Town" ideal could ultimately only be consummated by carrying out the type of development characteristic of Edinburgh's New Town. That development in the early nineteenth century consisted of dignified streetscapes of uniform terraces punctuated by churches. Whether the new mountainside subdivisions deserved the title so magnanimously alluded to by Norman Bethune, could only be borne out by the structures which would grace its streets and squares.

Montreal underwent a sharp commercial crisis towards the end of the decade. The rapid dismemberment of the old mercantilist system by Great Britain was felt most acutely among Montreal merchants. The stiff competition from New York merchants for the inland trade through the implementation of duty-free bonded shipments over the Erie Canal in 1845–46 also had its effect on the city's commercial position. Both factors froze population growth and real estate development for the time being (see Figs. 1, 2). The early 1850s brought only the addition of local disasters to further depress the situation. Fires ravaged the city repeatedly during 1850 and 1852 culminating in the Great Fire of 1852 which destroyed 1100 houses and the entire east end with it. Cholera plagues added to the misery during this period.

The commercial crisis lifted, however, as free trade brought its benefits to Montreal. The dredging of the river channel below the city brought trans-oceanic steamship service to the port for the first time in 1853, and simultaneously construction of the huge Grand Trunk Railway project centred on Montreal was begun. With these improvements in the city's competitive position, the import–export trade began to climb rapidly (see Fig. 1). The forces that transformed Montreal's commercial system in the 1850s also found their parallel in the city's housing. Montreal witnessed both a population and a housing boom during the decade, on a scale never before experienced except during those brief years of optimism between 1842 and 1844. During the 1850s, Montreal's population soared, effectively doubling between 1850 and 1861. The city's housing stock had climbed from 4406 units in 1842 to 7424 in 1852. It would leap to 14 313 units by 1861, and this figure did not take into account the substantial suburban growth occurring outside the city limits (see Fig. 2).

Montreal in the 1850s was quite clearly in the throes of a real estate development boom. The urban disasters of fire and plague probably heightened the boom, given the new influx of population and the shortage of housing. The most interesting observation to be made, however, is the fact that Old Montreal in 1850 was still the focal point for the homes of wealthy Montrealers. The merchants' homes were to be found in the western portion of the old city, along Great Saint James, Notre Dame and St. François-Xavier streets. These are not to be construed as merely business addresses as the 1850 directory clearly indicates that they were indeed domiciles. The simple fact that this area would witness a massive exodus of residents to the "New Town" by 1860, brings to light the most important catalyst in the suburban migration. Fires and disease had provided the psychological push for a suburban movement amongst the rich,[6] but the need for commercial expansion would furnish the ultimate rationale for the residential evacuation of the central area.

During the late 1850s and 1860s, Great St. James and Notre Dame streets were to be virtually transformed into the commercial core of Montreal. Since the 1820s, buildings intended solely for commercial purposes had spread out from the traditional waterfront/rue St. Paul location to infiltrate the mixed residential-institutional zone along those two streets. The commercial boom which began during the 1850s stimulated the expansion and multiplication of businesses while furnishing Montreal merchants with the necessary wealth to take up residence in the suburbs. As large prestigious commercial buildings superseded the small house-over-shop combination, an outward extension of the commercial district took place, swallowing up old houses and churches. The result was that Notre Dame Street during the 1860s became a corridor of tall arcaded facades housing the best of the city's retail and wholesale firms. Similar transformations altered the side streets as well, effectively producing a large exclusively commercial "downtown" by the 1870s where there had been a mixture of all possible urban land-uses only a few decades before. As such, the 1860s must be marked in the annals of Montreal's development as a decade of profound transformation. Up to 1850 it could be said there was an "old" Montreal. After 1850 a "new" Montreal emerged, mirrored in the dawn of a central business district and a new upper-middle-class suburb, the "New Town."

The factor which proved to be one of the best enticements, judging by the frequent mention in real estate advertisements, for the higher income residents of the city to move out of the central area was water servicing, a remarkable luxury in 1850s Montreal. The municipal government, horrified by the unchecked devastation wrought upon the city by the fires of 1850 and 1852 and dismayed by the ease with which disease was able to spread through the polluted urban drinking water, launched the great civic project known as the "Montreal Aqueduct" in 1852. The cost and scale of the Montreal Aqueduct project were enormous for a Municpal Government of twenty years' existence whose ventures into the realm of municpal services were still in the embryonic stage. But its effect on expansion of the city towards Mount Royal was profound if not decisive. The location of the reservoir high up the slope of Mount Royal suddenly gave the entire mountainside up to the level of the reservoir the potential of water servicing. As soon as construction on the aqueduct was assured in 1853, house-building activity began to surge forward on the mountainside after the eight year slump since the subdivision of all the mountainside estates. By 1856, when the first water was pumped into the reservoir, housing construction was literally booming. House builders could offer the convenience of flush-activated water closets as a standard feature, once the laying of pipe and sewer lines was completed. The years 1853–54 marked the beginning of a housing construction boom which would result in the creation of a unique townscape on the southern slope of Mount Royal.

The steeper portion of the mountainside estates above Sherbrooke Street attracted individuals who could afford the high cost of land—the obvious result of the high desirability of the location—and occupy large lots themselves. Land on the flatter plateau area south of Sherbrooke Street was also expensive but attracted instead speculators who could pay the high price and make a profit by building high-density prestige dwellings. The accepted formula in the 1850s for the type of housing contemplated was the terrace. Although the terrace was relatively new to the Montreal urban scene, having first made its appearance in the 1840s along major arteries in the older suburbs, St. Antoine, de Bleury, and St. Denis streets, the idea was over a century old in British urban planning and by the 1850s was just beginning to wane. The terrace, quite simply, was the uniting of a homogeneous group of attached houses behind a single monumental façade. It was a conception of high taste and because of its grand design was viewed as a distinct improvement over the prevailing individually conceived attached houses of the urban wealthy. Montreal's early terraces, however, were actually little more than uniformly designed row houses dignified with a name, such as "Tecumseh Terrace," "St. Antoine Place" or "Cornwall Terrace."

British "New Town" development and upper-class suburban development in general had occurred almost exclusively in the form of elegant terraces and mansions gracing broad streetscapes, tangential crescents and terminal vistas. Such was the development of Edinburgh's New Town, as it was of new suburban areas in Glasgow, Liverpool or London. The architectural profession had grown considerably in Montreal during the 1840s with the arrival of trained young men from the British Isles (George Browne, George Dickinson, William Footner, James McFarlane, John Ostell, James Springle and John Wells). These men filled a professional void in the colonial city and brought to a newly affluent merchant population the expertise with which wealth might be translated into physical expressions of British middle-class values. The question of whether or not the area on the southern slope of Mount Royal would live up to the label of "New Town" ascribed during the 1840s depended therefore on what type of development graced its streets.

Of four terraces undertaken in 1855, one is noteworthy. Representing the first tangible evidence of the lot sales by McGill College, "Wellington Terrace" (1855–56) was erected along the entire block face of the south side of Ste Catherine Street between McGill College Avenue and Mansfield Street. For a city that had heretofore only known a very "provincial" version of the English terrace, this new building clearly established a whole new standard. "Wellington Terrace" was the conception of George Browne, probably Canada's greatest architect at the time. Born into an architectural family in Belfast, Browne was trained for the profession in that terrace-rich city. Emigrating to Canada in 1831, he distinguished himself early by founding the first known school of architecture in the country in Quebec City. Appointed Government Architect in 1841, Browne proceeded to endow Kingston with the most sophisticated public and commercial buildings the nation had ever seen, when that city was selected as capital for the united provinces. He moved with the Government to Montreal in 1843 where he remained to work in private practice.[7]

Finally, in 1855, George Browne made the bold move of involving himself in the housing boom, not simply as an architect, but as a speculative builder himself. He purchased land and took the financial risk. What he conceived was extraordinary for a city used to squat gable-roofed houses. "Wellington Terrace" was a magnificent two-storey stone structure executed in a very refined Classical Revival manner. In fact his style had evolved into the more exuberant Baroque Revival mode of the 1850s, also known as "Louis XIV." His building introduced many new features to middle-class housing in Montreal. Among these were the large stone porticos over each doorway, a dignified cornice and window trim, and the whole topped by a flat roof surmounted by statuary. Except for its modest height, it was the equal of anything available in the upper class districts of London's west end.

The financial panic of 1857, being short in duration, seems not to have had any damaging psychological impact on speculative builders. In fact it had quite the reverse effect as 1858–59 was the first of two peaks in terrace building. Ste Catherine Street was rapidly being built up as a terrace corridor, but now McGill College Avenue was similarly establishing itself. It was quite natural for these two arteries to become the focal points of terrace expansion for they were the first two streets to be serviced with water from the new reservoir. Terrace developers were taking up the challenge put forth by George Browne, as almost all adopted the flat-roof configuration with elaborate cornice decoration. Moreover, terraces were now being built to a height of three full storeys exclusive of the basement, instead of two. In style, the terraces had finally cast off the dour Classical Revival mode which had held sway over Montreal at least since the 1830s. Instead the newer Italianate form was adopted as architectural decoration became highlighted with bracketing and segmental arch windows. "Mount Royal Terrace" (1858–59) was the leading confection of the day and its constantly receding and projecting twelve unit mass sitting haughtily above a raised basement produced a formidable looking streetscape along McGill College Avenue.

A new phenomenon in middle class housing was becoming evident by 1858. That year saw the construction of a myriad of extremely elegant semi-detached houses with such pedantic names as "Southwell Place," "Greenfield Place," or "Leicester Place." The houses were not unlike a pair of terrace units detached from the main body and placed amidst a generous lawn. The idea of semi-detached housing had been conceived in the Georgian era. Like the terrace, it was merely taken over and expanded in the early Victorian period, by becoming a fashionable sort of residence for upper-class aspirants.[8] Curiously however, the semi-detached house in Montreal enjoyed only a brief and intermittent vogue, unlike the younger Toronto which forsook the terrace very early for a wholehearted subscription to the semi-detached house.

The new decade brought at first a remarkable vitality to housing construction in the "New Town." The visit by the Prince of Wales to Montreal in 1860 re-cemented the psychological break that had occurred with Great Britain in the 1840s. The warm feelings for the Imperial connection reached a new peak amongst the Anglo-Saxon element of the population, and those feelings were effectively mirrored in the appearance of the "Prince of Wales Terrace" in 1860. Closer to the English model than ever before, this terrace was to be the most palatial ever erected in Montreal. Set at the head of a block on Sherbrooke Street, it foretold great things for the largely undeveloped artery. "Prince of Wales Terrace" was the work of George Browne. The masterful Classical Revival edifice touched with the exuberance of the contemporary Baroque Revival was the mark of his style. Hardly stopping there, he added the equally magnificent "Holyrood Place" (1861) to the already distinguished streetscape on McGill College Avenue. Another beautiful "Louis XIV" confection, the sweeping fourteen-unit terrace looked directly across the street at the slightly earlier "Mount Royal Terrace."

The construction of 1860–61 marked the apex of terrace development and design in Montreal, but it hardly marked the end. The second boom of terrace building came in 1863. Great Terraces lined nearly all streets faces of the old McGill and McTavish estates. The 1854 bylaw prohibiting further burials in the huge Roman Catholic cemetery on the plateau brought terraces sweeping around its perimeter in 1863, once the transfer of graves to the new mountain-top was assured. The opening of new streets above Sherbrooke (Upper University and McTavish streets) attracted terrace builders to their steeply rising gradients. One such terrace, "Princess Royal Terrace" (1862–63), situated in the upper reaches of University Street also made evident a new trend in housing tastes which would ultimately close the lengthy chapter of the terrace. This new terrace style purposefully stressed the individuality of each unit of housing. Instead of a unified façade, here was a collection of individual units, each with a projecting bay window above the portico, a miniature peaked gable over the attic window breaking the cornice, and an octagonal cupola astride the ridgepole. It was a delightful and distinctive piece of work in the Italianate style then in vogue in Montreal.

While terraces were busily carving out a new townscape below Mount Royal, another type of housing gradually made its impression felt in the area. Mansions had traditionally been located far up the mountain towards Côte des Neiges Road. Under John Redpath's impetus, a line of mansions had formed along Drummond and Mountain streets on the plateau area in the 1840s. No new development occurred until 1854 when the large houses began appearing once again in the "New Town" coincident with the start of the terrace boom. The 1850s and 1860s marked the peak of popularity with the Italianate or "Bracketed Style" in architectural fashion. Popular especially with the merchant class in Great Britain, lofty stone villas were springing up in Victorian neighbourhoods from Bristol to Glasgow. In the United States, the style had fired the imagination even more as large Cubic Italianate houses, or "Tuscan villas," swept across both the urban and rural landscapes in the northern states during the prosperous Civil War era. Montreal's architects were equally conversant with the style and dotted the "New Town" with large luxurious mansions of limestone.

Mansion construction began almost everywhere in the "New Town" at once. New houses filled in the remaining generous mansion lots on Mountain and Drummond streets which developed into extremely graceful arteries, given the ample setbacks provided for each house and the enthusiastic tree planting fortuitously undertaken in the 1840s, apparently by John Redpath himself. Of the merchants who came to inhabit this part of the "New Town" many were to become influential names in Canadian business. The inhabitants included Alexander Galt, George Stephen, John Ogilvie, and several others.

The true direction of mansion building was established when a wave of stone "villa" building swept up the steeper slope of Mount Royal to capitalize on the view. Virtually all the planned streets leading up the mountain slope were opened in the 1850s and mansion lot sales were made at a constant and rapid rate. University Street was built up almost entirely with mansions and terraces in the early 1860s. McTavish and Peel streets up the slope saw some initial mansion building at this time also. As mansions dotted the hillside, Sherbrooke Street at its base gradually emerged as an impressive artery lined with large mansions along the north side which were usually set well back from the street.

Church development was the final large-scale factor in the emergence of a mature townscape below Mount Royal. The Unitarians, Congregationalists, and Church of Scotland Presbyterians had been the first sects to express confidence in the shift of urban development towards Mount Royal by relocating their churches to the Beaver Hall Terrace vicinity by 1850. When the old Neo-Classical style Anglican cathedral was burned to the ground on Notre Dame Street in 1856, a new site and style were chosen for the rebuilt church. Christ Church Cathedral rose amidst new terraces between 1857 and 1860 in the most splendid Gothic Revival style Montreal would ever witness. Following closely the architectural developments in Great Britain, this edifice was in the vanguard of contemporary taste and cast an undeniable Victorian stamp on the "New Town." Moreover, the choice of a "New Town" location for the cathedral as early as 1857 was a confident statement on the migration of its affluent parishioners.

The 1860s were a boom period for church building in Montreal, and the bulk of that growth was channelled directly to the "New Town." Mostly spaced out along Ste Catherine and Dorchester streets, nine new churches were built in 1869, virtually all in the Gothic style. Besides two new churches added to the Beaver Hall Terrace cluster, these included two Anglican parish churches and a large Methodist church. The heaviest contribution, however, was made by four new Presbyterian churches. This gave the area a predominantly Presbyterian stamp and helps to confirm the ascendancy of native Scots or people of Scottish descent in the "New Town." Moreover, this meant that by 1869, exactly half the Presbyterian churches in Montreal were located in the "New Town," Presbyterianism accounting for slightly over one sixth of all churches in the city.

It is instructive to note that church relocation and construction was generally a leading rather than a lagging element of urban development in the "New Town." This tendency is well illustrated in a Notman photograph taken from Mount Royal above "Ravenscrag" in 1866. The incentive to act fast in order to obtain a large plot of land for a new church building was no doubt a motive behind the anticipatory moves of several churches, but the desires of the members themselves to take up residence in the "New Town" must not be discounted in the relocation decisions.

**PHOTO 1** McGill College Avenue looking north from Ste Catherine Street at Mount Royal Terrace, built 1858–59, and Ste Sophie Place, built 1858. Photo: Walker, c. 1865. Source: McCord Museum, Montreal.

PHOTO 2 Prince of Wales Terrace at the corner of Sherbrooke and McTavish Streets, 1860. Source: McCord Museum, Notman Photo no. MP 082/74.

**Photo 3** Princess Royal Terrace on Upper University Street built 1862–63; from a Kilburn photo, c. 1865. Source: Archives of Ontario.

**PHOTO 4** Thornhill, home of Henry Lyman built 1859–60 on McTavish Street. Beside it on Peel Street is The Elms, erected for Alfred Savage, 1860; photo, c. 1875. Source: McCord Museum, Notman Photo no. MP 094/74.

PHOTO 5 View of Montreal from Mount Royal. Sir Hugh Allan's house Ravenscrag (1860–62) in foreground, McTavish Reservoir (1852–56) and McGill College (1839–43, 1861) beyond. Streets running up the mountain slope from right to left are Peel, McTavish, McGill College, and Upper University. In the background is Victoria Bridge (1853–59) spanning the St. Lawrence River. Source: Archives of Ontario/ACC 16630-16.

The Notman photograph serves as an excellent overview of the "New Town" at a stage of its development when the terrace had almost run its course. The mansion district may be seen taking shape above Sherbrooke Street. Here the architecture of the Picturesque, then at the height of its popularity in the mid-nineteenth century, prevails. Trees are preserved and integrated into the plan while houses are intended to capture the romantic sentiments toward the past, evident through the Italian Renaissance towers and cupolas, Mediaeval Gothic turrets and finials, Tudor chimneys and Grecian urns rising above the leafy crowns.

This almost chimerical townscape dissolves near Sherbrooke Street, however. From there the broad shelf of the plateau is evident in the photograph until it ends at a thin line of trees running through the middle of the print. Cleared of trees, this is the terrace townscape, the heart of the "New Town." The stiff formality of the orthogonal street pattern is mirrored in the long rows of houses. The work looks unfinished and indeed there is still much land to fill. But streets such as McGill College, Union, University and Ste Catherine are virtually complete, giving the area a certain maturity. Here Georgian symmetry, elegance and orderliness prevail. The finer terraces with their flat roofs sloping to the rear are hard to miss. Certainly the "Prince of Wales Terrace" is predominant in the lower right-hand side of the view. But the most noble streetscape of the entire "New Town" is McGill College Avenue with elegant, flat-roofed terraces lining both sides of the street. A conception of remarkable dignity, this is the finest street Montreal had to offer in the 1860s.

The end of the "New Town" as a townscape in the Georgian tradition came quickly. The new stress on individuality highlighted in the "Princess Royal Terrace" and certainly evident in mansion and church construction, underlined the fact that the "Romantic Movement" begun in the eighteenth century was finally filtering down to architect, builder and ultimately the public. It was anti-rationalist, hence anti-Georgian, and for mass housing it marked the beginning of a reaction against the imposed orderliness and symmetry of eighteenth-century planning. In architecture it sought relief from monotony, exaggeration of individuality.[9] Terraces, as the epitome of Georgian rationalist planning, were doomed to extinction. Terrace construction continued to the end of the 1860s but tapered off rapidly. By the early 1870s, the last named terraces, though no longer really terraces but simply elegant row houses, were completed. By 1894, the Montreal directories no longer listed the names and locations of terraces. They became faceless entities known only by a street address like any other house. Following the principles of Romantic planning, trees had been planted along all the "New Town" streets in the 1850s. While forging a whole new streetscape of shade and colour, they ran against the purpose of terrace architecture which was to expose the façade. As the trees matured, the terraces disappeared behind a barrage of foliage, demolishing their potent visual effect on the streetscape and probably hastening public disregard for them.

The intriguing fact about terrace development in what is now Canada is that a comprehensive terrace townscape occurred only in Montreal. While the reasons for this occurrence have been explored in the local context, it would be of value to consider the circumstance in relation to a broader milieu. What for example does the "New Town" tell us about Montreal in the nineteenth-century urban system in Canada? Can any parallels be drawn between Montreal and major cities in the United States? Finally, where does the Montreal terrace fit in the framework of urbanization in the English-speaking world?

The first component to consider is a time reference. The terrace flourished as a popular form of urban housing between the years 1770 and 1860. This period was in fact the beginning of widespread urban growth in both Great Britain and the New World. The terrace must be considered against this setting. It is tempting at this stage to introduce some notion of scale. As the terrace was manifestly a high-density type of accommodation, it is easy to suppose that some sort of threshold population was required to support the incidence of terraces. Yet cities both huge and small, as witnessed by London and Bath, had their terrace townscapes. But if only the size of the upper middle class of the social spectrum is considered, then the terrace townscapes may be placed in their proper context. A review of the cities in which terraces were prevalent reveals a prosperous and growing upper middle class. In terms of function, those cities fell into three basic camps: commercial centres, administrative centres, or a combination of both. Montreal flourished because of its prime commercial position in the Saint Lawrence system. New York did likewise through its Mohawk corridor. Boston thrived on a mixture of commercialism and public administration. Across the ocean, commercial cities like Bristol and Liverpool had their terraces, but Glasgow, with its leading commercial position in the nineteenth century, offered the most dramatic demonstration of the relationship between terrace and commerce. On the public administration side, Edinburgh offered an equally dramatic display of the links between terraces and that function.

A terrace townscape in an urban centre within the time frame considered was indubitably linked with a strong upper middle-class sector of the population. Administrative and commercial cities drew considerable numbers of government officials and merchant entrepreneurs respectively. These in turn were seconded by a huge lower middle class fulfilling ancillary functions to the basic roles of government and trade. Those people, while not sufficiently well-off to afford a terrace residence, did on occasion climb the social ladder. In contrast, in an industrial centre vast pools of working class labour under the aegis of a small handful of industrialists tended to congregate. Where manufacturing predominated there was little need for a middle class and the manufacturers themselves formed a very small segment of the total population. Hence cities such as Birmingham or Manchester in Great Britain had fine mansions and a profusion of row housing but no terrace townscape.

The sole remaining anomaly in the case of the terrace was its strong presence in small urban centres in the south-central and southwestern part of England. Bath and Leamington Spa were replete with terraces. Brighton and other coastal cities had their share as well. These centres were all resort areas for the idle rich, housing aristocratic and primarily upper middle class residents, mostly elderly, seeking the relief of the health spas. The resorts lay within 120 miles of London, and their terraces may even be considered as extensions of the terrace townscape of the metropolis.

London itself was omnipotent and ultimately all developments in the urban sphere were mirrored through it, even if it did not originate them itself. Hence the terrace saw its Georgian-era flowering in the small city of Bath, but it was in London that the terrace was modelled on a truly massive scale and exported throughout the British world. London's terraces were the result of the commercial and administrative capacities of a metropolis whose position in the late eighteenth and early nineteenth centuries was unassailable.

In British North America, the urban scene was not sufficiently mature to support terrace housing until the nineteenth century. Halifax, a large administrative, military and commercial centre, first saw terrace construction, albeit on a very minor scale, in the 1820s. It remained until the 1840s, however, for terraces to erupt simultaneously in virtually all major commercial and administrative centres in Upper and Lower Canada. Even then, by the 1860s, cities such as Toronto, Hamilton and Quebec had only a few isolated examples of fully developed terraces. It remained for Montreal alone to develop a comprehensive terrace townscape.

## Notes

1. Contracting activities were gleaned from various personal account books of John Redpath on deposit at the McCord Museum, Montreal.
2. The plan was probably issued sometime in the transition between the years 1841 and 1842 as city By-law 74 of 27 June 1842 refers to the completed plan. Unfortunately no copy of the plan and its recommendations appears to be extant. Possibly it was destroyed in the City Hall fire of 1922. The street dimensions quoted here were deduced from contemporary subdivision plans registered with City Hall.
3. Subdivision plan by John Ostell, on deposit at Archives Nationales du Québec, in Montreal.
4. The *Gazette*, 11 April 1845.
5. Christopher Tunnard, *The City of Man* (New York, 1970), 57.
6. Urban disasters have always prompted an exodus from the city. Just as the dreaded plagues of the thirteenth century onwards spawned the multiplication of villas outside the city walls, so do suburbanites today cite their quest for "a cleaner, healthier neighbourhood" as the prime reason for their flight from the city. Lewis Mumford, *The City in History* (New York, 1961), 487.

7. Unpublished information pertaining to George Browne available in Percy Nobbs Room of Blackader Library at McGill University.

8. Henry-Russell Hitchcock, *Early Victorian Architecture in Britain* (New Haven, 1954), 411, 414.

9. Mumford, *City in History*, 489.

# COMMUNICATIONS AND URBAN SYSTEMS IN MID-NINETEENTH CENTURY CANADA*

PETER G. GOHEEN

Our literature is rich with grand assumptions about communications in nineteenth-century Canada, but our systematic knowledge of how they were organized is limited. The necessity of organizing the transmission of information over long distances implies the idea of a communications system, however detailed or articulated. That cities are the fulcra of these systems has been acknowledged. A systematic assessment of the structure and content of communications flows among the major urban centres of British North America in the nineteenth century has not yet been contributed. It has seemed reasonable to assert that those cities which rose to metropolitan rank did so through their ability to control communications and trade with growing hinterlands, while less successful places tried or succeeded more modestly.[1] That a distinctly Canadian communications system characterized the British North American colonies has been maintained with great vigour. It has been declared to be a "system...which lasted as the dominant economic form for two centuries of Canadian history," an idea more recently recast as "an emerging central Canadian metropolitan system...to organize British North American hinterlands into a separate continental unit."[2] The argument has become entrenched. Restatements rely effortlessly on similar geopolitical assumptions, the literature containing propositions such as those proposing that Montreal possessed a "natural hinterland" and that Upper Canada after mid-century constituted an identifiable "urban system."[3] In this paper communications among the major cities and towns of the colonies during the middle decades of the nineteenth century will be examined by undertaking a content analysis of leading newspapers in 1845 and 1855. By measuring the availability in several cities of published information about other places such

* *Urban History Review/Revue d'histoire urbaine* XIV, 3 (February/février 1986): 235–45.

basic questions of communications as what is being said to whom and through what channels can be discovered.[4] What, in particular, were the sources of public information available in the more important urban centres just prior to and after the arrival of the telegraph and the railroad? How did the pattern of information circulation change during a significant decade?

Communications among cities during this period developed in the context of urbanization, a process which implies changing relations among cities and their societies. When, as in nineteenth-century North America, it accompanies the expansion of settlement, it is marked by significant increases in the number and population size of cites. In these decades growth was most pronounced in the addition of new urban places to the lower ranks of settlements, with stability among the higher ranking centres (see Fig. 1). In such conditions the role of cities as central places and the territorial imprint of their influence change through the growth of a web of communications among the growing number of centres. To consider towns in their relation to each other through this network of communications is to treat them as a system. The idea of a system focusses on co-ordination, communication and interdependence among the interacting elements within a territorial framework defined by the pattern and structure of the interactions. The whole functions in a distinctive manner, and not as the sum of its parts taken individually. Allan Pred has defined an urban system as

> a set of cities which are interdependent in such a way that any significant change in the economic activities, occupational structure, total income or population of one member city will directly or indirectly bring about an alteration in...one or more other set members.[5]

The application of the logic of systems to the study of ties among cities during periods of urbanization follows logically from Philip Abram's remark that cities are "implicated in a nodal manner in these larger systems" no matter the context of their influence, be it economic, social or political.[6] This approach to urbanization has been termed "structural" because the activities which give rise to it are those that "require the appearance of coordinators (social positions devoted to coordinating large-scale activities...), communications line (to permit coordinators to carry out this work) and cross-cutting relationships (social relationships that cross the boundaries of kinship, locality and traditional alliances)."[7]

Communications express the movement across time and space of information, in whatever form and through whatever medium, which it is in the mutual interest of sender and receiver to exchange. Their co-ordination requires centralized agencies to assure their effective collection and diffusion, especially when great distances must be bridged by complex connections among many places. The institutions undertaking this task will achieve their greatest comparative advantage by maximizing their accessibility to sources

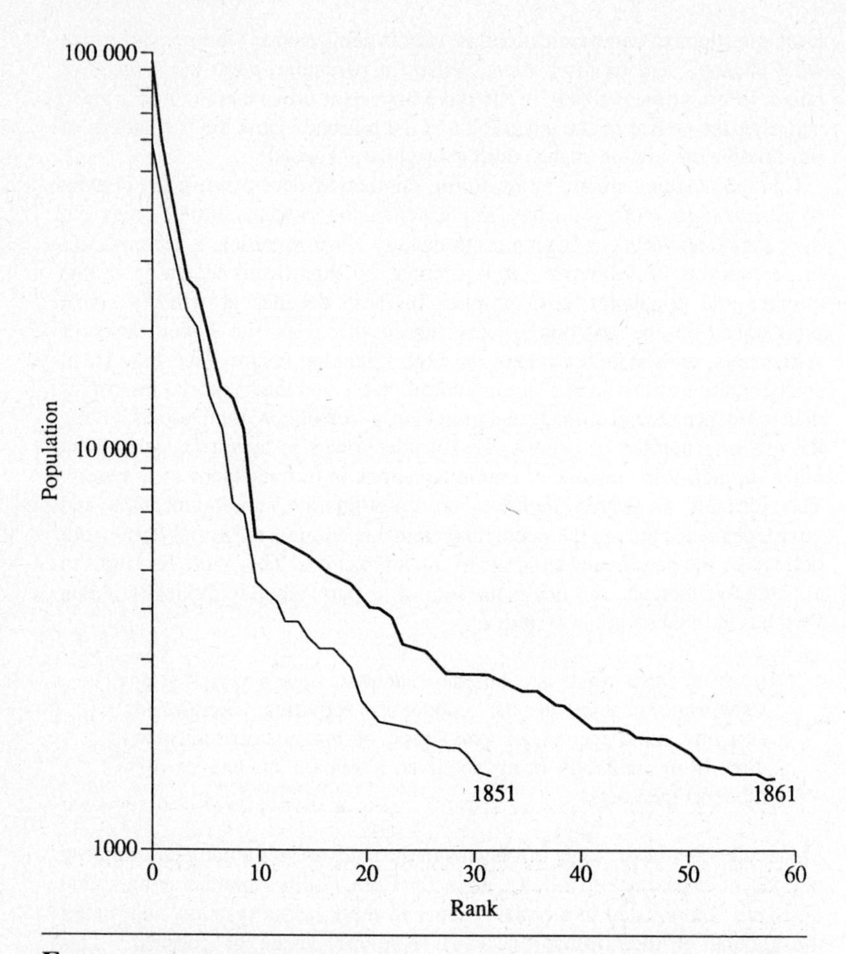


**FIG. 1** *Rank–Size Distributions of Towns with Population over 1500 in British North America.*

and markets. This advantage is locationally specific, so that communications systems focus on cities. They function within technological constraints as to the mode, speed and cost of their operation. Under conditions such as pertained during the nineteenth century, when access to information was relatively constrained by the cost of its acquisition and transmission, a few locations possessed great advantages of access to information. Communications were organized hierarchically under such circumstances and they relied on, and indeed helped engender, urban systems.

Communications is a broad concept. Communications exist in many forms. To generalize from the mass of specific messages in which it is manifested requires an unambiguous measure of information that will be capable of representing abstractly the principal qualities of the system. These include the spatial organization of information flows and the time required for their transmission. Information can be considered to represent a generalized measure of economic value, so that "the flow of information in a social unit has many of the same properties as the flow of economic values."[8] Geographers and social scientists studying the nineteenth century have examined numerous proxies for it. Transportation links have been an obvious choice, representing as they do specific channels for communication and implying the way there were used.[9] The town's potential for interaction within a network is no guarantee that maximum benefit will be achieved, however. The acquisition of new transport connections has been demonstrated to be insufficient to guarantee a town's growth.[10] The design of a transport system does not determine the way it will function. A useful and reliable index is one that measures flows directly. Michael Conzen analysed bank correspondent linkages, charting the organization of the urban system in the United States at its most integrated levels.[11] This is a splendid principle of articulation at the pinnacle of the hierarchy, but it relies on a pre-established coherent organization of national markets which cannot be assumed to have existed in nineteenth-century British North America. Pred adopts many measures, including notably newspaper datelines, postal and trade networks.[12] Measurement and synthesis become almost insurmountable obstacles to generalization across time and space because of the large number of somewhat different measures he used. The value of examining a single, unambiguous and broadly available source over the entire duration of a study is large.

Newspapers were published in every commercial centre of importance and in many aspiring to this status in British North America. By the 1840s they were crucial to the economic life of the colonies. They provided "the only regular pretelegraphic communications medium through which news of distant origin could be made locally available in the form of public information."[13] Bi-weekly and tri-weekly editions superseded weekly publications in the major centres while in Montreal the *Gazette* and *Herald* were appearing in daily editions during the summer months of heightened business activity. The number of papers published increased at a reckless pace, and many survived only a short time in an environment of unrestrained competition. As significant as the increase in the number of papers was the appearance of dailies in the largest centres and even in some of the smaller cities of Upper Canada.

The arrival of the telegraph meanwhile quickened the pace with which information, once received, could be dispatched to any point on the lines. Cities at the termini of lines had a clear advantage of access to the wires, especially in the early years when only a few wires, and hence few simultaneous messages, connected major centres. Intermediate points waited their turn to use the system. Communicating by wire remained expensive, and in 1855 only the most vital economic and political messages were relayed, and in the most abbreviated form possible. Summaries of prices in major markets were the most regularly printed telegraphic items, with international political stories appearing more irregularly.

The allocation of the content revealed the newspaper's market. In the era before mass literacy would make possible the appearance of the popular daily, the press's audience was limited to the business community and the social and political élite, usually not mutually exclusive groups. Editors reported and commented on politics with gusto and partisan passion. This was, in the years under study here, page 2 news, together with occasional social comment. In the middle decades of the century the majority of the paper was devoted to economic content. This coverage was often awarded top priority, editors frequently delaying the publication of other material if the volume of economic material, editorial or advertising, demanded it. The editorial content included, in addition to bulletins on prices in major markets, such other material as crop prospects, weather reports during growing seasons, harbour traffic, shipping intelligence, and trade reports from those regions of interest and importance to the local business community. Considering the total of economic items, advertising claimed much the greater share. In the then universal 4-page layout it was not unusual for all of page 1 to be devoted to advertisements, and standard for page 4 to be entirely claimed by paid copy. Advertising columns displayed notices for transportation services and schedules, the professions, commission merchants, manufacturers, importers, warehouses, wholesalers, and business services of every description, together with a few notices directed to a select retail clientele. From a count of lines of information printed in newspapers in Toronto and Montreal in 1849, Paul Rutherford has calculated that from 39 to 54 per cent of the content was devoted to advertising.[14] Many advertisements were placed directly by firms in distant centres wishing to compete for local business; other notices were placed by agents identifying the companies on whose behalf they solicited customers from the readership of the paper.

The aim here is to analyse the contents of leading newspapers in every major urban centre where at least a semi-weekly edition was published in 1845 and 1855 (see Table 1). Weeklies were excluded from the study; a selection was read and their editorial content discovered to reflect directly what was available from the more frequently issued regional papers published to which they had access. Not only was their news more dated than that appearing in semi-weeklies but they carried little of the more current market information to be found in the semi-weeklies. Furthermore, evidence available from the major papers suggests that their editions circulated at least among the businessmen of many smaller towns where weeklies were issued.[15] A problem limiting the completeness of any survey of newspapers at this date arises because many of the papers published have not survived. Where only a few issues of semi-weekly are extant it has been impossible to establish the representiveness of the few remaining issues, and these publications have necessarily been excluded from the list of those read.[16] The French-language press was less fully developed than the English, and semi-weeklies were published only in Montreal.

**TABLE 1** *Location and Frequency of Publication of Newspapers Analysed, 1845 and 1855*

| Location and newspaper | 1845 | 1855 |
|---|---|---|
| St. John's, Nfld. | | |
| *Public Ledger* and *Newfoundland General Advertiser* | s | s |
| Yarmouth, N.S. | | |
| *Yarmouth Herald* | s | |
| Halifax | | |
| *Morning Chronicle* | t | t |
| Saint John, N.B. | | |
| *Morning News* | t | t |
| Quebec | | |
| *Quebec Gazette* | t | t |
| Montreal | | |
| *Montreal Gazette* | t & d[a] | d |
| *La Minerve* | s | t |
| Kingston | | |
| *British Whig* and *General Advertiser for Canada West* | s | |
| *Daily British Whig* | | d |
| Toronto | | |
| *British Colonist* | s | |
| *Globe* | | d |
| Hamilton | | |
| *Daily Spectator* and *Journal of Commerce* | | d |
| Chatham, Ont. | | |
| *Western Planet*, and *Semi-Weekly Western Planet* | | s[b] |

NOTES: [a] Tri-weekly during 6 winter months, daily during 6 summer months.
[b] Weekly to 30 May1855 and then semi-weekly.

LEGEND: s = semi-weekly publication
t = tri-weekly publication
d = daily publication, Sunday excepted

Content analysis is a method for noting what symbols are used in available bodies of text where "enough attention is paid to the procedures of observation to make the operation replicable," and to develop "quantitative measures that are reasonably independent of the subjectivity of the observer."[17] Its requirements, as outlined by Ole Holsti, are objectivity, system and generality. Objectivity involves explicitly formulating rules and procedures; system implies consistently applied rules to govern the inclusion or exclusion of content or categories; generality refers to the theoretical relevance of the findings.[18] The symbols which it is designed to analyse are flows of words treated as expressions of attitudes: "content analysis operates on the view that verbal behaviour is a form of human behaviour, that the flow of symbols is part of the flow of events, and that the communication process is an aspect of the historical process."[19]

The non-local economic content of the papers, including both editorial and advertising matter, comprises the evidence for this investigation. The story, or the dateline, was the basic unit of editorial information counted; the advertisement was the item counted for paid content.[20] No purely political reporting was included. Much of the editorial content included in papers at this time was rewritten: if originating in Britain or Europe it could be copied from special news sheets which were précis of the latest intelligence. The most commonly cited of these was prepared in Liverpool and its publication timed for ships' sailings. In cases where these sheets were used as sources, internal evidence generally identified the specified place from which the story originated. Items containing such precise identification have been so coded and counted individually. Datelines have been recorded where given. Editorial and advertising content were recorded separately. Place of origin has been categorized for the purpose of preparing summaries by the following territorial categories: the Maritimes, including Newfoundland; the Canadas (Ontario and Quebec); Britain, including Ireland; the continental United States; and Other.

Random samples were drawn of all issues published for 1845 and 1855. For 1845, because the major English-language papers in Montreal published daily during the six months of summer and less frequently during the remaining six months, two seasonally stratified independent samples have been utilized. In each sampling period, two types of samples were employed: one consecutive week; and one "constructed" week, whereby randomly selected days, the number corresponding to the frequency of publication, were drawn[21] (see Table 2). The sample size varied with the frequency of publication of each paper, thereby constituting a constant fraction of the number of issues published.[22] A pre-test sample, comprising two consecutive and two constructed weeks for 1845 was tested for coding consistency.[23]

Published communications in 1845 placed every major centre in British North America within both international and regional networks. Editors of all the principal papers published a substantial amount of information from sources outside the colonies, its quantity often far surpassing the number of

**TABLE 2** *Sampling Schedules, 1845 and 1855*

| 1845 | | | | |
|---|---|---|---|---|
| Sampling period | Week of year | Week of | Day of publication | Type |
| I | 04 | 27 Jan. | 2d day | Constructed week |
| | 05 | 3 Feb. | whole week | Consecutive week |
| | 08 | 24 Feb. | 3d day | Constructed week |
| | 20 | 17 Nov. | 1st day | Constructed week |
| II | 07 | 23 June | whole week | Consecutive week |
| | 08 | 30 June | Tues., 1 July | Constructed week |
| | 09 | 7 July | Thurs., 10 July | Constructed week |
| | 10 | 14 July | Mon., 14 July | Constructed week |
| | 12 | 28 July | Wed., 30 July | Constructed week |
| | 12 | 28 July | Fri., 1 Aug. | Constructed week |
| | 15 | 18 Aug. | Sat., 23 Aug. | Constructed week |

| 1855 | | | |
|---|---|---|---|
| Week of year | Week of | Day of publication | Type |
| 07 | 19 Feb. | Fri., 23 Feb. | Constructed week |
| 14 | 9 Apr. | Tues., 10 Apr. | Constructed week |
| 19 | 14 May | whole week | Consecutive week |
| 35 | 3 Sept. | Thurs., 6 Sept. | Constructed week |
| 36 | 10 Sept. | Sat., 15 Sept. | Constructed week |
| 38 | 24 Sept. | Wed., 26 Sept. | Constructed week |
| 42 | 22 Oct. | Mon., 22 Oct. | Constructed week |

items from the region of publication appearing in the press (see Table 3 and Figure 2). Never less than 31 per cent of the total quantity, the "foreign" economic content was as high as 83, 78 and 72 per cent in the papers issued in Saint John, Halifax and Quebec respectively.[24] Only to the west of Montreal did it constitute less than half of the total volume of items, this fraction decreasing significantly the farther west the paper was published. The international information appearing in the colonial press originated in two great source regions: Britain and the United States; only in St. John's did a significant proportion of the content come from elsewhere, notably the Caribbean. The spatial pattern of the influence of these sources is clear. Britain's relative significance diminished regularly as distance from Saint John or Halifax increased; the relative frequency with which sources in the United States were printed increased west of Quebec. Liverpool, the British port in closest and most regular contact with the colonies, was the centre where commodity prices for important colonial export staples were fixed, and her commerce was widely reported. Stories containing great detail about activity in her port were regularly carried. Quebec, the old port for the export trade of the Canadas, was uniquely tied to Britain, and only selectively was intelligence from the United States available as public information in her press. The Quebec paper contained references to Boston and New York. By contrast, the Montreal and Toronto press regularly published prices received in the markets not only in these cities but in all the important commercial centres on the southern shores of the Great Lakes. In the Maritimes a strong American content was obvious in the press: Halifax and Saint John papers regularly published shipping news from ports as far south as Georgia and west to New Orleans.

**TABLE 3** *Newspaper Contents, 1845*

| | | Per cent of total number of items by regions | | | | |
|---|---|---|---|---|---|---|
| | | M | C | B | U | O |
| St. John's, (49) | *Public Ledger* and *Newfoundland General Advertiser* | 34 | 1 | 28 | 8 | 29 |
| Yarmouth, (28) | *Yarmouth Herald* | 50 | 2 | 15 | 30 | 3 |
| Halifax, (27) | *Morning Chronicle* | 26 | 2 | 39 | 26 | 6 |
| Saint John, (50) | *Morning News* | 16 | 1 | 47 | 33 | 3 |
| Quebec, (68) | *Quebec Gazette* | 6 | 16 | 65 | 9 | 4 |
| Montreal, (63) | *Montreal Gazette* | 2 | 44 | 37 | 16 | 1 |
| Montreal, (29) | *La Minerve* | 1 | 48 | 24 | 19 | 8 |
| Kingston, (33) | *British Whig* and *General Advertiser for Canada West* | 3 | 58 | 22 | 14 | 3 |
| Toronto, (50) | *British Colonist* | 3 | 66 | 7 | 24 | 0 |

LEGEND: M — Maritimes; C — The Canadas; B — Great Britain and Ireland; U — United States; O — Other

Brackets under city names give the mean number of non-local economic items per issue.

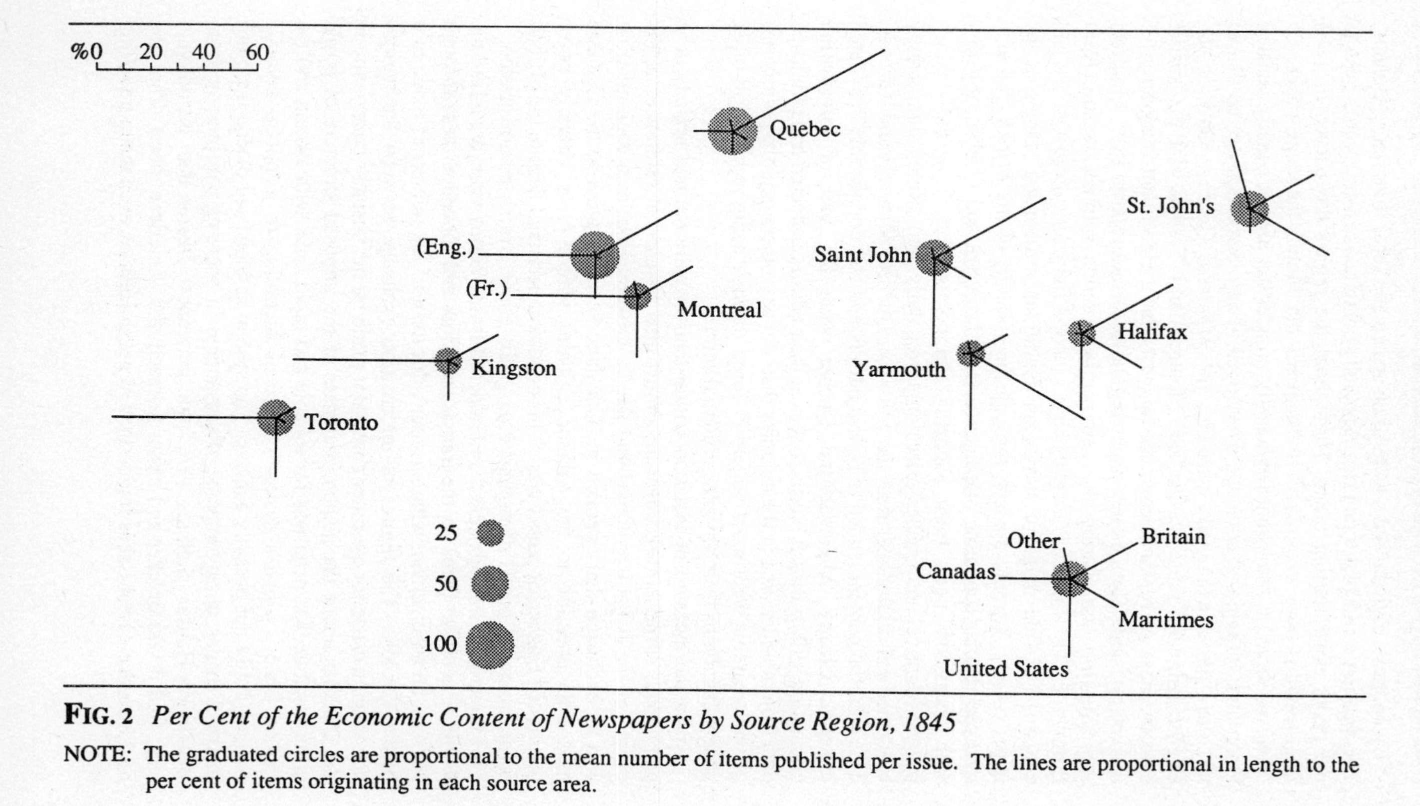


**FIG. 2** *Per Cent of the Economic Content of Newspapers by Source Region, 1845*

NOTE: The graduated circles are proportional to the mean number of items published per issue. The lines are proportional in length to the per cent of items originating in each source area.

By contrast, regional links were often sparce and local hinterlands isolated. The St. John's and Maritime press especially contained few references even to the major neighbouring cities. Throughout the region the pattern of local fragmentation was extreme.[25] In Montreal the French-language paper, *La Minerve*, served a somewhat territorially broader but almost equally isolated hinterland. Its regional coverage overlapped in any significant degree that of no other paper examined, including the *Montreal Gazette*. Only in the English-language press at Quebec, Montreal and Toronto did the spatial extensiveness of regional coverage suggest that a significant integration of markets existed. The Quebec paper regularly carried reports from Montreal and Kingston and, during the commercially active summer season, from Bytown.[26] The *Montreal Gazette* carried reports frequently from Quebec and contained a wide range of stories on conditions influencing staples in the upper colony. Toronto readers, through the columns of the *British Colonist*, received regular economic intelligence from Montreal and Quebec, together with occasional news from Kingston and points west. Kingston's editor printed Montreal and Quebec prices only irregularly, and offered significantly less dated editorial matter than the editors in Quebec, Montreal and Toronto. This editorial content tended to be less current and less comparable than dated material. Clearly, Montreal and Quebec were the foci of information circulation within British North America: their editors collected and published data from a wider area in the colonies than did any others, and the summaries of their markets were more widely diffused through being reprinted in other papers than items from any other colonial source.

Given the measure of isolation within their broadly defined regions, it is perhaps no surprise to discover an almost total absence of references in the papers of the Atlantic colonies and the St. Lawrence basin to each other. It was an exclusion that operated in both directions: the press in the Canadas paid little attention to the Atlantic colonies whose press virtually never mentioned Quebec or points west. This condition pertained despite the official organization of postal communications, still under British administration.[27] This imperial system, designed and imposed from Westminster, organized the whole network to focus on the transatlantic link and funnelled these through Halifax, an arrangement which accounts for most of the references made to it in the Canadas. The figures of information exchange between the regions document a cause for the bitter complaint made by the business community in the Canadas about the inappropriateness of the imposed structure of postal arrangements. The need was for reliable and rapid links with Britain and the United States, which a system conceived according to a unitary colonial outlook could not possibly achieve. The system as legislated placed the cities in the Canadas at an immense disadvantage in securing information from Britain via Halifax. Sailings were more frequent to Boston than the colonial city, and it was quicker and easier to reach the American coast from the St. Lawrence–Great Lakes region than to get to Halifax, even when travelling by sea from Quebec.[28] Other means of securing content information from Britain were found, and these included principally the use of the U.S. mails to reach Boston or New York and then, Britain. Private couriers, an even more legally irregular but still quicker means of getting to Boston or New York, were also resorted to at least on occasion. Inasmuch as the official arrangements for the colonial post office took no account of the interchange of mails with the United States, the colonies were simply left to make their own arrangements, entirely unofficially.

Reflecting the spatial bias noted in the circulation of information, the mean time lags of published, dated items indicate clearly the functional structure of communications.[29] (See Table 4.) Reading the cells indicates the dramatically long lapse between the despatch of news and its publication. The figures average items moving in both directions between the pairs of colonial cities. Between Halifax and Montreal the elapsed time to publication was 13.5 days; 10.5 days separated public information exchanged between Quebec and Halifax. The 12-day average direction required between Quebec and Toronto is also remarkable. The frequency of publication of the two cities' papers, semi-weekly in each case, may account for a day or two of that time but cannot explain the total, nor the 8 days to reach publication of dated items travelling between Kingston and Toronto. Some of the delay was undoubtedly also a result of the irregularity and unreliability of the mails, a more serious problem in late autumn or late winter than in summer. Summer travel was quicker, as between Quebec and Toronto, but obstacles did not altogether disappear. When it is remembered that only the most important and recently received news was dated in the press, and that the vast majority of news was printed without dates being given, these figures become more extreme. The likelihood was that most news published in any of these cities about any of the others would have been more dated than is indicated by these figures.

The contrast in the figures between the speed of access to information from other colonial cities and to data from American Atlantic coast seaports is striking. For purposes of presentation only Boston and New York are included, although dated entries from Oswego, Buffalo, Rochester, Philadelphia, New Orleans and other American cities frequently were published, as is implied by the data on U.S. material published in the colonial press. On the average, Halifax, Montreal, Quebec and Toronto could all receive news from American port cities in a shorter time than they could be in contact with each other. The single exception to this generalization among these cities was the Montreal and Quebec link which was quicker than Quebec's access to Boston or New York. Montreal, however, had news from Boston faster than news from Quebec. The magnitude of the time advantage which these cities enjoyed when in communication with Boston or New York, in contrast to the internal pace of travel, is clear from the figures calculated from the time-lag date (see Table 5). Quebec received news from Boston 9 days, on average, ahead of material sent at the same time from Halifax. Even

**TABLE 4** *Mean Time Lags for Published Information, 1845*

| | Halifax | Saint John | Quebec | Montreal | Kingston | Bytown | Toronto | Boston | New York |
|---|---|---|---|---|---|---|---|---|---|
| Halifax | | | | | | | | | |
| Saint John | 3.5 | | | | | | | | |
| Quebec | 10.5 | 10 | | | | | | | |
| Montreal | 13.5 | | 3 | | | | | | |
| Kingston | | | 5 | 6 | | | | | |
| Bytown | | | 6 | | | | | | |
| Toronto | | | 12, 7.5* | 4 | 8.5 | | | | |
| Boston | 5.5 | | 4.5 | 2 | | | 4.5 | | |
| New York | 6.5 | | 7, 2.5* | 4.5 | | | 4.5 | | |

NOTE: *The first figure is winter months, the second summer.

the Boston to Montreal trip was likely to be speedier than that from Montreal to Quebec.[30] Boston, where the British mails to the United States were landed, was favoured over New York. It is the generality of this advantage that is significant, and which contributes toward understanding the spatial bias of communications revealed in the content analysis of the British North American press. Access to the Atlantic ports involved two advantages. First, it provided a preferred route by which the colonial population could secure the latest British economic intelligence, and offered them the quickest route by which to send messages to Britain. Second, it provided a comparative advantage to any who wished to conduct their business with the United States, in contrast to those who relied on colonial communications linking the colonial cities. Here was a direct incentive not to rely on colonial establishments and not to organize business services on a colony-wide basis.

Between 1845 and 1855 the arrival in British North America of the telegraph opened the possibility of a radical new technology of communications. Information could now move faster than the pace of travel. By late 1846 American border cities were wired and in December a line from Toronto to Hamilton was in place, on its way to link these centres with the American system at the Niagara frontier. The lines joined in the early days of 1847.[31] Montreal was soon thereafter in telegraphic touch with Toronto, and by the close of 1847 this line—belonging to the Montreal Telegraph Company—operated 540 miles of wire and had opened nine offices.[32] In 1849 Montreal's ties to the American system became more direct when a line was built south across the 45th parallel to Troy, N.Y. where it joined with the trunk system.[33] Construction proceeded quickly throughout the length of the Canadas.[34] In just the one year, 1855, by which time the Montreal company controlled the route to Troy, this company built or acquired 541 miles of line and 101 offices were in operation. The Company controlled lines stretching from the Atlantic to Detroit.[35] In the Maritimes, the impetus to string wire came from the United States, from the metropolitan American press who sought the quickest possible access to British news. By the end of 1849 Halifax was in telegraphic communication with New York, via Amherst and Saint John.[36] By 1855 telegraphy made possible a radical spatial and temporal redefinition of information circulation in British North America.

**TABLE 5** *Mean Time Advantages from Canadian Cities to Boston and New York*[a]

| | From Boston | From New York |
|---|---|---|
| Toronto from Montreal | 2 | |
| Toronto from Quebec | 3 | |
| Toronto from Kingston | 4 | 4 |
| Montreal from Halifax | 8 | 7 |
| Montreal from Quebec | 1 | |
| Montreal from Toronto | 2 | |
| Quebec from Halifax | 9 | 5.5 to 11 |
| Halifax from Quebec | 5 | 4 |

NOTE: [a]Difference (in days) in the time lag of published information from Boston and New York over items from other Canadian cities

Evidence of the consequences of this fundamental change in accessibility can be found in the growth in volume and changing sources of non-local economic material published in the leading papers in 1855. In Toronto, Halifax and Montreal English-language papers, the per cent change in the decade was greatest (234 per cent, 144 per cent, and 82 per cent). By 1855, the Hamilton *Daily Spectator* printed, by the measure employed, the third largest volume of information in the colonial press. Each of these cities enjoyed direct access by telegraph not only to regional information but more importantly to American sources. Not coincidentally, 52 per cent of the editorial content of the Toronto and Hamilton press originated in the United States.[37] Kingston and Saint John papers, publishing a significantly higher volume of material then ten years previously, likewise secured high proportions of their editorial matter from American sources (77 per cent and 46 per cent respectively). By contrast, the Quebec press published scarcely any more non-local material then it had in 1845 (a 6 per cent increase) and in St. John's the volume had declined (by 16 per cent).[38] Both cities had lost locational advantage in two ways: with the reorientation of communications as a consequence of an integrated North American telegraph network, and with the upheaval to traditional trading patterns following the collapse of old policies of colonial preference in Britain.[39]

The American penetration of colonial information channels was universal; from St. John's to Chatham, Ontario, the proportion it constituted of the total increased in every single instance and doubled in several (see Table 6, Figure 3). Its volume overshadowed the Canadian content in the *Montreal Gazette* and the Quebec *Gazette* as well as the Maritimes content published in the St. John's *Public Ledger* and the Saint John *Morning News*. To attribute such an increase in American news and advertising to a mere improvement in the ability to gather information is to miss the fundamental point: the colonial cities were becoming absorbed into an American communications system at the cost of improved access to the circulation of information internally within the colonies or among them. The point is all the clearer when the availability in the press of regular commercial reports—market summaries and port records in the main—is examined. The press in each of the principal cities reported on an almost daily basis the market prices in New York, while commercial data from other colonial cities were reported only infrequently and often irregularly. In the *Montreal Gazette* and Toronto *Globe* telegraphed market items from New York were printed the following day. The *Daily Spectator* carried the same reports. In Halifax and Saint John the press carried regular and extremely detailed items on shipping activities in all the major Atlantic ports. Items from neighbouring cities appeared, by contrast, with far greater infrequency, and sometimes less often than reports from smaller American cities such as,—in the Toronto, Hamilton, Chatham and Montreal papers—Boston, Rochester, Oswego, Buffalo, Detroit, and Chicago among others.

In the colonies no more evidence of an exchange of information between the Canadas and the Maritimes existed in 1855 than in 1845. In the absence of direct rail or telegraph connections, and with American cities serving as termini for trans-Atlantic mails to the Canadas, ties with Halifax continued to atrophy. *La Minerve*, of Montreal, of all the papers, devoted its columns most exclusively to its region. In the upper colony news and advertising, facilitating a rapidly expanding commerce in the local hinterlands, occupied large portions of each issue of the local papers. Here at least the former isolation of individual trade area was disappearing, and more integrated circulation patterns were becoming established.

While the volume of information in circulation increased, and while trading areas became less isolated a process of stratification in the functions served by the press was also operating. Regular, dated commercial reports were conspicuously missing from several papers in 1855, notably those published in Kingston and St. John's, and appeared infrequently even in the Quebec *Gazette*. Montreal and Toronto papers circulated widely in the Canadas, as

**TABLE 6** *Newspaper Contents, 1855*

| Location | Newspaper | Per cent of total number of items by regions | | | | |
|---|---|---|---|---|---|---|
| | | M | C | B | U | O |
| St. John's, (41) | *Public Ledger* | 20 | 2 | 27 | 23 | 28 |
| Halifax, (66) | *Morning Chronicle* | 37 | 3 | 18 | 29 | 13 |
| Saint John, (69) | *Morning News* | 17 | 1 | 34 | 44 | 4 |
| Quebec, (72) | *Quebec Gazette* | 7 | 22 | 43 | 24 | 4 |
| Montreal, (115) | *Montreal Gazette* | 3 | 26 | 23 | 44 | 4 |
| Montreal, (30) | *La Minerve* | 1 | 65 | 6 | 24 | 4 |
| Kingston, (49) | *The Daily British Whig* | 0 | 46 | 18 | 35 | 1 |
| Toronto, (167) | *The Globe* | 0 | 55 | 2 | 43 | 0 |
| Hamilton, (91) | *Daily Spectator & Journal of Commerce* | 0 | 57 | 9 | 33 | 1 |
| Chatham, (58) | *Western Planet & Semi-Weekly Western Planet* | 2 | 45 | 10 | 38 | 5 |

NOTE: M — Maritimes; C — The Canadas; B — Great Britain and Ireland; U — United States; O — Other

Brackets under city names give the mean number of non-local economic items per issue.

judged from the territorial scope of notices placed in their advertising columns. The internal markets, at least in the Canadas, were becoming better organized as the reach of papers from the principal commercial centres extended into formerly largely autonomous hinterlands and into the expanding regions of settlement north and west of Toronto. In the Maritimes few signs of such a trend yet existed, although Yarmouth, its paper having ceased bi-weekly publication, would seem to have been losing its ability to compete

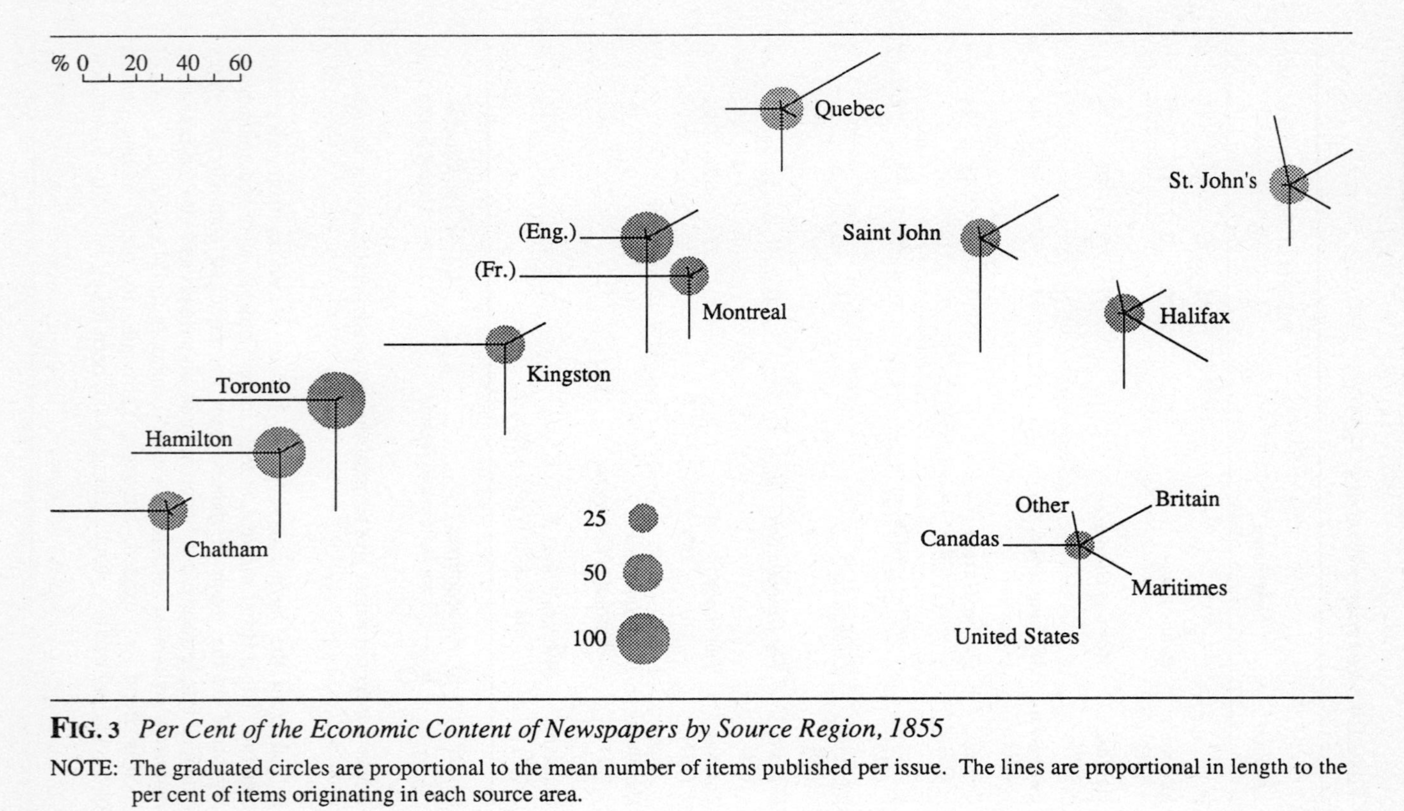


**FIG. 3** *Per Cent of the Economic Content of Newspapers by Source Region, 1855*

NOTE: The graduated circles are proportional to the mean number of items published per issue. The lines are proportional in length to the per cent of items originating in each source area.

with Halifax or Saint John for access to channels of information. These findings may be partially a result of both the increasing accessibility of the principal papers to wider hinterlands as internal communications improved. Telegraphy offered for the transmission of information a technological advantage comparable to that which railroads provided in the distribution of goods, including newspapers. In each case the gain was maximized in the centres where control resided, and especially in Toronto and Montreal. Significantly, the mails, always heavily burdened by the weight of the papers they had long been committed to carrying, utilized the railways as soon as even short stretches were operational.[40] By 1855, with the building of several trunk lines already well advanced, the promise of direct rail lines from Quebec and Montreal to Sarnia and from Toronto to Niagara and Detroit was in prospect.

Through a systematic and objective examination of the public economic information routinely published in the more important urban centres of the British colonies it has been established that at mid-century the communications channels employed by editors and advertisers reached well beyond national political limits and simultaneously remained isolated within regional boundaries. During the ten-year period studied, the importance of international sources of information increased, even as the value of the cities' hinterlands increased consequent to the growth of their population and a quickening of commercial activity. Some progress toward creating effective regional markets was registered, especially in the mutual exchange of current economic news among the few leading cities. In Canada West the trend could be detected among smaller centres as well. That a communications system, or systems, functioned, and functioned increasingly effectively, in reducing the lag of time over distance, is clear. That institutions in the principal urban centres organized and managed the system is also clear. It would be to misinterpret the evidence to conclude from this evidence that an autonomous Canadian communications systems had developed. The degree of closure necessary simply was not present; the trend of increasing reliance on American market information does not support it. A distinctive quality of urban communications systems in the colonies was precisely their international character, operating not in the place of colonial information channels but as an organizing principle, on a larger territorial framework, within which the growth of regional communications networks were possible.

# Notes

1. This point has been demonstrated in many studies, among which R.G. Albion's ranks highly. Robert Greenhalgh Albion, *The Rise of New York Post* (New York: Scribner, 1939).

2. The quotations are found in: Donald Creighton, *The Empire of the St. Lawrence* (Toronto: Macmillan, 1956), 15; and J.M.S. Careless, "Metropolis and Region: The Interplay Between City and Region in Canadian History Before 1914," *Urban History Review* 7 (February 1979): 103, respectively.

3. George A. Nader, *Cities of Canada*, Vol. 1 (Toronto: Macmillan of Canada, 1975), 152.

4. This is the model Harold Laswell constructed in the 1940s. Harold D. Laswell, "The Structure and Function of Communications in Society," in *The Communication of Ideas*, ed. Lyman Bryson (New York: Cooper Square Publishers, 1948), 37–51.

5. Allan R. Pred, *Urban Growth and the Circulation of Information: The United States System of Cities, 1790–1840* (Cambridge, Mass.: Harvard University Press), 187.

6. Philip Abrams, "Towns and Economic Growth: Some Theories and Problems," in *Towns in Societies*, ed. Philip Abrams and E.A. Wrigley (Cambridge: Cambridge University Press, 1978), 24.

7. Jan de Vries, *European Urbanization, 1500–1800* (Cambridge, Mass.: Harvard University Press, 1984), 12.

8. Richard L. Meier, *A Communications Theory of Urban Growth* (Cambridge, Mass.: M.I.T. Press, 1962), 128.

9. This has been a popular theme in the geographical literature. The writing in this vein includes: C.F.J. Whebell, "Corridors: A Theory of Urban Systems," *Annals*, Association of American Geographers 59 (1969): 1–26; Michael P. Conzen, "A Transport Interpretation of the Growth of Urban Regions: An American Example," *Journal of Historical Geography* 1 (1975): 361–82; Edward K. Muller, "Selective Urban Growth in the Middle Ohio Valley, 1800–1860," *Geographical Review* 66 (1976): 178–99; W. Randy Smith, *Aspects of Growth in a Regional Urban System: Southern Ontario 1851–1951*, Geographical Monographs 12 (Downsview, Ont.: Atkinson College, York University, 1982).

10. Robert Higgs, "The Growth of Cities in a Midwestern Region, 1870–1900," *Journal of Regional Science* 9 (1969): 369–75.

11. Michael P. Conzen, "The Maturing Urban System in the United States, 1840–1910," *Annals*, A.A.G. 67 (1977): 88–108.

12. In addition to Pred's earlier volume (see n. 5), see: Allan Pred, *Urban Growth and City-Systems in the United States, 1840–1860* (Cambridge, Mass.: Harvard University Press, 1980); and Pred, *City-Systems in Advanced Economies* (New York: Wiley, 1977), chap. 2.

13. Pred, *Urban Growth and the Circulation of Information*, 20.

14. Paul Rutherford, *A Victorian Authority: The Daily Press in Late Nineteenth-Century Canada* (Toronto: University of Toronto Press, 1982), 39.

15. The *Montreal Gazette*, for instance, printed lists of hotels and public places outside Montreal where its issues were regularly available.

16. The author has been unable to locate any copies of semi-weekly papers published in Ottawa for 1845 or 1855. The surviving issues of London papers are too few and scattered to be incorporated into this analysis.

17. Ithiel de Sola Pool and others, *The Prestige Press: A Comparative Study of Political Symbols* (Cambridge, Mass.: M.I.T. Press, 1970), x, xi.

18. Ole R. Holsti, *Content Analysis in the Social Sciences and Humanities* (Reading, Mass.: Addison-Wesley, 1969).

19. Pool, *The Prestige Press*, 26.

20. There is a choice among counting units when undertaking content analysis. This research adopted a standard measure, employed frequently. See: Guido H.

Stempel III, "How Newspapers Use the Associated Press Afternoon A-Wire," *Journalism Quarterly* 41 (1964): 380–84; G. Cleveland Wilhoit and David Weaver, "Foreign News Coverage in Two U.S. Wire Services: An Update," *Journal of Communication* 31 (Spring 1983): 132–48.

21. This procedure is widely adopted as a means to stratify random sampling. See: Richard W. Budd, Robert K. Thorp and Lewis Donohew, *Content Analysis of Communications* (New York: Macmillan, 1967), chap. 1; David H. Weaver and G. Cleveland Wilhoit, "Foreign News Coverage in Two U.S. Wire Services," *Journal of Communications* 31 (Spring 1981): 55–63.

22. Leslie Kish, *Survey Sampling* (New York: Wiley, 1965), 35.

23. William A. Scott, "Reliability of Content Analysis: The Case of Nominal Scale Coding," *Public Opinion Quarterly* 19 (1955–56): 321–25.

24. "Foreign" refers to sources outside British North America.

25. The fragmentation of the Maritimes was extreme, and the *Yarmouth Herald* provides an excellent example of it. Its Maritime content focussed on the immediate southern shore of Nova Scotia and as far as Digby.

26. Reports on the harvesting of the forests in the Ottawa valley regularly appeared, from Bytown, in the *Quebec Gazette* during the commercial season.

27. A classical history of the Post Office in British North America, largely written from the perspective of its colonial administrators, is: William Smith, *The History of the Post Office in British North America, 1639–1870* (Cambridge: Cambridge University Press, 1920).

28. Advertisements in the Montreal and Toronto papers regularly announced the services of express companies that provided quick carriage of mail to the American ports. The firms and their services were well known, and the postal authorities tolerated it.

29. The data in Table 4 have been calculated from the newspaper datelines. Where, as was frequently the case in the press in the smaller centres, information was often provided without dates, it has not been possible to calculate mean time lags. Other cells in the table may be empty for lack of regular contact between the centres, as in the case of Saint John and Bytown, or Halifax and Kingston.

30. The figures on time lags before publication accord with Glazebrook's interpretation of transportation developments in the 1840s. See: G.P. de T. Glazebrook, "Nationalism and Internationalism on Canadian Waterways," *Essays of Transportation in Honour of W.T. Jackman*, ed. H.A. Innis (Toronto: University of Toronto Press, 1941), 1–16; Glazebrook, *A History of Transportation in Canada*, I, Carleton Library no. 11 (Toronto: McClelland and Stewart, 1964), 154–55.

31. Ernest Green, "Canada's First Electric Telegraph," *Papers and Records*, Ontario Historical Society 24 (1927): 366–72.

32. John Murray, *A Story of the Telegraph* (Montreal: John Lovell, 1905), 110.

33. James D. Reid, *The Telegraph in America* (New York: Derby Brothers, 1879), 330.

34. Before Reid (see n. 33) wrote his comprehensive study, many other studies had been published chronicling the spread of telegraphy in North America. See: Alexander Jones, *Historical Sketch of the Electric Telegraph* (New York: Putnam, 1852); "British-American Telegraph System," *American Telegraph Magazine* 1, 4 (31 January 1853)—an advertisement of routes and rates; and the more recent study focussing on the United States: Robert Luther Thompson, *Wiring a Continent* (Princeton: Princeton University Press, 1947), 253–54.

35. National Railways, RG 30, vol. 10484, pp. 184, 202–204, Public Archives of Canada. This volume contains records of the Montreal Telegraph Company.

36. Murray, *A Story of the Telegraph*, 111–12.

37. The Montreal paper, *La Minerve*, equalled this figure, the highest in the colonial press.

38. The *Yarmouth Herald* had become a weekly by 1855 and, although it was read, was not included in the 1855 calculation.

39. Reciprocity in 1854 did not suddenly disrupt trading patterns, according to McDiarmid. Orville John McDiarmid, *Commercial Policy in the Canadian Economy* (Cambridge, Mass.: Harvard University Press, 1946), 71–84. Tucker has stressed that the St. Lawrence waterway system failed on its own merits and not suddenly because of changes to British Imperial policy. Gilbert N. Tucker, *The Canadian Commercial Revolution*, Carleton Library no. 19 (Toronto: McClelland and Stewart, 1964), 43–44.

40. Smith, *The History of the Post Office in British North America*, 277–79.

# THE MERCANTILE–INDUSTRIAL TRANSITION IN THE METALS TOWNS OF PICTOU COUNTY, 1857–1931*

L.D. McCANN

From the 1880s through to the early 1900s, many communities in the Maritimes successfully made the transition from mercantile to industrial capitalism: trading centres developed manufacturing enterprise; resource communities acquired new technologies to process staples; entirely new industrial towns were established. But urban well-being was not sustained during the economic crisis of the 1920s, which forced factories to close, unemployment to increase, and people to migrate. The interpretation of this cycle of growth and decline has produced conflicting explanations of the urban-industrial collapse. Some have stressed entrepreneurial failure;[1] others technological change in shipping,[2] or a marginal location and poor resource endowment.[3] The forces of continentalism have also been emphasized. According to this interpretation, freight rate alterations,[4] failed political prowess,[5] business reorganization and concentration,[6] and advantages accruing to external economies[7] all favoured the growth of central Canadian cities over their Maritime counterparts. From these studies, something is known of the collapse in Cape Breton, Halifax, Saint John, Yarmouth, and several other places, but a consensus has yet to emerge in this debate about the precise explanation of the region's urban-industrial failure.

In the mid-nineteenth century, Nova Scotia's mercantile economy was tied closely to the production and trade of staple commodities.[8] The structure of colonial manufacturing was dominated by staple processing and commerce-serving industries. In 1861 sawmilling and shipbuilding together accounted for just over 60 per cent of the total value of manufacturing. There was some grist milling and tanning, a little brewing and distilling, and the rudiments of local market manufacturing, but demand usually exceeded supply. Of necessity, most of Nova Scotia's requirements for hardware, machinery, textiles, furniture, glass, cordage, leather products, sugar, confectionery, and tobacco were satisfied by British and American imports. Even when production did take place, the scale of output was small. The

**Acadiensis* 10 (Spring 1981): 29–64.

largest industrial enterprise of the period, an iron works at Londonderry in Colchester County, employed fewer than forty men on a regular basis and turned out annually only about $40 000 worth of iron products.[9] Few manufacturers employed a work force of more than ten men, although some of the sawmill and shipyard operators did on a seasonal basis. The spatial pattern of this manufacturing activity was itself typical of a mercantile economy. Every county in Nova Scotia processed staple commodities for both domestic and export markets. Numerous grist mills were employed in grinding grain for local markets. The colony's sawmills shipped most of their products directly to foreign markets. The lumber trade was a rural industry which had only a limited impact on urban development in Nova Scotia.[10] Urban ties with shipbuilding, though not strong, were somewhat more pronounced, but provincial centres suffered stiff competition in the ancillary trades from Saint John, which had long controlled the Bay of Fundy economy.[11] Local market manufacturing that did exist was concentrated in the more populous communities. Halifax dominated all, manufacturing over one-half of the colony's products.[12]

It is clear that before Confederation the towns and cities of Nova Scotia had yet to experience the transforming effects of industrialization. Nova Scotia's policy of short-term tariffs and bounties was ineffective for fostering sustained industrial development, since these measures not only frequently conflicted with Imperial trade regulations, which were designed to restrict colonial manufacturing, but they also pandered to merchants who were often hostile to manufacturing enterprise.[13] Indeed, the press of the period often printed words to the effect that "what our manufacturers want, is not a high protective duty, but a market."[14] When petitioning the government for assistance, many manufacturers in all branches of industry cite the limited domestic market as the major deterrent impeding expansion.[15] Further exacerbating the problem was the geographical fragmentation of the region: "a parcel of little principalities, everyone of them pulling a different way, while the parent state has been pulling against them all."[16] Beyond these local limitations were the comparative advantages of foreign competitors. The United States and Great Britain had access to larger capital markets and cheaper industrial materials; both countries possessed more advanced technologies and skilled labour and they were able to enforce an effective protective tariff.[17] By Confederation, however, there was mounting evidence to suggest that Nova Scotia would overcome these obstacles and make the transition to industrial capitalism: manufacturing production doubled in the 1860s as the domestic market finally grew and machine-oriented technologies were introduced; merchants appeared more willing to support new manufacturing ventures; coal and iron deposits were claimed sufficient to provide the basis for an industrial "take-off"; and political union with the Canadas promised a railroad to create access to larger markets.[18]

The transformation of Nova Scotia's economic structure and the growth of its towns and cities in the post-Confederation period occurred simultaneously with the province's integration into the continental economy. Coal, iron, and steel industries, stimulated by external demand, spearheaded the transition from a mercantile to an industrial economy.[19] All were essentially urban activities aided substantially by the National Policy of industrial incentives and tariff protection. Indeed, urbanization was greatly affected by this pattern of development. In 1871, only 17 per cent of Nova Scotia's population lived in places of 1000 or more people. The proportion stood at 24 per cent in 1891, just over 35 per cent twenty years later, and 44 per cent in 1931. During the early stages of industrialization, between 1871 and 1891, the trading communities of the mercantile era maintained leadership in size and business importance. By 1911, however, urban growth was more selective. The transition to industrial capitalism was most pronounced across the Cape Breton, Pictou, and Cumberland coal fields where the mining and manufacturing towns were typically either newly settled or considerably expanded in size. Glace Bay, New Waterford, Stellarton, Westville, and Springhill were essentially the products of externally controlled corporations. Industrial capitalism also made an impact on long-established commercial centres situated along the route of the Intercolonial railroad. Halifax headed the list of growing manufacturing cities on the strength of its entrepôt function; Dartmouth produced rope and hardware; Yarmouth manufactured cotton duck; Truro turned out hats and caps, woolens, and butter and cheese; Sydney and Sydney Mines manufactured primary steel; New Glasgow specialized in secondary steel products; and Amherst built railway cars, pianos, boots and shoes, foundry products, and woolen goods. Each place had expanded beyond its earlier mercantile function.[20]

The impact of the transition to an industrial economy was ultimately only short-lived. Some trading centres, which were never really part of the transition, experienced decline as early as the 1880s, and as a group they continued to do so thereafter (Table 1). In the 1890s and 1900s, several staple producing communities suffered losses as a consequence of depressed markets. By the 1920s, a region-wide collapse was clearly evident. Towns and cities that had previously grown rapidly now halted their progress either to stabilize in size or even to lose population. In fact, population reversals were experienced by eighteen of the province's thirty-seven urban communities. For the first time, once prosperous manufacturing centres fell upon difficult times. Amherst, Sydney Mines, New Glasgow, and Trenton were the most notable examples. The fragile structure of the new industrialism stood revealed.

Pictou County exemplifies well the cycle of growth and decline associated with the mercantile-industrial transition (Table 2).[21] The county is a natural and functional region which focusses on Pictou Harbour. Settlement has generally shunned the hills which surround the harbour to concentrate on the coal fields and to run along the several river valleys which flow north into the sea. In the mercantile period, this environment supported a fairly prosperous staple economy. Exports to foreign countries consistently exceeded

**Table 1** *Sources of Urban Growth and the Mercantile–Industrial Transition in Nova Scotia, 1871–1931*

| Dominant source of growth | Urban place | Pop. 1871 | Rate of population growth (%) 1871–1881 | 1881–1891 | 1891–1901 | 1901–1911 | 1911–1921 | 1921–1931 | Pop. 1931 | Date place became urban |
|---|---|---|---|---|---|---|---|---|---|---|
| *Traditional mercantile* | | | | | | | | | | |
| Wholesale-trading complex (includes primary fishing and lumbering) | | | | | | | | | | |
| | Coastal | | | | | | | | | |
| | Annapolis Royal | 747 | 37.2 | -6.4 | 6.2 | .0 | 17.9 | -11.7 | 739 | 1881 |
| | Antigonish | n.a. | | | 164.7 | -2.7 | 2.2 | 1.0 | 1764 | 1901 |
| | North Sydney | 1200 | 26.7 | 65.3 | 84.9 | 16.6 | 21.5 | -6.8 | 6139 | *1871 |
| | Louisburg | n.a. | | | | -3.8 | 14.5 | -15.7 | 941 | 1901 |
| | Parrsboro | n.a. | | | 41.7 | -17.8 | -2.8 | -11.2 | 1919 | 1891 |
| | Digby | 942 | 35.7 | 8.1 | -16.7 | 8.4 | -1.4 | 14.8 | 1412 | 1881 |
| | Bridgewater | 1687 | 20.1 | 10.3 | -1.4 | 6.2 | 34.5 | 3.7 | 3262 | *1871 |
| | Lunenburg | 1777 | 24.0 | 22.1 | 8.3 | -8.1 | 4.1 | -2.8 | 2727 | *1871 |
| | Mahone Bay | | | | | | | -9.5 | 1065 | 1921 |
| | Pictou | 2883 | 18.0 | -11.9 | 7.9 | -1.7 | -6.0 | 5.5 | 3152 | *1871 |
| | Liverpool | 2204 | .9 | -8.0 | -5.3 | 8.9 | 8.8 | 16.3 | 2669 | *1871 |
| | Lockeport | 1011 | 21.5 | -.6 | -8.4 | -29.8 | 8.1 | 14.3 | 973 | *1871 |
| | Shelburne | 1423 | -18.8 | 12.6 | 11.1 | -.6 | -5.2 | 8.3 | 1474 | *1871 |
| | Wedgeport | n.a. | | | | 35.7 | 2.3 | -9.1 | 1294 | 1901 |
| | Canso | 704 | | 25.7 | 30.8 | 9.3 | .5 | -3.1 | 1575 | 1891 |
| | Inland | | | | | | | | | |
| | Bridgetown | 974 | 8.1 | 6.1 | -23.1 | 16.1 | 9.0 | 3.7 | 1126 | 1881 |
| | Kentville | 1779 | 19.4 | -20.6 | 2.7 | 33.1 | 17.9 | 11.6 | 3033 | *1871 |
| | Wolfville | 1697 | 10.8 | 4.4 | -28.1 | 3.3 | 19.5 | 4.3 | 1818 | *1871 |

| | | | | | | | | | | |
|---|---|---|---|---|---|---|---|---|---|---|
| *New industrialism* | | | | | | | | | | |
| Wholesale-trading and new or enlarged manufacturing | Sydney | 1700 | 28.2 | 11.3 | 308.3 | 78.9 | 27.2 | 2.4 | 23089 | *1871 |
| | Truro | 2114 | 63.8 | 47.8 | 17.5 | 1.9 | 23.8 | 4.5 | 7901 | *1871 |
| | Amherst | 1839 | 23.7 | 66.3 | 31.3 | 80.1 | 11.4 | -25.5 | 7450 | *1871 |
| | Oxford | 1034 | 20.8 | 14.3 | -10.0 | 8.3 | .7 | -19.2 | 1133 | *1871 |
| | Dartmouth | 2191 | 72.8 | 17.6 | 8.0 | 5.2 | 56.2 | 15.2 | 9100 | *1871 |
| | Windsor | 2281 | 11.1 | 11.6 | .7 | 1.5 | 1.8 | 2.9 | 3032 | *1871 |
| | New Glasgow | 1676 | 54.8 | 45.5 | 17.8 | 43.5 | 40.5 | -1.3 | 8858 | *1871 |
| | Yarmouth | 2500 | 39.4 | 74.7 | 5.6 | 2.6 | 7.1 | -.2 | 7055 | *1871 |
| New or enlarged staple production | Dominion | n.a. | | | | 67.5 | -7.7 | 19.1 | 2846 | 1901 |
| | Glace Bay | n.a. | | | 182.4 | 138.5 | 2.7 | 21.7 | 20706 | 1891 |
| | New Waterford | n.a. | | | | | | 37.9 | | 1921 |
| | Joggins | n.a. | | | | 51.4 | 5.1 | -42.3 | 1000 | 1901 |
| | Springhill | n.a. | | 434.8 | -5.3 | 25.3 | -.5 | 11.9 | 6355 | 1891 |
| | Inverness | n.a. | | | | | 9.0 | -2.1 | 2900 | 1911 |
| | Stellarton | 1750 | -8.6 | 50.7 | -3.1 | 67.5 | 35.8 | -5.8 | 5002 | *1871 |
| | Westville | 1675 | 31.5 | 43.1 | 10.1 | 27.3 | 3.0 | -13.2 | 3946 | *1871 |
| New or enlarged staple production and manufacturing | Sydney Mines | 1494 | 56.6 | 4.3 | 30.7 | 134.1 | 11.5 | -6.7 | 7769 | *1871 |
| New manufacturing | Trenton | n.a. | 6.8 | 51.2 | 55.7 | 41.7 | 101.1 | -8.1 | 2613 | 1901 |
| Regional centre | Halifax | 29582 | 22.0 | 6.5 | 6.2 | 14.2 | 25.2 | 1.5 | 59275 | *1871 |

SOURCE: Calculated from data in *Census of Canada*, 1931, vol. 1, Table 13.
NOTE: *Attained urban status (1000 or more population) by 1871.
n.a.: data not available

international imports. At first the export trade was based on timber sales to Great Britain, but after mid-century coal shipped to the United States predominated (Fig. 1). The town of Pictou, settled late in the eighteenth century by Presbyterian Scots, prospered through the early nineteenth century as a wholesale-trading centre. Its importance was challenged after Confederation by the growth of the coal industry at Stellarton (Albion Mines) and Westville, and by the emergence of Canada's first integrated metal-making and metal-working complex at New Glasgow, Trenton, and Ferrona (Figs. 2–5). The transition from a mercantile to an industrial economy was stimulated by several factors. After the monopoly of the General Mining Association was broken in 1857, American and Quebec capitalists invested heavily in the coal potential of the county. They were prompted by regional railway development, by Reciprocity with the United States (1854–1866), and by the expanding St. Lawrence market. The metals industry, in contrast, was the product of indigenous capital and entrepreneurship. From its beginning, New Glasgow serviced the surrounding agricultural community and built ships for the carrying trade. Several of its merchant families prospered, and when ship building was on the verge of collapse in the early 1880s, they invested substantially in the new industrialism. Teaming with skilled craftsmen, they used local resources to develop the Nova Scotia Steel and Coal Company which remained as the leader in the Canadian metals industry until early in the twentieth century. Founded in early 1870s, by World War I Scotia was a vertically integrated corporation of some 6000 employees which mined iron ore and coal, produced primary pig iron and steel, and manufactured a wide array of secondary metal products.[22] By the close of the 1920s, however, Scotia was no longer a separate corporate entity, and its demise forced the loss of urban population in the county.

Scotia Steel had its origin in 1872 as the Hope Iron Works when two Pictou County tradesmen of Scottish descent, Graham Fraser and George Forrest MacKay, formed a partnership to produce marine and railway forgings. MacKay had learned the blacksmith's trade in his father's New Glasgow shop. Fraser, by contrast, served his apprenticeship in blacksmithing at the Rhode Island Locomotive Works in Providence.[23] The growing demand for forgings encouraged both men to form a new enterprise in 1874, the Nova Scotia Forge Company.[24] This also prospered until the inadequacy of New Glasgow's water supply forced the company to relocate, in 1878, in Smelt Brook (renamed Trenton in 1882), a rural community situated two miles north of New Glasgow. Like other forges, Scotia used wrought and scrap iron, but during the 1870s and 1880s technological changes in the metals industry influenced the course of local production. Pig iron and steel were increasingly used in quality forge work, but obtaining these materials regularly and in sufficient quantity was difficult. Nevertheless, it was considered uneconomical in the mid-1870s to produce either material in Pictou County because an integrated iron and steel complex would create a surplus in excess of local needs which was too costly to ship to extra-regional markets. Later,

**TABLE 2** *Economic Development and Urbanization in Pictou County, 1871–1931*

| | 1871 | 1881 | 1891 | 1901 | 1911 | 1921 | 1931 |
|---|---|---|---|---|---|---|---|
| Total county population | 32 114 | 35 535 | 34 541 | 33 459 | 35 858 | 40 851 | 39 018 |
| Total urban population | 8 381 | 10 223 | 12 977 | 14 486 | 19 303 | 24 668 | 23 571 |
| Per cent population urban | 26.1 | 28.7 | 37.6 | 43.3 | 53.8 | 60.4 | 60.4 |
| Population of urban places | | | | | | | |
| Pictou | 2883 | 3403 | 2998 | 3235 | 3179 | 2998 | 3152 |
| New Glasgow | 1676 | 2595 | 3776 | 4447 | 6383 | 8971 | 8858 |
| Trenton | 397 | 424 | 641 | 998 | 1414 | 2844 | 2613 |
| Stellarton | 1750 | 1599 | 2410 | 2335 | 3910 | 5312 | 5002 |
| Westville | | | | | | | |
| Value of coal production ($000s) | 600 | 651 | 878 | 961 | 2563 | 2869 | 2081 |
| Value of urban manufacturing ($000s)[a] | n.a. | n.a. | n.a. | 1001 | 5158 | 16 132[b] | 8071 |
| Per cent population, farmers | 16.0 | 13.9 | 14.2 | 10.5 | 9.7 | 8.1 | 7.5 |
| Per cent population, miners | 2.9 | 3.6 | 4.0 | 4.6 | 5.5 | 5.1 | 4.8 |
| Per cent population, urban manufacturing | n.a. | n.a. | n.a. | 3.4 | 6.8 | n.a. | 2.8 |

SOURCE: *Census of Canada*, 1871–1931; and *Report ... for the Year, 1871–1931*, Department of Mines, Nova Scotia.

NOTE: [a] Places of 1500 or more population.
[b] Value is for 1917.

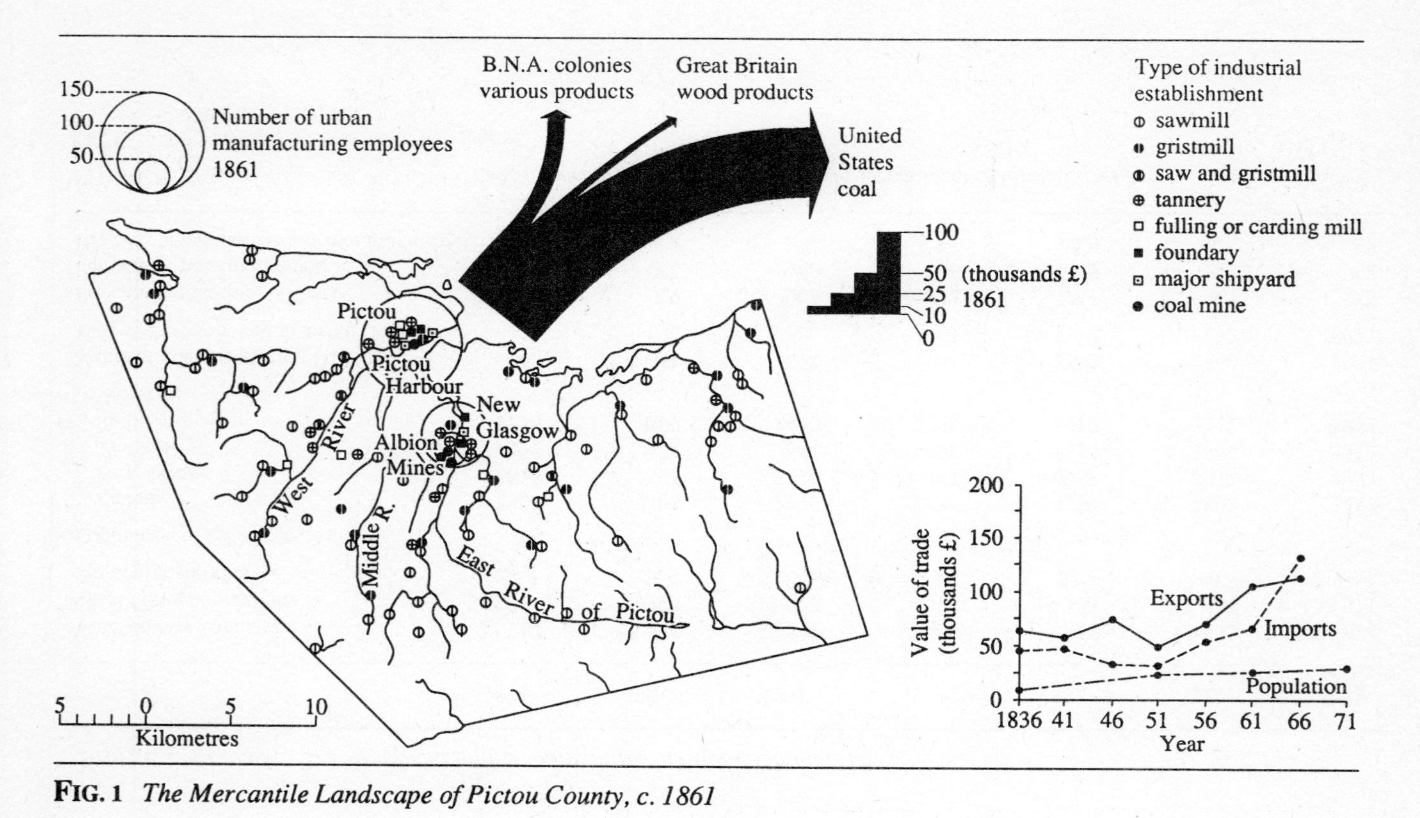


FIG. 1 *The Mercantile Landscape of Pictou County, c. 1861*

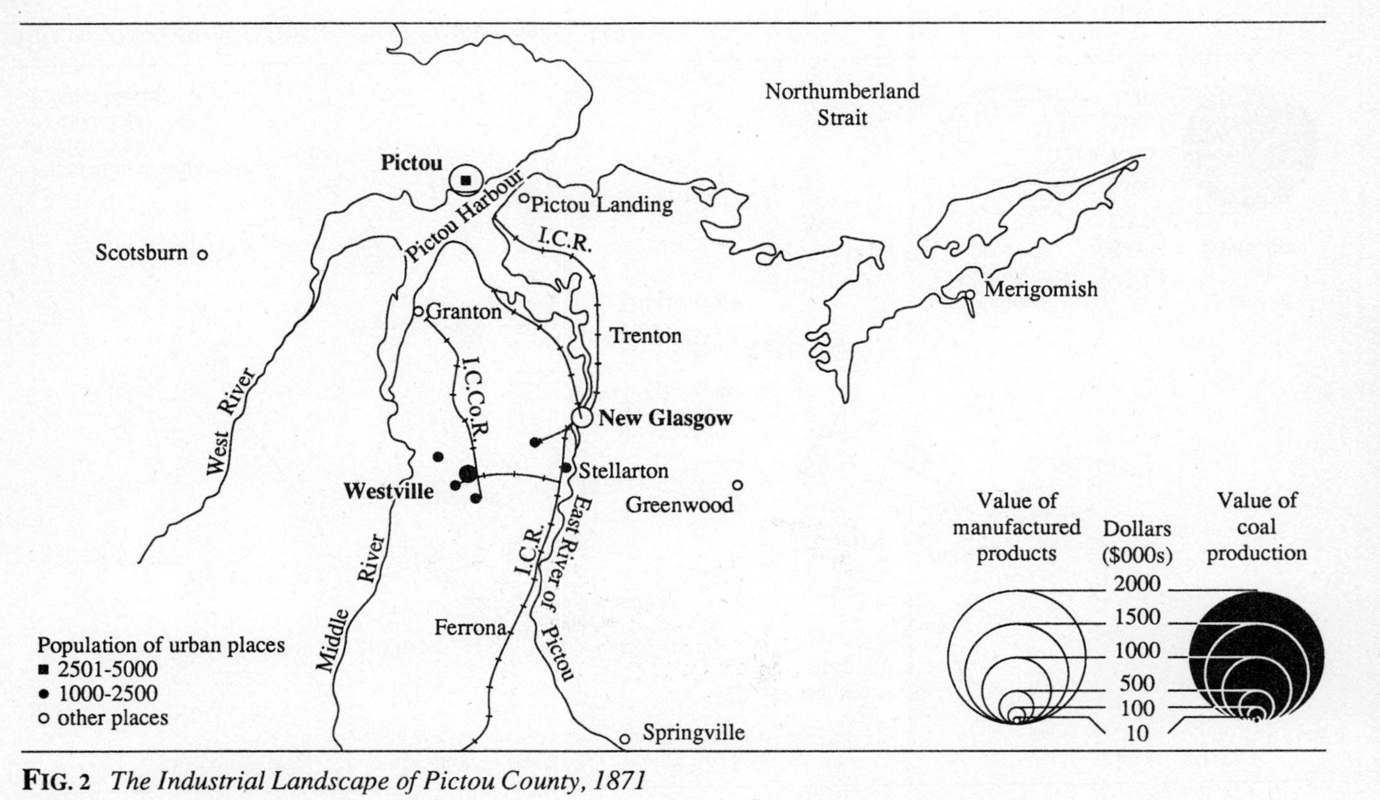


FIG. 2 *The Industrial Landscape of Pictou County, 1871*

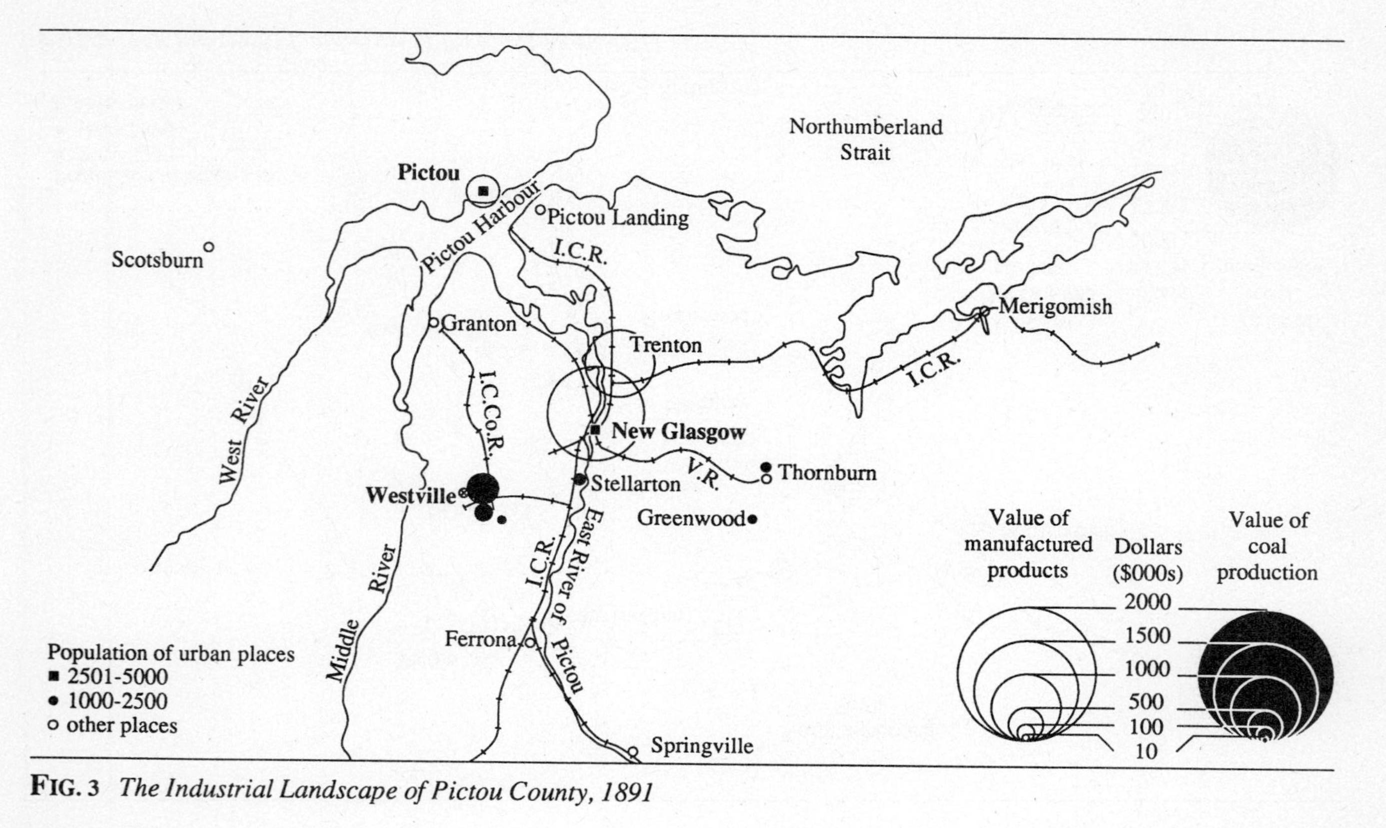


FIG. 3 *The Industrial Landscape of Pictou County, 1891*

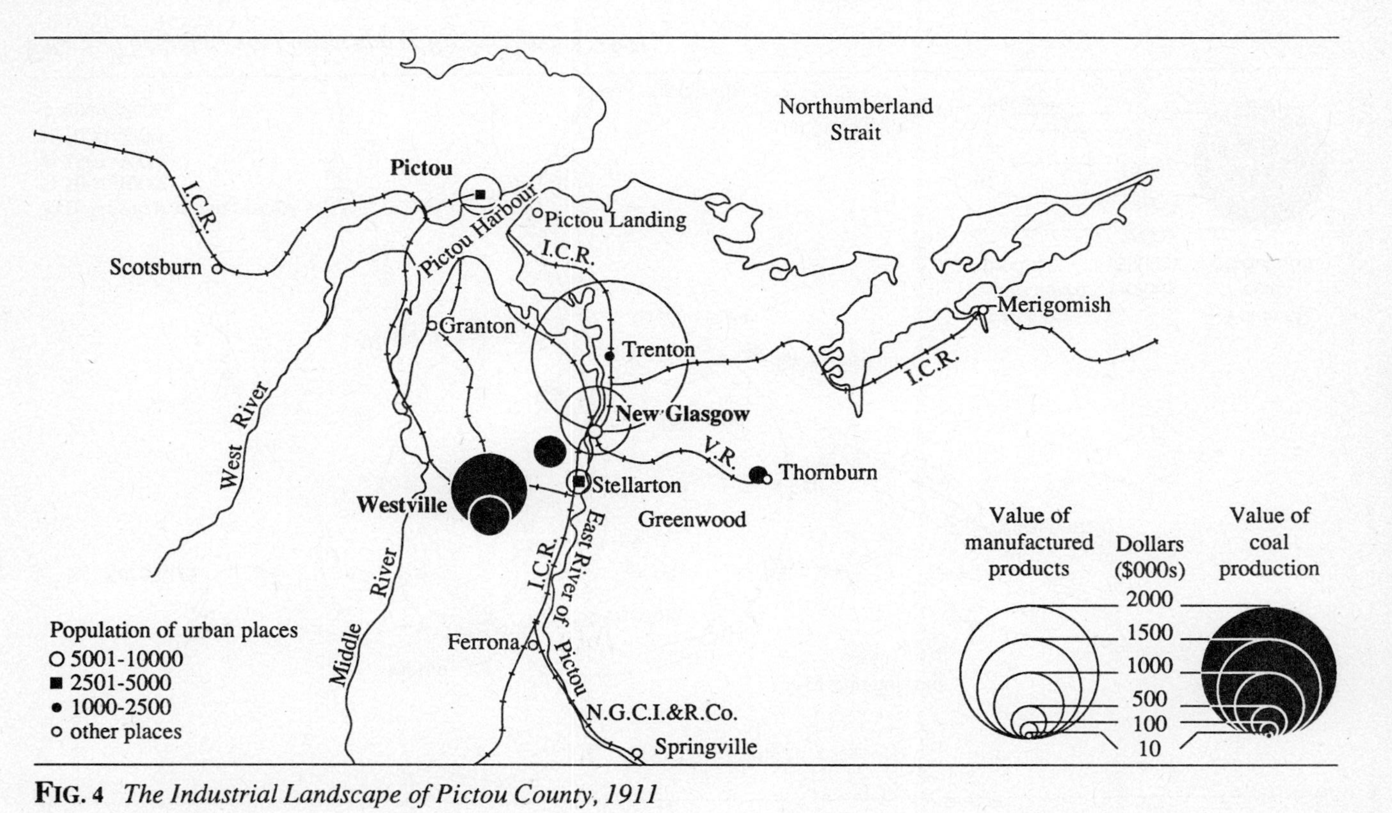


**FIG. 4** *The Industrial Landscape of Pictou County, 1911*

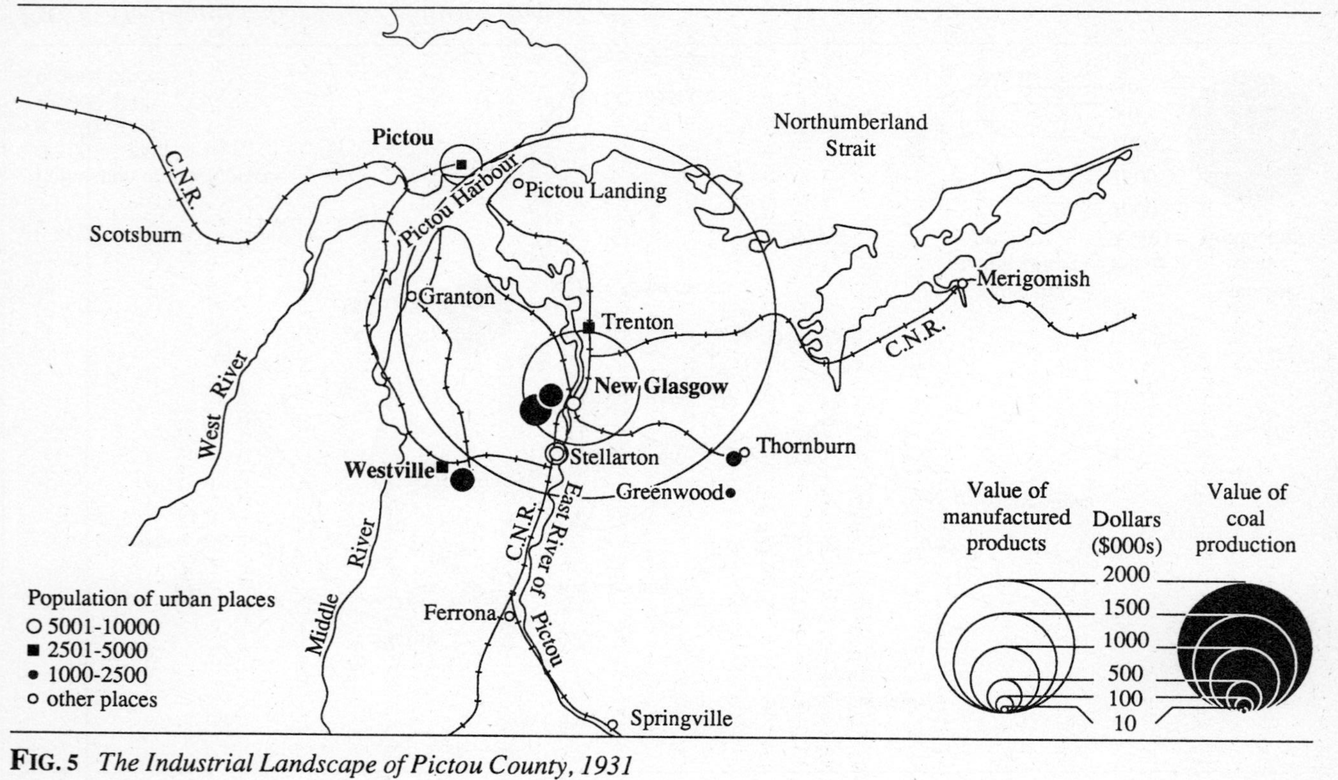


FIG. 5 *The Industrial Landscape of Pictou County, 1931*

however, the National Policy's 1879 tariff schedule of $5 per ton on steel ingots made the proposal of establishing at least a steel plant more realistic. A profit could be earned because the freight rate for shipping steel products from Nova Scotia to the major market in Ontario averaged $4.50 per ton.[25] To raise the capital for such a steel-making venture, Fraser and MacKay turned to the local mercantile community.

Foremost among their backers were two of New Glasgow's leading merchant families, the Carmichaels and the McGregors.[26] James C. Carmichael first established a general store at the head of navigation on the East River in 1809, anticipating correctly the future growth of New Glasgow as a market town. The business prospered and Carmichael's son, James William, subsequently expanded and diversified the business. The firm of J.W. Carmichael and Company eventually rose to become the community's principal shipyard, constructing thirty-nine vessels before the demise of ship building in the early 1880s. As well, the firm managed a trading fleet in support of the regional coal industry and served as agents of the Bank of Nova Scotia.[27] The McGregors likewise erected a substantial trading and shipping business. Roderick and James McGregor, sons of Rev. James D. McGregor, D.D., the first Presbyterian minister in the county, entered the wholesale-retail trade in 1830. By 1843, they had diversified their interests. James formed McGregor and Company and expanded into the hardware business. Roderick, in a separate and more prosperous venture with his sons, James Drummond and Peter Archibald, established R. McGregor and Sons. They became wholesale and retail grocers, provision dealers, general merchants, and shippers.[28] By the early 1880s, the Carmichaels and the McGregors were New Glasgow's leading merchant families.[29]

Within New Glasgow, these two families were the cornerstones of a cohesive group which was sustained by intermarriage and reinforced by shared social and community interests. James C. Carmichael married Christian McKenzie, sister of Captain George McKenzie, New Glasgow's most successful early shipbuilder, who was himself married to Sarah McGregor, sister of Roderick and James, the merchants, and daughter of Rev. James D. McGregor. The town's two wealthiest families thus became interrelated through marriage into the McKenzie family. A similar pattern emerged in the next generation. When James W. Carmichael married Maria McColl and James D. McGregor married Elizabeth McColl, and his sister, Ann, married Jeffrey McColl, shipping merchant and banker, the Carmichaels and the McGregors once again became related through an intermediate family. The social network now embraced three of the four shipping and mercantile families who remained active into the 1880s: the Carmichaels, the McGregors, and the McColls. The alliance was strengthened further when the fourth active shipper, Andrew Walker, married Georgina McKenzie, daughter of Captain George McKenzie and niece of James C. Carmichael. The mercantile élite of New Glasgow were thus part of an extended family.[30]

That Fraser and MacKay should turn to this mercantile community for financial support was not surprising. Co-operation, certainly not opposition, was characteristic of the mercantile–industrial transition in Pictou County. After his apprenticeship in Rhode Island, Fraser was first employed in 1867 as a blacksmith at the Carmichael shipyard where his father, Thomas Fraser, was the construction foreman. When he left in 1869 to set up his own smithing business, J.W. Carmichael and Company awarded him several contracts. Fraser was also known to the McGregors, because his great, great grandfather, Simon Fraser, had been one of three elders who emigrated to Pictou County with Rev. James D. McGregor.[31] George Forrest MacKay, in turn, married Mary J. Walker, sister of Andrew Walker.[32] Together, Fraser and Mackay had developed one of the province's leading industrial operations whose assets had increased, in less than a decade, to equal those of the most successful mercantile houses in Pictou County.[33] The merchant fraternity was well aware of this, and of the coal and iron producing potential of the region.[34] Moreover, some of its members, as politicians, had debated the merits of the new National Policy.[35] Perhaps of most importance, this was a period of transition in shipping technologies, a passing from sail to steam; and the likely success of the proposed steel works promised the merchants a new source of earnings.[36] Of the leading New Glasgow mercantile families, the Carmichaels, the McGregors, and the Walkers purchased shares in the new steel company (Fig. 6). The McColls did not, apparently because Jeffrey McColl was suffering financial duress in connection with the operation of the Pictou Bank.[37] In all, Pictou County investment accounted for 84 per cent of the subscribed shares; the remainder was raised principally in Halifax, and also in Guysborough and Antigonish counties and in Montreal.[38]

The steel works, which began operations in July, 1883, was the first in Canada to produce steel ingots.[39] Despite a glutted domestic market in 1883 and reduced prices in 1884 and 1885, which fell even more in 1886, the demand for Scotia's products was enough to warrant increased production. Prices had sufficiently improved by 1887 that one year later Scotia paid an 8 per cent dividend on preferred shares.[40] Of course, a favourable tariff schedule was essential to attain this rate of profit. New negotiations in 1887 had resulted in a duty of $9 per ton on puddled bars, $4 on pig iron, and $2 on scrap iron; imported iron and steel ingots, billets, blooms, and slabs were also charged $9 per ton.[41] This arrangement placed a discriminatory duty against goods competing with Scotia's output, but allowed the company's material inputs to be imported at relatively low rates.[42] By the close of 1888, the steel works was operating at full capacity. So, too, was the Forge Company, which was its largest customer. Considering their complementary operations, common location, and overlapping directorships, as well as their desire for greater efficiency in management and operation, it was logical for the two enterprises to amalgamate in 1889 to become the Nova Scotia Steel and Forge Company.[43]

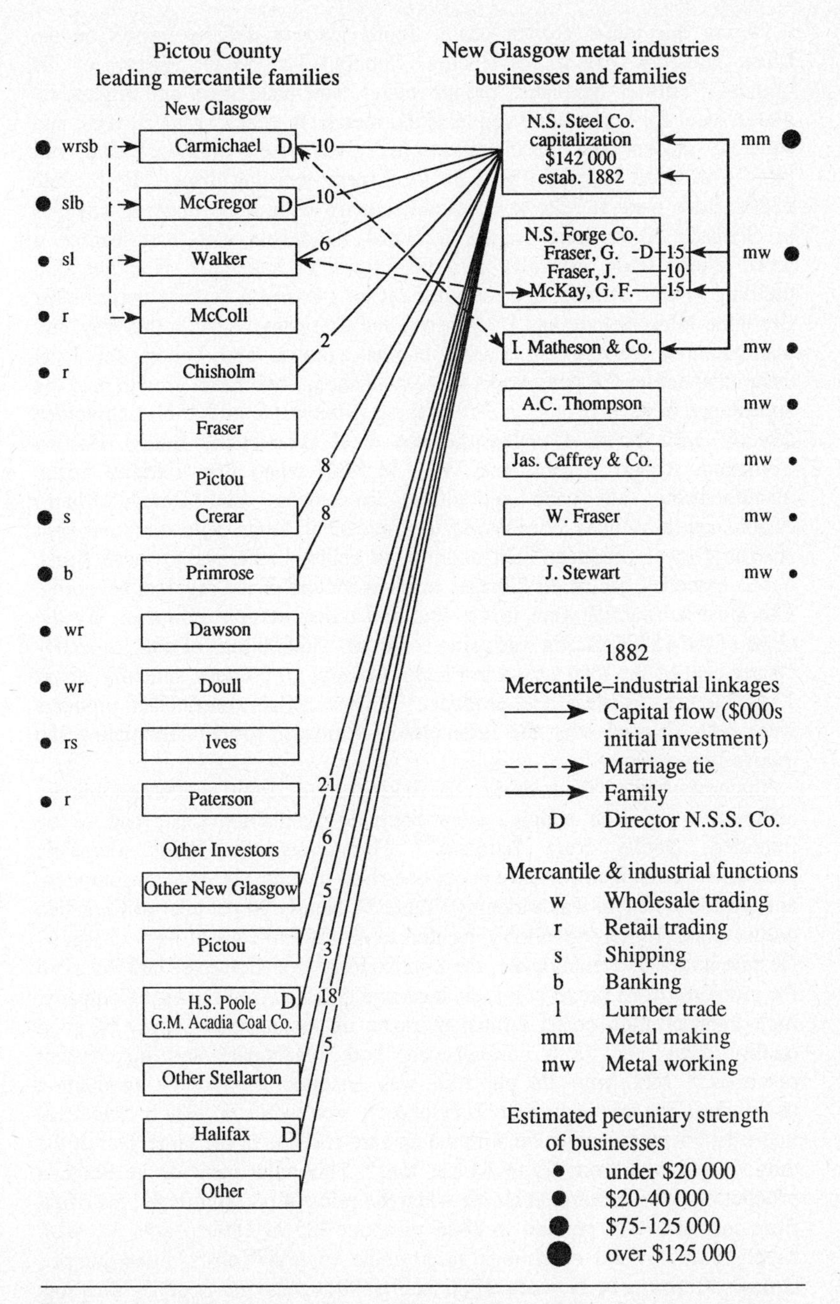


**FIG. 6** *The Mercantile–Industrial Transition in Pictou County, 1882*

During this initial growth phase, Scotia made a definite impact on the urban-industrial pattern of Pictou County. The wide variety of its output—"railway fishplates, plough plates, nail plate, bars and angles, tie plates, steel for agricultural implements, merchant steel in rounds, flats, and squares, angles and special sections, rivet steel, tramway and rail pits"—provided material inputs for local metal-working firms.[44] By the late 1880s, there were at least seven establishments with direct material linkages to Scotia.[45] Most were started by local Pictonians who had learned a metal-related trade, typically as a blacksmith or machinist, in either ship building or coal mining, and then had set up a business of their own. Fraser Brothers, John Stewart, and I. Matheson and Company began in this way, and manufactured respectively marine engines, plows, and boilers for local customers before the steel works was established. Their rapid growth, and the appearance of several other metal-working firms in the mid-1880s, coincided directly with Scotia's expansion into steel production. Bailey Harrow Company, Robert Brown, and W.P. McNeil, when they initially began manufacturing, all made agricultural implements, and Donald Munro established the Munro Wire Works to fabricate all kinds of fencing and light structural steel products.[46] In addition to selling materials to these firms, Scotia extended backward linkages to other sectors of the regional economy. The most substantial were to the coal and transportation industries. By the close of the 1880s, Scotia was using some 30 – 36 000 tons of coal, or nearly 10 per cent of the total raised in Pictou County, to produce annually about 13 000 tons of finished steel products.[47] Raw materials and finished products were both shipped over the Intercolonial Railway, further stimulating the industrial economy.

The proximity of Scotia to the coal fields created certain economies, but the company's pig iron supply, a considerable production cost, had to be imported, chiefly from Scotland.[48] Throughout the 1880s, domestic production accounted for only about one-third of total pig iron consumption, and by 1890 the gap was widening (Table 3). Nearly 90 per cent of Canadian output came from Londonderry, located some 150 km west of New Glasgow. Despite its relative importance, the Londonderry Iron Company had inherited the problems of its predecessor, the bankrupt Acadian Iron Furnace Company: high transportation costs; limited markets; an inconsistent supply of good quality coke; and as a consequence, both inadequate and inconsistent revenues.[49] Moreover, its pig iron was unsuited to Scotia's production techniques. The takeover of the Londonderry iron works in 1887 by Montreal interests, however, coincided with the upward revision in the same year of the duty on pig iron from $2 to $4 per ton.[50] This adjustment drove Scotia's production costs upward, at a time when the price of pig iron itself was rising from just over $19 per ton in 1886 to about $25 in 1890 (Table 3). With supply and demand conditions so unstable (material costs alone jumped almost 40 per cent between 1886 and 1890), some of Scotia's directors embarked on a programme of diversification to create an iron works.

**TABLE 3** *Imports, Production, and Prices in the Canadian Pig Iron Industry, 1884–1900*

| Year | Imports of pig iron (tons) | Canadian pig iron production (tons) | Scotia pig iron production (tons) | Pig iron prices quoted on Toronto market[a] British | Bayview American | Londonderry | Ferrona | Hamilton |
|---|---|---|---|---|---|---|---|---|
| 1884 | 52 184 | 29 593 | | $21.25 | | $19.67 | | |
| 1885 | 43 398 | 25 770 | | 19.44 | | 19.25 | | |
| 1886 | 45 648 | 26 180 | | 18.94 | | 18.88 | | |
| 1887 | 50 214 | 39 717 | | 22.13 | | 20.75 | | |
| 1888 | 48 973 | 22 209 | | 21.63 | | 22.13 | | |
| 1889 | 72 115 | 24 823 | | 23.75 | | 24.38 | | |
| 1890 | 87 613 | 25 697 | | 24.49 | | 24.25 | | |
| 1891 | 81 317 | 20 153 | | n.q.[b] | $23.00 | n.q. | | |
| 1892 | 68 918 | 30 294 | 12 519 | | 23.00 | 22.00 | | |
| 1893 | 63 522 | 46 948 | 22 725 | | 23.00 | 20.00 | $19.50 | |
| 1894 | 45 790 | 62 867 | 29 867 | | 21.50 | 20.00 | 19.50 | |
| 1895 | 35 060 | 31 692 | 17 447 | | 19.88 | 20.00 | 19.50 | |
| 1896 | 37 141 | 52 052 | 14 702 | | 19.50 | 20.00 | 19.50 | |
| 1897 | 28 940 | 33 254 | 22 500 | | 19.50 | 20.00 | 19.50 | |
| 1898 | 40 995 | 19 576 | 21 627 | | 19.50 | 20.00 | 19.50 | |
| 1899 | 48 594 | 31 861 | 31 100 | | n.q. | 20.00 | 19.50 | $20.33 |
| 1900 | 65 330 | 34 618 | 28 133 | | | n.q. | n.q. | 25.00 |

SOURCE: Donald, *The Canadian Iron and Steel Industry*, 327–28; Nova Scotia Steel and Coal Company, *Report of the Directors ... 1892–1900*; *Monetary Times*, 1884–1900.

NOTE: [a] Prices are the yearly averages, calculated from the price quoted in the *Monetary Times* at the end of each month.
[b] n.q.: not quoted.

The county's potential for iron production had been recognized for some time. The availability of coal was an obvious attraction. Other necessary raw materials, including iron ore and limestone, were known to the General Mining Association which had established an ill-fated and short-lived iron works in 1829.[51] By the 1880s, the various deposits of iron had been fully mapped and assessed to reveal an iron content ranging from 50 to 68 per cent.[52] E. Gilpin, the province's Inspector of Mines, was convinced that "the iron deposits...are more varied and of greater extent than elsewhere in the province, and from their relation to shipping and fuel flux are destined to play an important part in the future."[53] These opinions were confirmed in 1890 by Robert Chambers, the mining engineer of the prospective New Glasgow Iron,

Coal, and Railway Company, who judged that the deposits along the East River alone were capable of supplying a furnace of 20 000 tons annual capacity for fifteen years. When mixed with other regional ores, pig iron could be produced "at a price entirely below any competition."[54]

Substantial capital was required to establish the iron works. The blast furnace was estimated to cost $500 000. A railway to connect the ore deposits to the potential furnace site at Ferrona would require an additional $50 000. To secure this capital, a new pattern of financing and management emerged in Scotia's development. The mercantile interest, particularly J.D. McGregor and J.M. Carmichael, urged caution, arguing that if pig iron production were to be undertaken, then an entirely new and separate company should be formed, rather than risking Scotia's resources in the event the iron venture failed.[55] This strategy was eventually accepted and pursued by Graham Fraser in 1888.[56] When the necessary capital could not be raised, however, and this particular incorporation attempt failed, John F. Stairs in Halifax, an industrialist and federal politician, and J. Walter Allison, also of Halifax and a financier, were newly enlisted as directors for the company's successful 1891 incorporation and capitalization drive.[57] New Glasgow interests—Fraser, MacKay, and Harvey Graham—retained control of the company, but the period of local entrepreneurial capitalism was at an end. There was not sufficient capital within Pictou County to finance entirely a new round of industrial expansion. Scotia would hereafter be dependent on national and foreign money markets for its development capital.

The blast furnace was "blown in" at Ferrona in 1892 and soon achieved a stable market despite a number of obstacles. Ferrona, located on the Intercolonial and situated approximately equidistant from the Bridgeville ores, coking coal at Westville, and the Trenton steel works, provided optimal accessibility to reduce production costs (see Fig. 4). After an initial year of partial operation, the blast furnace was soon averaging an annual output of about 20 000 tons, or between one-third and one-half of the total Canadian production. Over half was consumed by Scotia's forge and newly upgraded steel plant; the remainder was sold elsewhere, chiefly to foundries in Ontario.[58] To capture this particular trade, different strategies were advanced. Low prices were offered during periods of slack demand, such as the early 1890s.[59] Overcoming high transportation costs was more troublesome. The Intercolonial Railway did offer competitive freight rates from the Maritimes to Quebec, but through charges on the Grand Trunk and Canadian Pacific lines were uncontrollably higher. Shipment by water, at best seasonable, was considered; but the central Canadian railways threatened to retaliate by cancelling the preferential rates they had given to some of Scotia's largest Ontario customers, which would naturally force these foundries to purchase materials elsewhere.[60] Price stability was therefore essential. To achieve this, the New Glasgow Iron, Coal, and Railway Company and the Londonderry Iron Company, Canada's major pig iron producers, entered into an agreement in 1896 "...for the regulation of prices, conditions, and terms upon which these companies shall sell their pig iron in the Province of Ontario and Quebec."[61] Government assistance, however, remained critical. The tariff on imported wrought iron scarp was boosted from $2 to $3 per ton in 1894, while a newly introduced bounty provided $2 for each ton of puddled iron bars or steel billets the company produced.[62] The various strategies proved successful, prompting the merger of the forge and steel works with the iron company in 1895 to create the Nova Scotia Steel Company. The reconstituted board included from Pictou County, Graham Fraser, J.D. McGregor, G. D. MacKay, and H.S. Poole, from Halifax, J.F. Stairs, J. McNab, Adam Burns, and J.W. Allison and from Quebec, Frank Ross.[63] The merger was entirely logical. As an integrated unit, the new corporation would be more efficient, not only in administration and management,[64] but also in planning material flows and in devising marketing strategies.[65]

During this period of diversification in the 1890s, Scotia continued to influence the process of urbanization in Pictou County. The company's labour force at the forge and steel works rose from about 420 in 1890 to 750 in 1898.[66] Most workers lived in New Glasgow, but others resided in neighbouring Trenton, which doubled in population to almost 1000 people. Some 250 men were employed at the blast furnace site, swelling the size of Ferrona.[67] The hamlets of Springville, Bridgeville, and Sunnybrae grew in support of nearby iron mining activity. In a similar way, employment in the coal and transportation sectors was supported by Scotia's business. The company annually purchased about 130 000 tons of coal, or up to 15 per cent of the County's total output; and in some years it paid out more than $100 000 in freight charges on the Intercolonial.[68] Without Scotia's presence, the urbanization process in Pictou County would have been arrested through the 1890s. Stellarton actually lost population between 1891 and 1901, and the growth of other urban places was at a low ebb (see Table 2). Sectors of the New Glasgow and Trenton economy, which in the 1880s had multiplied in scale, now either stabilized in size or subtracted strength (Table 4). Even Scotia experienced a temporary financial crisis in 1896 when severely depressed prices and reduced bounties caused financial losses which forced the company to reduce the wages and salaries of all workmen and officials.[69] By the close of the decade, however, with the stimulus of markets opening on new resource frontiers across Canada, the "volume of business...done was larger than in any previous year in the Company's history."[70]

Despite the upturn in business, weaknesses had appeared in the structure of the regional metals industry. Foremost, the manganiferous character of the East River ores made it difficult to produce foundry pig iron at the Ferrona iron works.[71] To overcome this problem, Scotia tapped its holdings at Brookfield and Arisaig, and purchased ore from the Pictou Charcoal Iron Company and the Torbrooke Iron Company; but the use of these ores was not entirely satisfactory, which led Scotia to examine other sources.[72] One of these included the red hematites at Wabana on Bell Island, Newfoundland, which the company first tested in 1892 and purchased the next year for only $5000. Within two years, Wabana ore comprised the major supply of iron for the Ferrona furnace. Despite the extra transportation costs of shipping from Newfoundland to Pictou County, a more economical pig iron was produced.[73] Scotia continued to search for additional sources of ore, since the payment of federal bounties on foreign ores, including those of Newfoundland, remained in question during the initial years of the Laurier administration, and the issue was not fully resolved until 1899.[74] Moreover, Scotia sold some of its Bell Island properties in 1899 to the newly formed Dominion Iron and Steel Company for a reported $1 000 000, but by 1904, it was realized that the best iron deposits had been sold inadvertantly.[75] A flurry of exploration followed, chiefly in mainland Nova Scotia and on Bell Island, but also in Cuba and Brazil.[76] In the end, the vast submarine deposits under Conception Bay off Bell Island were judged best, and indeed they provided enough ore for Scotia's own use and for export abroad.

**TABLE 4** *The Urban Economy of New Glasgow–Trenton, Selected Years, 1882–1930**

| Business sector | Pecuniary strength ($000s) | | | | | |
|---|---|---|---|---|---|---|
| | 1882 | 1892 | 1901 | 1912 | 1921 | 1930 |
| Metals manufacturing | 54 | 1082 | 710 | 1281 | 1425 | 222 |
| Other manufacturing | 112 | 160 | 158 | 203 | 219 | 225 |
| Construction | 7 | 19 | 25 | 63 | 176 | 61 |
| Trade | 185 | 299 | 350 | 458 | 884 | 727 |
| Transportation and communication | 323 | 412 | 412 | 500 | 662 | 250 |
| Community and business services | 38 | 40 | 48 | 93 | 105 | 65 |
| Totals | 719 | 2012 | 1718 | 2598 | 3471 | 1550 |

SOURCE: Calculated from data in Dun, Wiman and Company and R.G. Dun and Company, *Mercantile Agency Reference Books, 1882–1931*.

NOTE: *Estimated pecuniary strength

The profits realized from the sale of its Bell Island properties were used by Scotia to overcome another shortcoming of the Pictou resource base, the inadequacy of local coal for coking purposes. By the late 1890s, the Ferrona blast furnace was purchasing up to 80 000 tons of fuel annually from regional collieries. The company did not mine its own coal because central Canadian and foreign interests had gained control of the best reserves before Scotia's officials embarked on their expansionary drive in the 1880s. They did work several leases, but these failed to yield coal of sufficient quality or quantity to warrant development.[77] This situation created several problems. A protracted strike in 1887 cut off Scotia's fuel supply, forcing the temporary closure of the melting furnace at the steel works and a consequent loss of orders.[78] Prices were also subject to fluctuation. A more serious concern, however, was the quality of coke produced from mainland coal. Fuel efficiency was critical in the pig iron industry, and substantial economies could be won if a high grade coke were used. Early experiments with coke processed at the Intercolonial Coal Company's Drummond Mine at Westville did not prove successful; nor did a combination of Drummond and Springhill coal. Both were high in sulphur and ash content.[79] By 1898 a solution had been found: Cape Breton coal, purchased from the Dominion Coal Company yielded a satisfactory coke which resulted in greater efficiency and substantially reduced production costs.[80] Nonetheless, since an essential link in Scotia's integrated chain of operations remained in the hands of other interests, Scotia used the money earned from the sale of its iron holdings to the Dominion Iron and Steel Company to purchase, in 1900, the Cape Breton coal mining holdings of the General Mining Association.[81] Although the press criticized this takeover as foolish and extravagant, by 1904 coal mining was the most profitable sector of the company.[82] A coal washing plant and coke ovens were built at Sydney Mines in 1901 to supply the Ferrona blast furnace. By shipping coke, a less bulky and cleaner product than coal, significant handling and transportation costs were saved.

Nevertheless, the geographical dispersion of Scotia's various activities remained a matter of concern. As early as 1897, the company had considered locating a blast furnace in either Sydney or Louisburg to minimize the costs of assembling materials. A new company, the Scotia Steel and Iron Company was incorporated for this purpose, but achieved little because Scotia's directors failed to convince the federal government to extend the pig iron bounties beyond 1902.[83] Several joint ventures were considered during 1898 and 1899, including discussions with H.M. Whitney about Scotia's participation in the formation of the Dominion Iron and Steel Company, but when these, too, went unrealized, Scotia pursued a careful policy of self-management and vertical integration.[84] The company was reorganized in 1901 as the Nova Scotia Steel and Coal Company, and with increased capitalization in hand, set about the task of building a fully integrated iron and steel making complex at Sydney Mines.[85] There were good reasons for choosing this site. Cost analyses undertaken by the company during the 1890s suggested that a ton of pig iron could be produced for $5.50 at Sydney Mines, compared to actual costs of $10.50 at Ferrona (Table 5). Further savings of 20 per cent could be realized in the conversion of pig iron to steel billets. When completed in July 1905, the complex was judged the most efficient and technically advanced in Canada. By the close of the decade, Scotia employed some 2300 coal miners and 700 iron and steel workers in Cape Breton alone.

Sydney Mines was itself a "Scotia" town; rows of company-built cottages housed many of the town's 7500 residents.[86]

**TABLE 5** *Estimated Costs of Pig Iron and Steel Production at Ferrona and Sydney Mines*

| | Ferrona[a] | | | Sydney Mines[b] | | |
|---|---|---|---|---|---|---|
| Item | Required amount | Cost per ton | Total | Required amount | Cost per ton | Total |
| Iron ore | 2.0 tons | $1.75 | $3.50 | 1.80 tons | $1.00 | $1.80 |
| Coke | 1.4 tons | 3.00 | 3.75 | 1.25 tons | 1.52 | 1.80 |
| Limestone | .5 tons | 1.00 | .50 | .75 tons | .53 | .40 |
| Repairs | | | 1.00 | | | |
| Labour | | | 1.30 | | | 1.50 |
| Incidentals | | | .40 | | | |
| Cost: one ton pig iron | | | 10.50 | | | 5.50 |
| Cost: conversion to steel | | | 8.00 | | | 5.00 |
| Cost: one ton steel | | | 18.50 | | | 10.50 |

SOURCE: RG 21, vol. 25(d), PANS; P.T. McGrath, "The Manufacture of Iron and Steel in Cape Breton," *The Engineering Magazine* 2 (June 1901): 582–83.

NOTE: [a] Based upon actual production costs at Ferrona (pig iron) and Trenton (steel) using Pictou County materials during 1892–1893.

[b] Based upon production costs at Ferrona using Wabana ore and Cape Breton coke during 1896–1898.

The growth of Scotia's Cape Breton interests had immediate repercussions on the economy of Pictou County. Closure of the blast furnace and iron mining operations greatly reduced the population of Ferrona; and the removal of the open hearth furnaces had a similar effect on Trenton. Both closures, and the simultaneous opening of Scotia's Marsh Colliery at Coalburn, resulted in lost orders for the county's coal industry (although these losses were concealed by the substantial and simultaneous increase in the extra-regional demand for the county's coal at this time).[87] On balance, however, the initial impact of Scotia's internal reorganization upon Pictou County was positive. With expansion, the company's primary iron and steel output doubled in size to average over 70 000 tons annually; and virtually all of this was shipped from Sydney Mines to the metal-working factories of New Glasgow and Trenton for use in either forging or conversion to steel products. Bounties, protective tariffs and preferential freight rates, so essential to the metals industry, encouraged the distribution of a varied range of goods to distant markets. For example, the steel products of New Glasgow and Trenton firms went mainly to the agricultural implements manufacturing industry in Ontario; Scotia's marine forgings were shipped to Victoria, Vancouver, Owen Sound, Levis, and some Maritime cities.[88] Scotia Steel's competitiveness in these markets was facilitated by an efficient and productive plant at Trenton where a number of improvements were made between 1906 and 1912:[89] the forge was entirely rebuilt and equipped with the most advanced hydraulic presses available; a new railway axle plant was developed which immediately supplied over 60 per cent of the Canadian market; a new 28-inch cogging mill was added; expensive heating furnaces were replaced; and most other operations, including the plate mill and nut and bolt division, were either expanded or upgraded. The company's labour force at these facilities, which totalled about 800 in 1910, increased by some 900 employees shortly after the Eastern Car Company was organized in 1912 as a wholly owned subsidiary of Scotia.[90] This move towards further diversification and vertical integration can be justified solely by the growing demand for railway rolling stock both in Canada and abroad; in the process, Scotia also improved its internal economies of scale by securing a guaranteed buyer for its steel products in a market which was becoming increasingly dominated by Hamilton's newly organized Steel Company of Canada (Fig. 7).[91]

Throughout this period, Scotia's rolling mills continued to supply specialized materials to local metal-working industries. These firms had grown substantially since the business downturn of the mid-1890s to produce a wide variety of finished goods for regional and national markets.[92] Bailey-Underwood and the Brown Machine Company made agricultural implements, while bridges and structural steel work were produced by both W.P. McNeil and John Stewart. I. Matheson and Company continued to make boilers and engage in foundry work, and J.W. Cumming Manufacturing Company supplied mining equipment and forgings. The products of the Steel Furnishing Company included springs, mattresses, and office furniture. The Munro Wire Works manufactured various kinds of fencing. Finally, the Fraser Machine and Motor Company built marine engines for fishing boats, and the Canada Tool and Specialty Company filled custom orders for tools and other items. The labour force of these firms in 1912 totalled some 850 workers, an increase of almost 50 per cent since the late 1890s. Clearly, the continued growth of these smaller metalworking firms was assisted by Scotia's ability to supply specialized materials quickly and with minimal transportation costs. Other relationships, however, including family ties, the interchange of personnel, and capitalization assistance, should not be overlooked (Fig. 7). In fact, these types of linkages were not limited to Pictou County. At Sydney Mines, H.T. Sutherland, President of Thompson and Sutherland and brother-in-law of Thomas Cantley, then General Manager of Scotia, built a foundry and used Scotia's materials to make stoves for the company's chain of hardware stores.[93]

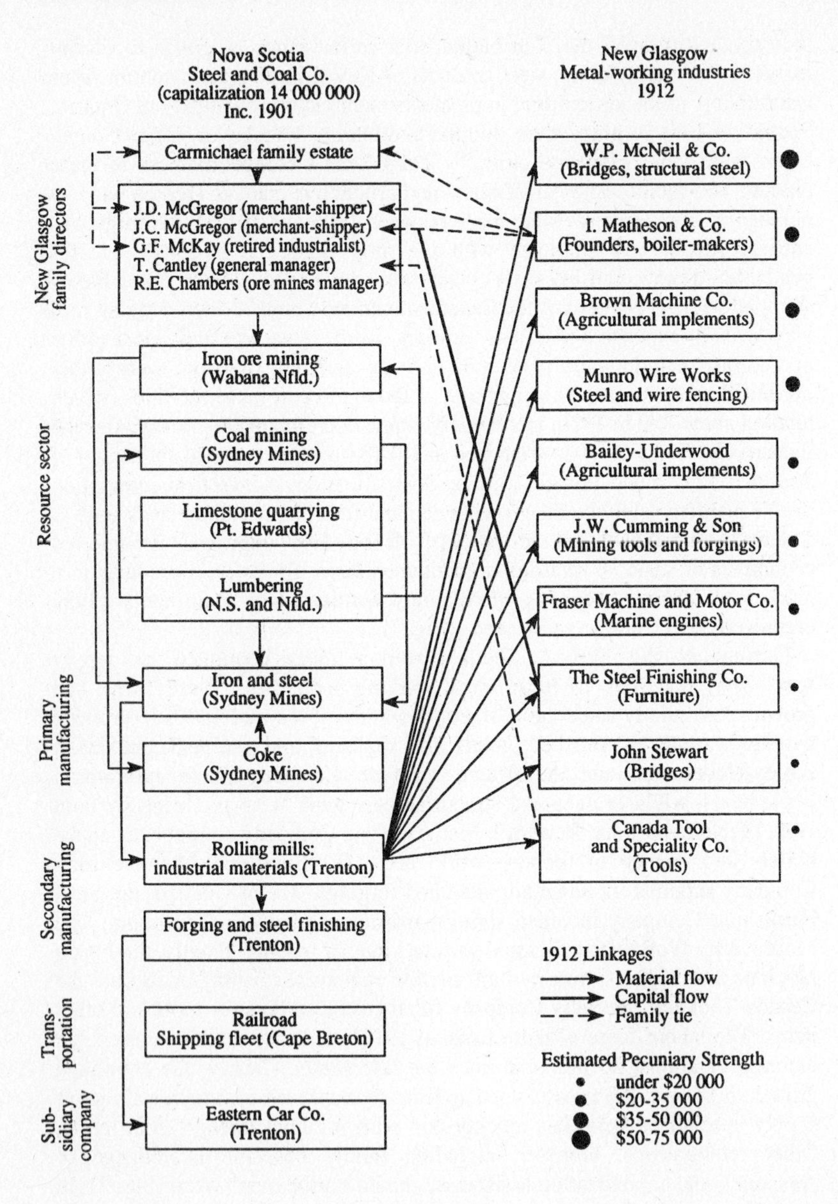


**FIG. 7** *The Organization of the Nova Scotia Steel and Coal Company and Linkages with Metal-Working Industries, 1912*

The development of the metals industry in the early twentieth century propelled a new round of town growth in Pictou County. Spurred by extra-regional demand and the artificial stimulus of war, the manufacturing output of New Glasgow and Trenton multiplied more than tenfold between 1900 and 1917, the peak of wartime production. As early as 1911, a factory survey by the provincial government had revealed that fully two-thirds of New Glasgow's industrial labour force and more than 90 per cent of Trenton's were engaged in the metals industry;[94] and this position of dominance was compounded during the war as factories turned to the production of munitions and Scotia embarked on a limited programme of shipbuilding.[95] Factories in Pictou County produced nearly $32 000 000 in war-related goods, or about 4 per cent of the Canadian total.[96] Scotia alone was awarded munitions contracts totalling at least $30 000 000, and the fact that Thomas Cantley served on the federal government's Shell Committee was no doubt instrumental in Scotia's ability to attract this type of manufacturing.[97] As a consequence of this concentrated wartime effort, New Glasgow's population doubled and Trenton's tripled between 1901 and 1921. The war effort had pushed the manufacturing labour force of both towns to an all-time high in 1917 of 3156 men and women, and town growth occurred simultaneously. The temporary thrust of wartime production, however, was quickly withdrawn: manufacturing employment dropped to 2655 in 1918 and stood at only 1284 in 1919.[98] Unemployment became a common experience. There was a slight recovery during the 1920s, so that by 1931 Trenton provided industrial jobs for 784 workers and New Glasgow for 604; but even this advance failed to recapture the prewar level of employment in 1911 when New Glasgow recorded 776 manufacturing employees and Trenton 1182.[99] As a result, the urban economies of both towns suffered considerably, forcing almost all sectors to decline in financial strength (see Table 4). It was therefore inevitable that New Glasgow and Trenton should record population losses between 1921 and 1931. The urban-industrial economy had begun to collapse.

The cessation of wartime contracts alone is not sufficient to explain the decline of the metals industry and the consequent loss of urban population in Pictou County. Nor was the local resource base a decisive factor; Scotia's move to Cape Breton demonstrated that at least metal working was still economically feasible in the county. While the immediate postwar recession lessened the external demand for marine forgings, mining equipment, and railway axles and cars—all key products in the region's export base—these same products were again in demand by the late 1920s, and a share of the market, albeit a smaller one, had been recaptured. Therefore, the most plausible reasons for the urban-industrial collapse are likely associated with the removal of the very incentives that initially propelled the metals industry to prominence: entrepreneurial initiative and the social milieu of community; government assistance in the guise of freight rate preferences, bounties, tariff protection, and grants-in-aid for infrastructural development; the internal economies of scale of Scotia, a vertically integrated organization; and the external economics of an integrated industrial complex, such as New Glasgow-Trenton.

Following Confederation, Pictou County was pulled incessantly into the national economy. Indeed, the basic contours of Canada's heartland–hinterland space economy were drawn in the late nineteenth and early twentieth centuries. As an industrial heartland emerged in southern Ontario and Quebec, the competitiveness of the periphery, comprised of highly localized regions such as Pictou County, was placed in jeopardy. From a theoretical perspective, it can be argued that advantages of external economies will gradually accrue to a developing heartland economy, forcing competitors in the periphery out of production. To test this proposition, data have been assembled which measure these economies as well as costs of production in selected towns and cities that competed in the Canadian metals industry (Tables 6 and 7). Because of certain deficiencies, these data must be interpreted carefully;[100] but they do suggest the comparative advantages and competitive position of New Glasgow and Trenton. Manufacturing establishments in the selected communities were generally comparable in average size, capitalization, and output. In terms of scale economies, therefore, there was little initially to differentiate New Glasgow and Trenton from, say, Hamilton. Only in the 1920s did Hamilton move ahead in average plant size, which is helpful in explaining the decreasing ratios there of material costs/output and labour costs/output. In the Hamilton case, this process of reducing costs was aided by the nearby automobile industry's demand for metal products,[101] and by the Ontario government's assistance in acquiring access to cheaper coal and iron ore.[102] By contrast, the industrial market for steel in the Maritimes was quite limited, and the Nova Scotia government did little to compensate the provincial steel industry for the loss of federal bounties in 1911. In addition, the federal government's policy of granting rebates on coal imports after 1907 meant that Nova Scotia's metal manufacturers lost the cost advantage of native coal.[103] Thus, faced with rising costs as a result of the loss of incentives previously awarded under the aegis of the National Policy, the industrial economy of New Glasgow and Trenton needed to maintain an efficient and productive industry to compete successfully in national markets. That this was partially accomplished is indicated by advances in certain structural indices—capital/labour, output/capital, and output/labour—but relative to other places, notably Hamilton, the competitive position of the Pictou metals towns deteriorated considerably between 1910 and 1930. Indeed, by 1930 Hamilton's ratio of net output to capital investment—that is, its manufacturing productivity—was twice as great as that of the Pictou metals towns. In 1910 there was only a marginal difference.

To compensate for growing losses in comparative advantage, a favourable freight rate structure was essential. The Intercolonial Railway pursued such a

**TABLE 6** *Structural Indices of Manufacturing in Selected Metal-Making and Metal-Working Towns and Cities, 1910–1930*

| | Average of establishments | | | | | |
|---|---|---|---|---|---|---|
| Date and place | Labour | Capital ($000s) | Output ($000s) | Capital/ labour | Output/ capital[a] | Output/ labour[a] |
| 1910 | | | | | | |
| New Glasgow-Trenton | 68 | 101 | 115 | 1489 | .20 | 303 |
| Sydney Mines | 85 | 3225 | 423 | 3817 | .30 | 11 156 |
| Sydney | 195 | 1251 | 470 | 6330 | .22 | 1397 |
| Hamilton | 58 | 159 | 151 | 2743 | .26 | 725 |
| Sault Ste Marie | 22 | 234 | 44 | 10 742 | .04 | 493 |
| 1920 | | | | | | |
| New Glasgow-Trenton | 35 | 169 | 241 | 4801 | .24 | 1169 |
| Sydney Mines | 21 | 117 | 299 | 6564 | .53 | 2970 |
| Sydney | 24 | 264 | 307 | 11 009 | .38 | 4156 |
| Hamilton | 40 | 182 | 217 | 4586 | .32 | 1463 |
| Sault Ste Marie | 28 | 401 | 306 | 14 398 | .32 | 3306 |
| 1930 | | | | | | |
| New Glasgow-Trenton | 49 | 381 | 270 | 7767 | .15 | 1135 |
| Sydney Mines[b] | | | | | | |
| Sydney | 72 | 865 | 468 | 11 979 | .20 | 1867 |
| Hamilton | 70 | 488 | 380 | 6909 | .31 | 1657 |
| Sault Ste Marie | 49 | 1485 | 441 | 30 309 | .11 | 3196 |

SOURCE: Calculated from data in *Census of Canada, 1901–1931* and *Canada Yearbook 1922 and 1933.*

NOTE: [a] Output equals net output (value of products less cost of labour and materials).
[b] Sydney Mines was no longer engaged in metals production in 1930.

policy from the early 1870s until it was merged into the Canadian National Railway. Thereafter, postwar inflation and the levelling of the Intercolonial's rates with other Canadian lines drove rates upwards by as much as 140 to 216 per cent.[104] This made it more costly for Pictou County's metal firms not only to reach distant markets, but also to purchase industrial materials, even from Cape Breton. The case of the J.W. Cumming Manufacturing Company illustrates well the predicament facing local industries.[105] With wartime profits and stock market financing, Cumming was the first metals company in the Maritimes to invest in the development of a steel foundry equipped with an electric melting furnace. Besides engaging in structural steel work for regional construction projects, the firm had become the major Canadian producer of wheels and axles for mining cars. It even maintained an office and warehouse in Lethbridge, Alberta to service its western Canadian customers. By 1922, however, control of this nation-wide market was severely threatened by the change in freight rates. In fact, Cumming's chief competitor, a firm in Liverpool, England, could enter the Kootenay mining district over the

Canadian Pacific rail line at a more competitive rate. Moreover, the firm's production costs had risen because the Trenton steel works could no longer supply Cumming with all of its required materials. These came instead from the Dominion Steel plant in Sydney, which itself had been forced to increase prices to accommodate the changing structure of intra-regional freight rates. Less than carload lots were particularly expensive. Clearly, the increase in transportation costs was a major liability to sustained economic growth in Pictou County.

**TABLE 7** *Manufacturing Production Costs in Selected Metal-Making and Metal-Working Towns and Cities, 1900–1930*

| | 1900 | 1910 | 1920 | 1930 |
|---|---|---|---|---|
| New Glasgow-Trenton | | | | |
| Average size of establishments | 20 | 68 | 35 | 49 |
| Material costs/output | .45 | .54 | .64 | .59 |
| Labour costs/output | .36 | .28 | .16 | .20 |
| Total costs/output | .81 | .83 | .80 | .79 |
| Sydney Mines | | | | |
| Average size of establishments | | 84 | 21 | |
| Material costs/output | | .65 | .71 | |
| Labour costs/output | | .11 | .08 | |
| Total costs/output | | .76 | .79 | |
| Sydney | | | | |
| Average size of establishments | 30 | 195 | 24 | 72 |
| Material costs/output | .52 | .18 | .54 | .44 |
| Labour costs/output | .32 | .23 | .13 | .19 |
| Total costs/output | .84 | .41 | .67 | .63 |
| Hamilton | | | | |
| Average size of establishments | 44 | 58 | 40 | 70 |
| Material costs/output | .52 | .51 | .49 | .45 |
| Labour costs/output | .23 | .21 | .24 | .23 |
| Total costs/output | .75 | .72 | .73 | .68 |
| Sault Ste. Marie | | | | |
| Average size of establishments | 50 | 22 | 28 | 49 |
| Material costs/output | .24 | .40 | .54 | .46 |
| Labour costs/output | .40 | .34 | .16 | .18 |
| Total costs/output | .62 | .74 | .70 | .64 |

SOURCE: See Table 6.

The 1920s thus appears as the critical decade in the devolution of the metals industry. Freight rate increases stole business elsewhere when Hamilton was emerging as the most productive and cost efficient steel centre in Canada. Nonetheless, several firms such as Cumming Manufacturing pursued new corporate strategies and technologies to maintain a competitive edge. The prevailing Canadian tariff structure provided generally adequate protection for these specialized firms and even for Scotia's forge and steel fabricating operations.[106] But other adaptations created negative consequences. On 21 March 1921, the Nova Scotia Steel and Coal Company was merged into the realm of the British Empire Steel Corporation (Besco). The entrepreneurs who originally developed Scotia had previously either retired or assumed less responsibility in company management: tradesmen, G.F. MacKay in 1889 and Graham Fraser in 1903; mercantile backers J.M. Carmichael in 1894 and J.D. McGregor in 1914.[107] The New Glasgow dominated board had withstood a Montreal-based takeover attempt in 1910, but control was eventually relinquished in 1917 to the American investment firm of Hayden, Stone and Company which had supplied Scotia with considerable amounts of working capital. Scotia's president, Thomas Cantley, was replaced by an American steelmaker, F.H. Crockard. Although "one of the bright stars of the United States Steel Corporation's galaxy of subsidiary corporations," Crockard possessed only limited experience in managing a fully integrated company. Subsequently, in an attempt to effect great economies of scale and efficiency in coal mining and steel manufacturing along the lines practised by U.S. Steel, Scotia was merged into the Besco conglomerate along with the Dominion Steel Corporation and the Halifax Shipyards Limited.[108]

The consequences of this merger proved disastrous for the metals industry in New Glasgow and Trenton. The cogging mill was dismantled in favour of the Sydney facilities, and although the rolling mills, forge, and axle and car plants remained in operation, they were neither expanded nor improved after 1917.[109] The primary iron and steel facilities at Sydney Mines were also closed, thereby ending the specialized material exchange between Scotia's operations in Cape Breton and Pictou County, and within the New Glasgow and Trenton metal-working complex itself. This ultimately affected efficiency and productivity as the analysis of the structural indices revealed (see Table 6). Of equal importance, the merger also dismantled the economies of vertical integration so carefully worked out by Scotia prior to World War I. It further destroyed the network of social connections in Pictou County—the initial organizing force of the metals industry—as a factor of development. Although a few of the sons of the founders of Scotia had followed their fathers into the company,[110] such relationships would play little part and were of limited importance within an international corporate structure. Besco subsequently experienced financial difficulties, and in 1926 it was placed in receivership; by 1928, the Dominion Steel and Coal Corporation had been formed to take over the company.[111] Circumstances of external control and financial difficulties obviously contributed to Scotia's diminished role and forced Pictou County's metals industry to assume a more peripheral position within the Canadian economy.

"Increase of population is rather the result of mercantile prosperity than the cause of it...and in accordance with this law of city growth, neither Halifax nor any other town in the Province can become a great commercial emporium, unless as a pre-requisite it becomes a seat of manufacturing activity."[112] This statement, written in 1874 by Duncan Campbell, author and industrial promoter, emphasized forcibly that for towns and cities of the Maritimes to grow and prosper, they had, of necessity, to develop a manufacturing base. Certainly this was the path to importance followed by the large cities of the North American seaboard. Many Maritime communities did, of course, make the transition from mercantile to industrial capitalism. Against the background of regional economic transformation, this transition was particularly evident in the metals towns of Pictou County. Building on entrepreneurial initiative and certain initial comparative advantages, including a relatively rich resource base of coal and iron ore, experience in marketing and distributing products abroad, and cheaper industrial materials and labour, local tradesmen and merchants joined together to develop one of Canada's first and largest vertically integrated corporations, the Nova Scotia Steel and Coal Company. But entrepreneurs in Nova Scotia were obliged to work within the necessary framework of government support. Freight rate concessions and tariff protection were essential to compensate for the long haul to distant markets and the existence of strong external competition. These measures became increasingly more important and essential as Pictou County's comparative advantages in manufacturing diminished in favour of Ontario's emerging heartland economy. With mounting political pressure, chiefly from western Canada but also from central Canadian steel makers, these devices of regional integration were pared away and the metals industry in Pictou County suffered steady decline, forcing population losses upon New Glasgow and Trenton.

As communities of a hinterland region, the towns and cities of the Maritimes could only grow in size mainly by trading goods with external markets. Usually the goods sent from a hinterland region are staple commodities rather than manufactured products. This is so because, theoretically, heartland cities possess advantages which render the production of secondary manufacturing cheaper and more productive and efficient than in their hinterland counterparts.[113] According to this particular law of city growth, it can be argued that without government assistance which compensates hinterland manufacturing cities for their comparative disadvantages in producing secondary products, it was inevitable that an urban-industrial collapse would take place in the Maritimes. The mercantile–industrial transition could not be sustained. Efforts to stave off decline during the 1920s, such as the attempt by Besco to rationalize its internal economies of scale by concentrating iron and steel production solely in Sydney, might have worked, but only if government policies continued to facilitate the export of regional products. Pictou County's metals industry suffered, therefore, not only from its growing inability to remain competitive within an integrated national market, but also from its inability to remain an essential link in the metals economy of Nova Scotia. In Besco's scheme of corporate reorganization and concentration, the industrial complex of New Glasgow and Trenton was assigned secondary status. The innovative role of Pictou County's community minded entrepreneurs was banished, to be replaced by an external agent of management. Thus, the bases of effective and sustained growth had been stripped, one by one and gradually over time, from the county. By the close of the 1920s, the accumulated disadvantages of a peripheral location were clearly apparent as factories closed, unemployment increased, and people moved away from New Glasgow and Trenton.

# Notes

1. T.W. Acheson, "The National Policy and the Industrialization of the Maritimes, 1880–1910," *Acadiensis* I (Spring 1972): 2–28; D. Frank, "The Cape Breton Coal Industry and the Rise and Fall of the British Empire Steel Corporation," *Acadiensis* VI (Autumn 1977): 3–34; D. Macgillivray, "Henry Melville Whitney Comes to Cape Breton: The Saga of a Gilded Age Entrepreneur," *Acadiensis* IX (Autumn 1979): 44–70; D.A. Sutherland, "The Personnel and Policies of the Halifax Board of Trade, 1890–1914," in *The Enterprising Canadians*, ed. L.R. Fischer and E.W. Sager (St. John's, 1979), 203–204.

2. E.W. Sager and L.R. Fischer, "Patterns of Investment in the Shipping Industry of Atlantic Canada, 1820–1900," *Acadiensis* IX (Autumn 1979): 19–43.

3. D. Alexander, "Economic Growth in the Atlantic Region, 1880–1940," *Acadiensis* VIII (Autumn 1978): 47–76; R.H. Babcock, "Economic Development in Portland (Me.) and Saint John (N.B.) during the Age of Iron and Steam, 1850–1914," *American Review of Canadian Studies* IX (Spring 1979): 1–337; R.E. Caves and R. Holton, *The Canadian Economy: Prospect and Retrospect* (Cambridge, Mass., 1959), 140–94; L.D. McCann, "Staples and the New Industrialism in the Growth of Post-Confederation Halifax," *Acadiensis* VIII (Spring 1979): 47–79; S.A. Saunders, *The Economic History of Maritime Provinces* (Ottawa, 1939), 14–33 and 90–99.

4. E.R. Forbes, "Misguided Symmetry: The Destruction of Regional Transportation Policy for the Maritimes," in *Canada and the Burden of Unity*, ed. D.J. Bercuson, (Toronto, 1977), 60–86.

5. E.R. Forbes, *The Maritimes Rights Movement, 1919–1927* (Montreal, 1979).

6. J.D. Frost, "Principles of Interest: The Bank of Nova Scotia and the Industrialization of the Maritimes, 1880–1910" (M.A. thesis, Queen's University, 1979).

7. B.S. Keirstead, *The Theory of Economic Change* (Toronto, 1948), 269–81; McCann, "Staples and the New Industrialism in the Growth of Post-Confederation Halifax."

8. In 1861, the agriculture, fishing, forestry, and mining sectors absorbed about two-thirds of the colony's labour force; their products and the sale of ships totalled nearly three-quarters of the value of exports. Calculated from data in *Census Report of Nova Scotia, 1860–61*, Appendix 5; and *Journals and Proceedings of the House of Assembly, 1862*, Appendix 1, Nova Scotia.

9. *Census Report of Nova Scotia, 1860–61*, Appendix 8.

10. In New Brunswick, by comparison, the timber trade had strong impact on urban development. See G. Wynn, "Industrialism, Entrepreneurship, and Opportunity in the New Brunswick Timber Trade," in *The Enterprising Canadians*, ed. Fischer and Sager, 7–20.

11. T.W. Acheson, "The Great Merchant and Economic Development in Saint John, 1820–1850," *Acadiensis* VIII (Spring 1979): 3–27; J.M.S. Careless, "Aspects of Metropolitanism in Atlantic Canada," in *Regionalism in the Canadian Community, 1867–1967*, ed. M. Wade (Toronto, 1969), 117–29.

12. Calculated from data in *Census Report of Nova Scotia*, 1860–61, Appendix 8.

13. A.A. Lomas, "Industrial Development of Nova Scotia, 1830–1854" (M.A. thesis, Dalhousie University, 1950), 129–49.

14. *Novascotian* (Halifax), 12 June 1848.

15. Lomas, "Industrial Development of Nova Scotia," 311–16.

16. *Novascotian*, 12 June 1848.

17. D. Campbell, *History of Nova Scotia* (Montreal, 1874), 506–8.

18. Discussion of the progress made in the economy at this time can be found in Campbell, *History of Nova Scotia*, 506–17; A. Gesner, *The Industrial Resources of Nova Scotia* (Halifax, 1849), 255–59 and 267–80. See also I. McKay, "Capital and Labour in the Halifax Baking and Confectionery Industry during the Last Half of the Nineteenth Century," *Labour/Le Travailleur* 3 (1978): 65–108.

19. The following comment, made in 1913, indicates the degree, if not the fragility, of the region's economic transformation: "When it is remembered that each wage earner represents, on the average, a family of four members, it follows that over 30 000 persons in Nova Scotia are directly dependent for their means of livelihood on this [steel] industry; or, including the associate industry of coal, in which case the number of men employed is increased to 26 000, over 100 000 persons resident in the Province are dependent on the steel industry. In other words, if for any cause, the two largest companies discontinued operations, one out of every five persons living in the Province would be deprived of his or her present means of livelihood." C. Cantley, "A Sketch of the Development and Present Operations in the Iron and Steel Industry of Nova Scotia," *Transactions of the Canadian Mining Institute* 16 (1913), 350.

20. *Journals and Proceedings of the House of Assembly, 1911*, Appendix 15, Nova Scotia; Canadian Manufacturer's Association, *Evidence of the Industrial Ascendancy of Nova Scotia* (Halifax, 1914).

21. For an overview of the industrial development of Pictou County, see R.M. Guy, "Industrial Development and Urbanization of Pictou County to 1900" (M.A. thesis, Acadia University, 1962); J.M. Cameron, *Industrial History of the New Glasgow District* (New Glasgow, 1970) and *The Pictonian Colliers* (Kentville, 1974).

22. Nova Scotia Steel and Coal Company, *Scotia: How Canada's Pioneer Steel Corporation was Evolved from a Country Forge* (New Glasgow, 1912); P.K. Parker, "The Nova Scotia Steel and Coal Company: Entrepreneurship and Industrial Development" (B.A. thesis, Mount Allison University, 1979).

23. Cameron, *Industrial History*, chap. 4; C.W. Parkers, ed., *Who's Who and Why in Canada, 1914*, V (New York, 1915), 346.

24. "Articles of Copartnership," G.F. MacKay MSS File, Public Archives of Nova Scotia (hereafter PANS).

25. W.J.A. Donald, *The Canadian Iron and Steel Industry* (New York, 1915), 85 and 93.

26. The importance of family and kinship ties in establishing businesses and the role of merchant families in funding nineteenth-century industrial enterprise are discussed in: P.D. Hall, "Family Structure and Economic Organization: Massachusetts Merchants, 1700–1850," in *Family and Kin in Urban Communities, 1700–1930*, ed. T.R. Hareven (New York, 1977), 38–61; H.C. Livesay and

G. Porter, "The Financial Role of Merchants in the Development of U.S. Manufacturing," *Explorations in Economic History* 9 (1971): 63–87.

27. *Eastern Chronicle* (New Glasgow), 4 May 1903; *Montreal Standard*, 5 May 1917; *Teare's Directory*, 1879 (Pictou, 1879), 94–95.

28. H.C. Ritchie, "Geneological Records" (Unpublished typescript, New Glasgow Regional Library, 1952); *Teare's Directory*, 95.

29. In 1882, the Carmichaels and the McGregors each had an estimated pecuniary strength of over $75 000; their closest competitor was rated at less than $40 000. Dun, Wiman and Company, *The Mercantile Agency Reference Book, 1882* (Montreal, 1882), 840.

30. The reconstruction of marriage patterns has been compiled from information in Ritchie, "Geneological Records." I am indebted to Paul Parker for discovering this rich source of information.

31. Cameron, *Industrial History*, chap. 6.

32. Ritchie, "Geneological Records."

33. Dun, Wiman and Company, *Mercantile Reference Book, 1882*, 840.

34. J.W. Carmichael was one of the first people to take out a coal lease in Pictou County after the monopoly of the General Mining Association was broken in 1857. He did so in 1861, but by 1864 the lease had lapsed. RG 21, vol. 4, Coal Leases, PANS.

35. For example, J.W. Carmichael represented Pictou as a Liberal from 1867 to 1872, and again from 1874 to 1878. J.P. MacPhie, *Pictonians at Home and Abroad* (Boston, 1914), 209.

36. Rosemary E. Ommer, "Anticipating the Trend: The Pictou Ship Register, 1840–1889," *Acadiensis* X (Autumn 1980): 67–89.

37. J.M. Cameron, "The Pictou Bank," *Nova Scotia Historical Quarterly* 6 (June 1976): 129.

38. "Prospectus of the Nova Scotia Steel Company, 1882" and "Letters Patent Incorporating the Nova Scotia Steel Company, Limited, 1882," Hawker Siddeley Papers, MS 4–106, Dalhousie University Archives (hereafter DUA).

39. Scotia initially made steel by the Siemens-Martin open-hearth process using acid linings, but several years later introduced basic linings which permitted a wider range of material inputs. The Siemens-Martin process was favoured over the Bessemer method because it produced a stronger, higher quality steel which could sustain higher transportation costs. For an economist's perspective on innovations in the steel industry, see P. Temin, *Iron and Steel in Nineteenth Century America: An Economic Enquiry* (Cambridge, Mass., 1964), 138–41.

40. Nova Scotia Steel Company, *Report of Directors ... 1883–1887* (New Glasgow, 1884–1888). With few exceptions, Scotia continued to pay at least an 8 per cent dividend on preferred shares until World War I.

41. Donald, *The Canadian Iron and Steel Industry*, 99 and 336; "Bounties for the Canadian Iron and Steel Industry," *The Iron Age*, 25 October 1906.

42. Graham Fraser's reaction to the new tariff schedule reveals something of the business attitudes of the New Glasgow industrialists: "On the whole the duty is very favourable to us. I believe the Montreal people are now squealing very hard about having to pay such a large duty on steel billets." G. Fraser and T. Cantley, 16 May 1887, Thomas Cantley Papers, MG I, no. 174, PANS. Thomas Cantley provides another illustration of the New Glasgow social network. He was a native of New Glasgow who had joined Scotia in 1885 as a salesman at the invitation of Simon A. Fraser, his friend and Graham Fraser's brother. Previously, Cantley had worked in B.S. McCurdy's store and then formed a business of his own with McCurdy as a

silent partner. Later, he would rise to attain the positions of general manager and president of Scotia Steel. Parker, *Who's Who*, 1778–79.

43. Nova Scotia Steel and Forge Company, *Report of Directors ... 1889*, 22.

44. Nova Scotia Steel and Forge Company, *Report of Directors ... 1890*, 33.

45. *Teare's Directory, 1879*; Dun, Wiman and Company, *Mercantile Reference Books, 1882–1890*.

46. Of these firms, the one which grew most rapidly was I. Matheson and Company. The firm itself illustrates well the continuing relationship between business success and New Glasgow's social network. Isaac Matheson, the firm's founder, was born at West River in Pictou County in 1814. He learned the blacksmith's trade in the coal mining industry, later married J.W. Carmichael's sister, and by the mid-1860s was the proprietor of the Acadia Foundry. Family ties were bound even tighter in the 1880s. James Matheson Carmichael married Christian Matheson, while his sister Christian Carmichael married William Grant Matheson. William, who had studied engineering at the University of New Brunswick and served his apprenticeship in Dundee, Scotland, succeeded his father, Isaac, as the head of the company. When the company was incorporated in 1896, however, James M. Carmichael was named as President and James C. McGregor as Vice-President. *Eastern Chronicle*, 12 September 1930; Cameron, *Industrial History*, chap. 1; Ritchie, "Geneological Records."

47. *Report ... for the Year 1880–1890* (Halifax, 1881–1891) Department of Mines, Nova Scotia; Nova Scotia Steel Company, *Report of Directors ... 1882–1888*.

48. Scotia purchased most of its pig iron through the firm of William Jacks and Company of Glasgow. William Jacks also contracted with Scotia to supply skilled labour. Hawker Siddeley Papers, MS 4–106, DUA.

49. Donald, *The Canadian Iron and Steel Industry*, 106–107 and 327; J.H. Bartlett, "The Manufacture of Iron in Canada," *Transactions of the American Institute of Mining, Metallurgical and Petroleum Engineers* 14 (1885–86): 439–41; C.O. Macdonald, *The Coal and Iron Industries of Nova Scotia* (Halifax, 1909), 233–48.

50. Donald, *The Canadian Iron and Steel Industry*, 336.

51. Bartlett, "The Manufacture of Iron in Canada," 538; Cantley, "A Sketch of the Iron and Steel Industry," 325; Gesner, *Industrial Resources*, 258.

52. See, for example, E. Gilpin, "The Iron Ores of Pictou County, Nova Scotia," *Transactions of the American Institute of Mining Engineers* (May 1895), 1–26 and *The Iron Ores of Nova Scotia* (Montreal, 1891).

53. E. Gilpin, "Report on the Iron Ores of Pictou County, Nova Scotia, 1890," RG 21, Series A, vol. 26, PANS.

54. R.E. Chambers, "Report on the New Glasgow Iron, Coal, and Railway Company Properties Outside the East River, 1890," Thomas Cantley Papers, MG 1, no. 174, PANS.

55. Nova Scotia Steel and Coal Company, *Scotia*, 9–11; Donald, *The Canadian Iron and Steel Industry*, 112; Cantley, "Sketch of the Iron and Steel Industry," 327.

56. Nova Scotia, "An Act to Incorporate the New Glasgow Iron, Coal, and Railway Company Limited" (Halifax, 1888). Besides Fraser, other directors included G.E.R. Burpee, W. Jacks, H. Aitken, and D.C. Fraser.

57. Nova Scotia, "An Act to Incorporate the New Glasgow Iron, Coal, and Railway Company, Limited" (Halifax, 1891).

58. Nova Scotia Steel and Forge Company, *Report of Directors ... 1892*, 39; Donald, *The Canadian Iron and Steel Industry*, 327; Guy, "Industrial Development," 122.

59. *Monetary Times* (Toronto), 31 August 1894.

60. J.F. Stairs to T. Cantley, 1 June 1894, Thomas Cantley Papers, MG 1, no. 174, PANS.

61. "Memorandum of Agreement ... 23 January, 1896," Hawker Siddeley Papers, MS 4–106, DUA. The prices quoted in this document are slightly less than those quoted on the Toronto market (see Table 3), and also indicate that the market was most competitive in southern Ontario.

62. Donald, *The Canadian Iron and Steel Industry*, 336.

63. Details of the merger discussions, which took place during 1893 and 1894, appear in the Thomas Cantley Papers, MG 1, no. 174, PANS.

64. Economies in the metals industry are discussed in A. Chandler, *The Visible Hand* (Cambridge, Mass., 1977), 258–72.

65. "The supply of pig iron being entirely under their own control enables them to secure orders which otherwise would have gone past them." Nova Scotia Steel Company, *Report of the Directors ... 1896*, 52.

66. Cantley to Gilpin, 7 October 1890, RG 21, vol. 25(d), PANS; G.E. Drummond, "The Iron Industry in 1898," *Canadian Mining Review* 18 (1899): 57.

67. J.S. Barrie, "The Coal and Iron Industries of Eastern Canada," *The Colliery Guardian*, 15 February 1901.

68. Nova Scotia, Department of Mines, *Report ... for the Year, 1890–1899*.

69. Nova Scotia Steel Company, *Report of the Directors ... 1897*, 58.

70. Nova Scotia Steel Company, *Report of the Directors ... 1899*, 76.

71. Donald, *The Canadian Iron and Steel Industry*, 112.

72. Nova Scotia, Department of Mines, *Report for the Year, 1893, 1894, and 1896*.

73. "An Appreciation of Robert E. Chambers," Thomas Cantley Papers, MG 1, no. 167, folder 2, PANS.

74. "Bounties," *The Iron Age*, 25 October 1906, 1074–75.

75. *Monetary Times*, 5 August 1904, 106.

76. "An Appreciation of Robert E. Chambers," Thomas Cantley Papers, MG 1, no. 167, folder 2, PANS: "Preliminary Report of Brazilian Iron Ores," Hawker Siddeley Papers, MS 4–106, DUA.

77. Before World War I, Scotia held five different coal leases in Pictou County. See RG 21, vol. 4, Coal Leases, PANS.

78. Nova Scotia Steel Company, *Report of the Directors ... 1887*, 14.

79. *Monetary Times*, 12 January 1898; Cantley, "Sketch of the Iron and Steel Industry," 328–29.

80. *Maritime Mining Record*, 22 November 1899, 10; Canada, House of Commons, *Debates* (1903), 7934.

81. The sale was negotiated by Thomas Cantley in London during 1899. Cantley also spent much time in Europe, particularly in Scotland and Germany, during the early 1900s signing iron ore and coal contracts and examining new forge and steel making technologies. Parker, *Who's Who*, 179; Nova Scotia Steel and Coal Company, *Souvenir 1908* (New Glasgow, 1908), 15.

82. *Maritime Mining Record*, 20 February 1901, 12; and Nova Scotia Steel and Coal Company, *Report of the General Manager ... 1909*, 7.

83. Canada, House of Commons, *Debates* (1903), 7933.

84. *Maritime Mining Record*, 22 November 1899, 10.

85. The company remained dominated by Nova Scotia financiers and industrialists. For a succinct discussion of the events leading to the incorporation, see D. Frank, "The Cape Breton Coal Industry," 13–14.

86. Nova Scotia Steel and Coal Company, *Report of the General Manager ... 1910*, 17.

87. Cameron, *Pictonian Colliers*, 98; *Monetary Times*, 19 August 1904. The mine was in production from 1902 to 1909, averaging about 40 000 tons of coal annually.

88. Thomas Cantley Papers, MG 1, vol. 167, folder 1913, PANS.

89. Cameron, *Industrial History*, chap. 5; Nova Scotia Steel and Coal Company, *Report of the General Manager ... 1905–1912*.

90. MG 1, no. 398, Eastern Car Company file, PANS; Cameron, *Industrial History*, chap. 7; New Glasgow et al., Town Councils, *Nova Scotia's Industrial Centre* (New Glasgow, 1916), 53–55.

91. D. Kerr, "The Location of the Iron and Steel Industry in Canada," in *Geographical Approaches to Canadian Problems*, ed. R.L. Gentilcore (Toronto, 1971), 59–68; Donald, *The Canadian Iron and Steel Industry*, 219–22.

92. Canadian Manufacturer's Association, *Industrial Ascendancy of Nova Scotia*; R.G. Dun and Company, *The Mercantile Reference Book, 1912*.

93. *Eastern Chronicle*, 24 January 1935.

94. *Journals and Proceedings of the House of Assembly, 1911*, Appendix 15, Nova Scotia.

95. The federal government provided financial assistance between 1917 and 1920 for Scotia to build seven small freighters of up to 2800 tons in size. Larger ships could not be built at Trenton because of the restricted size of the shipyard and Scotia's limited steel fabricating facilities. Scotia was even incapable of building ships that the company itself could use in the Wabana to Cape Breton iron trade. In fact, Scotia favoured Halifax as the province's most suitable shipbuilding location. "Resources of the Province of Nova Scotia as Regards Steel-Ship Construction," Thomas Cantley Papers, MG 1, no. 167, folder 7, PANS; and "Shipbuilding," Hawker Siddeley Papers, MS 4–106, DUA.

96. By comparison, Montreal was awarded contracts totalling $162 203 807; Toronto, $153 155 974; and Hamilton, $68 896 058. MG 30, B4, vol. 36, F.E. Hirschfile, Public Archives of Canada. I am indebted to Peter Rider, National Museum of Man, for drawing my attention to the source of these data.

97. Cameron, *Industrial History*, chap. 6; M. Bliss, *A Canadian Millionaire* (Toronto, 1978), 245.

98. Census of Industry, "Preliminary Report: Industrial Statistics of the Maritime Provinces for 1919" (Ottawa, 1922).

99. *Census of Canada, 1911*, vol. 3, Tables 7 and 111; Census of Industry, "Manufacturing Industries of the Maritime Provinces, 1931" (Ottawa, 1933).

100. Because it is impossible to obtain data for only metal-making and metal-working industries in individual cities, we are forced to rely on aggregate data for all manufacturing types. This problem is not too serious, because the metals industry in the selected towns and cities clearly dominated the manufacturing structure.

101. T. Traves, "The Political Economy of the Steel Tariff," in *The State and Enterprise: Canadian Manufacturing and the Federal Government, 1917–1931* (Toronto, 1979), 121–54.

102. O.J. McDiarmid, *Commercial Policy in the Canadian Economy* (Cambridge, 1946), 220; H.V. Nelles, *The Politics of Development* (Toronto, 1974), 125–31.

103. *Report of the Royal Commission on Coal, 1946* (Ottawa, 1947), 575–77.

104. Forbes, "Misguided Symmetry," 67.

105. The case of the Cumming Manufacturing Company has been developed from Evidence, Board of Railway Commissioners, 1926, vol. 483, 397–98, typescript, Provincial Archives of New Brunswick; Parker, *Who's Who*, 244.

106. Traves, "The Political Economy of the Steel Tariff," 139–47.

107. Fraser and Carmichael both left Scotia over disputes concerning financial matters. MacKay, who quit plant supervision in 1889, and McGregor both remained as directors until World War I, but their initial leadership role had been relinquished earlier to Robert Harris, the Halifax financier, and Thomas Cantley. See J.M. Carmichael to J.F. Stairs, 9 October 1894, MG 2, no. 330, PANS; Cameron, *Industrial History*, chap. 4; Nova Scotia Steel and Coal Company, *Annual Reports, 1882–1915*.

108. This takeover is assessed succinctly by D. Frank, "The Cape Breton Coal Industry," 13–17. Crockard had undertaken a similar task for United States Steel when the giant conglomerate took over steel-making operations in Birmingham, Alabama. I am indebted to Professor Alfred Chandler for this information, personal communication, 5 November 1980.

109. Hawker Siddeley Papers, MS 4–106, DUA.

110. Ritchie, "Geneological Records."

111. Traves, "The Political Economy of the Steel Tariff," 132–37.

112. Campbell, *A History of Nova Scotia*, 508.

113. McCann, "Staples and the New Industrialism," 48–52.

# THE FAMILY ECONOMY AND WORK IN AN INDUSTRIALIZING CITY: MONTREAL IN THE 1870s*

BETTINA BRADBURY

The impact of industrial capitalism on the structure, size, and nature of the family has recently been attracting the interest of historians, demographers, sociologists, and anthropologists.[1] The topic has produced some lively debates between feminists and family historians, between historians and sociologists, and between marxists and liberals.[2] Did industrialization lead to the emergence of the nuclear family as early sociologists believed?[3] Was the separation of home and workplace and the creation of a separate sphere in the home a result of industrialization?[4] Was the family a passive agent automatically adjusting its size and structure to economic change?[5] Was the advent of capitalism or industrialization the important factor?[6]

This paper aims to cast light on some of these broad questions. It examines how class position, cultural values, and changes in the nature of production influenced the family economy in the period of early industrial capitalism. It attempts to relate the work of family members to the particular nature of industrialization in one place at one time—Montreal in the 1870s. The aim is to see what data from the manuscript census reveals about the family economy in a period of transition, and to examine beyond the figures of census-based material the interaction between the family as an institution and the economy. The link between the two, here, is in the paid work of family members. Other important aspects of the family economy and family life—unpaid work at home, socialization, reproduction—are not dealt with in this paper.

To illustrate the inter-relationships and relative importance of class, cultural tradition, and the nature of production, five topics are studied. The first

* Canadian Historical Association, *Historical Papers/Communications Historiques* (1979), 71–96.

section briefly examines major aspects of Montreal's industrialization. The following three sections examine aspects of the family economy: the relationship between the number of workers per family and the father's occupation, the prevalence and nature of work by young children, and the work of wives and mothers. Finally, household structure is examined to see whether sharing housing offered an alternative survival strategy for families.

The major sources for the study are random samples taken of households resident in two Montreal wards, Sainte Anne and Saint Jacques, in 1871.[7] This data is complemented by a complete survey of all working wives in these two areas and of the manuscript returns of the industrial census.[8] Thus, while much of what is argued is relevant to all of Montreal in this period, the data is specifically focussed on the immigrant, industrial, working class suburb of Ste. Anne and the predominantly French-Canadian and more artisanal suburb of St. Jacques. Ideally, families and industrial change should be traced over several decades at least. Even a static examination of one period, however, begins to show important patterns.[9]

## Industrialization

Families living in Montreal in 1871 were part of a city in transition. For two to three decades industrial capital had unevenly but persistently been reshaping the geography of the city, the organization of production, and the nature of work.[10] The rhythm of people's lives and the bases of family life were radically altered. In trades like shoemaking, carpentry, and tailoring, old forms of production and apprenticeship had largely disappeared. Most workers were collected together under the control of one master, often manufacturing only a single part of a whole commodity.[11] Artisans had not been eliminated in most trades, but were increasingly confined to certain lines of luxury production, to repair work, and to the less industrial parts of town. The transition from mercantile to industrial city involved both the growth of large-scale industries and the proliferation of small-scale ones. Highly mechanized factory production co-existed with small workshops and artisanal production. Machine work in many cases multiplied the amount of hand work that had to be done.[12]

The city became increasingly differentiated by function. The residential areas of the bourgeoisie were concentrated together, separate from the homes of workers and from commerce and industry. Commerce was still centred largely in the old city, but retail merchants were beginning to move their shops up the hill toward Ste. Catherine Street. In the west of the city, Canada's first major concentration of industry was clustered around the basins and locks of the Lachine Canal, which the government had developed to produce water power for the emerging industrial bourgeoisie. Stretching along both sides of the canal among and beyond the factories was Ste. Anne, the first industrial working class suburb. Within its boundaries was Griffintown, the Irish immigrant area. Here were housed what remained of those people H.C. Pentland has identified as forming Canada's early proletariat two decades earlier.[13] Now they were supplemented by their children and by an influx of French Canadians and newer immigrant families from Ireland, England, and Scotland.

On the eastern boundary of Montreal, Ste. Marie was beginning to emerge as the major French-Canadian industrial suburb.[14] Between it and St. Laurent ward lay St. Jacques. It and Ste. Anne were like two different worlds in 1871. The first was definitely an immigrant suburb, a mixture of Irish, English, Scots, and French Canadians. Ste. Anne was Montreal's industrial area, whereas in St. Jacques production was largely artisanal or at a handicraft stage. The most common enterprise there was a small workshop, with between one and four employees—often the craftsman, an apprentice, and members of the family. The crafts that predominated were woodworking ones, especially carpentry and joiners shops; food processing, including small bakers and butchers with stalls at the local markets; and shoemaking and dressmaking.

The contrast between Ste. Anne and St. Jacques clearly illustrated three major aspects of Montreal's industrialization. First, the scale of enterprises was growing steadily. More and more workers were involved in large factories. Work processes were constantly being modified, old skills were rendered obsolete, and new ones created. Machinery, especially powered by steam or water, was increasingly being used.[15] Mechanization and the application of power to one part of the labour process usually created the need for additional and often tedious hand work in unchanged parts. Some of this was done in departments of the factories. In shoemaking and clothing, much was "put out," especially to women and children working at home. It was into this kind of work that the women and children of St. Jacques were drawn in large numbers.

Secondly, despite the overall increase in scale, industrial capitalist and pre-industrial forms continued to co-exist for a long period of time. In Ste. Anne, the presence of a few, large, mechanized, primary processing plants for flour and sugar seemed to have spurred the growth of small baking and confectionery establishments in the neighbourhood. Coopers and blacksmiths continued to run their shops, despite the fact that most of the large foundries and factories had coopering and blacksmith departments. The whole ward of St. Jacques existed as an almost pre-industrial, artisanal enclave in the changing city. Two-thirds of its productive establishments employed under five workers. Yet, even there, one large tobacco factory and two tanneries employed nearly half the ward's enumerated "industrial" workers.[16]

A third feature of Montreal's industrialization, and one most important for its families, was the heavy reliance on child and female labour. As work processes were cut down into their component parts, women and children were drawn into sections of the production process. In the city's type foundry, for example, a complex machine cast type "so rapidly that 200 small type could be cast in a minute." However, a small "jet" remained on the type. These were broken off by young boys. Then

> the type is next given over to a number of girls, who sit around a circular stone table. These young women rapidly pick up a type each and rub it upon the table...to smooth the surface. The dexterity...is astonishing.[17]

Or in Lyman's chemical plant, where most of the workers were men, and waterpowered machinery operated powerful presses and complicated cutting systems, women were "kept constantly employed in the washing of bottles."[18] Similarly, in De Witt's Buckskin Glove Factory on the Lachine Canal:

> A machine at one stroke takes out pieces the shape of the thumb and fingers of the human hand...In an adjacent room a number of young women, operating on sewing machines stitched them together with great rapidity.[19]

In shoemaking, cigar making, and confectionery, the story was the same. A cigar maker complained in 1889 that

> in 1863 there was a mould invented...Before that time we did not know what it was to have a lot of apprentices in the shops. The system of making cigars by moulds caused a great many children to go to work at the trade. Manufacturers found they could get cigars more cheaply by children.[20]

Women and children thus came to constitute a vital element of Montreal's industrial labour force.[21] In 1871 three types of production dominated in Montreal: leather, boots and shoe manufacture; clothing manufactures; and metal work and transportation related industry. In the first two, the proportion of women and children was 50 per cent and 80 per cent, respectively. Overall, women and children made up nearly 42 per cent of the industrial workforce reported in the 1871 census. Montreal's industries appear to have employed significantly more women and children than did Toronto's where the proportion was 33 per cent.[22] Thus, although the employment of large numbers of women and children appears to have been a general characteristic of early industrial capitalism everywhere, the proportions involved varied immensely. In a mill town like Lowell, Massachusetts, for instance, women constituted 56 per cent of the workforce, compared to Montreal's 33 per cent. In Preston, Lancashire, England, by the time boys were fourteen, 88 per cent of them were working. In Montreal around 25 per cent of boys eleven to fifteen years old worked.[23] Obviously, the different opportunities for work for family members in any one locale conditioned the particular nature of the impact of industrialization of the family.

## The Family Economy: Average Numbers of Family Workers

Montreal's labour market was characterized by seasonal and cyclical unemployment and by low wages. In the winter many workers were without jobs. The Port, which in summer fed both commerce and industry, was open only seven to eight months a year. With its closure, the rhythm of business and employment for the whole city slowed down. Labourers and carters found themselves seeking alternative winter employment although there was very little work available. City lumber yards closed down between November and May. Even shoemakers and moulders expected to lose two or three months during the winter. Competition for jobs became tough. Winter wages in most jobs dropped. "When they don't find work at anything else," explained a moulder in the 1880s, "they walk the streets and wait till work commences, and when the bosses see they are hard up for work, they try to reduce wages and put them as low as possible."[24]

While winter wages dropped, living expenses usually soared. The winter of 1871–72 was exceptionally severe and fuel costs rose to what was reported as "famine prices" of between ten and fifteen dollars a cord.[25] Obviously a labourer earning between one and two dollars a week could not afford to pay such a price, when a cord of wood would heat the home for only a week.[26]

Given the need for extra money in the winter for fuel, clothing, and food, and the low wages that prevailed in most jobs, it is not surprising that it was fairly generally accepted that many working class families needed more than one worker if they were to survive adequately. Employers and charity workers alike agreed on this a decade later before the Royal Commission on the Relations of Labor and Capital. Some, while arguing that young children should not work, admitted that "many are necessitated to do so from the fact that their parents probably earn very little, not sufficient to keep a large family unless the little fellows are sent to work at tender years."[27] Employers pleaded pressure from widows and poverty-stricken parents as the reason for hiring very young children.[28]

In 1871 families in Ste. Anne and St. Jacques averaged 1.6 workers each. Averages, however, are generally deceptive, masking more than they show. The father's occupation was crucial in influencing the work of other family members. In the few Ste. Anne families that were headed by proprietors, the average number of workers was only 1.2. In both wards, semi-skilled and unskilled workers in contrast averaged 1.8 workers each. Skilled workers averaged only 1.5. The one divergence between the wards interestingly reflected the fundamental difference in the nature of production in the two wards. St. Jacques' proprietors averaged more workers per family than did local skilled workers or "white collar workers" (see Table 1). The reason lay in the nature of their enterprises. For these artisans and small shopkeepers, their business was often a family undertaking. Few employed large numbers of workers. Most were helped by apprentices, sons, daughters, or wives.[29]

**TABLE 1** *Average Number of Workers in Families Classified by the Father's Occupational Group, 1871*[30]

| | Ste. Anne | St. Jacques |
|---|---|---|
| Professionals | 1.0 | 1.3 |
| Proprietors | 1.2 | 1.6 |
| "White collar" workers | 1.2 | 1.4 |
| Skilled workers | 1.5 | 1.5 |
| Semi and unskilled workers | 1.8 | 1.8 |

If the apparent strong relationship between class and the number of family workers is examined further, to see actual rather than average numbers of workers, roughly 40 per cent of unskilled families in St. Jacques had more than one worker compared to 30 per cent of skilled and 20 to 25 per cent of white collar and professional families.

## The Family Economy: Working Children

Both St. Jacques and Ste. Anne were working class wards, with 60 to 80 per cent of their residents involved in manual wage labour, skilled or otherwise. French Canadians predominated in skilled trades in both wards, while the Irish of Ste. Anne clustered significantly in unskilled positions, especially as labourers and carters. Small proprietors, artisans and shop owners were much more prevalent among St. Jacques's workers, especially within the small non-French-Canadian population (see Table 2).

It was definitely the norm in families of all classes and backgrounds for the husband to be the primary breadwinner. Two-thirds of all workers in both wards were the male heads of their family. Virtually all husbands listed an occupation in the 1871 census, although this did not imply that they had steady work or were currently employed. Nor did it mean that the occupation listed was their only one. "Certain establishments," the writer of the 1871 census monograph explained,

> do not employ workmen or labourers during the whole year, nor in a regular manner...men following certain occupations are successively engaged in the course of the year in various employments.[31]

The few husbands not listing a job were either retired and living with one of their adult children, or they were newly married and living, together with their bride, with one of the families of origin.

**TABLE 2** *Occupational Groups by Origins: Ste. Anne and St. Jacques Wards Compared, 1871*[33]

Ste. Anne

| | French-Canadian | | Irish | | Other | | Overall |
|---|---|---|---|---|---|---|---|
| | No. | % | No. | % | No. | % | % |
| Professional | 1 | 1.1 | | | | | .3 |
| Proprietor | 3 | 3.3 | 8 | 6.2 | 8 | 9.9 | 5.0 |
| Commercial employee | 1 | 1.1 | 10 | 7.7 | 8 | 9.9 | 6.3 |
| Public service | | | 2 | 1.5 | 1 | 1.2 | 1.0 |
| Service | 2 | 2.2 | 5 | 3.8 | 4 | 4.9 | 3.6 |
| Skilled | 58 | 63.7 | 43 | 33.1 | 41 | 50.7 | 48.3 |
| Semi & unskilled | 26 | 28.6 | 60 | 46.2 | 18 | 22.2 | 34.5 |
| Other | | | 2 | 1.5 | 1 | 1.2 | 1.0 |
| Total | 91 | 100.0 | 130 | 100.0 | 81 | 100.0 | 100.0 |
| Per cent of total population | | 26.5 | | 50.0 | | 23.5 | |

St. Jacques

| | French-Canadian | | Other | | Overall |
|---|---|---|---|---|---|
| | No. | % | No. | % | % |
| Professional | 16 | 3.2 | 10 | 11.0 | 4.4 |
| Proprietor | 43 | 8.6 | 20 | 22.0 | 10.5 |
| Commercial employee | 45 | 9.0 | 11 | 12.1 | 9.5 |
| Public service | 9 | 1.8 | 1 | 1.1 | 1.7 |
| Service | 18 | 3.6 | 13 | 14.3 | 5.3 |
| Skilled | 241 | 48.3 | 15 | 16.5 | 43.5 |
| Semi & unskilled | 97 | 19.4 | 17 | 18.7 | 19.3 |
| Other | 30 | 6.0 | 4 | 4.3 | 5.8 |
| Total | 499 | 100.0 | 91 | 100.0 | 100.0 |
| Per cent of total population | | 82.5 | | 17.5 | |

Older sons still resident at home were the most usual second wage earner. Almost all sons over twenty worked, while only half the daughters of that age did. About 75 per cent of sixteen to twenty year old sons had jobs, while only around 40 per cent of daughters did. If there were boys in the family, the older girls were likely to remain at home to help with housework and care of younger children. At all ages sons were much more likely to work than daughters (see Table 3).

More interesting is the number of children between the ages of eleven and fifteen who worked. It was the work of children of these ages in factories and sweatshops that was to capture the imagination and elicit the horror of reformers a decade or so later. Newspapers, Royal Commissions, and labour unions would all proclaim the evils of child labour. Laws would be passed attempting to control it, not always with great success. In 1871, however, there was no legislation to prevent the work of young children and there was little public outcry compared to the reforming voices of subsequent decades.[32] Graphic descriptions of the hours and conditions of child labour exist, but little real idea of how widespread it was, of what families it occurred in, of the role that it played in the economy of businesses and families, and of what parents thought about their young children being involved in wage labour.

Around 25 per cent of boys aged between eleven and fifteen reported an occupation to the 1871 census taker, while about 10 per cent of girls did so (see Table 3). Focussing on those families which had these youngsters at work, the following section will attempt to describe the work they were doing and some of the factors that determined whether or not children of this age would work in any particular family.

**TABLE 3** *Children, Work, and School Attendance, 1871*[34]

| | Work | | School | | Neither | | |
|---|---|---|---|---|---|---|---|
| | No. | % | No. | % | No. | % | Total no. |
| **Ste. Anne** | | | | | | | |
| Sons | | | | | | | |
| 0–5 | | | 6 | 8 | 67 | 92 | 73 |
| 6–10 | 1 | 2 | 38 | 67 | 18 | 31 | 57 |
| 11–15 | 9 | 24 | 22 | 58 | 7 | 18 | 38 |
| 16–20 | 40 | 75.5 | 1 | 2 | 12 | 22.5 | 53 |
| Daughters | | | | | | | |
| 0–5 | | | 4 | 5 | 74 | 95 | 78 |
| 6–10 | | | 48 | 76 | 15 | 24 | 63 |
| 11–15 | 5 | 7 | 32 | 48 | 33 | 47 | 70 |
| 16–20 | 21 | 40 | 4 | 7.5 | 28 | 52.5 | 53 |
| **St. Jacques** | | | | | | | |
| Sons | | | | | | | |
| 0–5 | | | 8 | 6 | 124 | 94 | 132 |
| 6–10 | 2 | 2 | 48 | 54 | 39 | 44 | 89 |
| 11–15 | 25 | 26 | 43 | 45 | 28 | 29 | 96 |
| 16–20 | 61 | 75 | 5 | 6 | 15 | 19 | 81 |
| Daughters | | | | | | | |
| 0–5 | | | 8 | 6 | 132 | 94 | 140 |
| 6–10 | | | 54 | 60 | 46 | 40 | 90 |
| 11–15 | 12 | 13 | 39 | 42 | 47 | 45 | 92 |
| 16–20 | 41 | 40 | 1 | 1 | 60 | 59 | 102 |

First, it should be reiterated that a demand for child labour existed in Montreal. A large proportion of the city's major industries were dependent on children's cheap labour. With industrialization Montreal appears to have developed a variety of jobs that were age specific, which children did for a while until they became too old or too experienced to be paid such cheap wages.

Most of Ste. Anne's young worked in factory jobs—in the local cotton mill or tobacco factories, or as typecasters or nailers. A Ste. Anne cotton mill reported twenty-four workers aged under sixteen to the 1871 census taker, although there may well have been more. Two-thirds of the employees were female.[35] Young children in the mill were confined to specific tasks such as carrying thread and hose or working in the mule and spinning rooms as "doffers." Most of the women and children were French Canadians. Several of the working families had been brought from the rural Saguenay country as cheaper "green" labour. Many children in the mill also had brothers and sisters there and sometimes fathers or widowed mothers as well.[36]

Fines in cotton mills were high and a daily experience, especially for the children. As a result the pay they took home was often drastically reduced.[37] Fines were also the standard method of disciplining youngsters in the tobacco factories of both wards. There, too, children tended to work on specific jobs, often separate from the skilled tradesmen who might have taught them the trade. While some were technically employed as apprentices, indentureship for most children did not guarantee induction into the mysteries of a trade. Most "apprentices" in cigar making spent their time watching a machine or only rolling cigars. In St. Jacques ward in 1871, there were still some children who appear to have been apprenticed to a small master running his own shop, some to their father. They worked in trades such as tinsmithing, not in cigar making or shoemaking, both of which had radically altered over the decades.

It was from the semi- and unskilled Irish and French-Canadian families of Ste. Anne, St. Jacques, and other areas of Montreal that the bulk of the city's young workers were drawn. These families were more than twice as likely to have children under sixteen at work as were skilled families. Such children worked in around 30 per cent of unskilled families compared to 12 per cent of skilled. In Ste. Anne, the children of non-manual workers seldom had jobs, whereas St. Jacques's artisans and entrepreneurs did put their children to work at an early age (see Table 4). Family work for the latter was part of an old tradition, but was also necessary because of the increasing competition they were experiencing from industrial production.

In large families, especially those with an unskilled father, it was much more common for young children to be sent out to work. In families of four (that is, with two children) only 5.5 per cent had eleven to fifteen year olds at work, while 30 per cent of families of eight did so. The presence of older siblings does not seem to have mitigated against a younger child also being sent out to work. Indeed, the opposite seemed true. Where older brothers or sisters worked, children between eleven and fifteen were more likely to also work than those who had older siblings who did not. Certainly, the wages of one working child were not high enough to give much of a boost to family income in large families. The larger a family, the more likely a young child would be sent out to work.

**TABLE 4** *Percentage of Non-Manual, Skilled, and Unskilled Families with Working Children under Sixteen*[38]

| Age | Ste. Anne, 1871<br>11–15 | St. Jacques, 1871<br>11–15 |
|---|---|---|
| Non-manual | 0% | 22.5% |
| Skilled | 11.8% | 13.6% |
| Unskilled | 33.3% | 29.0% |

French Canadians appear to have been somewhat more likely to send their younger children to work than other groups. In St. Jacques, nearly 25 per cent of French-Canadian families with children aged between eleven and fifteen had at least one of them at work in 1871, compared to only 13 per cent of non-French Canadians. More French-Canadian families had children of all ages at work than other groups. Studies of families from Quebec in the United States have shown similar patterns. In Cohoes, New York, during the 1880s for instance, 27.3 per cent of female French-Canadian workers in textile plants were under fourteen compared to 13.5 per cent of English and 15.6 per cent of Irish workers.[39] Similarly in Manchester, New Hampshire, in the early twentieth century, Tamara Hareven found that French Canadians had more textile workers per family than other groups. She argues that the

> basic tradition of family work and of the economic role of each member...was carried over from the agricultural background. The important continuity was in the perception and experience of the family as a work unit, even when the location of the job and the work processes were different.[40]

Cultural attitudes to work and to the idea of the role of children certainly seemed to have supported child labour in French-Canadian families. The relationship between ethnicity and the work of young children, however, should not be overstressed. Class was still more important than ethnic background. In Ste. Anne, where the Irish constituted most of the unskilled workers, more of their families had children at work than did French Canadians—even unskilled French Canadians. The family economy had been part of rural Irish life too, although most of Ste. Anne's residents with young children were second generation immigrants, brought up far from the land. For families of all backgrounds, basic need arising from the insecurities of a father's work was as important as cultural values and tradition, so that for all groups unskilled families were more likely to have their children at work than other families (see Table 5).

**TABLE 5** *Ethnicity and Working Children**

| | Ste. Anne | | St. Jacques | |
|---|---|---|---|---|
| | French-Canadian | Other | French-Canadian | Other |
| Non-manual | 0 | 0 | 55 | 38 |
| Skilled | 80 | 82 | 58 | 25 |
| Unskilled | 86 | 94 | 77 | 50 |

NOTE: *The percentage of families with children over age eleven who have at least one child at work.

Finding work for these children appeared to have been a family responsibility. In the textile industry especially, capitalists preferred to hire whole families. Indeed, they advertised for families in the newspapers, specifying that young children would be welcome.[41] And they recruited whole families of "green labour" from the rural areas. Manufacturers saw it as a distinct advantage to hire whole families and by the 1880s were providing "cottages, so as to give the employees of the mill nice comfortable homes." Girls working in such factories were assumed to be living with their parents. They "would not undertake the work otherwise," an employer pointed out.[42] For parents, it was desirable to have their young children in the same workplace. It enabled mothers to work. Traditional ties between children and parents could be maintained, even though the family as a unit of production which had once worked their land together had been transformed. Employers often argued that the hiring of very young children resulted from parental pressure. A mill overseer explained:

> ...a man will be working at the mill, and his daughter working there also, and he may have a small child, whom he desires to have there, for instance, in the spooling room. Often you don't want to take the child, but if you do not, he and his daughter will go out, and they will go to some mill where the whole three will be employed.[43]

It was apparently common for mothers to seek work for their daughters and for sons to act as go-betweens. For instance, when Madame Sara Fontaine's two daughters were dismissed, first from the Ste. Anne Mill and then from the Hudon Mill at Hochelaga, it was she who went to the "boss" asking "Why did you dismiss my daughters? I have need of their assistance to live."[44] The manager explained that when girls came to the mill their "mothers often come with them, and beg the chance of getting them on to work."

> For instance, there was a mother brought a girl the other day. I said she was small. The mother replied: 'I went into the mill about that age.' I told her...at first she would get very little pay. She replied that she understood that.[45]

The relationship between young working children, their employer, and the parent or parents was complex. Work for whole families offered a chance for the family unit to stay intact, at least within the confines of one factory. It also meant that the employer could pay lower wages and that parents could be expected to exercise some discipline over their children. The whole family could thus be moulded to the demands of industrial work with minimum friction. Family employment appeared, however, to have been largely limited to the textile trade. Elsewhere, fathers and sons, or several siblings, frequently worked in the same plant. Mothers and daughters often worked at home as sewing girls. In the situations where children worked alone, parents appeared to have endowed the employer with the patriarchal and disciplinary powers usually attributed to the father. In the 1880s, Mr. Fortier, Montreal's infamous exploiter and abuser of child labour, claimed that parents asked him to discipline their children. When "apprentices" in his factory failed to turn up on time, they first notified the parents, then "had the child arrested. We have had parents come to us over and over again," he argued, "and threaten to hold us responsible if we did not make the apprentices attend to their work." Other tobacco manufacturers reported having been requested by parents "to correct the children." Still others sent the children home to their parents when they did wrong.[46]

Obviously children needed discipline to conform to the demands of factory routine. Adults too had to learn the punctuality and application that these new work processes demanded. In the relationship between children, employer, and parents, however, the latter apparently assumed that employers performed the same role as masters of apprentices had done in former times. Yet most employers were concerned only with employing and disciplining a cheap labour forces. The family and the child did not gain the benefits of a trade well learned in return. They merely earned some money. This, the employer appeared to have considered a family responsibility. Fines, one employer explained, were imposed

> in order that the parents may see it marked on the envelope, that it may thus attract the parent's attention—they see 10¢ marked as a fine and they will know about it. They will then find out from the children how it occurred, or they will go to the overseer and speak about it and that generally effects the result we desire.[47]

How parents felt about sending their young children to work in factories and workshops is hard to determine. Certainly French Canadians and Irish immigrants from rural backgrounds were used to labouring together as a family. Many children had meant many hands to work the land. The farm economy had been a family economy. Even where children had left the land to work elsewhere, it was apparently common for French-Canadian children to return much of their earnings to their father. Fathers, in return, had been responsible for finding land, employment, or dowries for those children who would not inherit.[48]

In the city this family economy was fundamentally undermined, but did not disappear totally. For most families production and ownership were no longer linked. Now they had only their labour to sell, at whatever price the capitalists were offering. Only those with sufficient capital or skills could set up small family businesses or artisanal shops, and the latter were increasingly suffering from the competition of industrial capital. The old values of family work, however, may well have continued to function. They served well in a situation where many fathers could not earn enough to support a family. Need and tradition seemed to have combined to maintain the idea of family work and the fact of child labour within the growing and changing city.

Until reformers reacted against child labour and legislation was passed to control it in the 1880s and 1890s, the work of many family members continued to be a feature of the urban family economy. "The working family" continued to "suffer generally from lack of means, and there is no doubt that in the families of working people, where the average of children is 8, 9, or even 10, there is need of the handwork of children under 14."[49] Until well organized unions began to push for a working wage adequate to nurture a whole family, child labour would continue to be vital to family survival. What the parents thought about it in private could have no influence until they had the means to express their wishes.

Research on attitudes about the family and children in English Canada suggests that ideas about childhood may have undergone a fundamental transformation in the years following the 1870s. Whether similar changes occurred in Quebec remains to be studied. Before the 1890s English Canadians generally showed little awareness of children as individual persons with an emotional life of their own. Children were viewed by many as partially formed, potential adults.[50] Or, for men like Egerton Ryerson, as small men differing from adults in the need for greater restraint. Work was seen as crucial to the formation of character, as one of the best forms of education. Childhood and education were part of a brief, passing phase which, to the dismay of educators, many parents expected to be quickly finished so that children could "enter the working world."[51]

The widespread practice of child labour in Montreal suggests that attitudes there were similar. Whatever the ideal was, the labour of children was obviously vital to the economy of many of the city's families. Many children did not work, however. Despite the fact that there were no compulsory school laws in Montreal, around one-half of the boys and girls between the ages of eleven and fifteen reported attending school in 1871. Once boys reached sixteen, "the working world" was the major educating agent, while for girls the home was more important. At all ages large numbers of children neither worked nor went to school (see Table 3). Some of them may have had jobs that were not reported to the census taker. Others may have swelled the ranks of the "Arabs of the street" who worried contemporary middle class observers. Some of these street children were reported to earn "a few pence by retailing newspapers or, as is sometimes the case, supplement[ing] the labour of begging by the sale of daily journals," forming an "irregular squad of urchins who may be seen around the printing offices at the hour of publication." Others, observers believed, were "thrust forth this morning from a comfortless home" to beg or to steal.[52]

## The Family Economy: Working Wives

Not all families could rely on the work of their children to prop up the family income, as many had no children old enough to work. In both Ste. Anne and St. Jacques over two-thirds of the families were dependent on the wages of only one worker at the time the 1871 census was taken. Of these, 75 per cent of Ste. Anne's and 65 per cent of St. Jacques's families were at the stage of their life cycle when all children were under eleven years old. This was a period in the process of family formation when a steady income was more needed than ever, but when children were too young to help supplement it. Where the income of the father was insufficient, alternative survival strategies had to be followed. Either the wife and mother could go to work, or housing could be shared with friends, relatives, or boarders to cut down on rental and heating costs.

A few wives took on steady jobs and reported an occupation to the census taker. Still more probably worked occasionally, taking in washing, ironing, sewing, mending, or babysitting for neighbours, relatives, or friends. Their work, and the day to day labour of women in the home, is absent from the statistics and from most of the observations of the period. Likely even steady work for wages by married women was under-enumerated by census takers.[53] Yet even if under-enumeration was common, the wife was clearly the one family member least likely to have a paid job at any period of her married life. Only 2.5 per cent of all wives resident with their husbands reported an occupation.[54] Despite its relative infrequency, the work of these women is worth examining in some depth, as it clearly illustrated the way family economies were both influenced by, and interacted with, the particular nature of industrialization in any area.

Working wives were clustered in the poorer sections of both wards. Virtually all had husbands with unskilled or skilled jobs. Nearly 25 per cent were married to labourers. Shoemakers in St. Jacques (21 per cent) and factory workers in Ste. Anne (25 per cent) were the next most common occupation of husbands. Sixty per cent of the wives worked as seamstresses

(73 per cent in St. Jacques and 53 per cent in Ste. Anne), another 11 per cent as chars and washerwomen, and 5 per cent as labourers of an unspecified nature. A few wives in both wards worked as grocers or traders and in other small corner businesses, often helping their husbands.

Fairly similar patterns of occupations in the two wards masked a basic difference in the relationship between the work of mothers and their families. While dressmaking and sewing occupations predominated in both wards, they were more prevalent and of a different nature in St. Jacques. There, sewing at home appears to have been part of the putting out system so basic to Montreal's clothing industry. While in Ste. Anne only two of the wives worked as dressmakers along with their children or other relatives, in St. Jacques 31 per cent of the women had other members of the family who listed the same occupation. Work at home was a family enterprise enabling the mothers to keep an eye on their young children while working, and to work with their daughters. The former was important as 20 per cent of the women who worked had children under the age of two and 45 per cent had children under five.

In the clothing trade, mechanization revolutionized production both in and outside the growing number of factories. In a trade that was particularly unstable in the years before the initiation of the National Policy's tariffs, capitalists sought ways to keep costs as low as possible.[55] "Putting out," "sweating," or "homework" saved on overhead rental, machinery costs, and labour costs. As the old craft of the tailor or seamstress was deskilled, as immigrants from the countryside and abroad were drawn into the city, homework especially for women and children multiplied. Thus, labour that resulted directly from the mechanization of some parts of the labour process brought to these women no separation of work and home, but rather the increased likelihood of work for wages at home.

Most employees in the clothing trade worked outside the factory. Work was shipped both to families in the city and as far as twenty or thirty miles away to St. Jerome, St. Hyacinthe, and Ste. Rose, where there were reported to be "hundreds of hands."[56] Employers often knew little of what went on outside their factory. "We don't know how many hands work at it," explained one Montreal clothier who employed seventy to one hundred people preparing the work to go out. "We only know one woman, but don't know how many she employs." He believed that in 1874 he probably employed a total of seven hundred to one thousand people including the hundred or so "inside."[57]

Mr. Muir, a Montreal clothier, explained the relationship between factory work and home work. In his factory there was

> a 15 horsepower engine running three machines having 50 needles each, and a knife which cuts cloth by steam, so that four cutters will do the work of from twelve to fifteen.

In homes around Montreal the next stage was carried out:

> We employ a large number of women who live in their own homes. These women sit down when their breakfasts, dinner and supper is over, and make a garment, but are not exclusively employed at this work all day.[58]

It was convenient for employers to believe that for these mothers and daughters, sewing was a secondary family occupation, something done in their spare time. They could thus justify the extraordinarily low wages paid. "Those people who work in their own homes work very cheap," Mr. Muir explained, "and they will earn comparatively little" compared even to unskilled factory hands who were earning only $1.50 to $2.00 a week in his factory. He told the 1874 Select Committee that "most of them are wives and daughters of mechanics, who earn enough to keep the house." The women were, he argued, earning enough money which enabled them "to buy finery...which they would not be able to buy but for this industry."[59]

The working wives of St. Jacques and most of those of Ste. Anne were certainly not in this position. The majority of their husbands listed their occupations as labourers, workers in the building trade, factory workers, or shoemakers. The first two had always been highly seasonal and precarious jobs. The latter had been rendered precarious by technological and organizational change.[60] Work by wives thus appears to have been much more the result of necessity than of the desire or need for extra finery.

Homework brought minimal pay, with wages almost always paid by the piece. The more people who could work, therefore, the better for the family. In one-third of the families in St. Jacques where the mother was a seamstress, daughters worked with her. It was not uncommon to find three to four sisters, ranging in age from eleven to twenty-eight all working, presumably together, as sewing girls. In the Aliron family, for instance, Demithilde and her four daughters aged fourteen to nineteen worked as sewing girls, while the father worked as a saddlemaker.[61] In some families daughters but not the mothers worked. Thus, in the Moisan family four daughters all worked as sewing girls, the wife did not work, and the father worked when he could as a labourer.[62] For widows, work at home offered both a means of support and a way to remain with their children.

The clothing industry was thus a vital part of the life of many St. Jacques's families. Not surprisingly, seamstress was the ward's leading occupation, ranking even above labourer. It was definitely women's work, and employers were able to take advantage of the large numbers of families desperately needing work for their members. Virtually all those involved were French Canadian, as was typical in the industry. "Your labour supply is chiefly French?" clothier Muir was asked by the 1874 committee:

> It was almost exclusively French
> —You have a surplus population in Montreal which enables you to get cheap labour? —Yes, in fact it makes my heart ache to have the women come crying for work.
> —Then your labour is very cheap? —Yes; too cheap.
> —I fancy that from the surplus in Montreal, you get labour cheaper than you could in any other part of the country? —We think so...Irish women, for instance, if they come to this country and do not get the wages they want, will emigrate.[63]

The demography of the Quebec family, the exhaustion of easily available good land in the Province, and the tradition of family work thus combined to enable capitalists in clothing and other trades to count on a steady supply of cheap labour.

Families working at home were not only involved in handwork. By 1872 advertisements in the newspapers for sewing machines for family use were common.[64] A journalist for the Montreal *Daily Witness* explained how families were contacted by sewing machine salesmen:

> A set of canvassers are first sent out in order to induce workingmen's wives to buy a machine. In reality they do not buy the machine, but are induced to sign a form of lease by the terms of which, without the intervention of a lawyer, this machine can be taken back again within any period of time, if the entire amount cannot be paid. If, therefore, by sickness or death...the poor woman is unable to pay the installment when due, she loses all that she has paid upon the machine.

How many of the women listing themselves as dressmakers had sewing machines is hard to tell. Definitely in this category were two sisters in Ste. Anne, Philomene and Aurelie Leduc. They each reported ownership of a sewing machine valued at sixty-five dollars to the industrial census taker. Working on "cloth etc. furnished by merchants," they produced around four hundred and three hundred dollars worth of coats, pants, and vests each. Unlike most St. Jacques women, these sisters appear to have employed one extra woman each, to whom they paid a total of $276 in wages annually.[66]

Probably some of Ste. Anne's working wives worked as seamstresses in the local merchant tailor's shops which employed three to nine people, or in the larger workshops of clothiers, dressmakers, and milliners in the neighbourhood. Some may have worked in one of the large clothing or hat-making factories. Only three of the married women dressmakers of Ste. Anne ran establishments of their own that were reported to the industrial census taker. Of these one reported an annual production of fifty dollars worth of dresses, the other two, three hundred dollars.[67] Not one of St. Jacques's women was reported as proprietor of her own establishment. The six hundred to nine hundred dollars capital mustered by the three Ste. Anne women was probably well beyond most of their saving abilities. Homework for them would continue to be the piecework of the putting out system.

Why these married women worked and how they viewed their participation in wage labour can only be surmised. Some of those who had no children may have worked because they wanted to, because they enjoyed their work, or to help save up money for the future. Most probably worked, however, because they needed to. That married St. Jacques women took the opportunity offered by homework suggested the importance placed on being near growing children. Many of the other women's occupations—charwoman, housekeepers, and small traders—were the ones that did not require a full time absence from the family and home. Some of the sewing women may have worked in factories, although not one listed an easily identifiable factory occupation. Such work would have meant a full day away from the home.

Most importantly, the work of wives provided a supplement or stabilizer to the father's income at those stages of the life cycle when children were too young to work (see Table 6). In Ste. Anne, most wives appear to have stopped work once their children were old enough to find jobs. There, under 20 per cent of the wives had working children. In St. Jacques, in contrast, most working wives did have children old enough to work. They continued to work largely because they could do so at home sewing.

**TABLE 6** *The Life Cycle Stages of Working Wives*[68]

| | Ste. Anne | | St. Jacques | |
|---|---|---|---|---|
| | No. | % | No. | % |
| No children | 21 | 27 | 13 | 17 |
| Children 1 and under only | 15 | 19 | 14 | 18 |
| Children all 10 and under | 12 | 15 | 5 | 7 |
| Some children 11-15, none older | 19 | 25 | 11 | 15 |
| Some children over 16 | 11 | 14 | 32 | 43 |
| Total | 78 | 100 | 75 | 100 |

## The Family Life Cycle and Household Structure

Both Michael Anderson and John Foster, in studies on mid-nineteenth century English working class families, have stressed that few were permanently free of poverty. Work by several family members there, as in Montreal, could ensure a less precarious survival. For those families who only had children too young to work, however, over one-half fell below the poverty line.[69] No poverty line has as yet been established for Montreal in this period. Clearly, however, large numbers of Montreal families were vulnerable to poverty at this stage. Certainly, until children were old enough to work, most families relied on one worker (see Table 7).

**TABLE 7** *Average Number of Workers at Different Stages of the Family Life Cycle*[71]

| | Ste. Anne | | St. Jacques | |
|---|---|---|---|---|
| | Average no. of workers | No. of families | Average no. of workers | No. of families |
| Wife under 45, no children | 1 | 13 | 1.1 | 50 |
| 1 child under 1 | 1 | 12 | 1 | 19 |
| All children 10 and under | 1.03 | 55 | 1.03 | 94 |
| Half or more 15 and under | 1.83 | 36 | 1.7 | 67 |
| Half or more over 15 | 3.05 | 19 | 3.2 | 34 |
| All over 15 | 2.5 | 13 | 2.3 | 28 |
| Over 45, no children at home | 1 | 5 | .8 | 24 |
| Single Parents | | | | |
| Half children under 15 | 2.0 | 2 | .75 | 4 |
| Half children over 15 | 2.5 | 2 | 2.75 | 10 |

Some may have turned to charity to survive. Figures from Protestant and Catholic organizations attest to vast numbers of families who were visited in their homes and given relief, especially during the winters. In February of 1872, 279 families received firewood, clothing, blankets, and provisions from the Board of Outdoor Relief of the Protestant House of Industry and Refuge alone.[70] The Grey Nuns and Sisters of Providence probably visited and provided help to three times that number of needy Catholic families.[72] Others, especially in St. Jacques, shared their living space with other families or relatives, or took in boarders.

Michael Katz has argued that in Hamilton in 1861 the "presence of boarders and relatives in any given household appears to have been largely accidental."[73] This was not so in Montreal in 1871. There, household structure was closely related to the family life cycle.

Over one-half the couples in Ste. Anne and St. Jacques began their married lives sharing their household, especially with unrelated families and couples. As children were born and grew older and as the family's size grew they were more likely to live alone. Seventy-five to 80 per cent of families lived alone when half their children were fifteen and under. For most families this was a crucial and difficult stage. Most children were too young to work and families were at their largest. As families grew, the strain of sharing cramped quarters appears to have become intolerable for all but the most needy. While only 20 per cent of families shared with relatives or other families at this stage, more took in boarders. Boarders provided some income without extreme overcrowding. As children left home families were once again likely to share living space, especially with relatives—often their married children (see Table 8).

**TABLE 8** *The Family Life Cycle and Household Structure*[76]

| Ste. Anne | Simple family (%) | Extended family (%) | Multiple some related (%) | Multiple not related (%) | Total no. of families |
|---|---|---|---|---|---|
| No children | 46.7 | | | 53.3 | 15 |
| 1 under 1 | 75.0 | 8.3 | | 16.7 | 12 |
| All under 11 | 71.4 | 5.4 | 3.6 | 19.6 | 56 |
| Half under 15 | 81.1 | 8.1 | 2.7 | 8.1 | 37 |
| Half over 15 | 85.0 | 0 | 0 | 15.0 | 20 |
| All over 15 | 60.0 | 6.7 | 26.7 | | 15 |
| No children | 66.7 | | | 33.3 | 6 |
| Overall household structure | 71.9 | 5.4 | 2.4 | 20.4 | 167 |
| With boarder(s) | 16.6 | 11.1 | 25.0 | 20.6 | 18.4% |
| **St. Jacques** | | | | | |
| No children | 40.8 | 4.1 | 14.3 | 40.8 | 49 |
| 1 under 1 | 36.8 | 5.3 | 15.8 | 42.1 | 19 |
| All under 11 | 63.4 | 8.6 | 5.4 | 22.6 | 93 |
| Half under 15 | 74.6 | 4.5 | 0 | 19.4 | 67 |
| Half over 15 | 50.0 | 8.8 | 2.9 | 38.2 | 34 |
| All over 15 | 57.1 | 14.3 | 17.9 | 10.7 | 28 |
| No children | 33.3 | 0 | 8.3 | 58.3 | 24 |
| Overall household structure | 56.4 | 6.7 | 7.3 | 29.3 | 328 |
| With boarder(s) | 17.2 | 16.0 | 22.2 | 11.7 | 15.7% |

At all stages of the life cycle it was the unskilled families who were least likely to live alone. Only 47 per cent of St. Jacques's unskilled families, compared to 66 per cent of professional families, lived in a simple nuclear household (see Table 9). People were sharing houses not because they wanted to, but because they needed to. A contemporary citizen observed that "under the present state of things, overcrowding is inevitable and only the cheapest and most inferior class of rookeries can be paid for out of the current rate of wages." He stressed the double and linked need for "better dwellings for the working classes and increased income for all wage earners of the city."[74]

**TABLE 9** *St. Jacques, 1871—Household Structure and the Occupation of the Father*

| | Professional & proprietor | | Service | | Skilled | | Unskilled | | Other | |
|---|---|---|---|---|---|---|---|---|---|---|
| | No. | % | No. | % | No. | % | No. | % | No. | % |
| No family | 1 | 2 | 1 | 3 | 1 | 1 | 1 | 1 | 1 | 14 |
| Simple family | 40 | 66 | 19 | 59 | 78 | 53 | 40 | 47 | 3 | 44 |
| Extended family | 4 | 6 | 1 | 3 | 10 | 7 | 7 | 8 | 1 | 14 |
| Multiple—some related | 4 | 6 | 1 | 3 | 14 | 10 | 5 | 6 | 1 | 14 |
| Multiple—none related | 12 | 20 | 10 | 32 | 43 | 29 | 32 | 38 | 1 | 14 |
| Total | 61 | 100 | 32 | 100 | 146 | 100 | 85 | 100 | 7 | 100 |

The percentage of nuclear families classified as occupying a whole household in both St. Jacques and, to a lesser extent, Ste. Anne was much lower than that found in other studies in Canada or elsewhere in the western world. It is also much lower than the 76 per cent found by Louise Dechêne in Montreal two centuries earlier in 1681.[75] In Hamilton, Upper Canada, Katz found that nearly 80 per cent of households contained only a simple nuclear family in 1851 and 1861.[77] This compares with 56.4 per cent in St. Jacques and 63 per cent in Ste. Anne in 1871. Anderson's work on Lancashire led him to suggest that industrialization, rather than leading to the decline of the nuclear family as early sociologists had posited, led to an increase in the importance of kinship. Kin, he argued, chose to live both with and near each other, helped each other find jobs, and provided essential support in critical situations. Yet, even there, 72 per cent of married couples occupied a whole house, 15 per cent shared with non-relatives, 5 per cent shared with kin, and 8 per cent lived as lodgers.[78] Thus, the high proportion of Montreal families sharing dwelling space with other couples, families, and boarders appears to have been peculiar to that city.[79]

There are several possible explanations. First, French-Canadian family-oriented values were probably very important in leading to the sharing of households by relatives. As an example, in St. Jacques, the French-Canadian suburb, the percentage of families sharing with relatives was double that of Ste. Anne. Furthermore, the residents of Ste. Anne, like those of Preston, Lancashire, and Hamilton, were largely immigrants who were less likely to have large numbers of kin near at hand. French Canadians in Montreal, in contrast, would have constantly been augmented by kin from the rural areas. Certainly in both wards, French Canadians were less likely to live as a single nuclear family than the Irish or other groups (see Table 10). Yet there were differences too in the extent of sharing. All St. Jacques families were more likely to double up with others than were those of Ste. Anne. This may have been a result of the nature of housing in the two areas. Or it may have reflected the fewer work opportunities near the St. Jacques area.

**TABLE 10** *French-Canadian and Others' Household Structure Compared*

| | Ste. Anne | | | | St. Jacques | | | |
|---|---|---|---|---|---|---|---|---|
| | French Canadian | | Other | | French Canadian | | Other | |
| | No. | % | No. | % | No. | % | No. | % |
| Solitaires | | | | | 2 | 1 | 3 | 5 |
| Simple family | 37 | 69 | 78 | 76 | 145 | 53 | 35 | 61 |
| Extended family | 1 | 2 | 6 | 6 | 20 | 7 | 2 | 4 |
| Mulitple—some related | 4 | 7 | | | 23 | 8 | 3 | 5 |
| Multiple—not related | 12 | 22 | 19 | 18 | 84 | 31 | 14 | 25 |
| Total | 54 | 100 | 103 | 100 | 274 | 100 | 57 | 100 |

Secondly, it is possible that the high percentage of families sharing households was not a real phenomenon at all, but the result of fuzzy definitions of households on the part of the census takers, who may have called all people resident in one dwelling, with separate apartments, a "household." This does not, however, appear to have been the case.[80] Qualitative evidence of overcrowding lends support to the statistical data. Fifteen years later "doubling up" was described as common and did not appear to be viewed as a recent phenomenon, although increased migration to the city as well as the effects of the Depression may well have exacerbated it. A doctor testifying before the Commission on the Relations between Labour and Capital suggested then that the average labourer's tenement would have three to four rooms and would be occupied by

> two or three families, or sometimes two families using one stove between them, and if there are several families, each family will have one room for a sleeping room, and use the kitchen for a dining room—the kitchen and stove in common with others.

An even greater number of families would share the same water closet or privy outside.[81] The same doctor reported finding as many as "seventeen or eighteen souls residing in a house of five or six rooms."[82]

## Conclusion

Class position, the stage of the family life cycle, and cultural values thus combined to condition not only the number of workers in any family and the age at which the children would be sent to work, but also the very composition of the households within which they would grow up. Many of the children in the families of Montreal's unskilled workers, at least those of Ste. Anne and St. Jacques wards, were likely to go to work before they were fifteen and to grow up in families that at some point of their life shared living space with large numbers of other people. Children in such families were also less likely than others to spend much of their life in school.

In what Pollard has referred to as the transformation of a "society of peasants, craftsmen and versatile labourers" into "modern industrial workers," the family played an important role.[83] The hiring of whole families in the textile trade, the continued use of outmoded apprenticeship contracts, systems of fining children, the putting out arrangement, and indeed, the very employment of children: all drew on old ideas and familial traditions within a new context. Families thus served as a medium of socialization to new and strange work habits.

Montreal in 1871 appears to have been in a phase common to most nineteenth-century communities undergoing an "industrial revolution." Labour was viewed as a commodity to be bought as cheaply as possible. Workers' families were not seen by producers as potential units of consumption. There was thus little impetus to raise individual worker's wages to the level necessary to properly support a family. Low wages, the changing organization of production, and the large numbers of jobs opened up to women and children combined to make the work of several family members both possible and necessary in all but the best paid of skilled working class families.

The desire of capitalists for cheap female and child labour coincided with the need of families with children old enough to send them out to work. The surplus of such unskilled labour helped in turn to keep wages down. Thus for a while the needs and values of working class families and of capitalists coincided to shape both the family economy and some of the characteristics of industrial production.

## Notes

1. For reviews of recent historical literature on the family and industrialization, see especially *Journal of Marriage and the Family* XXXV (August 1973); Elizabeth Pleck, "Two Worlds in One—Work and Family," *Journal of Social History* (Winter 1976); and Lise Vogel, "'The Contested Domain: A Note on the Family in the Transition to Capitalism," *Marxist Perspectives* I (Spring 1978). For books

dealing explicitly with the topic, see Michael Anderson, *Family Structure in Nineteenth Century Lancashire* (Cambridge: University Press, 1971); William Goode, *World Revolution and Family Patterns* (New York: Free Press of Glencoe, 1963); Peter Laslett and Richard Wall, *Household and Family Formation in An Age of Nascent Capitalism* (New York: Academic Press, 1977); Edward Shorter, *The Making of the Modern Family* (New York: Basic Books, 1975); and Neil J. Smelser, *Social Change in the Industrial Revolution* (London: Routledge and Kegan Paul, 1959).

2. For a feminist rejoinder to Shorter's work, see Louise Tilly and Joan Scott, "Women's Work and the Family in Nineteenth Century Europe," *Comparative Studies in Society and History* XVII (1975); and Louise Tilly, Joan Scott and Miriam Cohen, "Women's Work and European Fertility Patterns," *Journal of Interdisciplinary History* VI (Winter 1976). For Shorter's rejoinder to the earlier article, see "Women's Work: What Difference Did Capitalism Make?" *Theory and Society* III (Winter 1976). For Marxist critique, see Veronica Beechy, "Some Notes on Female Wage Labour in Capitalist Production," *Capital and Class* III (Autumn 1977); Jane Humphries, "The Working Class Family, Women's Liberation, and Class Struggle: The Case of Nineteenth Century British History," *The Review of Radical Political Economics* IX (Fall 1977); Jane Humphries, "Class Struggle and the Persistence of the Working Class Family," *Cambridge Journal of Economics* I (1978); and Lise Vogel, "The Contested Domain."

3. Talcott Parsons, "The Social Structure of the Family," in *The Family's Search for Survival,* ed. S.M. Farber et. al., (New York: McGraw Hill, 1965). For sociologists questioning this view, see especially Goode, *World Revolution and Family Patterns* (1963), and Laslett and Wall, *Household and Family in Past Time* (1972).

4. Pleck, "Two Worlds in One."

5. Humphries, "The Working Class Family"; and "Class Struggle and the Persistence of the Working Class Family"; Tamara Hareven, "Cycles, Courses and Cohorts: Reflections on Theoretical and Methodological Approaches to the Historical Study of Family Development," *Journal of Social History* XII (Fall 1978); Virginia Yans McLaughlin, "Patterns of Work and Family Organization: Buffalo's Italians," *Journal of Interdisciplinary History* II (Autumn 1971); and "A Flexible Tradition: South Italian Immigrants Confront a New Work Experience," *Journal of Social History* VII (Summer 1976).

6. Berkner, "Recent Research"; and Vogel, "The Contested Domain."

7. A 5 per cent random sample was taken of households enumerated in Ste. Anne ward in 1871, using a standard table of random numbers and taking one household in twenty at random from within each census subdivision, thus ensuring geographical coverage. In St. Jacques the same process was followed, except a 10 per cent sample was taken. The latter proved more adequate, as at times the numbers involved in Ste. Anne proved too small for some analyses. The samples taken approximated published material on the two wards as regards place of birth, origins, and age and sex structure.

8. Because of the small number of working wives in the two samples, I skimmed the returns for the two wards pulling out all working wives, resident with their husbands. All institutions enumerated by the 1871 industrial census takers in these two wards were studied. It should be noted that industrial returns for Subdistrict 8 of Ste. Anne ward are missing, so that the amount of industry in that ward is consistently underestimated by about 10 per cent. Manuscript Census, 1871, Schedule 6, Microfilm Reels Numbers 10041, 10042, 10044, 10045, Public Archives of Canada.

9. On the importance of longitudinal family studies, see Tamara Hareven, "The Family as Process: The Historical Study of the Family Cycle," *Journal of Social History* VII (Spring 1974). In my doctoral thesis I hope to be able to trace families from 1861 to 1881. This paper represents an initial attempt to sort out some elements of the relationship between families and industrialization from the information in the 1871 manuscript census.

10. For an excellent description of the unevenness of industrial change and the co-existence of highly mechanized and very labour intensive industries in the 1850s and 1860s in Great Britain, see Raphael Samuels, "The Workshop of the World: Steam Power and Hand Technology in Mid-Victorian Britain," *History Workshop* III (Spring 1977). On early industrial development in Montreal, see especially Gerald J.J. Tulchinsky, *The River Barons: Montreal Businessmen and the Growth of Industry and Transportation, 1837–1853* (Toronto: University of Toronto Press, 1977), especially chapter 12.

11. Joanne Burgess, "L'industrie de la chaussure à Montréal: 1840–1870—Le passage de l'artisanat à fabrique," *Revue d'Histoire de l'Amérique Française* XXXI (September 1977), 198.

12. Ibid., 204; and *Manuscript Census*, Industrial Schedules 1861 and 1871.

13. H. Clare Pentland, "The Development of a Capitalistic Labour Market in Canada," *Canadian Journal of Economics and Political Science* XXV (1956), 456.

14. C. Goucy-Roy, "Le Quartier Sainte-Marie à Montréal, 1850–1900," (M.A. thesis, Université de Québec à Montréal, 1977).

15. Just over one-third of Ste. Anne's manufacturing and industrial enterprises reported the use of steam or water power in 1871. In St. Jacques, in contrast, under 5 per cent used any kind of motor power.

16. Manuscript Census, 1871, Schedule 6, St. Jacques ward.

17. *The Montreal Gazette*, 19 July 1864, p. 4; and *Montreal Business Sketches ... with a description of the city of Montreal, its Public Buildings and Places of Interest*, (Montreal: M. Longmoore and Co., 1865), 18–19.

18. *Montreal Business Sketches*, 13.

19. Ibid.

20. Royal Commission on the Relations of Labor and Capital, *Quebec Evidence*, 1889, p. 369. (Hereafter RCRLC, 1889, *Quebec Evidence*).

21. For women's role in the Montreal economy from 1871 to 1891, see Suzanne Cross, "The Neglected Majority: The Changing Role of Women in 19th Century Montreal," Susan Mann Trofimenkoff and Alison Prentice, eds., *The Neglected Majority: Essays in Canadian Women's History* (Toronto: McClelland and Stewart, 1977).

22. Greg Kealey, *Hogtown: Working Class Toronto at the Turn of the Century* (Toronto: New Hogtown Press, 1974), 4.

23. The Lowell figure is from a personal communication from Francie Anderson, *Family Structure in Early Nineteenth Century Lancashire*, 75.

24. RCRLC, 1889, *Quebec Evidence*, 313.

25. "Report of the United Board of Outdoor Relief for Winter 1871–72," *Ninth Annual Report of the Montreal Protestant House of Industry and Refuge* (1872), 1.

26. The Montreal Council of Social Agencies estimated that a family required one cord of hard, best wood per week, and one cord of soft wood and coal and coal oil. See Terry Copp, *The Anatomy of Poverty: The Condition of the Working Class in Montreal 1897–1929* (Toronto: McClelland and Stewart, 1974), Appendix A. On the variable availability and price of fuel, see Huguette Lapointe Roy, "Paupérisme et assistance sociale à Montréal, 1832–1865" (M.A. thesis, McGill University, 1972).

27. RCRLC, 1889, *Quebec Evidence*, 290.
28. Ibid., 4 and 18.
29. Evidence from matching personal and industrial returns.
30. The figures presented in Table 1 and in all following tables are derived from the random samples of personal returns for each ward. The classification of occupations is based on that in Michael Katz, "Occupational Classification in History," *Journal of Interdisciplinary History* III (Summer 1972), Table 2, modified taking into account the work of the Philadelphia Social History Project, *Historical Methods Newsletter* IX (March–June, 1976). In this table public service, private service, and commercial employee have been arbitrarily collapsed to form the "white collar" category.
31. Canada, *Census of 1870–1871*, Vol. III, p. 5.
32. On subsequent legislation and its supplementation, see Roger Chartier, "L'inspection des éstablissements industriels, 1885–1900," *Relations Industrielles* XVII (January 1962).
33. See note 30. The percentage of the total population is from Canada, *Census of 1870–1871*, Table 3, Origins of the People, 288–89.
34. This table refers to all children resident in two wards, not just those resident with their parents.
35. Manuscript Census, 1871, Schedule 6, Ste. Anne, Subdistrict 9, p. 2.
36. RCRLC, 1889, *Quebec Evidence*, 281, 315, 318, 348, 393. Evidence of Ste. Anne cotton mill workers.
37. Ibid., 279, 280, 317, 392.
38. Here the categories Professional, Proprietor, Commercial Employee, and Service, Public and Private, are collapsed to create the non-manual category.
39. Daniel J. Walkowitz, "Working Class Women in the Guilded Age: Factory, Community and Family Life Among Cohoes, New York, Cotton Workers," *Journal of Social History* V (Summer 1972), 474.
40. Tamara Hareven, "Family Time and Industrial Time: Family and Work in a Planned Corporation Town, 1900–1924," *Journal of Urban History* I (May 1975), 371.
41. *Le Canadien*, 27 July 1889, cited in Jean Hamelin and Yves Roby, *Histoire économique du Québec, 1851–1896* (Montreal: Fides, 1971), 307.
42. RCRLC, 1889, *Quebec Evidence*, 380, 397.
43. Ibid., 394.
44. Ibid., 641.
45. Ibid., 397.
46. Ibid., 103, 140.
47. Ibid., 392.
48. Attempts to describe traditional family economies may be found in Gauldrée-Boileau, *Le paysan de Saint-Irénée* (1861), cited in Léon Gerin, "The French-Canadian Family—Its Strengths and Weaknesses," in *French-Canadian Society*, ed. M. Rioux and Y. Martin (Toronto: McClelland and Stewart, 1964), 34. On the family economy in twentieth century rural Quebec, see Gerald Fortin, "Socio-Cultural Changes in an Agricultural Parish," in *French-Canadian Society*, ed. Rioux and Martin, 94; Everett Hughes, *French Canada in Transition* (Chicago: University of Chicago Press, 1943, 1964), 172; and Horace Miner, *St. Denis: A French-Canadian Parish* (Chicago: Phoenix, 1939), 64.
49. RCRLC, 1889, *Quebec Evidence*,4.
50. Neil Sutherland, *Children in English-Canadian Society: Framing the Twentieth-Century Consensus* (Toronto: University of Toronto Press, 1976), 6, 10–11.

51. Alison Prentice, *The School Promoters, Education and Social Class in Mid-Nineteenth Century Upper Canada* (Toronto: McClelland and Stewart, 1977), 35–36.
52. *The Saturday Reader*, Montreal, IV (1867), 22.
53. On this problem see Sally Alexander, "Women's Work in Nineteenth Century London: A Study of the Years 1820–1850," in *The Rights and Wrongs of Women* ed. Juliett Mitchell and Ann Oakley (England: Penguin Books, Ltd, 1976), 63–66.
54. The following section is based on analysis of all working wives in the two wards. They numbered seventy-five in St. Jacques and seventy-eight in Ste. Anne.
55. *Report: Select Committee on the Manufacturing Interests of the Dominion*, Journals, House of Commons, Appendix III, 1874, pp. 8, 22. (Hereafter, *Report: Manufacturing Interests,* 1874).
56. RCRLC, 1889, *Quebec Evidence,* 284, 295.
57. *Report: Manufacturing Interests*, 1874, p. 23.
58. Ibid., 36.
59. Ibid.
60. See Burgess, "L'industrie de la chaussure".
61. Manuscript Census, 1871, Personal Returns, St. Jacques, Subdistrict 6, Household 137.
62. Ibid., Subdistrict 2, Family 53.
63. *Report: Manufacturing Interests*, 1874, p. 38.
64. *La Minerve*, any day in April, 1872, for example, 20 April, p. 1. "George Harvey, marchand de toutes éspèces de Machines à coudres de première classe à point nué pour familles et manufactures." In the same paper he advertised for a bilingual agent collector with good references.
65. RCRLC, 1889, *Quebec Evidence,* 603–4.
66. Manuscript Census, 1871, Schedule 6, Ste. Anne, Subdistrict 5, p. 1.
67. Manuscript Census, 1871, Personal Returns and Schedule 6, matched, Subdistrict 3, Households 105, 128, and 156.
68. This table based on *all* working wives, not a sample.
69. Anderson, *Family Structure*, 37; John Foster, *Class Struggle and the Industrial Revolution, Early Industrial Capitalism in Three English Towns* (London: Methuen and Co., Ltd., 1974), 96.
70. *Ninth Annual Report of the Protestant House of Industry and Refuge*, 1872, p. 1.
71. This table is based on the samples of families. This explains why the average number of workers at stage 2 can be one, while in the previous table some working wives had children under one. The stages of life cycle are based on those developed in Anderson, *Family Structure*, 202, modified so that whether children work or not is not defined within the life cycle.
72. On their work in the previous decade, see Roy, "Paupérisme et assistance sociale," 115–16. Between 1856 and 1863 she reports that the Grey Nuns helped an average of 225 families in their own homes annually. The Sisters of Providence helped as many as five hundred.
73. Michael B. Katz, *The People of Hamilton, Canada West: Family and Class in a Mid-Nineteenth Century City* (Harvard: University Press, 1975), 244.
74. RCRLC, 1889, *Quebec Evidence,* 732.
75. Louise Dechêne, *Habitants et Marchands de Montréal au XVII Siècle* (Paris: Librairie Plon, 1974), 416.
76. The categories of household structure are derived from those of Peter Laslett, "Introduction: The History of the Family," in *Household and Family in Past Times*, by Laslett and Wall, 31.

77. Katz, *The People of Hamilton*, 223.
78. Anderson, *Family Structure*, 49.
79. Taking in boarders was not unique to Montreal. Tamara Hareven has suggested that "at any particular point in time" the proportion of households in American cities having lodgers was between 15 and 20 per cent. "Urbanization and the Malleable Household: An Examination of Boarding and Lodging in American Families," *Journal of Marriage and the Family* (August 1973), 460. What was apparently unique to Montreal was the high percentage of families sharing houses.
80. Generally the census takers appear to have been careful to make the distinction between a shared address (building) and a shared household.
81. RCRLC, 1889, *Quebec Evidence*, 606.
82. Ibid., 609.
83. Sydney Pollard, *Genesis of Modern Management* (London: Edward Arnold, 1965), 160, 208.

# THE NORTH AMERICAN SHELTER BUSINESS, 1860–1920: A STUDY OF A CANADIAN REAL ESTATE AND PROPERTY MANAGEMENT AGENCY*

MICHAEL DOUCET AND JOHN WEAVER

Olivier Zunz recently has suggested that "change rather than continuity...marked northern American industrial society from 1880 to 1920."[1] His study of Detroit provides ample evidence to support this claim, at least in terms of that city's evolving social and spatial structures. Not all aspects of city life, however, changed as dramatically as those emphasized by Zunz. The property development industry, for example, was characterized during this period by a marked degree of continuity that was periodically overlain by subtle and gradual changes. In most North American cities, as Robert Barrows has pointedly reminded us, the industry continued to develop property in the traditional way—by erecting single-family housing, much of which would be occupied by renters and therefore would have to be managed.[2] This development process required a small and constant cast of actors including landowners, subdividers, lawyers, registry officers, builders, tradesmen and labourers, municipal officials, and real estate or land agents.[3] Our purpose in this article is to examine continuity and change in the property industry between 1860 and 1920 through the eyes of this last group.

The North American real estate business has evolved slowly over a fairly long period of time. Historian Pearl Davies cites the Cruikshank Company, founded in New York in 1794, as the oldest existing real estate firm in the United States, and suggests that New York was also the first city to obtain a real estate board when the New York Real Estate Exchange was founded in 1847. By the 1880s many cities had similar organizations that often were used by members to enhance local community growth and prestige.[4] But realtors were more than civic boosters even at that time. They quickly acquired an

*Business History Review 58 (Summer 1984): 234–62.

impressive list of duties and responsibilities including "appraisal, negotiating and making leases, collecting rents, making sales of real estate, and negotiating mortgage loans."[5] By the early years of the twentieth century, some firms had branched out into property development as well. The business, then, underwent a long, slow, and gradual process of professionalization.

Even the most fragmentary accounts of the practice of real estate agents place the business in an important social position mediating between a bourgeoisie with funds to invest and tenants residing in the investment dwellings. Their handling of mortgage capital, investments in shelter development, the collection of rents and management of rental properties, and the issuing of eviction notices allow insight not only into business cycles and structural changes in capitalism, but also into important social relationships. Early real estate agents were principal figures in the investment and social history of urban North America; they were the flesh and blood behind the distilled statements of land-use theory.

The fundamental obstacle to comprehending the real estate agent's significance to the history of capital markets and to the social history of housing is the scarcity of archival records. The office records of one Hamilton, Ontario, firm—Moore and Davis—for the period from late 1858 to early 1919 provide the necessary base for suggesting the general practices of the North American real estate business during important phases in its history. While Hamilton was in many respects a "typical" city during these decades, in older and larger metropolitan centres the timing of changes in business practices and the level of the agent's specialization may have differed.

The real estate and general agency business of William Pitt Moore and John Gage Davis began in August 1858 in offices located at King and James streets, Hamilton's central intersection. In 1866 the firm relocated one block to the north in the new Lister Block where it remained for more than a century. Records of the company's activities include letterbooks of correspondence sent from the firm, rent ledgers for properties managed by the firm, a mortgage ledger, general ledger books, estate books, diaries or day books, journals, and miscellaneous deeds and other documents.[6] Davis left the partnership at an unspecified date, and Moore retired in 1891. Moore's family has continued to manage the business to the present.

The home base for the firm—Hamilton, Ontario—is a port city, founded in 1816, and located at the western end (head) of Lake Ontario. Approximately forty miles from the provincial capital of Toronto, and sixty miles from Buffalo, New York, Hamilton has long been an important centre for commerce, industry, and transportation. Today the city is home to about half a million residents and is Canada's leading producer of steel. The population of Hamilton grew from 14 112 in 1851 to 114 151 in 1921. At the same time the area of the city more than doubled (from 3050 acres to 7130 acres) through annexations, and the number of occupied dwellings increased from 1950 to 28 984. These increases mask the fact that growth in Hamilton, as in other North American cities, was retarded periodically by external economic forces.

The depressed economic conditions that followed the panics of 1857, 1873, and 1891, the recession of 1907–1908, and the crash of 1914–1915 all had adverse effects on Hamilton's prospects, and were especially severe blows to the property industry. Throughout the study period, Hamilton remained as an important destination for immigrants to Canada. In 1871, 47.2 per cent of the city's residents had been born outside Canada, largely in the United Kingdom (40.2 per cent), the United States (4.6 per cent), and Europe (2.2 per cent). Half a century later the foreign born still constituted 38.8 per cent of Hamilton's population, with the United Kingdom (28.9 per cent), Europe (5.7 per cent), and the United States (3.4 per cent) continuing, albeit in slightly altered order, as the leading points of origin.[7] It was within these changing conditions that the real estate firm of Moore and Davis operated and prospered.

## The Contours of the Business

Initially Moore and Davis had to look beyond the land market to secure enough accounts to keep them solvent. The letters sent from the firm to its clients over the first seven years of operation illustrate this point (see Table 1). Collection notices, reports on the progress of collection activities, and notices of deposits made to clients' bank accounts constituted the largest single category of correspondence during those years. Other nonproperty-related matters included the location and sale of bonds and stocks, the sale of miscellaneous items such as leather (the Moore family had been associated with a tannery since the 1830s), the provision of and request for character references, and estate and personal affairs. In all, about 44 per cent of the letters written by the partners between 1858 and 1865 had nothing to do with real property. Later, much of the correspondence dealt with the insurance business, which today remains the sole activity of the firm.

Property was the major if not the sole concern of the firm in the early years. By 1863 the partners were publishing a monthly "land circular," and the firm provided a growing array of property-related services as time passed. These included selling property, composing advertising copy, posting for sale and for rent signs on property, letting buildings and houses and collecting rents, arranging mortgage money, preparing property valuations, recommending and then supervising repairs to property in their care, and conducting other property management duties such as the payment of taxes and water rates. Their attention to detail in these matters was remarkable. In 1862, for example, the partners informed Joseph Sudborough of Toronto that

> the roof of the house at the corner where White lives is rotted so that we shall be obliged to have a new roof and eve troughs, and also the boards of cellar in Grayson's mill will require to be new.

It will cost about $27 or $30 to put them in order. We have had a carpenter to look at them. Please let us know by return Post as they should be done before the Equinoxial Storms set in.[8]

**TABLE 1** *Moore and Davis's Outgoing Correspondence for Two Time Periods (1858–65 and 1912–14), by Category*

| | 1858–65 | | 1912–14 | |
|---|---|---|---|---|
| Category | Number | Percentage | Number | Percentage |
| Collections/financial | 542 | 37.4 | 647 | 48.0 |
| Sale of property/land values | 127 | 8.8 | 78 | 5.8 |
| Property management | 281 | 19.4 | 69 | 5.1 |
| Rental matters | 209 | 14.4 | 220 | 16.3 |
| Eviction notices/rent increase notices | 48 | 3.3 | 70 | 5.1 |
| Mortgages/titles | 106 | 7.3 | 150 | 11.1 |
| City property for sale | 16 | 1.1 | 36 | 2.6 |
| Farm property for sale | 26 | 1.8 | 2 | 0.2 |
| State of land market | 10 | 0.7 | 1 | 0.1 |
| Bonds and stocks available | 34 | 2.3 | 12 | 0.9 |
| Sale of miscellaneous items | 28 | 1.9 | 7 | 0.5 |
| Character references | 15 | 1.0 | 2 | 0.2 |
| Estate matters | 12 | 0.8 | 50 | 3.7 |
| Family matters | 4 | 0.3 | 5 | 0.4 |
| Total | 1448 | 100.0 | 1349 | 100.0 |

Such attention and service were especially popular with nonresident property owners and the executors of estates, even if Moore and Davis's advice was not always accepted at face value.[9]

The firm also examined rented dwellings when tenants vacated. If there had been damage, Moore and Davis went after the former residents. Having located Mrs. H. Jagoe in May 1891, Moore demanded that she either replace the glass in the front door and return a night latch or he would have it done "and look to you for payment."[10] Besides exercising vigilance with respect to tenants' conduct, the property agent kept a watch on civic and provincial affairs insofar as they impinged on real estate. The partners were among those who petitioned the provincial legislature in 1873 to incorporate a Hamilton Street Railway, and Davis served on the first board of directors. They pushed the city to reduce taxes levied against their clients and insisted that the municipal police force protect property owners from the annoyance and expense of vandalism. The windows of vacant houses, for example, had a terrible fascination that compelled "small boys" to throw stones.[11] Moore and Davis were politically active and knew enough about city neighbourhoods to be of some use to Hamilton's Liberal party. For example, they increased the number of eligible voters in a family by spreading out ownership on the assessment rolls to enable sons to meet the property qualification.[12]

As Liberals, they supported the moral reform measures of the Ontario government, such as a moderate liquor license act, but they definitely drew the line at legislation touching upon property rights and inheritance; they had no compunction about pressing Liberal M.P.P.s who owed them political favours, especially on matters of class legislation. After the 1886 provincial election, for example, William P. Moore wrote to Nicholas Awrey, M.P.P. for South Wentworth:

> I have noticed in the reports of proceedings in the house that there is a move made to do away with the Law of Distress for Rent. I know that the papers have been harping on the hardship of a Landlord having the power to Distrain for rent on poor people, particularly the Labour union has been at it for some time. My opinion is that they know very little about the matters.[13]

Moore went on to argue that if landlords could not seize a tenant's chattels it would be necessary to demand rent in advance. "A great many poor people would go to the poorhouse as they would not have money to pay the rent in advance."[14] The clarity and directness of these epistles establish the firm's attention to class interests and not just to details involved in managing parcels of property.

Overall, clients seem to have been satisfied with the services and judgment provided by the firm. Moore and Davis, in fact, came to represent a number of important corporate clients in Hamilton real estate matters, including the Colonial Securities Company, the Canada Permanent Building and Loan Company, and the Guardian Trust Company, all of Toronto; the Trust and Loan Company of Kingston; the Canada Life Assurance Company and the Gore Bank, both of Hamilton; and the Toronto, Hamilton, and Buffalo Railway.

Fees were levied for all services rendered to corporate and individual clients. These were specified in detail in the monthly land circulars.[15] The commission charge for property management usually varied according to some unstated appraisal of the degree of difficulty associated with collecting rents and attending to repairs. During the late nineteenth and early twentieth centuries, the firm charged a fee of 5 to 7.5 per cent. For property sales, the firm usually received a commission of between 2 and 2.5 per cent of the purchase price.

In matters concerning land sales, similarities with current real estate practice are evident. As would be the case today, Moore and Davis served as intermediaries between the buyer and the seller. The person interested in purchasing the property generally would submit a written offer to Moore and Davis, and they, in turn, would convey this offer to the owner or his agent. For example, in 1872 John Fox submitted the following offer for two parcels located in the east end of the city:

> I hereby offer you as agents for Dr. Rae, the owner, eight hundred dollars for Lots 114 & 115 on Victoria Avenue north of King Street, payable cash down, title to be satisfactory or no sale and taxes paid by owner to the time papers are completed and money paid. Vendor to furnish abstract and all papers in his possession for inspection only.[16]

A copy of this letter was sent to the Toronto barristers Maclennan, Downey, and Henderson, who acted as agents for Dr. Rae.[17] If the offer was rejected (as in this case), the party making it would be so informed and often would be urged to make a higher bid.[18] If the owner accepted an offer to purchase, Moore and Davis would inform the would-be purchaser of this fact and oversee the preparation of the papers needed to transfer the ownership of the parcel or parcels in question. Should financing be required, the firm might again be called upon to play the role of the go-between.[19] Apparently private lenders had to be particularly careful in the mortgage market, for the partners told Alex McNale of Owen Sound that "the money we loan principally belongs to an Estate and the Executor is not willing to loan except on city or farm property in this or adjoining counties." And in 1877 they suggested to Charles A. Blyth of the Canadian Bank of Commerce branch in New York City that "money is worth 8% interest payable half yearly, on mortgage security of double the value."[20]

The essential nature of Moore and Davis's business remained constant for half a century. Insight into the components of the business can be obtained by comparing the contents of letters at the beginning and near the end of the extant letterbooks. All 1448 letters leaving the firm from 1858 to 1865 were analysed; as were all 1349 letters from 1912 to 1914 using the same categories established in the review of the earlier correspondence (see Table 1). The technique is flawed in that it places no weight on the relative significance of one type of letter as opposed to another. For example, a letter requesting payment of an insurance premium entailed less background preparation than a letter reporting on repairs to a rental dwelling owned by an absentee landlord. Moreover, the firm used the telephone in much of its intracity business by 1900, though conversation seems to have been followed by confirmation in writing. Collections, including reports on mortgage installments and insurance premiums, constituted about one third to one half of the outgoing letters. A comparison of the sample periods suggests an increase in collection activity. The most appreciable shift in business, however, involved the decline in property management. Moore and Davis had been quite busy in the early period, supervising the repairs of houses and shops owned by absentee landlords. Quite likely the early volume of letters on this subject stemmed from the drastic collapse of the city's economy and the exodus of perhaps 20 per cent of the populace between 1857 and 1864. Property owners who departed often found it impossible to dispose of their Hamilton assets in a failing property market. Moore and Davis provided a service for these former residents, but over the years more and more of the land came to be owned locally. Indicative of the firm's increasing specialization in urban real estate concerns is the fact that a few business services decreased: these included farm property sales, sales of miscellaneous articles, and reports on the availability of bonds and stocks. Over time, then, the emergence of the firm as a modern professional real estate concern is apparent.[21]

The two sample periods yielded a common pattern of destinations; this is especially evident when the drop in correspondence to Wentworth County locations is seen as a likely result of the city's annexation of county territory beginning in 1891 (see Table 2). The city-bound letters constituted a special cluster because many were sent to tenants, mortgagors, and vendors of property. Letters sent outside the immediate area included reports to absentee landlords, statements for mortgages, and communications to former residents seeking to liquidate Hamilton assets. The geographic scope of this communications network suggests the considerable extent to which North American cities were economically and socially interdependent. For example, Toronto was the paramount destination for Moore and Davis letters sent outside the immediate vicinity because it was the head office centre for the insurance company represented by the firm and for several trust companies with Hamilton property. Also, numerous Hamiltonians had moved to the larger centre leaving behind unsold lots or dwellings. The steady 10 per cent flow of letters to the United States—frequently to Michigan and New York addresses—demonstrates the phenomena, well-known to social historians, of transiency, and underscores the significance of Hamilton's railway links with the border states. High turnover rates in the urban population, therefore, contributed significantly to the need for agencies like Moore and Davis.

TABLE 2 *Moore and Davis's Outgoing Correspondence for Two Time Periods (1858–65 and 1912–14), by Destination*

| | 1858–65 | | 1912–14 | |
|---|---|---|---|---|
| Destination | Number | Percentage | Number | Percentage |
| Hamilton | 297 | 20.5 | 429 | 31.9 |
| Wentworth county | 196 | 13.5 | 18 | 1.3 |
| Remainder of Ontario | 751 | 51.9 | 726 | 53.8 |
| Remainder of Canada | 68 | 4.7 | 30 | 2.2 |
| United States | 136 | 9.4 | 143 | 10.6 |
| Other | 0 | 0.0 | 3 | 0.2 |
| Total | 1448 | 100.0 | 1349 | 100.0 |

## The Mortgage Market

The mortgage market was quite limited in Canada during the nineteenth and early twentieth centuries. Chartered banks, the most important current source of funds, were legislatively excluded from issuing residential mortgages until the 1960s.[22] This left the field to life insurance companies, trust companies, building societies, mortgage loan companies, lawyers, real estate agents, and individuals. Precisely the same composition has been noted in studies in Boston and Pittsburgh during the late nineteenth century. Given this apparent fragmentation, it is not surprising that little is known about this area of finance, a point that Barrows has underscored for U.S. cities.[23] It does seem that most people tried to avoid mortgaging their property purchases whenever possible. One analysis of almost 1700 vacant Hamilton lots sold between 1847 and 1881 revealed that only 43 per cent were mortgaged at the time of sale, with the vendor or some other individual holding the mortgage in 93 per cent of the cases.[24] Another study of the sale of nearly 900 Hamilton houses during the same time period found mortgages in only 27 per cent of the transactions.[25] Such findings point to the existence of a localized and infrequently used mortgage market. Consequently, as the representative of several individuals and large estates, Moore and Davis were not insignificant players in the mortgage arena. It is plausible, moreover, to propose that, while thousands of investors made up the mortgage market in many contemporary urban settings, specialists like Moore and Davis co-ordinated the activity. They, and a few similar agents in nearby offices, determined the credit-worthiness of men of modest means or the strength of collateral. Mortgage brokers thereby affected the social and architectural shape of residential space, reinforcing notions about trustworthy character or desirable shelter.

When acting as mortgage broker, the firm sometimes worked for several interlocking commissions. Moore and Davis charged clients a fee of 2 per cent on any mortgage funds that it obtained. Such funds might have helped close a property sale for which the firm also charged a commission. Furthermore, Moore and Davis often sold the insurance policy that protected the mortgage against the loss of the property by fire. In 1912 Moore and Davis had to remind Toronto Dwellings, Limited, of the law that stated "that the Mortgagor will insure the Mortgaged premises in some insurance office to be approved of by the Mortgagee and that Miss Cummings requires it to be insured in the London and Lancashire Fire Ins. Co. in which Company it was insured at the time of purchase."[26] The London and Lancashire company was also the one fire insurance firm represented by Moore and Davis.

Beginning in the 1860s, the firm handled estate funds for trustees and widows. For Moore and Davis, six major estates seem to have constituted the bulk of the mortgage funds handled during the 1870s and 1880s; the ledgers for these funds provide a glimpse into the structure of mortgage lending.

Counting renewals, 706 mortgages with a total value of $1 073 268 were drawn from the funds of the six sources from 1860 to 1909. The most common values were $1000 (n=48), $2000 (n=38), $1500 (n=33), $500 (n=32), $600 (n=25), with the average value for all 49 years being $1560. These mortgages financed the purchase of small dwellings for owner occupants, revenue properties, and speculative lots.

Moore and Davis did not arrange mortgages with a blended payment scheme. Some of Hamilton's other property specialists, builders like Patterson Brothers, initiated such a plan for their clients in the 1880s as a means of easing the burden of financing homeownership.[27] Instead of having to secure savings or another loan to pay the principal at the end of the mortgage term, the mortgagor with a blended payments arrangement paid off the interest and principal together. The fifteen or twenty-year term was another feature of the blended payment system that made home ownership seem easier to attain. Yet, even as late as the 1920s, long-term blended payments were still regarded as relatively novel, and they applied only to the purchase of new houses.[28] In contrast, Moore and Davis made arrangements that fitted the traditional practice of home financing. Unlike a few major contractors, who sought to build a market of home buyers, brokers and local attorneys sought flexibility in the estates they guided. Of the 706 mortgages arranged by Moore and Davis, 221 (31.9 per cent) ran for three years; 204 (28.9 per cent) for five years; 102 (14.4 per cent) for two years, with the average term being only 3.6 years. Apparently the mortgagors of the day endeavoured to meet the principal due at the end of these fairly short terms, because 461 mortgages (65.3 per cent) were not renewed. Usually blended payments involved monthly installments, but Moore and Davis only drew up two mortgages on this basis. The half yearly payment was the most frequently arranged form, occurring 619 times (87.7 per cent). Each of these features appears to have been a standard practice throughout North America, and has been confirmed for Boston by Sam Bass Warner, Jr., in his *Streetcar Suburbs*.[29]

The rate of interest set by the firm dropped steadily throughout most of the study period, from an average of more than 7.5 per cent in the early 1870s to an average of less than 5.0 per cent in the early 1900s (see Fig. 1). This decline is hard to explain; the firm's papers reveal only vague comments about the relative availability of money. It may be that the local money supply was increased by British and American investment in Canada during the 1880s and especially in the early 1900s. Whatever the reason, the decline in interest rates may have contributed to the increase in the percentage of Hamilton householders owning homes: an increase from 25 per cent in 1861 to 33 per cent in 1901 to 50 per cent in 1911.[30] Other factors, including a period of industrial prosperity in the 1880s and the introduction of new building techniques and machined materials, may also have been significant. Nonetheless, the increased stability of the mortgage market by the late 1880s contrasted with financial instability in the late 1850s and early 1860s—a period when the trans-Atlantic credit system failed and interest rates soared.

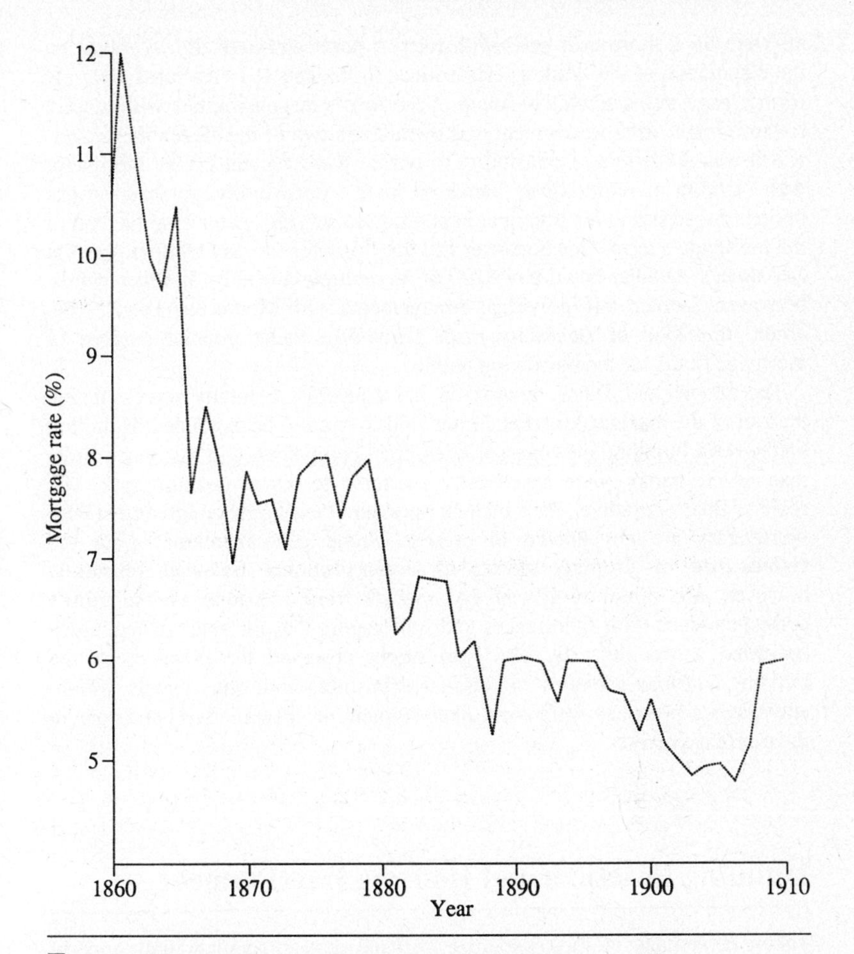


**FIG. 1** *Mortgage Interest Rates Charged by Moore and Davis, 1860–1909*

The lenders behind Moore and Davis's six principal sources of mortgage funds apparently curtailed their investments by the early twentieth century. The firm continued, however, to acquire clients with funds. No ledgers have been found for these later mortgages, but sufficient information remains in the firm's letterbooks to indicate that earlier trends continued. Estates and well-to-do widows once again supplied most of the money. In 1913, for example, Moore and Davis handled about $110 000 in funds for mortgage loans. About $40 000 came from the estate of Edgar H. Watkins, a deceased retail merchant; a Mrs. Mary Hopkins placed $26 300.[31] The three dozen mortgages in operation in 1913 had an average value of just over $3000, and all were on a short-term basis with interest paid semi-annually. A report on the disposition of the Watkins estate funds in January 1914 revealed a variety of mortgage terms as well as some of the firm's responsibilities with respect to those loans. Interest payment was overdue on two of the eleven mortgages, and it was the firm's responsibility to pursue these accounts. One mortgagor was "talking of requiring an increased loan." Each mortgagor had various options for repaying his principal in addition to settling accounts at the end of the mortgage's term. One borrower had the "privilege to pay all or any part at any time." Another could pay $100 or its multiple annually. In other words, borrowers worked out individual arrangements with Moore and Davis.[32] No doubt, this kind of flexibility made firms like theirs popular sources of mortgage funds for the borrowing public.

The Moore and Davis records do not constitute a totally representative portrait of the mortgage market. Other lenders need to be examined. Hamilton had several building and loan societies, trust companies, and insurance firms that, unlike banks, were specifically chartered to invest in mortgages. The scale of their operations, their interest rates, and their terms of agreement with mortgagors are not known at present. Some generalizations about the significance of property agents as noninstitutional financial operators, however, are possible. It can be implied from the tone of the firm's correspondence with mortgagees and mortgagors that the rates it negotiated prevailed across the city. The firm surely observed the practices of the building and loan societies and discussed business with other agents. Moore and Davis's practices were most likely typical of conservative behaviour in the mortgage market.

## Building Practices and Housing Development

Taking advantage of their expertise on such matters as changing property values, the state of local financing, and the capabilities of the city's building trades, Moore and Davis briefly expanded the scope of the firm's business activities by becoming land developers in 1884 and housing developers between 1907 and 1909. On a modest scale, Moore and Davis became producers of the basic urban commodity of housing. According to geographer David Harvey, who has examined the various participants in the urban real estate business and characterized the basic features of each, the housing developer or merchant builder made a special set of profit calculations. Unlike rental property managers, merchant builders worked, as they do today, at the margins of the city, hastening its suburbanization. They had no interest in restoring or rehabilitating older structures, for their primary function was the building and promotion of new units of housing. The merchant builder, moreover, should not be confused with the building contractor. While the latter tries to make money by selling both his artisanal skills and his ability to assemble and co-ordinate the manufacturing team that constructs the housing, the former tries to profit by purchasing land and enhancing its value through property development. The Moore and Davis records on suburban home construction indicate that their substantial profits came from their understanding of the many social, economic, and geographic factors that give housing value in addition to its basic function as shelter. A house's value as shelter (use value) would be constant to its occupant, but its value on the market place (exchange value) depended on the business cycle, the demographic and labour profile of the city, its location, and the interplay of its neighbourhood environment with the time-cost features of the journey to work. William Ghent Moore, as the son of the firm's founder William Pitt Moore, was in a good position to understand these factors intuitively, and recognized in 1907 that the widespread urban construction accompanying the industrial expansion of his city provided an opportunity to profit from the demand for housing by Hamilton's growing numbers of semi-skilled labourers and white-collar employees. He realized that the southeast side of the city, though relatively close to the exploding industrial district, was far enough away from the noise, fumes, and unsightly structures of the factories in the northeast to have some appeal for potential home buyers. Like scores of Hamilton developers active at the time, he helped create residential patterns with socially distinctive characteristics: immigrant labourers in the boarding houses of the northeast, semi-skilled labourers and clerks in the southeast, and the élite in the southwest.[33]

During the upswing in the business cycle that peaked around 1912 and 1913, William Ghent Moore built fourteen single-family homes (see Table 3). He entered into agreements with a building contractor, William Wray, who then co-ordinated the purchase of building materials and arranged for all the subcontracting: excavation, masonry work, carpentry, tinsmithing, plastering, painting, and glazing. Wray supervised and evaluated each phase of construction. If satisfied, he forwarded the subcontractor's request for payment to Moore. Agreements like this were typical of one important type of business arrangement for home production, but there were others. Many builders purchased lots themselves; and building-supply firms occasionally functioned as developers. Some people even built their own houses. The housing industry, unconsolidated and flourishing, attracted numerous combinations of investors and producers. Nevertheless, despite the variety of business arrangements, a handful of major property subdividers, a builders' association, and eventually a real estate board, provided the industry with the leverage necessary to enforce a measure of unity when setting prices and when dealing with construction unions. All the same, the Canadian urban housing industry remained dominated by flexible partnerships and co-ordinating associations until after World War II, when corporate integration and packaged suburbs began to challenge traditional ways of doing business in the industry.[34]

By the time Moore took an interest in housing ventures, the city's suppliers of building materials and the building trades had had about twenty years of experience with machine-manufactured housing components. Doors, sashes, mouldings, baseboards, newel posts, banisters, and other wood pieces were regularly being turned out by power equipment in the city's several major lumberyards. For an even longer period, builders had utilized pattern books for their house plans. Several homes built by Wray for Moore, for example, refer to a plan number seventy-three from an unspecified pattern book. By the time Moore entered the property development business, the standard house had become smaller, evolving toward what Gwendolyn Wright has termed the minimalist house.[35] Even though the business network organizing the housing industry remained both fairly traditional and scattered among numerous temporary partnerships, technology and standardization had taken a significant foothold.

**TABLE 3** *The Profitability of William Moore's Speculative Housing Ventures, 1907–1909*

| Construction costs | Norway St., 1907 Cost ($)[a] | %[a] | Central St., 1908 Cost ($)[b] | %[b] | Mountain St., 1909 Cost ($)[c] | %[c] | Cost ($)[d] | %[d] |
|---|---|---|---|---|---|---|---|---|
| Lumber | 442 | 26.8 | 298 | 22.1 | 335 | 20.9 | 425 | 23.7 |
| Carpenters' wages | 150 | 9.1 | 120 | 8.9 | 120 | 7.5 | 150 | 8.4 |
| Plasterers' contracts | 140 | 8.5 | 90 | 6.7 | 115 | 7.2 | 150 | 8.4 |
| Cellar contracts | 117 | 7.1 | 70 | 5.2 | 70 | 4.4 | 90 | 5.0 |
| Painting and glazing | 55 | 3.3 | 55 | 4.0 | 55 | 3.4 | 60 | 3.3 |
| Hardware | 27 | 1.6 | 25 | 1.9 | 25 | 1.6 | 24 | 1.3 |
| Chimney | 12 | 0.7 | 20 | 1.5 | 20 | 1.3 | 15 | 0.8 |
| Gas pipes | — | — | — | — | — | — | 9 | 0.5 |
| Tinsmiths' contracts | 14 | 0.8 | 14 | 1.0 | 14 | 0.9 | 14 | 0.7 |
| Other | 37 | 2.2 | — | — | — | — | — | — |
| Pump and well | 26 | 1.6 | — | — | 24 | 1.5 | 24 | 1.3 |
| Contractor's payment | 75 | 4.4 | 100 | 7.3 | 100 | 6.3 | 80 | 4.4 |
| Construction costs | 1095 | 66.3 | 792 | 58.6 | 878 | 54.9 | 1061 | 58.9 |
| Land cost | 300 | 18.2 | 300 | 22.2 | 360 | 22.5 | 392 | 21.8 |
| Profit | 255 | 15.5 | 258 | 19.2 | 362 | 22.6 | 347 | 19.3 |
| Sale price | 1650 | 100 | 1350 | 100 | 1600 | 100 | 1800 | 100 |

NOTE: Each unit took approximately forty days to build.
[a]Based on the construction of two two-story frame houses.
[b]Based on the construction of one frame cottage.
[c]Based on the construction of six frame houses.
[d]Based on the construction of five two-story frame houses.

As a consequence of these changes, dwellings could be erected quickly and for a relatively low price. In 1913, a Hamilton contractor demonstrated the principle of rapid construction using abundant prefabricated components by raising a twelve-room house in one day. More typically, houses were built over a five- to seven-week period, with the work sequence revealing both an appreciation of new technology and the persistence of old crafts. Advanced mass-production techniques were utilized at the lumberyard, where wood cut at mills in Northern Ontario or New Brunswick and owned by city dealers was finished into standard widths and shapes.[36] Horsedrawn drays hauled the supplies to construction sites, with punch clocks recording the departure time on the delivery ticket. When the materials arrived, the contractor signed the ticket, which then became the basis for the billings mailed to William Ghent Moore by the suppliers.

In contrast, the construction of basements remained technologically unsophisticated. Each basement was excavated by pick and shovel, a chore that appears to have required 100 man hours for completion. A masonry specialist arrived next to build the basement and, if required, the foundation footings for the verandah or for rooms lacking a cellar. The carpenters next arrived to put down the floor beams, install frames, raise the roof, and finally clad the exterior. A tinsmith then installed roof gutters; plasterers, painters, and glaziers finished the dwelling. About ten men appear to have worked on each of Moore's houses. In 1909, when five houses were being built for Moore on the same side of Mountain Street, Wray organized the construction around a work sequence, instead of building each unit concurrently. For the merchant builder, this type of staggered assembly spread out capital expenditures. Ideally, the completion and sale of one house would generate enough revenue to complete another. Good timing in the construction and sales could thus minimize the enterprise's credit requirements.[37] In sum, housing development was a sophisticated business involving a string of specialists. The developer decided what, when, and where to build. The contractor co-ordinated the suppliers and tradesmen. Timing was an essential consideration in every phase, from site selection to closing with a buyer.

The largest single item in the cost of Moore's houses was lumber, which accounted for about 25 per cent of all expenses, including land costs. In both 1907 and 1909, a two-story 30 by 22 foot frame house could be constructed for just under $1100. In his initial negotiations with Wray, Moore tried to hold construction costs to $1000. In 1908, Wray had been able to build very modest frame cottages for just over $790. Throughout this three-year period, lumber remained roughly 40 per cent of the construction cost, with carpenters' wages accounting for 14 per cent, and plastering contracts 13 per cent (see Table 3). Suggestively, construction costs remained stable overall, with lumber prices even declining slightly. The integrated and technologically progressive lumber industry thus seems to have been seeking profits through volume sales and technological improvements rather than through high unit costs.

The converse was true of the land itself. While its supply could be increased by creating new subdivisions, its value could not. In terms of amenities or even necessary facilities, building lots were not all alike and were sold under the assumption that the amount of good land was finite. The economics of materials, labour, and land were thus governed by different principles. The economics of building materials were based on a conception of renewable supply; the economics of construction labour revolved around the city contractors' ability to reduce craft union demands by threatening to introduce non-union labourers; and the economics of land rested in the assumption that accessible real estate existed in limited supply. Consequently, in a city with a rapidly increasing immigrant population, building supply costs fell, labour costs were held in check, and land prices often increased (see Table 4).[38] The rise from $300 to $392 per lot in two years demonstrated the significance of the concept of land scarcity and the ability of land developers to pass along the related costs. The profitability of the land-subdividers' business was demonstrated by increases in the price of property; the developers' ability to make a profit despite these increases was revealed by Moore's nearly constant 20 per cent net rate of return. Added costs were simply passed on to the consumer.

TABLE 4 *Changes in Costs and Profits for Similar Two-Story Frame Houses, 1907–1909*

| Year | Number | Construction costs | Land costs | Profit margin | Price |
|---|---|---|---|---|---|
| 1907 | 2 | $1095 | $300 | $255 | $1650 |
| 1909 | 5 | $1061 | $392 | $347 | $1800 |
| Change | | -3.2% | +30.7% | +36.1% | +9.19% |

It should be observed that the years William Ghent Moore acted as building developer were abnormal. The nearly 10 per cent rise in the cost of housing between 1907 and 1909 was exceptional. Over the longer period, from 1861 to 1911, the introduction of mass-produced building supplies, minimalist housing designs, and declining mortgage rates all helped to increase the percentage of homeowning households. Furthermore, it is probable that civic housing codes and public health campaigns improved the quality of the city's housing stock during the same period. A few pockets of slum dwellings and numerous overcrowded boardinghouses for immigrant labourers remained important exceptions to this pattern of long-term improvements; however, as Barrows reminds us, such structures were not typical products of the property industry in urban North America at this time.[39]

In the brief period William Ghent Moore worked as a housing developer, he demonstrated the ingenuity of a businessman able to respond quickly to opportunities and to frame cost-efficient contracts with suppliers and tradesmen. His work as developer also demonstrates the profitability of this business, although there is no denying its riskiness. The business cycle could not be forecast and repeatedly the housing industry would peak as the urban economy had already started to weaken. This happened in the late 1850s, in the early 1890s, and in the 1913–15 recession. It occurred again in 1930. Because they were involved in housing development for such a short period,

Moore and Davis avoided the over-construction and speculation that culminated in the 1913 Canadian economic collapse.

## Landlords and Tenants

If the preceding discussion of Moore and Davis's mortgage activity and housing development suggests social progress, or at least an increase in property ownership by wage earners, then the eviction notices, issued by the firm suggest a less happy theme. These notices permit an empirical investigation of a process that has been described theoretically by David Harvey. Harvey maintains that the landlord's rate of return on lower quality dwellings constitutes a class monopoly rent. Class action, he argues, is sometimes necessary to maintain this monopoly. One example of an action of this kind, Harvey contends, occurs when there is an oversupply of inexpensive rental housing. In this situation, "a rational landlord strategy is to reduce maintenance [until] scarcity is successfully produced....The class interests of landlord and tenant are clearly opposed to each other."[40] According to this thesis, Moore and Davis should have advised landlords to withdraw housing from the market and convert the vacant property to other revenue-yielding uses. Examination of the evidence, however, suggests that the existence of a class monopoly in the provision of housing did not always have such socially undesirable consequences.

Using city directories and assessment rolls, an effort was made to determine what happened to tenants receiving Moore and Davis eviction notices and to the dwellings from which they may have been evicted. Out of a total of 567 residential and commercial eviction notices issued between 1893 and 1918, all but 72 (12.7 per cent) could be traced to yield data about the tenants and the outcome of the notice. This data reveals that Harvey's claim that landlords withdrew rental housing to maintain a class monopoly is difficult to substantiate. In more than two-fifths of the cases, the original tenant stayed in the dwellings. There were only twenty-four instances (4.2 per cent of known outcomes) in which a tenant was, apparently, removed to facilitate the sale of the property. This instance represented the fourth most frequent outcome of the eviction notice (see Table 5). Furthermore, rental property was converted to building lots only six times (1.0 per cent). After the upsurge of concern about public health in the early twentieth century, it was occasionally civic authorities, not landlords, who forced the issue of reinvestment and intensified the housing crisis afflicting the urban poor.[41]

The behaviour of Moore and Davis thus does not support Harvey's thesis. Nor does the fact that it was the local government that intensified, at least in part, the housing crisis. As Harvey focussed on the contemporary housing situation, he did not have the advantage of historical hindsight. At best, the notices and related letters of advice to landlords sent by Moore and Davis suggest that landlords attempted during the periods of urban growth to function as a class monopoly to increase rents. Eviction threats were issued liberally during upswings in the business cycle, and must be considered as part of an investor strategy. In certain instances, eviction threats were coupled with rent increases: "If you are willing to pay the increased rental kindly call at our office and sign the lease. If you object to the payment of said increases in rent we wish you to consider this as a notice to vacate on the said 6 day of June 1913."[42] The contents of letters sent to tenants were not, however, sufficiently detailed to state conclusively that rent increases were the overriding issue. In 1916 and 1917, however, when the letters included more than routine information, thirty-two of fifty-six notices mentioned a rent increase. Evidence of another sort strengthens the rent-increase hypothesis. The three-year periods between 1886 and 1918 in which the most eviction notices were issued coincided with significant upward swings in the local business cycle (see Fig. 2). In contrast, during the depressed 1890s, the brief recession of 1907–1908, and the crash of 1914–15, Moore and Davis rarely issued notices.

**TABLE 5** *Outcomes of Eviction Notices Issued by Moore and Davis, 1898–1918*

| Outcomes[a] | Number | All cases (%) | Locatable cases (%) |
|---|---|---|---|
| Original tenant stays[b] | 244 | 43.0 | 49.3 |
| New tenant | 134 | 23.6 | 27.1 |
| House is vacant | 27 | 4.8 | 5.5 |
| House is sold to new occupant | 24 | 4.2 | 4.8 |
| New owner and new tenant | 17 | 3.0 | 3.4 |
| New owner and same tenant | 14 | 2.5 | 2.8 |
| Owner moved in | 13 | 2.3 | 2.6 |
| Property becomes lots | 6 | 1.0 | 1.2 |
| New owner and vacant | 4 | 0.7 | 0.8 |
| Sold to recipient of notice | 3 | 0.6 | 0.6 |
| Other | 9 | 1.6 | 1.8 |
| Could not locate | 72 | 12.7 | — |
| Total | 567 | 100.0 | 100.0 |

NOTE: [a] As traced in city directories and assessment rolls.
[b] In these instances, tenants apparently complied with demands for higher rents.

Of the threatened tenants who could be identified in the assessment rolls, 244 (49.3 per cent) remained tenants at the same location after the date of the threatened eviction. This was by far the most common outcome of the firm's action. It seems, therefore, that many tenants complied with new rental charges. New tenants were found in only 134 cases (27.1 per cent); vacant units in only 31 cases (6.3 per cent). In general, the notices were issued to

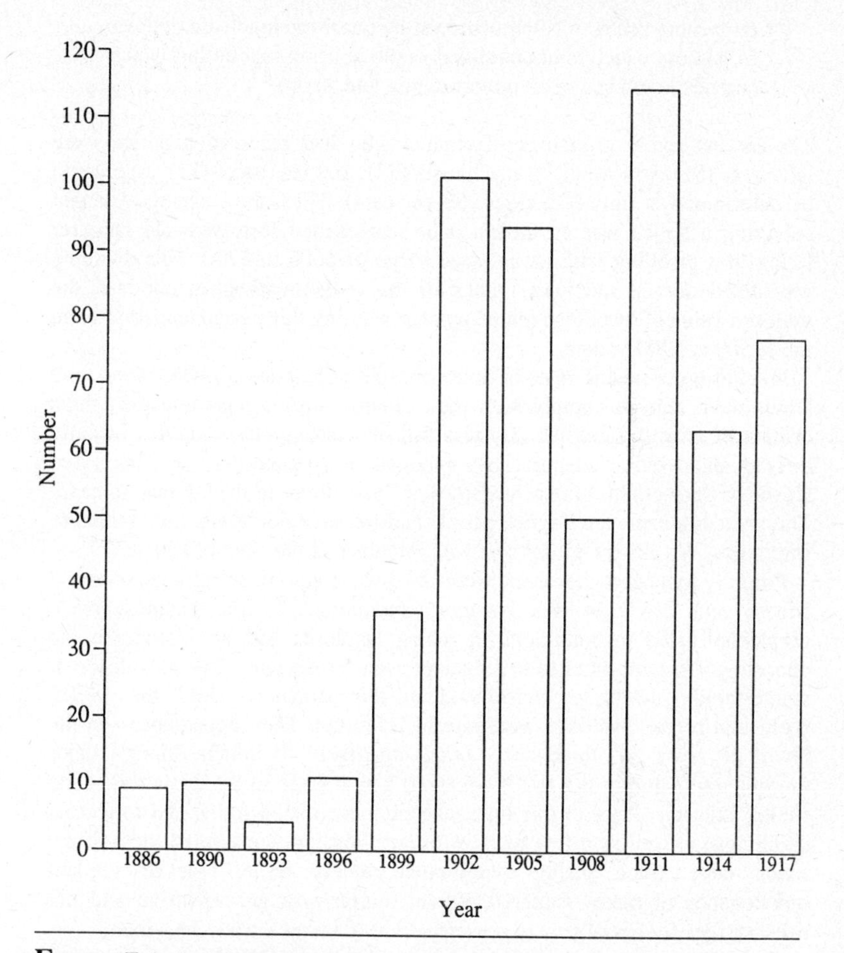


**FIG. 2** *Eviction Notices Issued by Moore and Davis by Three-Year Intervals, 1886–1918*

residential tenants. Property use could be determined definitely in 499 instances (88 per cent). Of these, 452 (90.6 per cent) were residential.

The residential tenants' profile fits David Harvey's description of the type of urban dweller most vulnerable to a monopoly class of landlords:

> In a sequential allocation of a fixed housing stock in order of competitive bidding power, the poorer group, because it enters the housing market last, has to face producers of housing services who are in a quasi-monopolistic position...Lack of choice makes the

> poor more prone to being squeezed by quasi-monopolistic policies (a process which is not confined to the housing market but which extends to job and retail opportunities, and so on).[43]

The largest social groupings of tenants who had received a notice were labourers (81), widows (32), machinists (23), and teamsters (21). Age could be determined in only 332 cases (59 per cent). Thus, the "average" tenant receiving a notice was an unskilled or semi-skilled forty-year-old labourer living in a dwelling with an assessed value of $600 to $700. This dwelling was decidedly on the lower rungs of the rental market. In contrast, the assessed value of dwellings rented by clerks during this period tended to be in the $1500 to $2000 range.

In addition to raising rents in times of rapid population growth, Moore and Davis were able to comply with their clients' wishes regarding the ethnic origins of tenants since the city was full of working-class families recently arrived and seeking shelter. They reported in August 1913 to Mrs. Ellen Keyes of Springfield, Massachusetts, that "your favor of the 9th inst. to hand. The present tenants are English people and we have not at any time rented to foreigners. We always do our best with reference to the class of tenants."[44]

Property managers, however, were not always able to select tenants as did Moore and Davis in this instance; undulations in the business cycle occasionally led to conditions in which landlords had no latitude in the choosing of tenants and had to reduce or even forego rents. The prevalence of single-family dwellings contributed to this situation. Until the 1920s, multi-unit rental dwellings were rare in Hamilton. Their appearance—in the form of rows of three-story brick apartment buildings along major thoroughfares during the 1920s—marked a new stage in the evolution of the shelter industry. Prior to this time, cheaply constructed frame and roughcast dwellings, as well as a few rows of terrace housing, constituted most of the rental units. Such shelter deteriorated rapidly if left vacant; vigilant maintenance of many scattered, vacant houses was an expensive and not necessarily a foolproof way to prevent serious damage during the winter.

As winter approached in the depression year of 1891, Moore and Davis worried about the situation of many houses that they managed. They wrote to John Storie of New York that his house was still vacant. "We have offered to fix it up and rent it at a low price but it seems impossible to get it rented. There are a great number of vacant houses in the City."[45] During the subsequent depression years—especially in winter—Moore and Davis recommended rent decreases, delayed payments, and house repairs. The prospects of burst pipes, broken windows, and vandalism were real; the firm suggested assorted concessions to keep houses occupied and hence protected.[46] When the firm could, it induced tenants to sign a year's lease in April to insure that the house would be occupied the following winter. In contrast, during boom eras, the preferred system was rental on a monthly basis, with increases levied in March and again in August or September. The following wisdom exemplified the firm's objective during hard winters: "It is much easier to keep a tenant than to get a new one especially at this season of the year [21 November]." Tenants recognized their leverage; they complained about the state of the dwellings, they moved out in search of better situations, and they withheld rent knowing that the firm preferred not to evict. In February 1893, Moore and Davis sent, in exasperation, a note to one tenant; however, they did not threaten eviction: "There is now three months rent past due, on the No. 31 West Avenue. We request that you will kindly let us have the amount in full. Yours truly, Moore and Davis."[47]

When depression struck the city in 1914, tenants once again appear to have recognized that the existence of surplus housing made landowners vulnerable. Of course, they well recognized the precariousness of their own incomes, and tried to roll back rents through threatened and actual relocations. In a report to the Guardian Trust Company of Toronto, Moore and Davis noted that "the prospect of renting or selling are not very bright at present." One consequence was that "the tenants in Nos. 9 and 15 Windsor Street want their rent reduced to $20.00 per month each. We have spoken to Mr. Alexander about it and we thought to try to get $22.00 but if not to reduce to $20.00 for the present rather than have them move and the houses remain vacant."[48] Not all absentee landlords appear to have listened to such advice. M.J. Cashmen of Port Huron, Michigan, for example, had to be given a second account of conditions: "We understand that the rent was to be increased after the winter...You will find it very difficult to get a desirable tenant especially in the winter at an increased rent."[49] While correlation of eviction notices with the business cycle has been mentioned, a further glimpse at the eviction pattern reveals its seasonal nature (see Fig. 3). This graph demonstrates the firm's reluctance to evict tenants in winter. By inference, it denotes a real, albeit limited and contingent, possibility for tenant leverage.

The advent of the apartment building signalled the start of a new era. As it forced a re-examination of land costs and required the participation of entrepreneurs and financial institutions, it helped undermine the well-established piecemeal gradualism of the residential rental business. From the landlord's perspective, an additional feature of the new order was the eradication of the power of unorganized tenants. When apartment structures sprouted throughout the city in the 1920s, and again in the 1960s, they signalled the arrival of a new level of sophistication in the landlords' monopoly. As corporate owner-operators replaced the network of landlords acting through the medium of the property manager, the nature of the landlord-tenant relationship also changed. Tenants now would seek to wield power through overt collective action and through government intervention. Despite these changes, Moore and Davis continued, until the 1970s, to manage rental homes. During that decade, the Moore family got out of the business altogether, concentrating instead on property insurance.

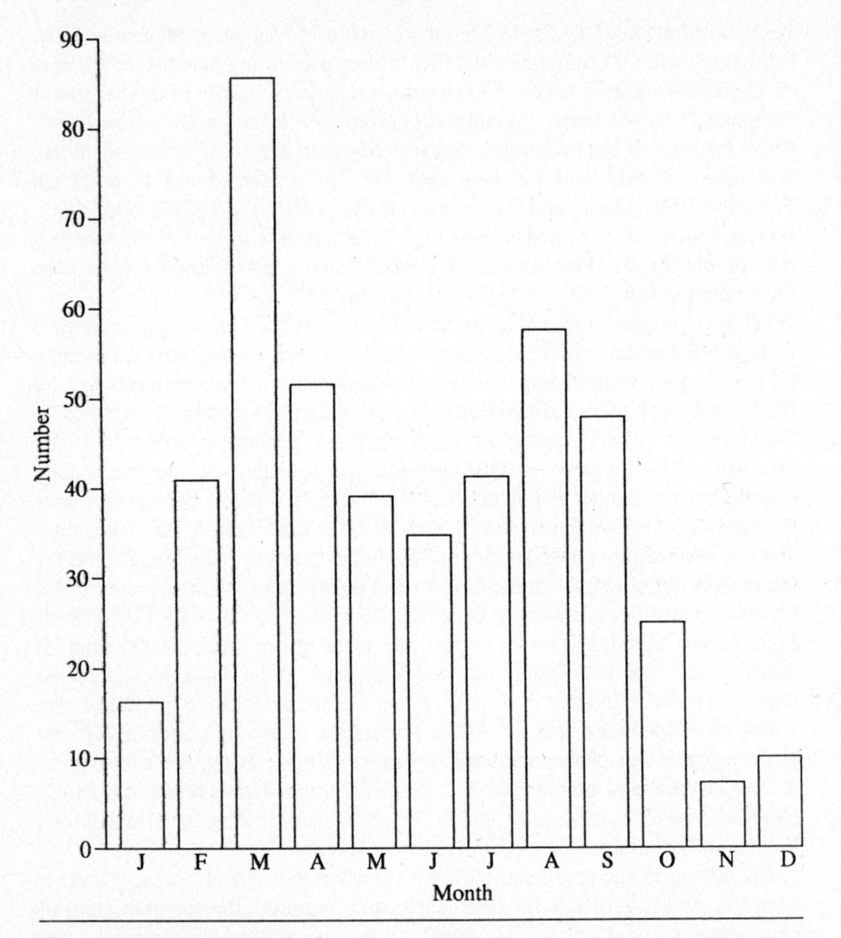


**FIG. 3** *Residential Evictions Ordered by Moore and Davis by Month, 1886–1918 (n=1)*

## Conclusion

The foregoing analysis of the records of Moore and Davis suggests that the North American urban property industry changed little between 1860 and 1920. To be sure, the firm become more professional as it devoted itself more single-mindedly to the property business; however, the basic product of the industry—the single-family house—remained through the period at the centre of the firm's activities. The single-family house was a familiar landmark in the North American urban landscape as a symbol of achievement and independence; less obviously it was, and largely remains, an urban staple whose construction and management requires varied talents. Moore and Davis's approach to property management, mortgages, and the sale of urban property did not change during the period of our study. There were good reasons for this continuity. Unlike many consumer durables, houses were costly; as an investment, units were less liquid and more expensive than stocks and bonds. To have survived many fluctuations of the business cycle required a cautious skepticism. Seldom did the firm write to clients in optimistic tones. Haunted by the cataclysmic recession of 1857–60, the first generation avoided "creative financing." In Hamilton, the worldwide economic collapse ruined many real estate speculators and left landlords with many vacant properties. As Moore and Davis entered the business at precisely this traumatic moment, it is likely they were struck with the follies of optimism and innovation. Their mortgage arrangements minimized risk. To landlords, they advised patience and discouraged rash evictions. Similarly, in his one isolated venture into property development and housing construction, William Ghent Moore chose to build familiar types of dwellings, whose price, appearance, and location were carefully calculated. With the exception of this venture—a venture that took place during a period of unprecedented local growth—the firm's business was consistently routine and prudent. In addition to these specific examples of the firm's conservatism is the general observation that the nature and destination of its written correspondence changed only slightly in more than half a century.

The agents' efforts to mediate, through activities like obtaining mortgage funds and renting dwellings, between the various groups in the property industry, gave them an important role in the city-building process. In this regard, similarity with current real estate practice is evident. This having been said, it must be added that these roles and influences have been generally ignored by students of urban development. For much too long, geographers and economists using economic models of land use have dominated the real estate literature. Only recently have many of these scholars stopped considering housing, in the tradition of land-use economics, as a single-value commodity—i.e., as mere shelter. Neoclassical and neo-Marxist scholars, critical of this formulation, have, it is true, tried to supplant it with more complicated models. Nevertheless, the real "bidders" or real "manipulators" hypothesized about in such models are too seldom seen. Business historians should have a far greater say than they have had in the past in describing the processes that have made the North American city.

Especially in recent decades, significant changes have taken place in the property business. Moore and Davis, however, did not change with the industry. For example, the trend toward vertical and horizontal integration in the housing business today contrasts dramatically with the limited range of activities undertaken by Moore and Davis. Furthermore, they participated in only the most limited fashion in the several significant changes in the housing industry that did take place in their era. During this era, modern mass-production technology was introduced into house construction through the prefabrication of numerous house components. Blended mortgage payment schemes were also introduced by developers to encourage home ownership. In addition, apartment buildings became more commonplace in urban North American cities, and class-based residential patterns replaced the heterogeneous neighbourhoods of the mid-nineteenth-century city. The fact that Moore and Davis became actively involved in neither blended payments nor apartments suggests the limitations of their conservatism. Who did instigate these changes and why they came about remain questions for future research.

By 1920 cracks were appearing in the formerly solid belief that private industry could provide all urban housing needs. In response to the housing crisis precipitated by World War I, the Canadian government made at that time its first, timid forays into the housing field.[50] Unfortunately, at present this nexus of change is only partially understood, though some elements, such as changes in house-building technology, have been explored in depth.[51] A more synthetic approach to these changes is essential if the evolution of the property industry and the implication of this process for the spatial and social ordering of urban places is to be properly understood. While insights gleaned from business history and historical geography offer an alternative to the limitations of theoretical abstraction, much room for historical inquiry remains. The Moore and Davis records document but one approach to property management in one city in one epoch in the history of the shelter business. Our findings parallel those in similar studies closely enough to venture the claim that Moore and Davis followed common practices. But many questions remain. Was their caution extreme, their survival unusual, and their refusal to innovate in the post-1920 period atypical? Did other established entrepreneurs, undeterred by precedents constraining the Moores, innovate successfully in new financial methods and shelter types? It will be necessary to study more firms over longer periods in different cities before a more dynamic portrait of housing as business history can be sketched.

# Notes

1. Olivier Zunz, *The Changing Face of Inequality: Urbanization, Industrial Development, and Immigrants in Detroit, 1880–1920* (Chicago, 1982), 400.
2. Robert G. Barrows, "Beyond the Tenement: Patterns of American Urban Housing, 1870–1930," *Journal of Urban History* 9 (1983): 395–420.
3. Michael J. Doucet, "Urban Land Development in Nineteenth-Century North America: Themes in the Literature," *Journal of Urban History* 8 (1982): 327–31.

4. Pearl J. Davies, *Real Estate in American History* (Washington, 1958), 18–21, 36.

5. Ibid., 39.

6. The inventory of Moore and Davis's records includes 22 volumes of letterbooks, 9 rent ledgers, 1 mortgage ledger, 12 general ledger books, and 7 estate books.

7. John C. Weaver, *Hamilton: An Illustrated History* (Toronto, 1982), 196–98.

8. Moore and Davis (hereafter M & D) to Joseph Sudborough, 13 September 1862, Moore and Davis's Letterbooks (hereafter Letterbooks), vol. 1. The Letterbooks are part of the Hamilton Collection in the Hamilton Public Library.

9. M & D to James McLlennan, 19 September 1865; M & D to the Reverend John Irvine, 6 December 1867; both in Letterbooks, vol. 3.

10. M & D to Mrs. H. Jagoe, 7 May 1891, Letterbooks, vol. 11.

11. M & D to W.R. Whately, deputy chief, Hamilton police, 17 July 1914, Letterbooks, vol. 16.

12. W.P. Moore to A.A. McKillop, 18 February 1887, Letterbooks, vol. 9.

13. W.P. Moore to N.A. Awrey, 24 March 1887, Letterbooks, vol. 9.

14. W.P. Moore to N.A. Awrey, 31 March 1891, Letterbooks, vol. 11.

15. M & D to S.J. Vankoughnet, 1 May 1862, Letterbooks, vol. 1.

16. John Fox to M & D, 30 September 1870, Letterbooks, vol. 5.

17. Fox's offer was rejected. The two lots in question were sold to a William Lemon in 1873 for $1000.

18. For example, see M & D to Richard Bull, 13 July 1869, Letterbooks, vol. 4.

19. M & D to D.F. Duncombe, 25 October 1867, Letterbooks, vol. 3.

20. M & D to Alex McNale, 14 September 1872, M & D to Charles A. Blyth, 25 June 1877, both in Letterbooks, vol. 5.

21. Moore and Davis Mortgage Ledgers, Estate of Gilbert F. Davis. For more on Hamilton mortgages during this period see Michael B. Katz, Michael J. Doucet, and Mark B. Stern, *The Social Organization of Early Industrial Capitalism* (Cambridge, Mass., 1982), chap. 4, and Michael J. Doucet, "Building the Victorian City: The Process of Land Development in Hamilton, Ontario, 1847–1881" (Ph.D. diss., University of Toronto, 1977), chap. 6.

22. Walter Stewart, *Towers of Gold, Feet of Clay: The Canadian Banks* (Toronto, 1982), chap. 6.

23. Sam Bass Warner, Jr., *Streetcar Suburbs: The Process of Growth in Boston, 1870–1900* (Cambridge, Mass., 1962), 118; John Bodner, Roger Simon, and Michael P. Weber, *Lives of Their Own: Blacks, Italians, and Poles in Pittsburgh, 1900–1960* (Urbana, 1982), 161–70; Barrows, "Beyond the Tenement," 415–18.

24. Doucet, "Building the Victorian City," chap. 6.

25. Katz, Doucet, and Stern, *The Social Organization*, chap. 4.

26. M & D to Toronto Dwellings, 5 June 1914, Letterbooks, vol. 16.

27. Moore and Davis Collection, pamphlet folder, *Advice to Tenants by Patterson Bros., The Builders of Homes* (n.p., n.d.).

28. John C. Weaver, "From Land Assembly to Social Maturity: The Suburban Life of Westdale (Hamilton), Ontario, 1911–1951," *Histoire sociale/Social History* II (1978), 411–40.

29. Warner, *Streetcar Suburbs*, 119–20.

30. Weaver, *Hamilton*, Table 4, 197.

31. 12 December 1912 to 10 September 1914, passim, Letterbooks, vol. 16.

32. M & D to E.D. Cahill, K.C., 14 January 1914, Letterbooks, vol. 16.

33. For a discussion of similar occurrences in a U.S. city, see Zunz, *The Changing Face of Inequality*.

34. James Lorimer, *The Developers* (Toronto, 1978).

35. Moore and Davis, vertical file box labelled Mountain, Central, Norway. In keeping with the image of merchant builders as businessmen who kept their records on the backs of envelopes, the estimates and running totals on actual costs were pencilled on the backs of envelopes. On minimalist design, see Gwendolyn Wright, *Moralism and the Model Home: Domestic Architecture and Conflict in Chicago, 1873–1913* (Chicago, 1980).

36. See for example, W.D. Flatt, *The Trail of Love: An Appreciation of Canadian Pioneers and Pioneer Life* (Toronto, 1916). Flatt was a Hamilton lumber baron with holdings in Michigan. He spread his business into building materials and real estate subdivision. According to the 1871 manuscript census, the largest building firm in Hamilton was that of C.W. and T.H. Kempster, which also was a manufacturer of sashes, doors, and window blinds.

37. For a candid, inside discussion of merchant builders' practices in the 1950s, see Ned Eichler, *The Merchant Builders* (Cambridge, Mass., 1982).

38. Doucet, "Urban Land Development," 300–302.

39. Barrows, "Beyond the Tenement," 395–97.

40. David Harvey, *Social Justice and the City* (Baltimore, 1975), 171.

41. M & D to Samuel Green, 5 June 1913 and 8 September 1913, Letterbooks, vol. 16.

42. M & D to H. Burch, 5 May 1913, Letterbooks, vol. 16.

43. Harvey, *Social Justice and the City*, 170.

44. M & D to Ellen Heyes, 11 August 1913, Letterbooks, vol. 16.

45. M & D to James Storie, 21 July 1891, Letterbooks, vol. 11.

46. M & D to Dr. G. Morton, 30 July 1891, Letterbooks, vol. 11.

47. M & D to James Bennett, 9 February 1893, Letterbooks, vol. 11.

48. M & D to Guardian Trust Company, 19 August 1914, Letterbooks, vol. 16; M & D to Messrs. Cohen and Sugarman, 10 September 1914, Letterbooks, vol. 11.

49. M & D to M.J. Cashman, 28 February 1913, Letterbooks, vol. 16.

50. Albert Rose, *Canadian Housing Policies, 1935–1980* (Toronto, 1980), 1–2.

51. Wright, *Moralism and the Model Home.*

# THE EVOLUTION OF SETTLEMENT SYSTEMS : A CANADIAN EXAMPLE, 1851–1970*

F.A. DAHMS

The topic of urban development has been addressed from a number of perspectives which have improved our understanding of the factors contributing to the processes operating in individual places and in systems of settlements. Works such as that by Artibise, Dyos, Johnson, Masters, and Warner have examined local political, economic, technological and human factors affecting the growth of individual cities.[1] At the other extreme, studies of national urban systems by Borchert, Conzen, Pred, Simmons, and Rozman have focussed on the long-term, large-scale technological and economic factors leading to integrated systems of major cities.[2] Theoretical concepts developed by Walter Christaller and elaborated by many others have helped us to understand the market functions, size, and spacing of settlements, but have done little to explain the evolution of settlement systems.[3]

The three approaches outlined above might roughly be categorized as temporal, spatial, and theoretical. Unfortunately, they have often been pursued independently, rather than combined in an effort to integrate the most useful features of each into one study.[4] It seems obvious that improved explanatory generalizations about the evolution of settlements will be achieved when we explicitly recognize their interactions with other places through time, the role of changing technology in these interactions, and the role of individuals in the total evolutionary process. Furthermore, a number of theoretical concepts must be integrated into our explanatory schemes if they are to have general applicability. It is possible to relate the processes of regional urban growth to the factors so often cited in individual urban histories, and to the general economic and technological evolution described in accounts of the development of national urban systems. Large-scale technological and

*Journal of Urban History 7, 2 (February 1981): 169–204.

economic factors have impinged upon the development of individual cities by influencing the activities of their politicians and promoters. Improving transportation has enabled metropolitan centres to expand their spheres of influence across vast areas and has led to differential growth among settlements at all levels of the urban hierarchy. Some of the principles of competition and organization suggested by central place theory may be applicable at various stages of settlement evolution.

This article integrates the approaches sketched above by tracing the evolution of a carefully defined urban system from its earliest development to the present day. It attempts to isolate the factors affecting the development of the settlements studied within a theoretical framework. This interdisciplinary approach should demonstrate the advantages of combining the historical analysis of individual cities with a concern for the interdependency and interaction among urban places within local, regional, and national systems. Rather than making conclusions about the evolution of small settlements on the basis of inferences derived from the study of large settlements, or from the retrospective application of theory, we will deal explicitly with the evolution of small places.[5]

## The Conceptual Framework

A number of scholars have developed conceptual frameworks outlining the evolution of settlement systems in areas varying in size from the continental United States to small sectors of the developing frontier (Table 1).[6] Although their terminology differs and specific dates obviously relate to the areas where such studies were made, there is an underlying similarity among the schemes. All reflect changing technology as it has affected transportation links between settlements and their hinterlands and the interaction among settlements at various levels of the urban hierarchy. They also reflect the effects of the mechanization of agriculture and the development of trade links that eventually integrated even the most isolated frontiers into national economies. Each emphasizes one or two important factors: Vance—wholesaling and long-distance trade; Careless—metropolitan influence on the frontier; Borchert—changing transport technology; Whebell—innovation, diffusion, technological change, and inertia; Muller—nodality and transportation; Bowden—urban-hinterland interaction; Hudson—immigration and competition; Mitchell—economic change; McKenzie—changing transport technology (Table 1). In many respects, these emphases result from the focus of each scheme upon a different scale of settlement from local to continental. Nevertheless, each contributes to an understanding of the evolution of settlement systems at all scales. Those most relevant to the case study are considered in more detail below.

**TABLE 1** *Selected Conceptual Outlines of the Evolution of Settlement Systems*

| Scale | Continental: Frontier to Development of a Settlement System | | |
|---|---|---|---|
| Author | James E. Vance Jr. | Maurice Careless | John R. Borchert |
| Periods and major characteristics | Mercantile model | Metropolitanism | American metropolitan evolution |
| | *Initial search phase* Search from Europe for economic information on North American coasts | *Superficial extractive frontier* Low levels of settlement, capital, technology: fishing, fur trading, square timber etc. Economic stimulus from transatlantic metropolis. Local colonial garrison towns established. | *Sail-wagon epoch 1790–1830* Major settlement on Atlantic coast; few inland trade centres. Small hinterlands; orientation to Europe; boom cities on inland waterways; no primate metropolis. |
| | *Test productivity and harvest natural products* Periodic staple production: fish, timber, furs to old country | | |
| | *Initial settlement at points of attachment* Settlers produce and export staples and consume manufactured goods from old country. | *Committed extractive state* Staple agriculture, settled inshore fishing, sawn lumber, stock breeding, mining. Older settlements extend commercial links to hinterland; rise of small urban places. | *Iron horse epoch 1830–1870* Regional rail networks converge at major ports on inland waterways, follow original water-routes. Rapid increase in low level urban centres; emergence of national transportation system and first order metropolis at New York. |
| | *Development of depots of staple collection* Settlements inland along water routes from points of attachment develop to collect staples from hinterlands. | *Processing economy* Flour milling, tanning, canning, box and shingle mills, smelting. Older centres control wide hinterlands, transport system, finance, investment, industry. Incipient manufacturing centres appear in hinterlands. | *Steel-rail epoch 1870–1920* Opening and commercialization of western resources and agriculture. Centralization of industry in old metropolitan areas; decline of some manufacturing centres at old water power sites; increase in number of low order cities. |
| | *Entrepôts of wholesaling* Depots become entrepôts and ultimately manufacturing cities. Linear settlement pattern. Central places develop in agricultural hinterlands. | *Regenerative stage* Frontier passed—local service activities, industrial production importation of material to process locally. Regional metropolitan development now organizing systems of urban places in hinterlands. | *Auto-air-amenity epoch 1920–* Regional and metropolitan dispersal; satellite cities, dense highway network; boom centres in south and southwest; large old places decentralize; suburban sprawl. |

| Scale<br>Author | Regional: Frontier to Development of a Settlement System<br>Charles F.J. Whebell | <br>Edward K. Muller | <br>Martyn J. Bowden et. al. |
|---|---|---|---|
| Periods and major characteristics | Corridor theory of urban systems<br><br>*Subsistence agriculture*<br>Migrants assess natural hazards and settle accessible areas; waterways are routes of ingress; little trade; subsistence production of timber, tanbark, furs. Urban places on main routes handle immigrants, judicial, administrative functions.<br><br>*Commercial agriculture*<br>Government promotes settlement; transport improvements, more social and economic interaction; capital accumulation, entrepreneurial activity. Settlement beyond river valleys; large urban places with banks, political power, provide conditions for railroad building.<br><br>*Railway period*<br>Local lines built, then amalgamated into regional or national networks as capital becomes available. Factory development in places with capital and rail service; upward growth spiral for older places.<br><br>*Automobile era*<br>Road system links major places on railways and extends into hinterlands. Metropolitanization begins in "senior towns."<br><br>*Metropolitanism*<br>Metropolitan centres and major throughways greatly increase metropolitan activities. Sorting of places analogous to effect of railway; fewer large metropolitan centres dominate. | Model of selective urban growth<br><br>*Pioneer periphery*<br>Subsistence agriculture, communication along natural routes; low population densities, little purchasing power or inter-regional trade. Urban growth at main transportation nodes to handle external trade relations, serve immigrants and produce some consumer goods. Some regional entrepôt development. Three level urban hierarchy develops.<br><br>*Specialized periphery*<br>Improvement in transportation; cash crop specialization. Rise of manufacturing at entrepôts; increased nodality of original places, some new nodes develop. Access and manufacturing increase importance of centres in older settled regions. Primary staple production and export.<br><br>*Transitional periphery*<br>Railways integrate region into continental economy. Improved staple export position. Structure of urban system reinforced by railway net. Some regional centres gain markets; old major places shift from commercial functions to manufacturing for regional markets. | Competition and settlement pattern<br><br>*Initial sorting*<br>Emergence of local centres of manufacturing and milling. Local regionalization of trade.<br><br>*Delineation of major regions*<br>Influence of major places expanded. Initial interaction of hinterlands followed by separation as competition leads to contraction.<br><br>*Subregional superimposition and establishment of ranking*<br>Emergence of intermediate centres at peripheries of major hinterlands and within larger hinterlands. Major regional centres increase in rank; extended spheres of influence and integration of subregional hinterland. Three level urban hierarchy develops. |

| Scale | Local: Frontier to Development of a Settlement System | | |
|---|---|---|---|
| Author | John C. Hudson | Robert D. Mitchell | Roderick D. McKenzie |
| Periods and major characteristics | Location theory for rural settlement | Developing frontier | Settlement eras |
| | *Colonization*<br>Settlers move into areas beyond original settlement as improving technology enable them to survive in a new area. | *Level 1*<br>Unspecialized farming and local commercialism. | *Pioneer settlement 1850–1880*<br>Water transportation and rim settlement. Mills formed nuclei of settlement; villages were creation of distant economic needs. |
| | *Spread*<br>Settlers fill up new area; population density increases. Colonization tends to produce uniformly spaced farms as settlers move in. | *Level 2*<br>Increasing commercialism and low order urbanization. Agricultural specialization and expansion of urban trade and manufacturing. | *Aggregation and urbanization 1880–1910*<br>Early railway-induced economic boom; concentration of population in urban places. Commercial agriculture and local manufacturing developed. |
| | *Competition*<br>An area fills up, agricultural prices determine minimum size of viable farm. Small farms are amalgamated into larger holdings. Urban centres compete for hinterland control. Large places often take over trade of smaller ones; small places decline. | *Level 3*<br>Centralization of local manufacturing and services. Agricultural regionalization; intensification of external contacts. | *Centralization and metropolitanism 1910–*<br>Increasing dominance of regional metropolis; decline of small urban centres. Integration of urban system through motor transport. |

SOURCE: Bouchert, "American Metropolitan Evolution"; Bowden, Bruce and LaRose, "The Development"; Careless, "Metropolis and Region"; Hudson, "A Location Theory"; McKenzie, "Ecological Succession"; Mitchell, "Shenandoah Valley Frontier"; Muller, "Regional Urbanization"; Vance, *The Merchant's World*, 148–67; Whebell, "Corridors."

For Canada, the theme of metropolitanism developed by Maurice Careless best exemplifies the process of urban systems development at a general level.[7] He suggested that the urban outpost was often at the cutting edge of the frontier as it projected trade, control, and settlement outward into the landscape. In his scheme, "metropolitan cities simply represent the top level of urban communities in interaction with their supporting regions. They may, of course, have numbers of lesser cities and towns in their own broad hinterlands, but beneath the preeminent metropolitan centers, these subordinate places have functioned within a similar pattern of relationships on a more limited and localized scale."[8] Careless went on to suggest that Canadian metropolitan centres controlled far-distant staple-producing areas "that were but thinly occupied and at rudimentary frontier stage of growth."[9] In his opinion, this metropolitan-hinterland analysis is much more applicable to Canada than the central place theory of Walter Christaller. In his refutation of Christaller's scheme as it relates to Canada, Careless concurred with James E. Vance who proposed a "mercantile model" of North American settlement (Table 1). In this model, Vance emphasized the critical importance of the wholesale function of settlements established inland from major ports. These "depots of staple collection" developed along major water routes to the interior to supply the wholesale merchants trading back to the ports and the mother country. As the system matured, "depots" eventually became "entrepôt cities" and ultimately manufacturing centres. He recognized the emergence of a central place hierarchy much later, after land had been cleared and farming began around settlements originally fostered by long-distance trading ties. According to Careless, "Vance's entrepôt city sounds a good deal like the commercial metropolis," but his theory "does not adequately examine the hinterland side of the rural-urban complex which is of importance in Canada."[10]

Closer to the scale of our case study is an important but neglected article by Charles F.J. Whebell.[11] In many respects, Whebell anticipated Vance's mercantile model and applied it successfully to the settlement of southwestern Ontario. Perhaps the two similar schemes were conceived in a parallel and independent process, since neither refers to the other.

Whebell proposed a "corridor theory of urban systems" which recognized: (1) the irregularity of the earth's physical surface and the irregular distributions of resources including fertile land; (2) the diffusion of technological and organizational innovations from a few points of origin at varying rates; and (3) that human achievement and decision making generally follow the principle of least effort, with the corollary of the inertia of fixed capital and socioeconomic structure. From these postulates he explained New World settlement as a process by which people and innovations moved inland along major transport corridors (usually waterways) to establish a linear series of settlements initially concerned with administration rather than manufacturing and commerce. Agriculture was initiated in the areas with good land most accessible to potential markets. During the five major settlement periods

(Table 1), places on the original corridors having initial advantages attracted technological and organizational innovations first, thereby enhancing their prosperity and influence. After initial settlement along the corridors, "inertia" of capital, power, and influence controlled subsequent development. Places having the initial advantage of early development and accessibility remained at or near the top of the urban hierarchy.

Avery Guest has examined regional urban growth at a scale even closer to that of our study area. He replicated Roderick McKenzie's early analysis of the effects of changing transport upon settlements in the Puget Sound area of Washington.[12] As suggested by Whebell's theory, Guest found remarkable stability in the ranks of urban places through time. Even the introduction of the car did not have the major effects on settlement growth anticipated by McKenzie. By the time motor transport was widely adopted, large places already on the railway network had attracted highways and perpetuated the pattern established earlier. Guest argued that places had more control over their own destinies in the early period when they could compete for railways and for control of hinterlands. In the auto era, the metropolis became the principal focus of economic life for the whole region as increased travel speeds enabled it to dominate a more extensive hinterland than was possible earlier. The effects of inertia proposed by Whebell were clearly evident in Guest's study area.

A number of important factors are implicit or explicit in most of the studies reviewed above. They include metropolitan–hinterland interaction; long-distance stimulus of local settlement; initial advantage and historical inertia; local political and entrepreneurial initiative; competition and evolution of a settlement system; and technological innovation in transportation and agriculture. Each will be considered in the following case study of a regional urban system small enough to be easily comprehended, yet complex enough to respond to many of the forces identified elsewhere at regional or even national scales.

## The Study Area

One might have chosen an arbitrarily defined study area such as Wellington County (Guelph is the county seat) or a group of townships for this research. The area used here is also arbitrarily chosen, but for reasons other than the ease of data collection provided by political divisions. In 1970 the Guelph Central Place System was defined using a method developed by John Marshall (Map 1).[13] In this context, a central place is any settlement that provides goods and services to persons living outside its borders; purely residential nucleations are therefore excluded from consideration. The study area contains all centres whose functional complexity is now affected more by the central city (Guelph) than by any of its major competitive centres. The

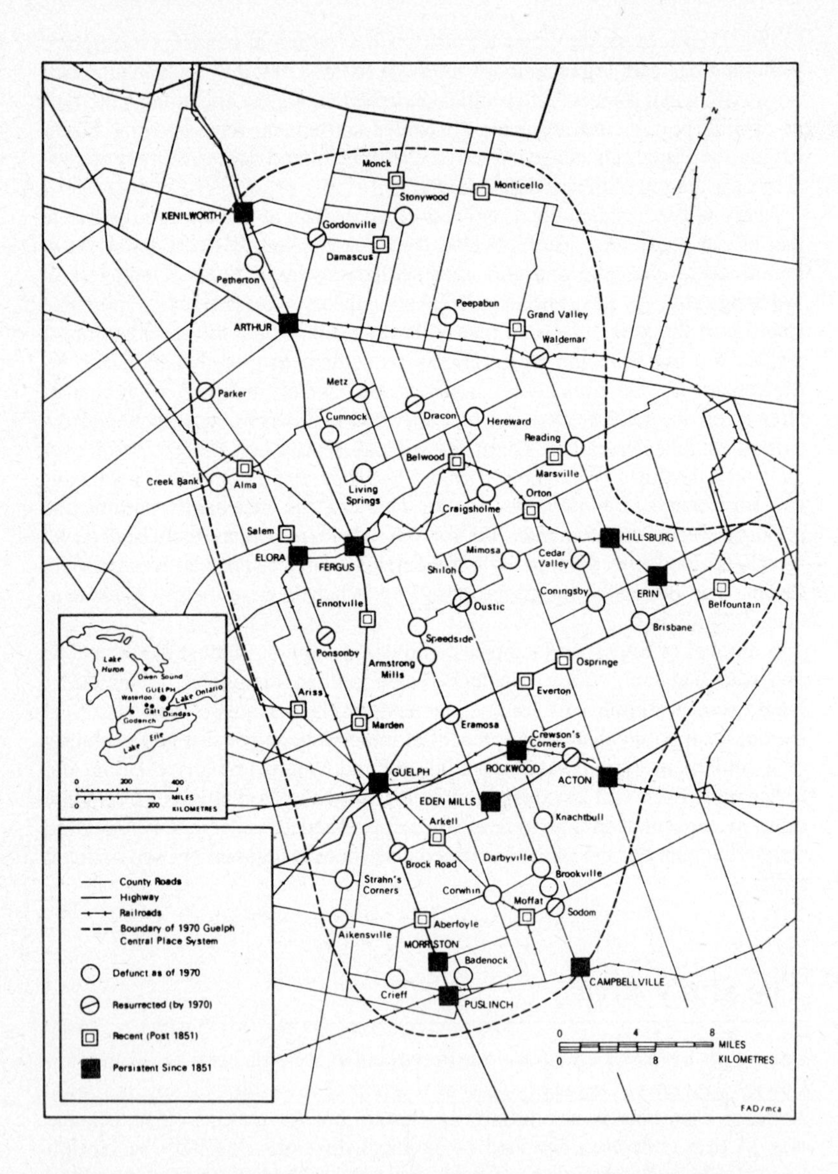


**MAP 1** *All Central Places That Have Existed within the Boundary of the 1970 Guelph Central Place System, 1851–1970*

system is defined by the interrelationships among the settlements in it, rather than on the basis of a previously selected boundary.

The use of a contemporary central place system for historical research is appropriate for several reasons. First, it enables us to explore temporal relationships within an area that now has functional, rather than merely political, coherence. Second, it encompasses an area large enough to contain all settlements that could conceivably have had any close trade links with Guelph in the past. Given the primitive transport technology of the pre-car and pre-rail eras, it is highly unlikely that any settlement not now part of the Guelph Central Place System would have been closely linked to Guelph in the past. Work by Marshall has shown conclusively that no central place systems existed in the "Queen's Bush" (now Grey and most of Bruce County) of Ontario before the use of the automobile became widespread. He suggested that "Central places appear to be organized into small and structurally distinct local hierarchies."[14] Poor roads and primitive transport technology severely limited the kind of interaction necessary to large hinterlands and the formation of major central place systems in Ontario before highway improvements occurred. The use of the area of the 1970 Guelph Central Place System as a laboratory in which to study the evolution of settlements makes no assumption that a central place system existed there before 1970.

Agriculture has been important in the vicinity of Guelph since its initial settlement in the late 1820s.[15] Urban places there have always existed principally as central places rather than as manufacturing, resort, or otherwise specialized settlements. Even now, only Guelph, Acton, and Fergus have well-established non-central place activities such as manufacturing and institutions (Map 1).[16] Most of these enterprises were established after 1845 when the urbanization and industrialization of southern Ontario accelerated.[17]

# Methods

The importance of settlements is measured through a comparison of the number of functions and establishments found in each period. A function is a distinct type of retail or service business, while an establishment is the building where such a business is conducted. A combined general store and grist mill would be one establishment with two functions. Early Ontario towns had many multifunctional establishments, necessitating consideration of both the number of functions and establishments to give a true picture of their importance. Here both are tabulated.

Dun and Bradstreet Reference Books provided data for all years considered except 1851 when the Canada Directory was used.[18] Unfortunately, some service functions such as medical doctor, lawyer, barber, and similar professions are not listed by Dun and Bradstreet. Since there was no comparable source for these activities in the early years, they were excluded.

Many early businesses such as cooper, tanner, miller, carriage maker or blacksmith combined retail, service, and industrial functions, and they have been included despite the fact that they had an industrial as well as service/retail component. With the proviso noted above, lists of all central place functions (providing goods or services to consumers) and establishments for each settlement at each time period were extracted from the directories. The choice of establishment total for designations such as town or village on maps is based on previous studies of central places in Ontario.[19]

Table 2 summarizes the growth and development of the study area from 1851 to 1970. During this period, 16 original settlements were joined by others to reach a total of 63 in 1891. By the end of our study period, however, only 45 central places remained. This and the changes in numbers of functions, establishments, and ratios noted on Table 2 can only be explained by the detailed historical analysis to follow.

## Early Settlement

Settlement in the Guelph area was promoted by the Canada Company which was established in 1826 to dispose of Crown Lands. In 1827, John Galt, a commissioner of the Canada Company, founded Guelph as his headquarters; an administrative centre to be situated conveniently between the company's large Huron Tract to the west and the capital Toronto. Guelph was laid out at the confluence of the Speed and Eramosa Rivers on a site at the head of navigation on the Speed where several falls provided excellent sources of power. Galt intended to insure the success of this new urban centre by providing an infrastructure before settlers arrived. In addition to pouring capital and tradesmen into the new town, he engaged in a major program of road building to link the settlement to the outside world and to encourage agricultural development in the nearby townships. By 1832 his workers had opened roads to Dundas at the head of Lake Ontario, to Waterloo, and to Owen Sound on Georgian Bay (Map 2).[20] Although but primitive tracks through the forest, these links provided access to the fledgling community and the potential to establish trade associations as the area developed. Early progress was rapid, and by 1832 Guelph Township had a population of over 700, about 400 of whom lived in the new town.[21] By 1843 Guelph has grown to 700 people and had a wide range of trades and shops including four distillers, three bakers, two saddlers, a coach maker, four wheelwrights, six blacksmiths, a tinker, three butchers, two coopers, two tanners, a watch maker, 20 carpenters, and 42 tradesmen.[22] Much of this early success was the direct result of Galt's carefully implemented economic planning.[23]

Other major places were established within a few years of Guelph's start, all at dam sites which supplied power for their mills. Erin was founded in 1824, Elora in 1832, Fergus in 1934, Acton in 1835, and Arthur in 1841.[24] By

**TABLE 2** *Study Area: 1851–1970*

| Year | 1851 | 1864 | 1871 | 1881 | 1891 | 1901 | 1911 | 1921 | 1931 | 1941 | 1951 | 1961 | 1970 |
|---|---|---|---|---|---|---|---|---|---|---|---|---|---|
| Number of central places | 16 | 31 | 41 | 62 | 63 | 61 | 62 | 42 | 37 | 38 | 35 | 34 | 45 |
| Population of study area | 21 341[a] | 49 200[b] | 56 324 | 63 515 | 57 648 | 54 397 | 54 930 | 54 181 | 57 145 | 59 428 | 65 434 | 83 147 | 97 508 |
| Number of establishments | 198 | 437 | 629 | 888 | 991 | 905 | 901 | 851 | 1005 | 918 | 1063 | 1081 | 1376 |
| Number of functions | 38 | 55 | 56 | 67 | 64 | 74 | 70 | 70 | 76 | 64 | 71 | 79 | 90 |
| Number of establishments per central place | 11.6 | 11.9 | 15.3 | 14.3 | 15.7 | 14.8 | 14.5 | 20.3 | 27.2 | 24.2 | 30.4 | 31.8 | 30.5 |
| Number of functions per central place | 2.4 | 1.8 | 1.4 | 1.1 | 1.0 | 1.2 | 1.1 | 1.7 | 2.1 | 1.7 | 2.0 | 2.3 | 2.0 |

SOURCE: *Upper Canada Personal Census by Origin*, 1861; *Census of Canada*, 1871–1970; Dun and Bradstreet of Canada Ltd., *Reference Book* (Toronto, 1864–1970); R.W. Mackay, *Canada Directory* (Montreal, 1851).

NOTE: [a] Because of slightly different definitions in the Census before 1871, data are for an area somewhat larger than the study area.
[b] Population for 1861. Area as above.

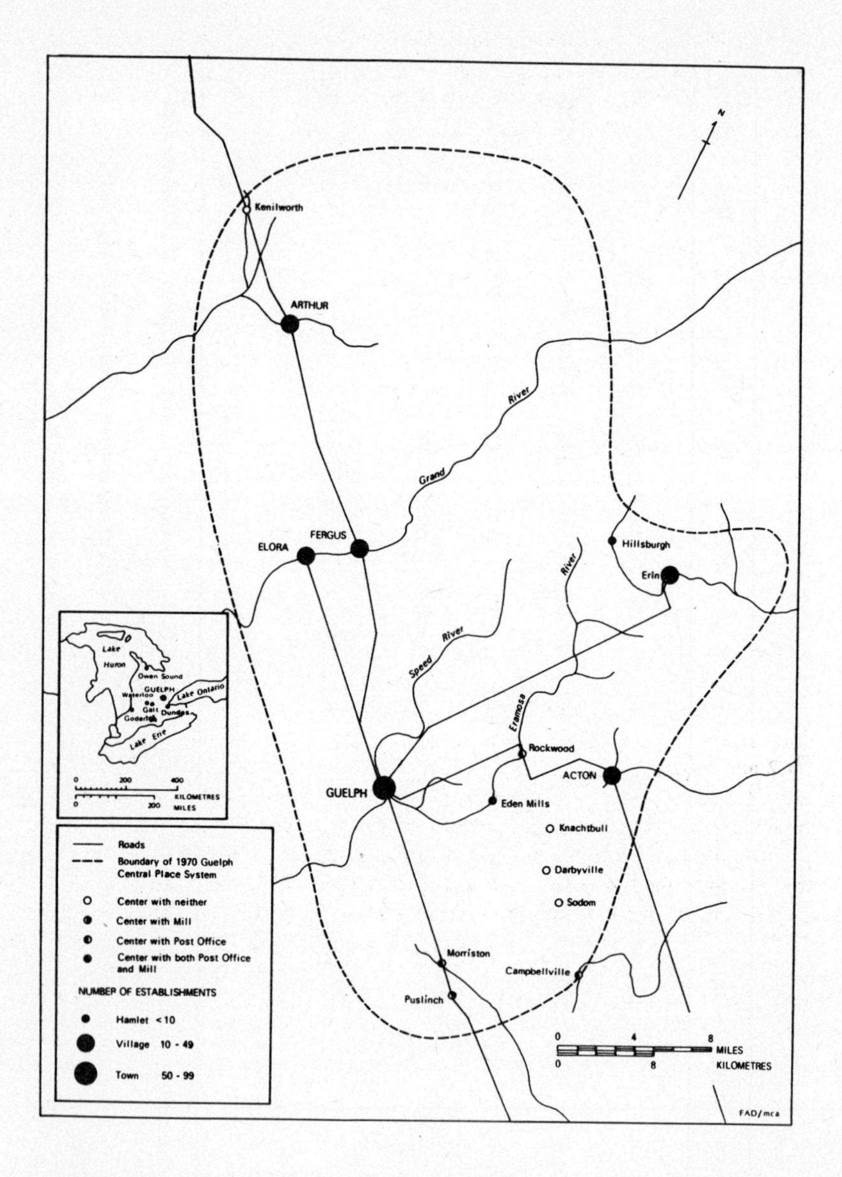


**MAP 2** *Central Places in the Study Area, 1851*

the late 1840s all had several mills, general stores, blacksmith shops, and churches. By the Census Year of 1851 each had a post office as well.[25]

Every one of these places was established at a dam where mills were built. Their initial function was industrial/service, for they transformed local raw materials (grain, logs, wool) into partially finished products such as flour, timber, or woollens. They were linked to each other by roads which had been built deliberately to promote the sale and settlement of land in the area. These widely spaced towns (19 to 40 kilometres apart; Map 2) initially attracted farmers from the immediate vicinity to their mills. Given the very slow travel speeds by horse and wagon (3.2 to 4.8 kilometres per hour), a trip to the mill often necessitated an overnight stay. Hence hotels and taverns were established, and then general stores, tanners, wagon makers, and other functions which took advantage of customers originally attracted to the mills. As time passed, an increasing number of consumer-oriented goods and services became available at what were originally "industrial" mill sites. Given the primitive state of early roads cut through the bush, and transport only by foot or animal, the first settlements served a limited and almost exclusive hinterland. Spelt has suggested that the maximum trade radius in the era was approximately 7.2 kilometers.[26] Consequently, only Elora and Fergus at 4.8 kilometres apart would have been major competitors in the early period of settlement (Map 2).

The early concentration of settlements of the southeastern part of the area occurred because settlers generally arrived from Lake Ontario along the Brock road which Galt's men had cleared, and encountered that area first (Map 2). The two largest places in 1851 were Guelph and Fergus having, respectively, 37.2 and 18.4 per cent of the establishments in the area (Table 3). The four largest centres (25 per cent of the total) included 77 per cent of all business establishments. The six largest settlements (37.5 per cent) contained about 90 per cent of establishments and had the greatest range of functions as well. On the average, the remaining 10 settlements (62.5 per cent) had only 1.2 establishments each. In most of these places the mill was still the only business. Settlements in the area were now clearly differentiated by size and functions with Guelph far in the lead (Table 3). Although it experienced subsequent economic problems, the foundation laid by Galt and the Canada Company has enabled Guelph to remain at the top of the local urban hierarchy to the present day.

## Railways and Urban Growth

Railway service was very important to the growth of settlements in the Guelph area (Map 3). In many, the coming of the railway was no accident as the deliberate action of groups or individuals often made the difference between railway-induced development or slow stagnation. Railway financing in Ontario between 1850 and 1881 depended heavily upon grants from municipalities competing for their services.[27] It was logical that the largest towns of the day could afford the most, and therefore attracted railway service first.

**TABLE 3** *Number of Settlements, Functions and Establishments in the Study Area, 1851*

| | | | Percentage of: | |
|---|---|---|---|---|
| Settlement | No. of functions | No. of establishments | Functions | Establishments |
| Guelph | 28 | 73 | 23.5 | 37.2 |
| Fergus | 22 | 36 | 18.5 | 18.4 |
| Elora | 18 | 29 | 15.1 | 14.7 |
| Acton | 12 | 14 | 10.1 | 7.1 |
| Arthur | 10 | 13 | 8.4 | 6.6 |
| Erin | 9 | 10 | 7.6 | 5.0 |
| Rockwood | 3 | 4 | 2.5 | 2.0 |
| Knachtbull | 3 | 4 | 2.5 | 2.0 |
| Campbellville | 3 | 3 | 2.5 | 1.5 |
| Sodom | 3 | 3 | 2.5 | 1.5 |
| Eden Mills | 2 | 2 | 1.7 | 1.0 |
| Morriston | 2 | 2 | 1.7 | 1.0 |
| Hillsburgh | 1 | 1 | 0.8 | 0.5 |
| Kenilworth | 1 | 1 | 0.8 | 0.5 |
| Puslinch | 1 | 1 | 0.8 | 0.5 |
| Darbyville | 1 | 1 | 0.8 | 0.5 |
| Total | 119 | 197 | 100.0 | 100.0 |

SOURCE: R.W. Mackay, *Canada Directory* (Montreal, 1851).

Guelph was in the forefront as its leading citizens promoted the building of a rail line to link it with Toronto. They persuaded the Municipal Council to purchase shares worth £25 000 in the proposed Toronto–Guelph Railroad which was taken over by the Grand Trunk Railway and opened to Guelph in 1856.[28] Not satisfied with this accomplishment, Guelph businessmen next took a hand in promoting the Galt and Guelph Railway to offset Galt's advantage as the northern terminus of the Great Western. Eventually the City of Guelph loaned the new railway £20 000 and it was opened to Guelph in 1857.[29] This placed Guelph at the northern extremity of the Great Western which took over the line in 1869.[30] After both routes were opened, Guelph experienced a boom as all freight and produce from the north passed through it to Toronto and Hamilton "making the Guelph market and stores exceedingly busy."[31]

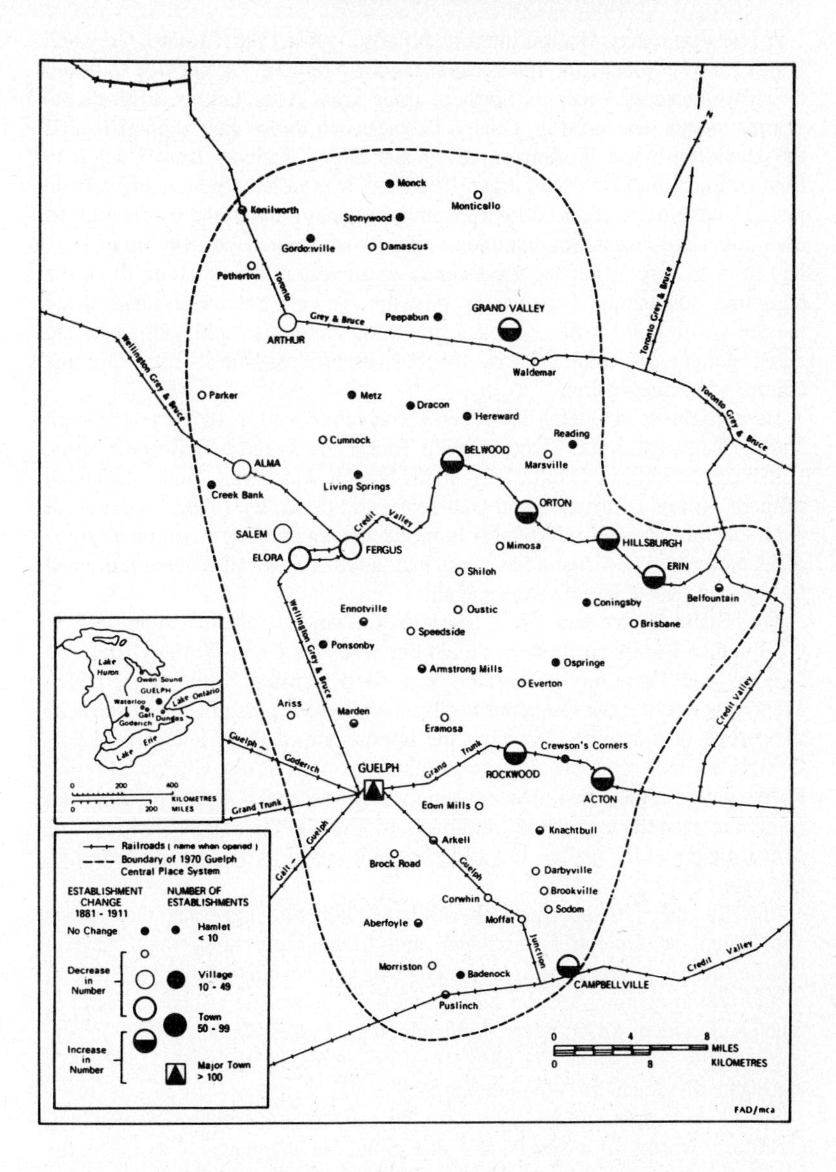


**MAP 3** *Changes in Numbers of Establishments in Central Places in the Study Area, 1881–1911*

A few years later, Guelph interests bitterly opposed the Toronto, Grey and Bruce Railway planned to run north of the town through Orangeville to Owen Sound to truncate Guelph's northern trade area. After failing to block the charter of this new railway, Guelph businessmen threw their support behind the Hamilton-based Wellington, Grey and Bruce Railway from Guelph to Southampton via Elora and Fergus. The rival lines were both built and opened in 1871 but Guelph reduced losses from its northern hinterland by creating its own direct rail link to Southampton. "The Town's whole strategy up to 1871 had been to make itself the great centre of attraction and radiation to all the adjoining townships, and to do this the Town's ratepayers had taxed themselves to build roads, railways, and a Market House, and had, again and again, fought off challenges by the businessmen of other centres for the control of its market area."[32]

Another threat to Guelph's prosperity was introduced in 1873 by the Credit Valley Railway to link Toronto with Elora, via Fergus, Belwood, Orton, Hillsburgh, and Erin (Map 3). Its main branch which ran south of Guelph through Milton, Morriston, and Galt began to operate by 1879.[33] It detracted from Guelph's former rail monopoly in the area and helped to stimulate some of its northern rivals. Just a few years later another new rail scheme prompted Guelph to take the initiative once again.

The Grand Trunk and Great Western Railways amalgamated in 1882.[34] Guelph then lost its position on a main line when the Great Western Route via London and Hamilton to Toronto was so designated. This route, which eventually became the Canadian Pacific main line, bypassed Guelph some 20 kilometres to the south. Knowing the importance of main line rail service, Guelph Council and businessmen quickly promoted the Guelph Junction Railway to join the new line near Campbellville (Map 3). Again, political and economic leaders in Guelph combined to finance the railway which was owned by the municipality. It was completed, leased to the Canadian Pacific, and opened in 1888.[35]

Initially the Guelph Junction Railway did not generate the profits anticipated, so Guelph businessmen and Council pressured the Canadian Pacific railway to extend it to Goderich. This was accomplished by 1906 and, in addition to opening a wider hinterland, the line became a financial asset to Guelph. Between 1890, when dividends were first declared, and 1926, the municipality realized $1 171 889[91] from its interest in the railway. By 1963, aggregate dividends had amounted to $2 995 803.[36]

Spelt's comment on the effect of the railway upon towns in southern Ontario is worthy of assessment at this point. He stated that: "as far as the urban centres were concerned, the railway was a matter of growth or decline...in general the villages and small towns which by this time had not become important enough or fortunate enough to attract a railway and which remained dependent on roads were doomed."[37] By 1881 all major railway construction in the Guelph area had ended, and enough time had passed for its effect on the settlements to be clear. An examination of changes in the study area between 1851 and 1881 provides evidence with which to test Spelt's assertion (Table 4, Map 3).

The places which were largest in 1851 had all attracted the railway before 1881. This was no accident as their sinuous routes reflect the care that railway builders took to satisfy settlements competing and paying for their services between 1851 and 1881. Of the 62 central places in 1881, 16 had existed before the railways' arrival, 10 developed with railway stimulus, and 36 were established without the benefit of the railway. Eleven of the original 16 settlements (68.8 per cent) had attracted railway service by 1881.

The data above indicate that the building of the railway had little to do with the foundation of the majority of settlements appearing between 1851 and 1881. But it did make the area easily accessible to settlers coming from the east. Indeed, many of the new places were the result of immigration and local population growth between 1851 and 1881. During that 30-year period, the number of people in the area almost tripled (Table 2).

If increasing population was the major factor accounting for the proliferation of places between 1851 and 1881, what was the effect (if any) of the railway upon the provision of goods and services there? The most striking fact is the major increase in the number of functions and establishments in the centres that existed in 1851 and had attracted the railway by 1881 (Table 4). The 252 per cent increase in establishments in these places accounted for fully 67 per cent of the total increase in the number of establishments in the area between 1851 and 1881. There was a 138 per cent increase in functions in the same 11 places. In contrast, new places on the railway by 1881 accounted for only 7.8 per cent of the establishment increase between 1851 and 12.9 per cent of the increase in functions. The five 1851 centres not on the railway by 1881 together added only 11 new establishments or 1.6 per cent of the total increase between 1851 and 1881, and only 0.3 per cent of the increase in functions. They were not all "doomed" as suggested by Spelt, but certainly did not share the prosperity enjoyed by their counterparts that did attract the railway. In fact, only 2 of the original 1851 settlements, Darbyville and Knachtbull, failed to survive as central places until 1970. The great proliferation of establishments in the original 11 places that attracted the railway emphasizes their increasing importance as centres of comparison shopping and domination of the local urban hierarchy (Maps 3 and 4).

An examination of the provision of some key goods and services in 1851 and 1881 sheds light upon the economic changes between those dates (Table 5). In 1851, mills were found in 14 of the 16 settlements (87.5 per cent). By 1881 only 25 of 62, or about 40 per cent, of the settlements had a mill as the provision of other services had surpassed the importance of milling as a settlement forming factor. By 1881, post offices were found in 95 per cent of settlements, and general stores in 69 per cent. Blacksmiths, shoemakers, and grocery stores were considerably more ubiquitous in 1881 than in 1851. On the other hand, tailors and bakeries, although more numerous in 1881, were found in a lower percentage of settlements than in 1851. Such

**TABLE 4** *Changes in Numbers of Functions and Establishments in Study Area by Railway Status of Settlement, 1851 and 1881*

| Settlement category | No. of places | Number of Fun. 1851 | Number of Est. 1851 | Number of Fun. 1881 | Number of Est. 1881 | Change in no. of Fun. 1851–1881 | Change in no. of Est. 1851–1881 | Percentage of Fun. in study area 1851 | Percentage of Est. in study area 1851 | Percentage of Fun. in study area 1881 | Percentage of Est. in study area 1881 | Percentage of increase in Fun. 1851–1881 | Percentage of increase in Est. 1851–1881 |
|---|---|---|---|---|---|---|---|---|---|---|---|---|---|
| 1851 settlements without railway by 1881 | 5 | 10 | 13 | 11 | 24 | +1 | +11 | 8.4 | 6.5 | 2.4 | 2.7 | 0.3 | 1.6 |
| 1851 settlements attracting railway by 1881 | 11 | 109 | 185 | 260 | 653 | +151 | +468 | 91.6 | 93.5 | 56.6 | 73.5 | 44.4 | 67.8 |
| Post 1851 settlements on railway by 1881 | 10 | 0 | 0 | 44 | 54 | +44 | +54 | 0 | 0 | 9.6 | 6.1 | 12.9 | 7.8 |
| Post 1851 settlements without railway by 1881 | 36 | 0 | 0 | 144 | 157 | +144 | +157 | 0 | 0 | 31.4 | 17.7 | 42.4 | 22.8 |
| Totals | 62 | 119 | 198 | 459 | 888 | +340 | +690 | 100.0 | 100.0 | 100.0 | 100.0 | 100.0 | 100.0 |

SOURCE: Calculated by the author.

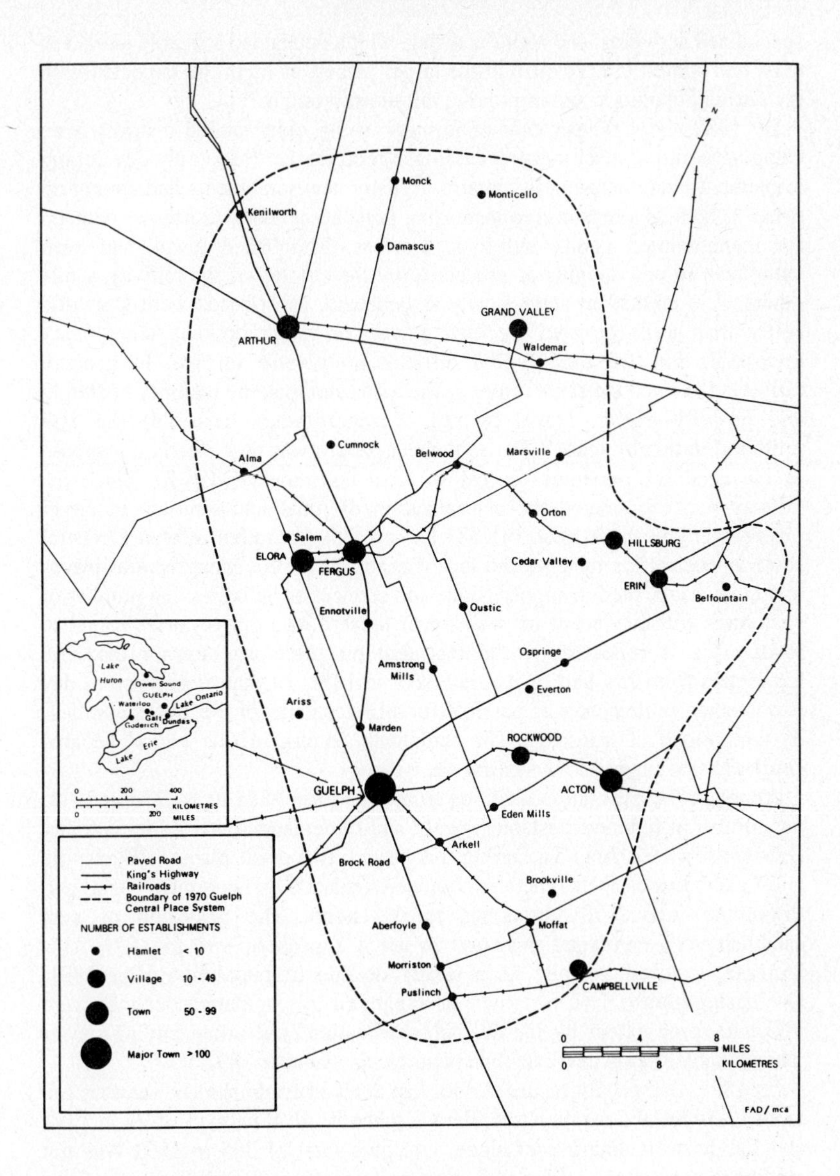


**MAP 4** *Central Places in the Study Area, 1941*

specialized activities, and manufacturing, which demanded a sizable market to exist had started to centralize in the larger places, as might be expected with increasing population and improving rail transportation.

By 1880 about 90 per cent of farmers in the older settled districts were using agricultural machinery, providing a good market for rapidly developing implement manufacturing in Ontario.[38] Many new settlements had sprung up (Map 3) both as a response to increasing population and to consumer demand for manufactured goods and local services. Established towns had been stimulated to new heights of prosperity by the coming of the railway, while others were created to serve newly settled land. Most roads were still little better than trails covered by dirt, gravel, or rough broken stone, many impassible for two months and difficult to traverse in five. In general, railways followed the same routes as the roads and took the majority of freight and intercity traffic. Travel by rail or water (where possible) was still preferred to that by road.[39] The settlement pattern was now clearly a response to the need for maximum access to local consumers (Map 3). Since the railway had encouraged the centralization of mills and industry in larger places, many of the hamlets of 1881 had no mill, but rather offered a general store or post office to serve the local farmer (Table 5). Many central places had to be established to supply goods and services to an increasing number of customers still dependent on walking or horse-drawn conveyances to get to town. This is reflected by the fact that no place was further than 5.6 kilometres from any part of its hinterland in 1881. At that time, a return day trip to some settlement was possible for all inhabitants of the area, regardless of their mode of transport. The settlement pattern in this period became similar to that suggested by central place theory.

Although the population declined from 63 515 in 1881 to 54 930 in 1911, the number of functions, establishments, and settlements remained remarkably constant (Table 2, Map 3). During this period, two small places (Aikensville and Crieff) lost all their functions, but were replaced by two others (Ariss and Ennotville) about 20 kilometres to the north. The provision of new establishments continued unabated to reach a peak of 991 in 1891. This increase occurred in spite of a steady decline in population after 1881. Decreasing numbers of customers as suggested by population declines were offset to some extent by inertia, industrialization, and urban buying power which enabled some new establishments to survive after 1891.

By 1891, Guelph, Elora, and Arthur had attained establishment numbers not to be exceeded for many years. Elora reached its all-time high of 72 in 1891 and has been declining ever since. Guelph's total of 305 in 1891 was not surpassed until 1931; Arthur's 90 stood as its peak until 1961. Fergus attained 84 establishments in 1901, a number not exceeded there until 1970. The minor settlements that survived until 1970 displayed similar fluctuations, albeit of a smaller magnitude. During the 1881–1911 period, Grand Valley became the second most important service centre (after Arthur) in the northern third of the area (Map 3). Its establishment total increased from 14 to 43 in the 30-year

**TABLE 5** *Distribution of Most Common Functions, 1851 and 1881*

| | 1851 | | | 1881 | | |
|---|---|---|---|---|---|---|
| Function | Number of establishments | Number of places with function | Percentage of places with function | Number of establishments | Number of places with function | Percentage of places with function |
| General store | 30 | 10 | 62.5 | 84 | 43 | 69.4 |
| Post office | 12 | 12 | 75.0 | 59 | 59 | 95.2 |
| Tailor | 12 | 5 | 31.3 | 31 | 11 | 17.7 |
| Grist mill | 11 | 8 | 68.8 | 10 | 8 | 16.1 |
| Hotel | 11 | 5 | 31.3 | 54 | 21 | 33.9 |
| Tavern | 10 | 5 | 31.3 | 22 | 16 | 25.8 |
| Blacksmith | 9 | 7 | 43.8 | 81 | 41 | 66.1 |
| Grocery store | 9 | 2 | 12.5 | 77 | 14 | 22.6 |
| Sawmill | 6 | 6 | 37.5 | 19 | 17 | 27.4 |
| Wagon maker | 6 | 5 | 31.3 | 32 | 20 | 32.3 |
| Footwear/shoemaker | 6 | 3 | 18.8 | 59 | 18 | 29.0 |
| Harness maker | 5 | 3 | 18.8 | 11 | 9 | 14.5 |
| Bakery | 4 | 4 | 25.0 | 19 | 9 | 14.5 |
| Cooper | 3 | 2 | 12.5 | 12 | 10 | 16.1 |

SOURCE: R.W. Mackay, *Canada Directory* (Montreal, 1851); Dun and Bradstreet of Canada Ltd., *Reference Book* (Toronto, 1881).

period under discussion. Elora and Fergus began to suffer from their mutual proximity as Fergus lost 20 establishments and Elora 23 by 1911. The local population was inadequate to support two major settlements so close together. A few kilometres further south, Guelph increased its share by 29 establishments by the end of these three decades. Slow stagnation and moderate centralization of services were the major processes between 1881 and 1911 as the full effects of the completed railway system were felt (Map 3). More dramatic changes occurred with the coming of the automobile after 1911.

## Centralization 1911–1941

Depression, war, and highway improvement all affected settlements between 1911 and 1941. Major local road improvements were demanded by farmers who owned more than a third of Ontario's 182 000 passenger vehicles by 1922. At the same time, city people insisted on better provincial highways to connect the larger places. A major road program resulted and produced 400 miles of new provincial highways and improvement of much of the rural system within three years.[40] The number of cars in Ontario increased from 1530 in 1907 to 114 376 in 1918 and to over 300 000 by 1926.[41] In this period, centres grew if they enjoyed good road access, but eight settlements on the railway lost service establishments. The great depression contributed to a decline of establishments from 1005 in 1931 to 918 in 1941. The variety of functions in the area dropped from 76 to 64 in the same period as saddlers, tanners, drovers, brewers, carriage works, sewing machine agents, and similar enterprises disappeared. The number of places with one or more functions fell from 62 to 38 between 1911 and 1941, while the area's population rose slowly from 54 930 to 59 428.

Before the car became widely available, and before roads were good enough to encourage extensive motoring, most central places served a small local hinterland. Few of them had much interaction with Guelph or with other large centres except by rail which served their manufacturing firms and agricultural export trade.[42] With the increasing mobility provided by the car after the major road building and improvements, it became possible for shoppers to bypass small local centres and seek more variety in the major places 19 to 23 kilometres apart. By 1930, most towns and villages were joined by paved roads.[43] As transportation improved, the smallest settlements lost their one or two establishments as shoppers bypassed them going to the newly accessible local town. In addition, the full effects of rural mail delivery, introduced in 1908, had been felt.[44] General stores lost much of their business after they ceased to be postal pick-up centres for the surrounding rural hinterland and catalogues began to offer a wide variety of goods by mail from Toronto. Well before 1941 many general stores closed for good. The disappearance of all central place functions in 24 of the smallest settlements between 1911 and 1941 clearly reflects the new transport realities and the added choice open to any rural dweller with a car (Map 4).

The largest places became increasingly important as providers of goods and services between 1911 and 1941 (Table 6). In 1941, Guelph had 44.6 per cent of all establishments in the study area and Fergus had 8.3. The addition of Arthur, Acton, Elora, Grand Valley, and Erin accounted for another 26.5 per cent of establishments. With the exception of Grand Valley, these places also had the most functions and largest populations. Grand Valley, slightly behind Rockwood in population, and equal to Hillsburgh in functions, exceeded both in establishments. Its location at the north of the area, far from major competitive centres, accounted for its ability to sustain a large number of establishments relative to its population. The remaining 31 settlements now shared only 21 per cent of the establishments among them.

Between 1911 and 1941, Elora continued its rapid decline in importance relative to Fergus. The influence of a Fergus politician ensured that the Guelph–Fergus road was declared a King's Highway and paved between 1922 and 1925.[45] Elora has never completely recovered from this blow which left it on a sideroad leading nowhere (Map 4, Table 6). The other major places, all commanding viable local hinterlands at their respective extremities of the study area, continued to grow in absolute terms.

## The Guelph Central Place System–1970

Continued centralization of functions and the increasing economic dominance of the largest and oldest settlements are the major characteristics of the 1970 Guelph Central Place System (Map 5). The other is the resurgence of the hamlets, whose numbers increased by 7 between 1941 and 1970. Their low point came in 1961, when only 34 central places were found in the study area. This was 11 fewer than the number in 1970 (Table 2).

By 1970, the major settlements had increased their domination of the system (Table 6). At this date, Guelph contained almost 50 per cent of establishments, while Fergus, Acton, Arthur, Erin, and Elora accounted for another 32 per cent. The remaining 38 settlements shared the other 18 per cent of the establishments in the system. The average number of establishments per central place had increased from 11.6 in 1851 to 30.5 in 1970. On the other hand, the average number of functions dropped from 2.4 to 2.0 (Table 2). The almost universal use of the car had greatly strengthened the economic position of the major places. As in most modern industrial societies, many consumers in the 1970 Guelph Central Place System travelled to the largest towns for their specialized purchases and for comparison shopping. The number of establishments there proliferated in response to the increased business, which in turn attracted more customers. The big (and old) became even larger while many small settlements languished or lost some of their functions.

**TABLE 6** *Number of Functions and Percentage of Establishments in Largest Settlements, 1851–1970*

| Year | 1851 | | 1881 | | 1911 | | 1941 | | 1970 | | | | |
|---|---|---|---|---|---|---|---|---|---|---|---|---|---|
| Number of settlements | 16 | | 62 | | 62 | | 38 | | 45 | | 1970 population | Mean rank 1851–1970 | Standard deviation |
| Place | No. Fun. | % Est. | No. Fun. | % Est. | No. Fun. | % Est. | No. Fun. | % Est. | No. Fun. | % Est. | | | |
| Guelph | 28 | 36.8 | 65 | 30.7 | 62 | 33.5 | 61 | 44.6 | 90 | 48.3 | 55 625 | 1.00 | 0.00 |
| Fergus | 22 | 18.2 | 34 | 9.0 | 32 | 6.7 | 37 | 8.3 | 64 | 8.6 | 5191 | 2.54 | 0.63 |
| Elora | 18 | 14.6 | 37 | 9.0 | 33 | 6.3 | 29 | 4.7 | 35 | 4.4 | 1766 | 4.23 | 1.31 |
| Acton | 12 | 7.0 | 26 | 5.7 | 35 | 6.6 | 34 | 6.9 | 64 | 8.4 | 4790 | 3.85 | 0.86 |
| Arthur | 10 | 6.6 | 30 | 7.8 | 36 | 7.6 | 30 | 6.9 | 46 | 5.3 | 1303 | 3.85 | 1.66 |
| Erin | 9 | 5.0 | 23 | 3.8 | 26 | 4.6 | 27 | 4.0 | 46 | 4.9 | 1284 | 6.38 | 1.15 |
| Rockwood | 3 | 2.0 | 15 | 2.0 | 15 | 2.4 | 19 | 2.6 | 21 | 2.2 | 985 | 8.69 | 1.14 |
| Hillsburgh | 1 | 0.5 | 16 | 3.2 | 23 | 3.2 | 26 | 3.5 | 23 | 2.1 | 505 | 8.15 | 1.10 |
| Grand Valley | – | – | 12 | 1.5 | 27 | 4.8 | 20 | 4.0 | 23 | 3.2 | 872 | 8.00 | 4.56 |
| Area total | 38 | 198 | 67 | 888 | 70 | 901 | 64 | 918 | 90 | 1376 | 97 508 | | |

SOURCE: Calculated by the author; *Census of Canada*, Population, 1970.

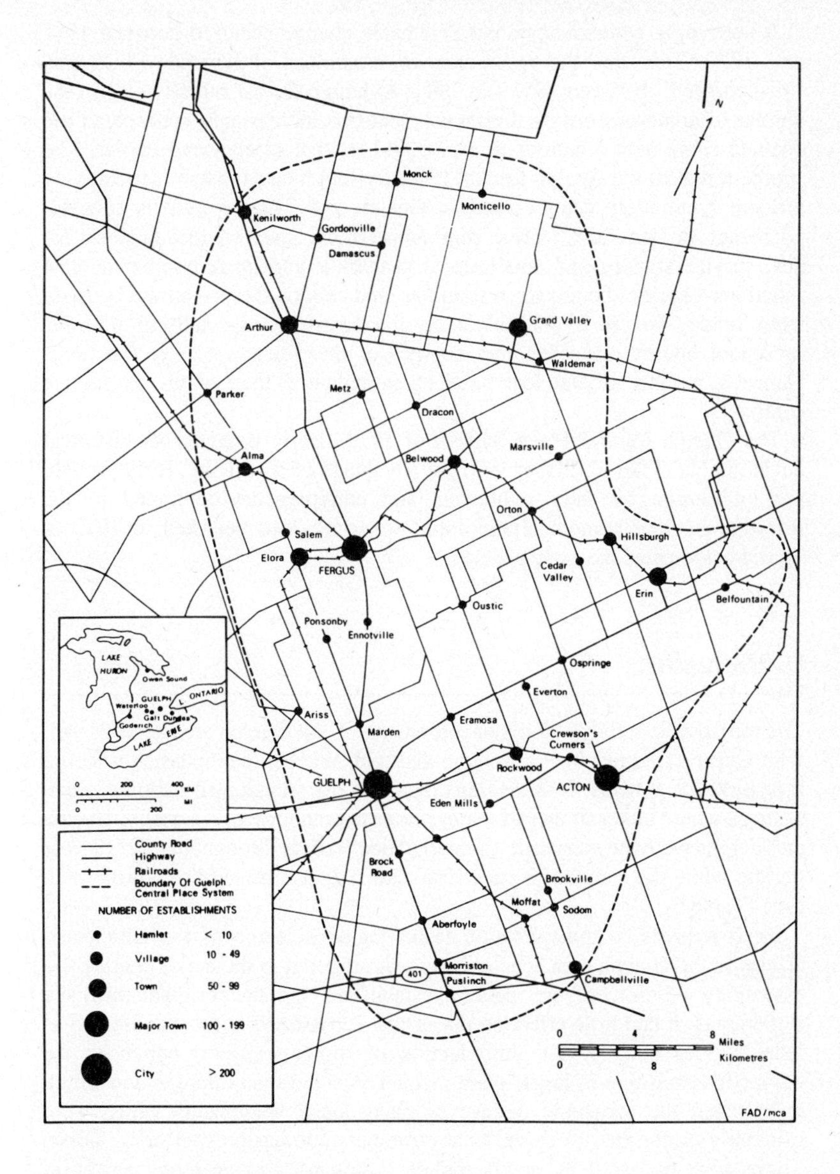


**MAP 5** *The Guelph Place System, 1970*

A seemingly contradictory, but explicable change occurred between 1941 and 1970. This was the resurgence of a number of hamlets which had "disappeared" between 1911 and 1941. Although the car initially caused the demise of numerous marginal establishments, its increasingly widespread use enabled some new functions to replace others that disappeared earlier. The southern half of the Guelph Central Place System housed numerous relatively affluent commuters who worked in Guelph and Toronto and its suburbs, Kitchener, or Hamilton.[46] These rural non-farmers have provided business for new service stations and small stores near their homes. A number of new functions—such as boutiques, restaurants, and antique shops—attract business from Sunday drivers. Reasonably accessible locations, especially in old mills or school houses, have become the sites of these new specialty functions. Hence a number of hamlets have again regained their status as service centres.[47]

The Guelph Central Place System of 1970 clearly reflected its historical development (Map 5). Places with the advantage of a mill site, early growth, and promotion by their politicians and entrepreneurs continued in the forefront of development. Their initial economic lead persisted to 1970 as inertia perpetuated the early patterns.

## Conclusions

The remarkable stability of major settlements in the Guelph area accords well with Guest's findings in Washington and with Whebell's emphasis on inertia in settlement systems. It is also analogous to the situation in national urban systems where rank stability of major places is pronounced.[48] Locally, Guelph and Fergus were the economic and population leaders throughout the 119-year period, while the status of Acton, Erin, and Arthur changed little during that time (Table 6).

Improvements in transportation technology had some of the anticipated effects in the Guelph area. The railway was attracted to the major centres and essentially reinforced the pattern established by the original mill-site settlements. It had little effect on places that it bypassed as most continued as local service centres. The introduction of motor transport enhanced the competitive position of larger places which received road improvements first. It hastened the economic demise of many small settlements which were originally established to serve local customers coming on foot or by horse. These were bypassed by newly mobile customers seeking more variety in larger towns.

Central place theory may help to explain the spatial pattern of settlements between 1871 and 1911, but has little relevance to their initial establishment or subsequent evolution. All the major places in the study area were established at dam sites in virgin forest and joined by roads built to open land to settlement.[49] Transportation was difficult at the best of times and certainly did not encourage competition or interaction in the early years. Only between the 1870s and 1920s did conditions approach those of perfect competition and no impediments to travel posited by classical central place theory. Before and after this period, initial advantage and promotion of individual settlements combined with transport improvements accounted for much of the urban growth.

The example of Guelph's development soon after its establishment and during the period of railway building supports the contention that local initiative and boosterism have had a major impact on urban systems development. Had Fergus been selected by Galt, it might well have become the major settlement in the system. Careless's thesis of metropolitanism and Vance's notion of long-distance impetus for local settlements are also supported by this study. The actions of Galt and the Canada Company in the Guelph area were a distant expression of British colonialism. Urban settlements in the Guelph area were at the cutting edge of the frontier and did indeed precede agricultural activities. There is ample evidence to indicate that staples such as wheat, wool, and timber were exported from the Guelph area in the early years.[50] Later, as the railway encouraged manufacturing for export, the Guelph area settlements became part of a larger Canadian urban system, dominated locally by Toronto.[51]

Finally, Whebell's corridor theory of urban systems describes the evolution of the Guelph Central Place System rather well. The area passed through all his phases with approximate local dates as follows: subsistence agriculture, 1820s to 1840s; commercial agriculture, 1840s to 1860s; railway era, 1856 to 1920s; auto era, 1920s to 1960s; metropolitanism, post-1966 (when a local throughway opened). The orientation of the major centres is clearly linear (Maps 2, 5) along the north-south axis of the original Brock Road. Guelph was established as an administrative centre and innovations initially came to it from London (via Toronto) through Galt and the Canada Company. Later, rail and road links to Toronto continued to send innovations to Guelph, just as it in turn diffused ideas and settlers to its hinterland via an ever-improving communications network. Staples, and later manufactured goods, flowed in the other direction.

To a large degree, Whebell's scheme subsumes the others in Table 1, and is adaptable enough to be applied almost anywhere in North America. Unless the Guelph area is unique (a highly unlikely possibility), the processes found here and generalized by Whebell provide a better explanatory framework for urban systems development than either classical central place theory or studies emphasizing only spatial or temporal factors. An integrated, interdisciplinary approach has provided greater insight into urban development in the Guelph area than would any narrow disciplinary treatment. Whebell's "corridor theory" should be tested elsewhere.

# Notes

1. Alan F.J. Artibise, *Winnipeg: A Social History of Urban Growth, 1874–1914* (Montreal, 1975); H.J. Dyos, *Victorian Suburb: A Study of the Growth of Camberwell* (Leicester, 1961); Leo A. Johnson, *History of Guelph 1827–1927* (Guelph, 1977); Donald C. Masters, *The Rise of Toronto 1850–1890* (Toronto, 1947); Sam B. Warner, *Streetcar Suburbs: The Process of Growth in Boston, 1870–1900* (Cambridge, 1962) are representative of the vast literature on individual city development.

2. John R. Borchert, "America's Changing Metropolitan Regions," *Annals*, Association of American Geographers 62 (1972): 352–73; Michael P. Conzen, "The Maturing Urban System in the United States, 1840–1910," *Annals*, Association of American Geographers 67 (1977): 88–108; Conzen, "A Transport Interpretation of the Growth of American Regions," *Journal of Historical Geography* 1 (1975): 361–82; Allan Pred, *City Systems in Advanced Economies* (London, 1977) which synthesizes much of his earlier work; James W. Simmons, "The Evolution of the Canadian Urban System," in *The Useable Urban Past*, ed. Alan Artibise and Gilbert Stelter (Toronto, 1979), 9–33; Gilbert Rozman, *Urban Networks in China and Tokugawa Japan* (Princeton, 1973); Rozman, *Urban Networks in Russia 1750–1800 and Premodern Periodization* (Princeton, 1976).

3. For example, Walter Christaller, *Die zentralen Orte in Suddeutschland* (Jena, 1933), translated by Carlisle W. Baskin as *Central Places in Southern Germany* (Englewood Cliffs, 1966); Arthur E. Smailes, "The Urban Hierarchy in England and Wales," *Geography* 29 (1944): 41–51; John Brush, "The Hierarchy of Central Places in Southwestern Wisconsin," *Geographical Review* 43 (1953): 380–402; Howard E. Bracey, "Towns as Rural Service Centres: An Index of Centrality with Special Reference to Somerset," *Transactions, Institute of British Geographers* 19 (1953): 95–105; Brian J.L. Berry, *Geography of Market Centers and Retail Distribution* (Englewood Cliffs, 1967); John U. Marshall, *The Location of Service Towns* (Toronto, 1969); F.A. Dahms, "The Evolving Spatial Organization of Settlements in the Countryside—an Ontario Example," *Tijdschrift voor Econ. en Soc. Geografie* 71 (1980): 295–306.

4. Many studies by geographers and economists have attempted to test some of the concepts suggested by central place theory: Harold Carter, *The Towns of Wales—A Study in Urban Geography* (Cardiff, 1966); Carter, "The Urban Hierarchy and Historical Geography: A Consideration with Reference to Northeast Wales," in *Geographical Interpretations of Historical Sources*, ed. Alan R.H. Baker, John D. Hamshere and John Langton (Newton Abbot, 1970), 269–86; Wayne K.D. Davies, "Towards an Integrated Study of Central Places: A South Wales Case Study," in *Urban Essays: Studies in the Geography of Wales*, ed. Harold Carter and Wayne K.D. Davies (London, 1970), 193–227; Christopher R. Lewis, "The Central Place Pattern of Mid Wales and the Middle Welsh Borderland" in *Urban Essays*, ed. Carter and Davies, 228–68; Gerald Hodge, "The Prediction of Trade Center Viability in the Great Plains," *Papers and Proceedings of the Regional Science Association* 15 (1965): 87–115; Hodge, "Do Villages Grow: Some Perspectives and Predictions," *Rural Sociology* 31 (1966): 183–96; James T. Lemon, *The Best Poor Man's Country: A Geographical Study of Early Southeastern Pennsylvania* (Baltimore, 1972); Carle C. Zimmerman and Gary W. Moneo, *The Prairie Community System* (Ottawa, 1971); John F. Hart, Neil E.

Salisbury, and Everett G. Smith, Jr., "The Dying Village and Some Notions About Urban Growth," *Economic Geography* 44 (1968): 343–49. Historians such as Maurice Careless, "Metropolis and Region: The Interplay Between City and Region in Canada Before 1914," *Urban History Review* 3, 78 (1979): 99–118; Careless, "Some Aspects of Urbanization in Nineteenth Century Ontario" in *Aspects of Nineteenth Century Ontario: Essays Presented to J.J. Talman*, ed. Fredrick H. Armstrong, Hugh A. Stevenson, and J. Donald Wilson (Toronto, 1974), 65–79; Leo A. Johnson, *History of the County of Ontario, 1615–1875* (Whitby, 1973); Blaine A. Brownell and Donald R. Goldfeld, eds., *The City in Southern History* (Port Washington, 1977); Eric Lampard, "The Evolving System of Cities in the United States: Urbanization and Economic Development" in *Issues in Urban Economics*, ed. Harvey S. Perloff and Lowdon Wingo (Baltimore, 1968), 81–139; Gilbert A. Stelter, "The Urban Frontier in Canadian History" in *Cities in the West*, ed. A.R. McCormack and Ian McPherson (Ottawa, 1978), 269–86; Richard C. Wade, *The Urban Frontier: The Rise of Western Cities, 1790–1830* (Cambridge, 1959); Jeffrey G. Williamson and Joseph A. Swanson, "The Growth of Cities in the American Northeast, 1820–1870" *Explorations in Entrepreneurial History* 4 (1966): 44–67 and Avery Guest, "Ecological Succession in the Puget Sound Region" *Journal of Urban History* 3 (1977): 181–210, have contributed much empirical detail and some theoretical interpretations of urban development at various scales.

5. For an example of the retrospective application of theory see Richard L. Morrill, *Migration and the Spread and Growth of Urban Settlement* (Lund, 1965).

6. Borchert, "Metropolitan Evolution"; Careless, "Metropolis and Region"; Guest, "Ecological Succession"; Martyn J. Bowden, Bruce La Rose and Brian Mishara, "The Development of Central Places on the Frontier: Vermont 1790–1830," *Proceedings*, Association of American Geographers 3 (1971): 32–38; John C. Hudson, "A Location Theory for Rural Settlement," *Annals*, Association of American Geographers 59 (1969): 365–81; Robert D. Mitchell, "The Shenandoah Valley Frontier" *Annals*, Association of American Geographers 62 (1972): 475–86; Edward K. Muller, "Regional Urbanization and Selective Growth of Towns in North American Regions" *Journal of Historical Geography* 3 (1977): 21–39; Roderick D. McKenzie, "Ecological Succession in the Puget Sound Region" in *Roderick D. McKenzie on Human Ecology*, ed. Amos H. Hawley (Chicago, 1968), 228–43; James E. Vance, Jr., *The Merchant's View of the World, The Geography of Wholesaling* (Englewood Cliffs, 1970), 138–67; Charles F.J. Whebell, "Corridors: A Theory of Urban Systems" *Annals*, Association of American Geographers 59 (1969): 1–26.

7. Careless, "Metropolis and Region."

8. Ibid., 110.

9. Ibid., 111.

10. Ibid., 112.

11. Whebell, "Corridors."

12. Guest, "Ecological Succession"; McKenzie "Ecological Succession."

13. Marshall, *Service Towns*, 78–79; Fredric A. Dahms and James A. Forbes, "Central Places in the Golden Triangle; The Guelph System 1970," in *The Waterloo County Area: Selected Geographical Essays*, ed. Andrew G. McLellan (Waterloo, 1971), 114–27.

14. John U. Marshall, "Central Places in the Queen's Bush" (M.A. thesis, University of Minnesota, 1964), 141.

15. Johnson, *Guelph*, 38–42.

16. Dahms and Forbes, "Central Places."

17. Jacob Spelt, *Urban Development in South Central Ontario* (Assen, 1955) reprinted in the Carleton Library Series (Toronto, 1972), 91. Spelt provides an excellent large-scale account of urban development which combines historical, spatial, and theoretical interpretations of the evolution of settlement systems in part of Ontario from its initial settlement to 1951. Donald W. Kirk, "Southwestern Ontario: The Area Pattern of Settlements in 1850" (Ph.D. diss., Northwestern University, 1949) is an excellent source for the early period.

18. Dun and Bradstreet, *Reference Book* (Toronto, 1864, 1871, 1881, 1891, 1901, 1911, 1921, 1931, 1941, 1951, 1961, 1970); Robert W. Mackay, *Canada Directory* (Montreal, 1851).

19. Marshall, *Service Towns;* Dahms and Forbes, "Central Places"; Spelt, *Urban Development.*

20. Johnson, *Guelph,* 13–19; James M. Cameron, "The Canada Company and Land Settlement as Resource Development in the Guelph Block," in *Perspectives on Landscape and Life in Nineteenth Century Ontario,* ed. J. David Wood (Toronto, 1975), 141–58, provides an excellent account of the early development of the Guelph area from the perspective of its potential return to investors in the Canada Company.

21. Johnson, *Guelph,* 30.

22. Donald McDonald, *Plan of the Town of Guelph* (Guelph, October 1847).

23. Johnson, *Guelph,* 3–51 and Cameron "Resource Development" discuss this aspect of Guelph's early success in some detail.

24. Ross Cumming, ed., *Historical Atlas of the County of Wellington* (Toronto, 1906; reprint edition 1972); Cumming, ed., *Illustrated Historical Atlas of the County of Halton Ontario* (Toronto, 1877; Reprint edition 1971).

25. Mackay, *Canada Directory.*

26. Spelt, *Urban Development,* figure 12.

27. Johnson discusses the local situation in detail in *Guelph,* 147–77. He covers the topic more generally in *The County of Ontario,* 282–316.

28. L. Bladen, "Construction of Railways in Canada to the Year 1855," *Contributions to Canadian Economics* 5 (1932): 46.

29. Johnson, *Guelph,* 171.

30. Bladen, "Construction," 47.

31. *The Daily Mercury,* Centennial Edition (Guelph, 1927), 24.

32. Johnson, *Guelph,* 217.

33. Bladen, "Construction," 50.

34. Ibid., 47.

35. Marvin W. Farrell, *The Guelph Junction Railway, 1884–1950* (Guelph, 1951), 4.

36. *Statement of Earnings of the Guelph Junction Railway Company Received by the Guelph Junction Railway Company from the Canadian Pacific Railway* (Guelph, 1963).

37. Spelt, *Urban Development,* 116.

38. Spelt, *Urban Development,* 120. James W. Gilmour, *Spatial Evolution of Manufacturing in Southern Ontario 1851–1891* (Toronto, 1972) provides a comprehensive large-scale interpretation of early manufacturing activities in Ontario.

39. Spelt, *Urban Development,* 116. See also Thomas F. Mellwraith, "Transportation in the Landscape of Early Upper Canada," in *Perspectives,* ed. J. David Woods, 51–63 for a more general discussion of early transportation.

40. Joseph Schull, *Ontario Since 1867* (Toronto, 1978), 244–45.

41. Joseph E. Middleton and Fred Landon, *The Province of Ontario: A History, 1615–1927* (Toronto, 1927), 713.

42. Spelt, *Urban Development*, 123.

43. R.M. Smith, "Kings Highways of Ontario," *Canadian Geographical Journal* 16 (1938): 159–93.

44. Spelt, *Urban Development*, 182.

45. *Daily Mercury*, 15.

46. Statistics Canada, "Census of Canada Special Tabultion; Place of Work by Place of Residence by Enumeration Area, Wellington County, 1971" (Ottawa, 1977).

47. Recent work by F.A. Dahms has examined the changing functions and revitalization of towns and villages in other parts of Canada. In most instances, former rural service centres with some combination of scenic amenities, heritage architecture, access to population and effective local entrepreneurs have increased in population and/or numbers of economic functions. Isolated single industry resource towns did not usually share in this revival. See for example F.A. Dahms, "Small Town and Village Ontario," *Ontario Geography* 7, 8 (1980): 19–32; "The Process of Urbanization in the Countryside: a Study of Bruce and Huron Counties, Ontario 1891–1981," *Urban History Review* 12 (1984): 1–18; "Demetropolitanization or the Urbanization of the Countryside—The Changing Functions of Small Rural Settlements in Ontario," *Ontario Geography* 24 (1984): 35–61; "Diversity Complexity and Change: Characteristics of Some Ontario Towns and Villages," *The Canadian Geographer* 30 (198): 158–66; "Settlement Dynamics, Migration and Commuting: Western Ontario, 1971–1985," in *Essays on Canadian Urban Process and Form III: The Urban Field*, ed. P.M. Coppack, L.H. Russwurm and C.R. Bryant (Waterloo, 1988), 157–91. A synthesis and extension of this research to Quebec and the Maritime Provinces is available in Dahms, *The Heart of the Country: From the Great Lakes to the Atlantic Coast—Rediscovering the Towns and Countryside of Canada* (Toronto, 1988).

48. Guest, "Ecological Succession"; Whebell, "Corridors"; Careless, "Metropolis and Region"; Pred, *City Systems*, 33.

49. Andrew F. Burghardt, "The Origin and Development of the Road Network of the Niagara Peninsula, Ontario, 1770–1851," *Annals*, Association of American Geographers 59 (1969): 417–40 found that milling in the Niagara Peninsula was often initiated before agricultural settlement reached the frontier. "Clearly mills did not seek to locate along roads; rather the good water power site created the roads leading to it," 434–35. The long-term stability of settlement rank and transport network in the Guelph area was certainly attributable to a large degree to the process described by Burghardt.

50. Kenneth Kelly, "Agricultural Landscapes of Wellington County" in *On Middle Ground—Landscape and Life in Wellington County 1841–1891*, ed. Elizabeth Waterson and Douglas Hoffman (Guelph, 1974), 39–47.

51. Dahms and Forbes, "Central Places."

# CANADIAN SUBURBANIZATION IN A NORTH AMERICAN CONTEXT—DOES THE BORDER MAKE A DIFFERENCE?*

PAUL-ANDRÉ LINTEAU

Comparative history is certainly one of the most stimulating areas of the historian's domain. But when it comes to comparisons between Canada and the United States, the venture is not easy: both sides of the road look so similar that one can easily miss the differences. After all, the two countries share the longest common border in the world and their inhabitants apparently have the same style of living. Canada is all too often seen as a mere extension of the United States, especially of its economy and of its culture. But a closer look reveals significant differences: size and ethnic composition of the population, economic specialization, and political institutions, to name but a few. Such similarities and differences are, of course, reflected in the urban milieu, and the urban historian must proceed cautiously. In fact, the image of an undifferentiated North American city has been increasingly challenged in recent years.

The slower development of urban history in Canada creates an additional difficulty. Although the field of Canadian urban history has expanded tremendously since the early 1970s, research has remained insufficiently articulated; in most instances it does not go beyond the individual case study.[1] Whereas the American historian can rely on numerous general histories or surveys of the evolution of the urbanization of the United States, there is still no matching synthesis in Canada.[2]

The problem is even greater for the history of suburbanization, because few Canadian historians have dealt with this peculiar subject. No equivalent to Kenneth T. Jackson's *Crabgrass Frontier*[3] is available. Although a systematic and thorough comparison is not feasible, it is possible to look at certain

**Journal of Urban History* 13, 3 (May 1987): 252–74.

aspects of Canadian suburban development and to compare these with their American counterparts. After an overview of the major developments in the study of Canadian suburbanization, this article will address the question of the differences.

## Some Aspects of Canadian Suburbanization

Suburban development in Canada has been dealt with largely through the history of the core city, where it is only one among numerous dimensions examined in urban biographies. Few studies focus specifically on the evolution of a suburb or on the suburbanization process. Yet, if not numerous, these studies nevertheless reveal some features of the Canadian suburban scene.

The suburbanization process appeared quite early in the history of the Canadian urban development. During the eighteenth century, the cities of Quebec and Montreal experienced the urbanization of areas lying outside their walls with the creation of the first *faubourgs*. Louise Dechêne has shown how, in Montreal, a growing social division of space took place: Merchants, professionals, and clergy lived in the city with their servants, while artisans and labourers were increasingly pushed to the suburbs. By the end of the century the population of the suburbs outnumbered that of the city itself.[4]

These early suburbs were integrated within the boundaries of the city in 1791 and later became wards. If suburbanization is seen as the process of extension of the urbanized area into the country, be it inside or outside the limits of the city, then we can say that the suburbanization process in Montreal and Quebec was set in motion during the eighteenth century and did not stop thereafter. But if we look only at the creation of distinct political units—the suburban towns, then we can say that the process really took off during the second half of the nineteenth century with the development of a system of municipal institutions and with the beginning of industrialization.

In the early stages the process was limited to a small number of towns, but it gained momentum during the second half of the century and by the turn of the century it was visible in a host of Canadian towns and cities. It was nevertheless much more important in Montreal than anywhere else.

## Montreal and Its Suburbs at the Turn of the Century

For a century and a half, from the late 1820s when it outnumbered Quebec City to the early 1970s when it was surpassed by Toronto, Montreal was the metropolis of Canada. The population of the city and its suburbs reached

100 000 in 1861; it attained the million mark in 1931 and now stands at 2.8 million.[5] Over the years, waves of suburban expansion resulted in the creation of a host of surrounding towns. Not surprisingly, the case of Montreal has attracted historians who have devoted numerous studies to the city and its suburbs, dealing especially with the great surge at the turn of the century.[6]

The most substantial study, to date, of the evolution of a Canadian suburb town deals with the town (city in 1913) of Maisonneuve, created in 1883 and annexed to Montreal in 1918.[7] Controlled by a handful of French Canadian promoters, it grew rapidly in the first decade of the century and boasted a population of 18 000 by 1911. The promoters attempted to attract those industries from the core city that were looking for expansion and cheap land. The ultimate objective was that the workers would follow the enterprise and become residents of Maisonneuve. The council advertised the town as the "Pittsburgh of Canada." By the eve of the First World War, its industrial output ranked it among the leading cities in Canada. Its population was mostly working class and 90 per cent of the heads of households were tenants. Around 1910, a new team of civic leaders launched a huge and costly beautification scheme that included large public buildings, elegant boulevards and a six-hundred-acre park. To finance the project and become the "Garden of Montreal," the city ran into debt and, unable to pay the interest, was forced into annexation by the provincial government.

The study of Maisonneuve led to some interesting findings and generated more general proposals. At the very centre of suburban development, the promoters emerged as the key players. They are truly entrepreneurs of spatial organization, being responsible for what can be seen as private planning of urban space. I came to see urban land development as one of the major sectors in capitalist economies, alongside manufacturing industries, commerce, and finance. Yet it rarely appears as such in official statistics. We have to shed the image of a shadowy activity congenitally defined as speculation. My argument is that speculation as such is not the only or the most significant basis of the land development sector. Speculation, of course, is present just as it is in many high-tech ventures of Silicon Valley, in some huge foreign loans of the largest and most reputable American banks, or in many stock exchange operations. But, as I see it, land development is fundamentally an industry in which, in the best capitalist tradition, numerous entrepreneurs, often in a very competitive environment, try to create, organize, and sell a town, a subdivision, a building, or simply a lot and to obtain the greatest possible profit out of it. This is not a risk-free activity; and, along with the manufacturers or the bankers, they can experience tremendous success or devastating failure. And as in the other sectors of the economy, since the nineteenth century, the land development industry has experienced a growing tendency toward concentration. In early twentieth-century Maisonneuve, the promoters were simply land subdividers, letting other agents build and sell the houses, whereas modern developers tend to integrate all these functions. The basic process of land development is nevertheless essentially the same, although the size, the scope, and the complexity of its operations has changed. This is why it is essential to go beyond the promoter as an individual decision maker and to look at land capitalism of the land development industry as a whole in order to draw fundamental patterns and trends.[8]

Another finding of the Maisonneuve study dealt with the ethnic origin of the promoters. In Montreal the majority of the population was French Canadian, while the whole economy of the city was dominated by a powerful white Anglo-Saxon Protestant minority. In Maisonneuve, as in many other suburb towns of Montreal, most of the promoters were French Canadians. This can be explained by the very nature of the land development sector. It does not require technological know-how, or international connections, but some long-term financing, easily available through mortgage and secured by the land itself. It also involves a knowledge of the local conditions and some political connections in order to influence or control the suburban town council. French Canadians could easily enter this field.[9] The nature of the land development thus permitted the rise of entrepreneurs from a modest background or from a nondominant ethnic group, although it also attracted investors from the wealthy upper crust society.

Maisonneuve is an example of a certain type of neighbourhood, quite common at the turn of the century: the industrial suburb with a working-class population. In Maisonneuve the promotional scheme was geared to the idea that residents would come to the town if it succeeded in attracting manufacturing enterprises. In exchange for municipal bonuses, industries accepted the condition that 80 per cent of the workers had to be residents of the town. The newcomers moving to Maisonneuve at the turn of the century were thus mostly from the working class and as salaries were low in the Montreal area, the overwhelming majority of these workers were tenants. The typical Maisonneuve house was a row house, two or three stories high, with three to five dwelling units. The owner usually lived on the main floor and rented apartments on the upper floors. Most of the owners were quite modest, although some merchants and professionals had acquired a certain number of adjoining houses. Another aspect of Maisonneuve life, also characteristic of many other suburbs and of many working-class neighbourhoods with the core city, was that some wealthy industrialists and most of the local merchants and professionals lived in the town. They owned handsome houses on a few elegant blocks and they formed a local élite concentrating in their hands the key positions on the town council, the school board, and the parish board, as well as in benevolent or religious associations. The industrial suburb town thus represented a microcosm of society as a whole, with its social ranking and its social division of space. Such a feature would disappear in the post-World War II era when the élites would leave the working-class neighbourhoods, thus achieving a complete separation between their daily work milieu and their residential environment.[10]

The study of Maisonneuve also permitted examination of the strategies of the privately owned public utilities corporations that, in the Montreal area, took advantage of the multiplication of suburban municipalities. Small towns such as Maisonneuve were no match for these financial giants that were able to obtain advantageous positions, and even to improve these over time, while resisting public pressure for better services.[11]

Maisonneuve was only one among numerous Montreal suburbs. Only a few of these have yet been studied.[12] Many of the suburbs shared with Maisonneuve the characteristics of an industrial and working-class area. But there were also some purely residential towns for the upper and middle classes. The best example is Westmount, located to the west of the city, on the slopes of Mount-Royal, which became at the turn of the century a decidedly bourgeois town, housing the most powerful and wealthy Canadian capitalists. The differences among various suburbs were reflected in the manner they were governed. In a stimulating study, Jean-Pierre Collin presented a comparative analysis of municipal regulations in two upper-class (Westmount and Outremont) and two working-class (Maisonneuve and St. Henri) suburbs between 1875 and 1920. He argued that municipal administrations represented a significant level of power and were able to adopt coherent policies in order to protect an exclusive residential milieu and life-style, in the first two cases, and to give a free hand to developers, in the other two.[13]

As elsewhere in North America, Montreal experienced the annexation movement. Between 1883 and 1918, twenty-two suburban municipalities were annexed to the core city, most of these between 1905 and 1910. Montreal thus integrated most of the urbanized territory at the time—with the exception of the two bourgeois enclaves of Westmount and Outremont—and even acquired large areas that would remain undeveloped until the post-World War II era. The process here was quite similar to what has been studied in the United States. There was nevertheless a singular aspect: as the suburbs were at that time mostly inhabited by French Canadians, their annexation strengthened French Canadian presence and power in the city council.

## Other Canadian Examples

The most significant study of a Canadian suburb outside the Montreal area is John Weaver's research on Westdale, in Hamilton, Ontario.[14] Developed from 1911 by a group of wealthy businessmen who owned eight hundred acres of land, Westdale was annexed early (1914) to Hamilton but retained the image of a distinct suburb. It was planned as a white Anglo-Saxon Protestant middle-class residential area, although the less attractive parts of the property were sold for working-class housing and the upper fringe was given an exclusive and élitist character. The developers used restrictive covenants to define "the minimum dwelling value and the building materials"—and even in some cases to retain the right to approve the plan—according to the type of subdivision they had envisioned and to bar some ethnic groups from buying or renting.[15] After a slow start, construction increased in the middle 1920s, to be halted by the depression and the war; it was resumed after World War II, and most of the land was occupied by 1951. According to the author, the history of Westdale parallels that of numerous North American residential middle-class suburbs. It also provides a case study "in the evolution of the property industry," as the developers carefully planned the areas but did not venture into the construction business itself, drawing upon "an array of traditional crafts and specialists."[16]

Ross Paterson had provided a similar case study for a Toronto suburban development, Kingsway Park, in Etobicoke. There, "between 1906 and 1912 Home Smith put together a 3000 acre land assembly" and was able to retain it until development opportunities materialized. Kingsway Park was a small portion of this huge tract of land. Designed for the upper-middle class, with the developer retaining the right to approve the plans, it was built up mostly in the late 1920s and during the 1930s, attracting professionals and managers of British origin.[17]

The history of the suburban development of Toronto in the first decades of the twentieth century still has to be written. The same thing can be said of most other major Canadian cities. Up to now, suburban development, and even the land development industry within the core area, has remained but one topic among many others included in the major urban biographies.[18]

## The Postwar Era

Between 1945 and 1980 a new wave of suburban development spread over all the major Canadian cities, and it was certainly the most significant trend in postwar urban growth. This phenomenon was already visible in the 1961 census returns, although there were sharp differences from one province to another.[19] It continued through the following two decades. For example, between 1951 and 1981, the population of the city of Montreal, even with the annexation of a few suburb towns, declined by 4 per cent (from 1.02 to 0.98 million), whereas that of the entire metropolitan census area rose by 103 per cent (from 1.4 to 2.8 million).

As in the United States, the individual family house in a suburb has remained the ideal image throughout the period. Most of the new developments were in fact characterized by the single-family, owner-occupied, detached house, although a significant number of multi-unit houses or apartment buildings have also been erected. And as in the United States, the construction of many new rapid-transit freeways in the major metropolitan areas has sped up the process of urban sprawl. In Canada, however, road building has been primarily a provincial rather than a federal responsibility, the only major federal intervention being the partial financing of the Trans-Canada Highway. There were nevertheless some differences in the patterns of suburbanization among the various regions and provinces, owing to differences in economic and political structures, to differentiated rates of growth and local conditions.

In addition, it is important to stress that although their population is declining, inner cities have not suffered such sharp and systematic decay as their American counterparts. Some areas have been torn down to make room for extended business districts. Others have been rejuvenated either by middle-or upper-income groups upgrading the old housing stock, or by new immigrants who proudly transformed their environment, like the Portuguese in Montreal. Some older areas remained appealing because they offered quite affordable rental opportunities, strengthened in some places by government regulation of the rental market.

Suburban expansion in Canadian cities cannot be explained only by the desire of the middle classes to flee from the city. Working-class people were pushed to the suburbs by the expansion of the business district and by the redevelopment of older areas. In addition, older suburban zones, close to the core, remained attractive for middle- and upper-class populations throughout the period and offered an alternative to the more remote suburban residential choice. Such phenomena are particularly visible in Montreal and Toronto but are also evident in Vancouver and Winnipeg. Suburban development thus took place in a complex environment.[20]

Almost no Canadian historian has ventured to study the evolution of urban or suburban development in the postwar era. Published works on this period are nevertheless numerous, and range from the radical essay attacking corporate developers and supporting citizens' participation to the official planning report issued by a municipal or governmental body. In fact, given the importance of suburban expansion during the period, most of the urban studies have a suburban-related component. Many of these, however, have limited historical—if not ahistorical—perspectives.[21]

Four major subjects emerge from these studies. One is the rise of the corporate developer and its consequences both on suburban expansion and on urban renewal. Another topic of concern is housing: its provision, its availability, its quality, and the role of federal and provincial governments in that field. A third concern is urban sprawl and its costly consequences. Finally, a fourth topic is the political battle between the various levels of government, and between various groups within the city, over the control of the urban scene.

This article does not attempt to survey systematically this kind of material. I will simply signal a few issues, significant for historians, stemming from some of these publications.

One of the major features of Canadian suburban development has been the emergence of the corporate developers. Although the interwar period provided a few early examples—Westdale and Kingsway Park—the 1950s opened a new era in the land development industry. The creation of Don Mills, on the eastern outskirts of Toronto, is usually seen as a landmark of that transformation. A development company controlled by E.P. Taylor, one of the most important Canadian financiers, launched in the early 1950s the project of a large planned suburban community of a two thousand acre piece of land. The plan included many novelties: neighbourhood organization, separation of car traffic and pedestrians, provision for green spaces, provision for work by attracting industries in specific areas, and control over the design of houses. Another innovation in the Don Mills project had the developer investing to service the lots and transferring the costs to the buyers, thus relieving municipal authorities from heavy investments, a policy that was to spread over large portions of suburban Canada. Don Mills was a complete success for its promoters; it set a new standard that was repeated in various places.[22]

In the span of a few years, suburban development in a majority of Canadian cities fell into the hands of a small number of corporate developers who were able to reap the profits of the housing boom. The key strategy of these developers was to gain control over vast pools of rural land surrounding the cities, years ahead of actual development. They then enjoyed monopolistic or oligopolistic control of the situation, pushing aside, to a marginal position, the smaller operators.[23] Whether or not this permitted developers to retain land and to raise significantly the price of the lots they sold is still a disputed issue. Lorimer argues strongly that such was the case when he compared the price of suburban land between Montreal and other Canadian cities.[24]

In fact, the situation in Montreal and in other metropolitan centres of the Province of Quebec was different. There, the corporate developers did not gain full control of the market, and a larger number of small- or medium-sized promoters were responsible for a higher proportion of new suburban projects than in other Canadian metropolises.[25] Consequently, the price of land was lower. One explanation lies in the great number of distinct suburban municipalities, which have quite extended powers over urban planning and development and whose officials usually want to give a distinct character or label to their peculiar community. The easy availability of cheap land and the fact that most towns retained the financial responsibility of servicing the lots permitted small operators, who were often French Canadians, to stay in business.[26] This situation did not prevent large corporate developers from being very active in Quebec, especially in Montreal downtown redevelopment projects, in the major shopping centres, and in some suburban areas; but they were never able to gain control of the quite competitive suburban market.[27]

The long-term trend was nevertheless toward greater concentration in the Canadian urban development industry, even if it was less pronounced in Quebec. According to many authors, federal government policies have been a determining factor in that direction. The creation in 1945 of the Central (later Canadian) Mortgage and Housing Corporation (CMHC) represented a major step. Its objective was to support the provision, by the private sector, of sufficient and adequate housing to Canadians and to maintain the level of employment in the construction industry. Over the years it acted as a mortgage lender, or it guaranteed mortgage loans made by private institutions,—thus permitting easier access to homeownership for a large number of families. It also influenced the type of housing by defining standard building specifications that were prerequisite to its support.

According to many authors, CMHC policies had a double effect. The standards they set were biased toward the individual owner-occupied family house for the middle-class population. Because of this, they contributed to the acceleration of the suburban expansion process and to the relative decline of core areas. Even when, under political pressure, CMHC was forced, from the late 1950s, to help develop low-cost housing for the working class and to invest in urban renewal, the bulk of its action remained concentrated on access to family home ownership.

The second effect of CMHC policies was to nurture the growth of corporate developers and builders. In supporting suburban expansion they strengthened the position of those who already controlled the large pools of land. In setting high construction standards, they favoured those builders who were able to put up many units in a standardized way.[28]

CMHC policies did not have the same effect in Quebec, at least in the postwar years, because they were ill adapted to the peculiar situation of the province. There the need was for less costly housing attractive to the working class and for multi-unit homes. The provincial government played a more significant role in devising policies to reduce the cost of such housing.[29]

In all provinces, provincial and municipal authorities were key participants in urban development. In the Canadian federation the responsibility for urban affairs is in the hands of the provinces. Their actions differed greatly: Some provinces had social-democratic governments that adopted progressive social measures, while others had very conservative administrations that preferred a laissez-faire attitude. For example, two provinces (British Columbia and Quebec) chose to freeze the urbanization of agricultural land, while others decided not to interfere with the market. Some provinces created rent control boards, but others resisted popular pressure to adopt such a measure. In spite of these differences in style and level of involvement, all provincial governments nevertheless kept a close eye on urban matters and did not hesitate to pass legislation even when local representatives disagreed. A good example is the forced merger, in 1965, of fourteen suburb towns of Montreal, located on Jesus Island, into a new suburban city of Laval.

Provincial governments were also instrumental in creating various types of metropolitan co-ordination governments, a crucial issue for suburb towns. The solutions adopted differed greatly from one province to another. In Ontario and Quebec a two-tier system was implemented with a division of power and responsibilities between the town councils and the metropolitan body, including the presence of elected representatives from the former to the latter. In the Prairies, in Winnipeg's Unicity, in Edmonton, or in Calgary, the general pattern has been one of amalgamation in a single-tier body, while on the Pacific Coast, Vancouver used special-purpose boards. The objectives also differed. In many Ontario metropolitan areas created in the 1950s and 1960s there was a need to involve the core cities in supporting the costly suburban extension of some basic services as roads, water, and sewage and in the planning of land uses. But, in Quebec's urban communities, created in 1970, the most important issue was to spread over the suburbanites the heavy operating costs of some core city services like public transportation and, in Montreal, police forces.[30]

Even with strong provincial intervention, which in the long run seriously limited municipal autonomy, many town councils resisted centralization and retained large powers in matters of urban planning and the provision of basic services.[31] Such a decentralization of powers added to the complexity of the situation by allowing significant differences from place to place. At the local level, town officials in a same area often had diverging attitudes vis-à-vis the kind of suburban development they envisioned.

It is not possible to draw in a few lines the global portrait of such diverse policies. Suffice it to say that in Canada, from 1945 to 1985, state intervention has been a major component of urban and suburban development; and generally speaking, it has operated, more often than not, in accordance with developers' plans rather than against them.[32]

### Canadian Histography and Suburban Development

This rapid survey of Canadian historiography dealing with suburban development has permitted a sketch of some of the key issues. Clearly, the land development industry and the role of the promoter or the developer occupies centre stage in most of the studies. Canadian scholars have provided a model to understand the role and the functioning of this industry and its evolution over time. A second major theme is the role of all levels of government, especially since 1945, but also in the early twentieth century. The importance of regional differences has also been acknowledged, especially in the case of Quebec, where French Canadians have followed a distinct course. Finally, some studies have demonstrated a concern for the historical significance of a specific type of suburb: the industrial and working-class town.

## Does the Border Make a Difference?

How can we compare these aspects of Canadian suburban development with the suburbanization of the United States? Quite evidently, given the state of the art in Canada, our answer can only be tentative and must necessarily remain incomplete. It is possible to draw some ideas about similarities and differences between the Canadian and American experiences, but it is also necessary to relate both cases to a paradigmatic model of the suburbanization process.

## Similarities and Differences

The history of urban and suburban development shows striking similarities between Canada and the United States. At the end of the nineteenth century both countries experienced sustained suburban growth linked to many common factors: the significant rise in urban population fueled by migrations; the redefinition of functions in the central areas, now devoted to business activities; the growth in size and number of manufacturing enterprises; the transportation revolution, particularly the advent of the electric street car; the ascent of the land promoter as an active agent of the urbanization of surrounding rural land; the emergence of a new image of the home and the multiplication of suburban towns, later to be annexed by the core city. Moreover, in both countries the tremendous suburban expansion that occurred after 1945 presented similar characteristics: improvements in personal income permitting more families to buy houses; the deeply felt impact of the automobile; the prevalence of the single-family owner-occupied home in the suburbs; the emergence of large-scale development and building enterprises; and, finally, extended urban sprawl. Such similarities would seem to support the idea of a paradigmatic North American city, although in Canada it would be smaller in size and would follow the U.S. mode with a certain time lag.

But this ill-defined idea of a North American city is at the same time challenged by a closer look at some of the discrepancies. Even before we can begin to formulate international comparisons, some problems arise from a purely internal point of view: Striking differences between the disparate regions of the country make it difficult to talk about any single model of a Canadian city. Although in recent years some of these differences might well have eroded, they remain as palpable today as they have certainly been in the past; a simple visit to Montreal and Toronto is revealing in this regard.[33]

History has forged the physical appearances of Canadian cities, and its long-term impact is probably still more visible today than in most American cities. The heritage of the colonial and commercial era has been felt strongly in places like Montreal and Quebec city or in the cities of the Maritime Provinces. Both the highly centralized urban system of the province of Quebec, under the heavy dominance of Montreal, and the more decentralized system of Ontario are deeply rooted in the initial forms that these systems and their components took in the eighteenth and early nineteenth centuries. Later development and a highly specialized economy explain the distinct features of the cities of the Prairies, although these also felt the influence of models imported from central Canada by the early developers.

Compared with the United States, the slower growth of Canadian population and economy, with the resulting smaller scale of cities, probably permitted a more orderly urban growth. The reshaping of Canadian cities not only involved fewer demolitions but, in general, allowed for the integration of the assets of the past in a smoother, less discontinuous, fashion. Consequently, the successive phases of suburban development evidenced a gradual evolution from downtown models and organization rather than a sharp break with tradition.

In Canada, history also means ongoing dependency: first with France, then with Great Britain, and now with the United States. Throughout its evolution, Canadian society has assimilated not only ideas and models but also capital and people from dominant societies. In the case of suburban development, Canadians were simultaneously influenced by American and British models, sometimes choosing one, sometimes the other, and sometimes trying to integrate parts of both traditions.

The importance of French Canadians in the evolution of Canada and their sheer numerical majority in the province of Quebec is also a distinct characteristic. Although their relative weight declined over the last two centuries they still represent a quarter of the Canadian population and four-fifths of the Quebec population. Over the centuries French Canadians have developed their own North American models of housing and community life.[34] It is a serious mistake to perceive this influence as purely rural. The formerly common image of the French Canadians as the last folk society north of the Rio Grande has been completely discredited by historians during the last two decades. The fact is that there is a longstanding and enduring urban tradition among French Canadians, demonstrated by their urban forms in Montreal, by their control of municipal institutions, and by their active role in the land development industry.

Aside from the significance of the French Canadians, the ethnic scene in Canada is very different from that found in the United States. In Canada, ethnic diversification has been a much slower process, although it has accelerated since 1945. People of black origin have always represented tiny minorities in Canadian cities, so that the racial factor was not a determining one in Canada whereas it gave a powerful impulse to American suburban expansion. Of course, prejudice and segregation were present in Canadian society and were expressed, for example, against Jews and Italians in central Canada and against Indians and Métis in the West. Nevertheless, it seems to me that class was as much a segregative factor as ethnic origin in the social division of Canadian suburban space.

The role and the evolution of local political structures are also significant factors differentiating Canada and the United States. Many observers, for example, have stressed the importance of the longstanding tradition of nonpartisan politics at the municipal level. More generally, state intervention at all levels of government has evolved under different conditions, and the impact of this phenomenon upon suburban development has to be researched more systematically. There is, for example, a significant difference in the fiscal treatment of homeownership: Canadians are not allowed to deduct local taxes and mortgage interest from their income tax, although they do get a tax break on their capital gains when they sell the house. As people go to the suburbs to live in their house rather than to think about selling it, the fiscal incentive to become a homeowner is not so strong and so immediate as in the United States.

In fact, the analysis of the differences between Canadian and American urban development has already attracted the attention of some scholars. The most significant contribution is that of John Mercer and Michael A. Goldberg, who challenge the concept of a North American city and focus upon social values as the key factor explaining the differences.[35] They argue, for example, that "values tolerating ethnic and racial diversity and values which contribute to a less violent milieu play a role in maintaining the superior livability of the Canadian central city." They also point to different political values, finding a greater acceptance of government intervention and collective action in Canada. This would explain the better managed cities and a more even distribution of the costs of urban growth. Although their article deals only with very recent urban evolution, the questions they raise merit further research over a longer historical time period.

But, as is generally the case with any revisionist approach, Mercer and Goldberg are probably going too far in the other direction and throwing out the baby with the bath water. Assessing the differences between the two countries does not mean that the concept of the North American city loses its explanatory powers. This paradigm permits us to stress the high degree of similarity in the fundamental patterns of urban and suburban development in both countries. At the same time, there are differences in the way these patterns are actualized. Sometimes it is only a matter of degree or size; sometimes it is the result of distinct historical evolution or social values.

Thus, alongside major similar or parallel phenomena there are some significant differences between the Canadian and American urban and suburban development. But what can we do with such an appreciation of distinctiveness?

## A Suburbanization Process?

Close scrutiny of the differences between Canada and the United States is necessary to understand the evolution of each society. But if the objective is to understand suburbanization itself should we not stress the similarities?

Clearly each country is unique. But each city within a country shows some degree of uniqueness. Despite these differences there are some converging factors; there is a pattern. There is a suburbanization process, or more accurately, a subprocess of the urbanization process. It is the centuries-long trend toward the expansion of the urbanized areas by the transformation of previously rural land. And even when they choose to live in splendid isolation from the core city, suburban territories and suburban population are inextricably linked to the metropolitan area of which they are a constitutive element.

This suburbanization process has seven major components:

1. Land: its availability, its price, its location and site, and its use by the land development industry
2. Transportation: its technological impact, its availability, and its price
3. Population trends: especially migration movements and the formation of new households
4. Economic structure: its nature, its evolution, and its historical heritage
5. Social structure: class divisions, composition of the work force, income, and the cost of housing
6. Cultural values: including perceptions of the ideal home but also and, more important, of class and race or ethnic solidarity and differences
7. Political structures: degree of local autonomy, resources available for community development, citizens' involvement and participation in the decision-making process.

All these components are everywhere present in the process of suburbanization, although their mix varies from one place to the other and, in the same place, from one period of time to the next. Finally, in any single place, country and time, the process is actualized in a unique manner. Yet the process nevertheless remains a process with its common features.

So, what should be stressed: process or local specificity? Among the social sciences one of the fundamental contributions of the historian has always been to show the distinctiveness of a situation, to be aware of a sense of time and place. In recent decades, historians have developed a greater awareness of the importance of understanding not only individual but also fundamental processes in the evolution of human societies. They nevertheless have retained a salutary cautious attitude toward broad generalizations by remaining aware of the individual case, of specificity. It is probably within this equilibrium between process and uniqueness that we should continue to seek the historian's contribution to the understanding of our societies.

# Notes

1. For an overview of Canadian urban history, see Alan F.J. Artibise and Paul-André Linteau, *The Evolution of Urban Canada: An Analysis of Approaches and Interpretations* (Winnipeg, 1983); see also Alan F.J. Artibise and Gilbert A. Stelter, *Canada's Urban Past: A Bibliography to 1980 and Guide to Canadian Urban Studies* (Vancouver, 1981).

2. Even if there is no survey book, there are four very useful collections of essays, all edited by Gilbert A. Stelter and Alan F.J. Artibise: *The Canadian City: Essays in Urban and Social History*, 2nd edition, revised and expanded (Ottawa, 1984); *The Usable Urban Past: Planning and Politics in the Modern Canadian City* (Toronto, 1979); *Shaping the Urban Landscape: Aspects of the Canadian City-Building Process* (Ottawa, 1982); *Power and Place: Canadian Urban Development in a North-American Context* (Vancouver, 1986).

3. Kenneth T. Jackson, *Crabgrass Frontier, The Suburbanization of the United States* (New York, 1985).

4. Louise Dechêne, "La croissance de Montréal au XVIIIe siècle," *Revue d'histoire de l'Amérique française* 27 (September 1973): 163–79.

5. Among the urban biographies of Montreal, see John Irwin Cooper, *Montreal: A Brief History* (Montreal, 1969); Kathleen Jenkins, *Montreal: Island City of the St. Lawrence* (Garden City, NY, 1966); Raoul Blanchard, *L'Quest du Canada français: Montréal et sa région* (Montreal, 1954); Paul-André Linteau, "Montréal" in *The Canadian Encyclopedia* (Edmonton, 1985); Jean-Pierre Collin, *Histoire de l'urbanisation de la paroisse de Montréal, 1851–1941* (Montreal, 1984).

6. The author is co-director of a research group on social history of Montreal, at the Université du Québec à Montréal; see: Paul-André Linteau and Jean-Claude Robert, "Montréal au 19e siècle: bilan d'une recherche," *Urban History Review/Revue d'histoire urbaine* 13 (February 1985): 207–23; since the early 1970s several other groups and individuals have become very active in the history of Montreal.

7. Paul-André Linteau, *The Promoters' City: Building the Industrial Town of Maisonneuve, 1883–1918* (Toronto, 1985). Originally published in French in 1981, the book is a revised version of my Ph.D. dissertation submitted at the Université du Montréal in 1974. See also P.A. Linteau, "The Development and Beautification of an Industrial City: Maisonneuve, 1883–1918," in Stelter and Artibise, *Shaping the Urban Landscape*, 304–20.

8. Linteau, *The Promoters' City*, chap. 2, "The Developers"; see also P.A. Linteau, "Le contrôle de l'espace et du bâti dans la banlieue montréalaise," in M. Garden and Y. Lequin, *Habiter la ville, XVe–XXe siècles* (Lyon, 1984), 153–74.

9. Paul-André Linteau and Jean-Claude Robert, "Land Ownership and Society in Montreal: An Hypothesis," in *The Canadian City*, ed. Stelter and Artibise, 39–56; Linteau, "Le contrôle de l'espace."

10. Linteau, *The Promoters' City*, chap. 6, "A Working-Class Town"; "Le contrôle de l'espace."

11. Linteau, *The Promoters' City*, chap. 5, "The Power of the Utility Monopolies."

12. Walter Van Nus, "The Role of Suburban Government in the City Building Process: The Case of Notre-Dame-de-Grâces, Quebec, 1876–1910," *Urban History Review/Revue d'histoire urbaine* 13 (October 1984): 91–103; Jean-Louis Lalonde, "Le village Saint-Jean-Baptiste: la formation d'un faubourg ouvrier à Montréal, 1861–1886" (M.A. thesis (history), Université du Québec à Montréal, 1985). There is also an interesting study of an early "New Town" within the limits of the City: David B. Hanna, "Creation of an Early Victorian Suburb in Montreal," *Urban History Review/Revue d'histoire urbaine* 9 (October 1980): 38–64.

13. Jean-Pierre Collin, "La Cité sur mesure: spécialisation sociale de l'espace et autonomie municipale dans la banlieue montréalaise, 1875–1920," *Urban History Review/Revue d'histoire urbaine* 13 (June 1984), 19–34.

14. John C. Weaver, "From Land Assembly to Social Maturity: The Suburban Life of Westdale (Hamilton) Ontario, 1911–1951," in *Shaping the Urban Landscape*, ed. Stelter and Artibise, 321–55.

15. Ibid., 333.

16. Ibid., 332.

17. Ross Patterson, "The Development of an Interwar Suburb: Kingsway Park, Etobicoke," *Urban History Review/Revue d'histoire urbaine* 13 (February 1985): 225–35.

18. Among the most important urban biographies for this period, see Alan F.J. Artibise, *Winnipeg: A Social History of Urban Growth, 1874–1914* (Montreal, 1975) and the various monographs published in The History of Canadian Cities series (Toronto): A.F.J. Artibise, *Winnipeg*; Max Foran, *Calgary;* P.E. Roy, *Vancouver;* John C. Weaver, *Hamilton;* J.M.S. Careless, *Toronto to 1918;* James Lemon, *Toronto Since 1918;* John Taylor, *Ottawa.*

19. Leroy O. Stone, *Urban Development in Canada* (Ottawa, 1967), 155–71.

20. For examples of diversity in a suburban area, see Gérard Divay and Jean-Pierre Collin, *La communauté urbaine de Montréal: de la ville contrale à l'île centrale* (Montreal, 1977).

21. For a survey of studies dealing with contemporary Canadian development see Artibise and Stelter, *Canada's Urban Past* and Canadian Council on Urban Regional Research, *Urban and Regional References, 1945–1969* (Ottawa, 1970), with supplements through 1976.

22. For a history of the Don Mills project, see "The Suburbs," a special issue of *City Magazine* 2 (January 1977): 28–38.

23. Peter Spurr, *Land and Urban Development: A Preliminary Study* (Toronto, 1976); James Lorimer, *The Developers* (Toronto, 1978); see also James Lorimer and Evelyn Ross, eds., *The Second City Book: Studies of Urban and Suburban Canada* (Toronto, 1977) and James Lorimer and Carolyn MacGregor, eds., *After the Developers* (Toronto, 1981).

24. Lorimer, *The Developers*, chap. 5.

25. Gérard Divay and Marcel Gaudreau, *La formation des espaces résidentiels. Le système de production de l'habitat urbain dans les années soixante-dix au Québec* (Montreal, 1984). This book is the offspring of a large-scale research project on the new residential areas of the province of Quebec in the 1970s. The project was conducted by INRS-Urbanisation, an urban research centre linked to the University of Quebec. A host of research reports were produced in the course of the project. See also Caroline Andrew, Serge Bordeleau, and Alain Guimont, *L'Urbanisation: une affaire* (Ottawa, 1981).

26. Divay and Gaudreau, *La formation*, chap. 3; Lorimer, *The Developers*, chap. 5.

27. One author has signalled the importance of foreign (mostly European) ownership of some of the large developing groups in the Montreal area: but he examined only a limited number of case studies; see Henry Aubin, *City for Sale: International Finance and Canadian Development* (Toronto, 1977).

28. On CMHC policies see Spurr, *Land and Urban Development;* Lorimer, *The Developers;* Divay and Gaudreau, *La formation;* Marc H. Choko, Jean-Pierre Collin, and Annick Germain, "Le logement et les enjeux de la transformation de l'espace urbain: Montréal, 1940–1960," *Urban History Review/Revue d'histoire urbaine* 15 (October 1986): 127–36.

29. Choko, Collin, and Germain, "Le logement"; Divay and Gaudreau, *La formation.*

30. For a survey of these issues see the seven broad essays (on Montreal, Toronto, Ottawa-Hull, Halifax, Vancouver, Winnipeg, and Edmonton) in Warren Magnusson and Andrew Sancton, eds., *City Politics in Canada* (Toronto, 1983).

31. On the loss of municipal autonomy see John Taylor, "Urban Autonomy in Canada: Its Evolution and Decline," in *The Canadian City,* ed. Stelter and Artibise (1984), 478–500 and Warren Magnusson, "Introduction: The Development of Canadian Urban Government," in *City Politics in Canada* by Magnusson and Sancton, 3–57. On municipal resistance to centralization in Quebec see Gérard Divay and Jacques Léveillée, *La réforme municipale et l'Etat Québécois (1960–1979)* (Montréal: INRS-Urbanisation, 1981).

32. See James Lorimer, "Citizens and the Corporate Development of the Contemporary Canadian City," *Urban History Review/Revue d'histoire urbaine* 12 (June 1983): 3–9. For a list of the major works on the governance of Canadian cities, see Artibise and Linteau, *The Evolution of Urban Canada*, 26–30.

33. In a very important survey article, Gilbert Stelter has gone beyond the local differences to suggest an interpretation of the city-building process in Canada; see Gilbert A. Stelter, "The City Building Process in Canada," in *Shaping the Urban Landscape,* ed. Stelter and Artibise, 1–29.

34. See, for example, Jean-Claude Marsan, *Montreal in Evolution: Historical Analysis of Montreal's Architecture and Urban Environment* (Montreal, 1981).

35. John Mercer and Michael A. Goldberg, "Value Differences and Their Meaning for Urban Development in Canada and the U.S.," in *Power and Place*, ed. Stelter and Artibise, 343–94; these authors have recently developed their ideas in *The Myth of the North American City: Continentalism Challenged* (Vancouver, 1986).

# ETHNICITY AND NEIGHBOURHOODS*

**ROBERT F. HARNEY**

The sesquicentennial anniversary of Toronto has inspired the publication of a number of books on its history as a city. Few deal with what has become the most salient feature of Toronto in its one hundred and fiftieth year, its role as a preferred target of migration for people from every corner of the globe, its polyethnic character and its reputation for tolerance of human variety.

At a time when public relations campaigns make much of the city's ethnic mosaic in order to encourage tourism and investment, and politicians seem almost to credit themselves for the growth of a civic ethos of multiculturalism, it seems useful to learn more about Toronto's ethnic and immigrant past, to examine the city's actual record, in terms of inter-ethnic encounter, tolerance and attitudes toward pluralism. ...

The current celebratory mood of the city and the remarkable flowering of immigrant cultures here since the Second World War lead to a false retrospect about the history of the ethnic groups in the city, one in which the past and the present are conflated into a single oversimplified story. In his superb pseudo-geography, *Invisible Cities*, Italo Calvino writes: "Beware of saying to them that sometimes different cities follow one another on the same site with the same name, born and dying without knowing one another, without communication among themselves."[1] The lack of comprehension to which Calvino refers is not just among ethnic groups, but occurs as well among the various generations or migration cohorts within each ethnic group. History as slogans and stereotypes flourishes when serious history has not been attempted, and little or no serious history of Toronto's different peoples and their lives in the city has been written until very recently. We have been abandoned to labels such as "Toronto the Good," which conjure up images of a totally homogeneous colonial city with all its immigrants from the British Isles. The inadequacy of that view of the past has spawned a newer view which sees the city through the eyes of its post-World War Two polyethnicity and assumes a Toronto past in which great numbers of non-British immigrants were forced to hide their ethnocultures, were

---

*Robert F. Harney, *Gathering Place: Peoples and Neighbourhoods of Toronto, 1834–1945* (Toronto: Multicultural History Society of Ontario, 1985), 1–24.

oppressed or shunted aside or quickly harried into Canadianness. Both views, of course, are rhetoric masquerading as history.

For Toronto, then, the past, in Marc Bloch's words, "is a given quantity that nothing can change," but "knowledge of the past is a thing in process." If that process is left to public relations officers and partisans to impose upon, in an anachronistic way, it becomes more useful as a text for reading the current struggle between pluralists and traditionalists in the city than as a picture of the city's past. One would think that study of the census and city directories would answer the two basic questions: Was Toronto a mere extension of Great Britain into the mid-section of the American continent, or had it, like equivalent American cities, received large-scale foreign immigration? If the latter were so, was it also so that, by what is now seen as a failure of civic virtue, the Anglo-Celtic host society and élite chose to suppress all manifestations of other ethno-cultures in the city? Behind the last question lurks the assumption that newcomers generally wished to maintain old-world ways and ethnic group coherence rather than seek well-being and integration through rapid acculturation.

Both forms of retrospective falsification confuse an overwhelming statistical predominance of immigrants from the British Isles with ethnic homogeneity. English, Scots, Irish Catholics, Irish Protestants and Welsh did display separate ethnic identities in terms of associational life, sometimes language, religion, culture and settlement patterns. To test the truth of this assertion, ask any Irish Catholic who tried to break the Orange Lodge monopoly on the better positions in city government or the police, or ask any English artisan who encountered Canadian nativism whether discrimination affected them in nineteenth century Toronto. Along with the 10 per cent of the population that did come from "foreign lands," these ethnic differences among immigrants from Great Britain created patterns of separateness which foreshadowed the post-First and Second World War ethnocultures and ethnic enclaves in the city.

One can then scan the census figures for the city in the pre-World War Two period either for evidence of the overwhelming British presence, or for a glimpse of the presence of other peoples. If it is valid to ask whether Toronto the Good was a uniquely British city in North America or an incipient polyglot one like New York or Chicago a fitting predecessor to the cosmopolitan giant of today, in absolute numerical terms the answer is unequivocal. Even in 1911, after twenty years of mass migration and countless warnings by social gospellers, nativist union leaders and frightened racists about the impending inundation of the city by foreigners, the figures still show Toronto with 80 per cent of its population of British descent. About 4 per cent of the population was Jewish. Perhaps 2 per cent was of German origin, many of them long in the city and acculturated. Only the 4000 Italians, the 1000 Chinese and various Slavic groups—Macedonians, Ukrainians, Poles—and the Finns lived in visible concentrations of population like the Jews.

Even by 1941 the percentage of the city claiming British descent had not declined much. Then in a city of almost 700 000, there was no non-British ethnic group, which made up more than 5 per cent of the population, other than the Jews. Nonetheless, more than 14 000 Italians, 11 000 Poles, 10 000 Ukrainians, several thousand each of Finns, Chinese, Greeks, and Macedonians, along with almost 50 000 Jews, did live in Toronto. They were made highly visible by their proximity to city hall and the commercial downtown or their concentration in certain industrial areas. Toronto, before 1945, had ethnic enclaves and was in certain areas a polyglot city, far more cosmopolitan than Wyndham Lewis's "mournful Scottish version of a North American city." On the other hand, it remained overwhelmingly British in terms of the origins of its people, its attitudes and, of course, the place of the English language.

While the census cannot tell us much about the sensibilities, identities and *mentalités* of ethnic groups, or about inter-ethnic encounters, it can do more than simply show us that 10 per cent of the population was non-British. Patterns of settlement record what sociologists call the residential segregation index and enable us to sense the degree of each group's dependence on immigrant ethnoculture, their "clannishness," or their exclusion from the mainstream. For instance, although immigrants from Scotland as well as those who gave German as their ancestry were almost equally distributed throughout the city's four census areas in 1911, Jews, Italians, Chinese, Ukrainians and Macedonians showed no such even dispersal through the city. Rather they were heavily concentrated in those neighbourhoods such as the St. John's Ward, the Kensington Market area, the Toronto Junction and the East End. ...

William Lyon Mackenzie King, the future prime minister, in a series of *Daily Mail and Empire* articles in 1897, made the first serious attempt to understand and study the ethnic enclaves of Toronto. King wrote:

> The presence of large numbers of foreigners in Toronto makes an inquiry into these conditions a subject as interesting as it is timely. Does their presence here portend an evil for this city such as the above statistics which have just come upon the cities of the United States, or is the class of foreigners in this city here cast in a better mould and are they likely to prove at once good citizens and a strength to the community? These are questions of more than vital moment to the city, and answers can only be found in examination of the present condition of the people, a comparative study of their numbers, occupations and methods of living, their relations to the civic, religious and industrial life, together with a retrospective glance into the past as to the causes which brought them here and a speculative forecast as to the probable increase in their numbers which may be affected in the future.[2]

King went on to write about Germans, French, Jews, Syrians and Italians among others and did so in what was a remarkably informed and fair manner for his time. He did, however, confirm a false dichotomy that remains a problem in migration studies. "The Irish, Scots, English, Americans and Newfoundlanders," he wrote, were "so nearly akin in thought, customs, and manners to the Canadians themselves...that in speaking of a foreign population, they have generally been disregarded altogether. For with the exception of maintaining a few national societies, their foreign connection is in no way distinctively marked in civic life."

In the more democratic and pluralistic language of our time, we would be unlikely to frame questions about immigration and ethnicity in the manner King did. Nonetheless, his agenda of study is not that far from the preliminary one necessary for a retrospective ethnography of the city now. Most of those who have followed him in commenting on "foreigners" in Toronto did so in a context in which they clearly took the presence of immigrant neighbourhoods, or "foreign quarters," to be a form of urban blight. *Missionary Outlook* in 1910 observed:

> Every large city on this continent has its fourfold problem of the slum, the saloons, the foreign colonies and the districts of vice. The foreign colony may not be properly called a slum, but it represents a community that is about to become an important factor in our social life and will become a menace in our civilization unless it learns to assimilate the moral and religious ideals and the standards of citizenship.[3]

Any useful studies of the mores and folkways of immigrants and their children were not likely to prosper within the perimeters of the social gospel camp. From 1897 until the last half dozen years, no one, except a few evangelists and immigration restrictionists who brought a special anxiety to their work, has followed King in the effort to study the ethnic minorities and the ethnic neighbourhoods of the City of Toronto.

James Scobie observes in the introduction to his study of the city of Buenos Aires that reams of research, "on urban services, such as paving, parks, sewage, police, lighting and garbage disposal, on the location, regulation and expanse of industry, on education, public health, morality and amusements,"[4] have been produced on cities, but little is written about the people of a city. Rather than try to understand the non-British of the city, most scholars writing about Toronto have naturally enough concentrated on those whom they see as affecting power relations and the economic development of the city or as significant in the city's mainstream cultural and political life.[5]

In fact, though evangelists, city nurses, police officials, academics and teachers turned attention to the immigrant neighbourhoods of the city between 1900 and 1940, they did so without any clear understanding of what those neighbourhoods were, nor did they ask the relevant questions. Were the immigrant quarters simply stepping-stones towards acculturation, breathing spaces for immigrants and their children until they could become Canadian? Were they working-class neighbourhoods, or were they, as they were believed to be by much of their own ethnic intelligentsia, self-appointed élites and officials from the lands of emigration, stratified sub-societies and colonies within a larger diaspora? Were they new communities created by people in need of creating local ascriptive worlds within the larger, colder space of a Canadian industrial city? Did the European and Asian immigrants who gathered in ethnic enclaves do so willingly in order to preserve their old-world cultural baggage intact, or would they have been willing to embrace Anglo-Canadian ways if made welcome? Were such neighbourhoods fossils of the old world, or places of regeneration where a new ethnicity and new set of emblems, new networks of acquaintanceship and new eclectic North American ideas and values could grow up?

The terms used then and now—immigrant quarters, working-class neighbourhoods, ethnic enclaves, ghettos, Little Italies, Chinatowns, ethnocultural community—create a problem. They do not so much describe the social system and cultural life of particular groups of people in the city as they delineate the categories which such groups are supposed to inhabit. If the validity of these categories is assumed, the observer is relieved from any attempt to learn about and understand these groups. For example, all immigrants in a working-class neighbourhood may not be in the working-class and those who are may not be so in terms of their class of origin, class of destination, or *mentalités*. Moreover, the ethnic enclaves are rarely made up uniformly of one ethnic group. Nor does consensus within the group necessarily follow from shared ethnicity. A sense of the variety of individual approaches to acculturation, personal and familial migration projects, sense of sojourning and settling, adjustment to the new world within the ethnic community, the persistence of sub-ethnicities, and so on, is lost when the usual nomenclature is imposed on migration and ethnicity in process.

Study of ethnicity in Canada as a North American process is best understood when integrated into a spatial, in this case an urban, frame. The obverse would seem to have equal merit. No great North American city can be understood without being studied as a city of immigrants, of newcomers and their children, as a destination of myriad group and individual migration projects. Describing city government or municipal politics, the building of an urban economy and the evolution of the city as polity obviously has value. To do so without understanding ethnicity in the city seems a bit like analysing the captain and crew of an ocean liner but not noticing the passengers, what they expect of the vessel and why they are travelling. Without knowing the networks, folkways and values of the city's immigrants, whether from the United Kingdom or not, studying the encounter between city officials and the people of the city is at best one-sided, at worst vacuous.

Since the possibility for a more deeply textured history of the city and its people exists, we must pursue it beyond the limited historiographical inheritance we have been given for the study of Toronto. The absence of traditional urban studies has spared Toronto some of the misdirection which came from the behaviouralists' emphasis on using the census, on rates of economic, social and geographical mobility as codes to measure acculturation and integration, a methodological tide which first buoyed and then set adrift urban studies in the United States.[6] Toronto's ethnic and social historians, by their late start, know that such an approach based on the host society's sources is particularly unfit as a full explanation of immigrant and ethnic communities. For the most part, they would agree with Mr. Dooley, Finley Peter Dunne's fictitious Irish American bartender, who remarked on academic history in his time to a friend: "I know history isn't true Hinnissy cause it ain't like what I see ivry day in Halsted Street. If anyone comes along with a histhry iv Greece and Rome that will show me the people fightin', getting dhrunk, makin' love, getting' married, owin' the grocery man, and bein' without hard coal, I'll believe there was a Greece and Rome, but not before."[7]

Mr. Dooley had it right. If we fail to plumb the depths of attitudes toward Canada, toward the old country, to understand ethnic identity and ethnocultures, to understand immigrants' reactions to rebuffs or their attitudes towards their culture and those they identified as their fellows, then immigrants to Toronto—once dismissed as migrant navvies, "sheenies," "bohunks," "wops," or just unskilled workers—will again be dismissed, this time by a generation of social, labour and urban historians who reduce them to statistics. The broad categories of social history, like the broad categories of prejudice, are conveniences for those too lazy to comprehend the complicated nature of man in the city and of individual migration projects or separate ethnocultures.

To call for an interior history of immigrant and ethnic communities in Toronto before the Second World War is not to suggest some autonomous substructure, which allows us to ignore the reality of the circumambient city. Quite the reverse; it requires that we find ways to understand all the actors in the city's history, to understand the trauma of encounter at the boundaries of identity in the classroom, the corner restaurant, the factory or at leisure on street corners.

Migration routes, projects and destinations are always in flux. The immigrant adjusts to new situations in new places, changing or resisting. With our current state of scholarship we can only wonder now why old-world styles and ideas were discarded or defiantly maintained after some calculation of the cost, or after repeated approval or disapproval by the Canadian host society. Obviously we have to know the significance of those ways and ideas for the immigrant before we can understand, not just the immigrant group itself, but the processes of acculturation and the nature of daily life in the city. If we remember that the immigrants were conscious participants in all intercultural encounters, then the study of ethnic boundaries can begin to yield to answers about identity and *mentalités* themselves—what Fredrik Barth dismissively calls "the stuff" inside the ethnic boundary.[8] For ethnic boundaries turn out to be penumbras of opinion, choice and situation, not just hard-edged perimeters between the immigrants and the old stock.

When, under the influence of the Irish national revival, W.B. Yeats set out to discover the common people of Ireland, he was startled to realize that their history was virtually unknown. "Ancient map makers wrote across unexplored regions: here are lions, across the villages of fishermen and turners of the earth. So different are these from us we can but write one line that is certain: here are ghosts."[9] Anyone who sets out in the 1980s to understand the ethnic neighbourhoods of Toronto before the Second World War may well believe, like Yeats, that Toronto's ethnic enclaves are uncharted, unexplored and little comprehended empty spaces on the map.

Separate settlement in this city, the creation of urban spaces that were somehow different from the Toronto mainstream and yet produced an ambience different from that of the country of origin, happened for a number of reasons. The sense of fellow-feeling, the in-gathering for reasons of language, both out of pride of language and out of pain produced by *diglossia*,* the need to maintain folkways and mores, the location of work, the price of housing and transportation, the need for coherence in the face of outside hostility—all these contributed to neighbourhood creation. In Toronto, the city that developed after the pioneer period increasingly took the form of a grid. Such a regular plan lent itself only grudgingly to the creation of ethnic nooks and crannies. For example, the history of the St. John's Ward, in the heart of the city, as an underdeveloped area and immigrant quarter to the west of Yonge Street and behind the city hall, was in fact very short lived. The completion of the grid with Bay Street and Dundas Street in the early twentieth century, along with the introduction of sewers, ended what had been essentially an encapsulated immigrant world. The development of commercial and public institutions followed and drove immigrants farther west into the back alleys that later produced Kensington Market and farther yet, in the case of the Italians, to the short, non-gridded streets around St. Agnes Church. At the same time, Poles, Macedonians, Finns and others settled in the small cross streets of the industrial sectors of the East End, the Niagara region, and later the Junction in the West End.

One remarkable feature of all of these neighbourhoods for the city explorer or urban archaeologist is the degree to which the sites do not now correspond to the general grid layout of the city but, if not extirpated by freeways or housing projects, have still the quality of an enclosed space conducive to close and familiar street life. Whether in Kensington Place, near Little Trinity Church in the East End, or around the Clinton Street area of the second Little

---

**Diglossia* is bilingualism in two languages of uneven status in society. Typically the family language, or immigrant language, is the more comfortable medium but the one valued less in the city. For immigrants from rural backgrounds, *triglossia* existed. Dialect, ethnic language and English were viewed in ascending order of value in terms of the host society, but descending order of affection by the immigrant.

Italy, there still clings a feeling that these were neighbourhoods in a very immediate and face-to-face sense.

Historical sources on immigrants in Toronto can be divided into three groups. First there are municipal records, statistical and circumstantial, ranging from assessment roles and city directories to pedlars' licence lists, arrest logs, police books and student cards in the various inner-city grammar schools. Such materials can be used to recreate the setting of encounter and much of the factual surroundings of immigrant life. Then there is the literature of the urban actors themselves. On the one side is the writing of those already in the land, ranging from evangelical pamphlets of the social gospel missions, reports of settlement houses, royal commissions, medical officers' reports, boards of education papers and the English-speaking press. Such sources obviously can provide a valuable picture of the interplay between perception and reality in urban history. To pass through ethnic boundaries to ethnic identities, however, the immigrant's own account of this urban experience is also necessary. For that there is oral testimony, the fragile memory of the immigrants themselves, to be used with the same caution one would apply to any kind of subjective written biography, reminiscence or memoir. There are church almanacs, jubilee volumes, the minutes of fraternal and mutual aid organizations, letters and guides to letter writing in English and in the old-country language. There are also the reports of officials, foreign consuls and intellectuals travelling from the countries of origin passing through Toronto.

The numbers of those immigrants who came to Canada before World War Two are thinning dangerously. The city's history will pay dearly if we neglect the systematic gathering of oral testimony and other ethnocultural materials which could enrich our knowledge of people in the city. As it was for Yeats, so for us the most important source of information will be the people who, as immigrants and the children of immigrants, lived in ethnic neighbourhoods and who possess in their collective memory, personal papers, or as guardians of the records of now defunct ethnic associations, the history of those places.

Immigrants need no longer be depicted either as pro-Torontonians or proto-Canadians, as people on the threshold of acculturation, or as potential fossils, living in colonies of an old country, maintaining cultural baggage which changed little until it fell away like scales from the eyes in a healing Canadian environment. Instead, scholars may begin to see the immigrant colony itself as having a history, a process of development. Improved ways of observing group ethnicity may lead to more comprehension of the nature of personal ethnicity so that immigrants may come to be seen neither as simply the pre-articulate masses of Toronto, nor as Italians, Finns, Poles, etc., but as specific kinds of Torontonians—Italian, Finish, Polish Torontonians—who underwent individually and as groups a variety of urban experiences, met a variety of receptions which affected their strategies for living here and contributed in a variety of ways to the city's growth.

The new emphasis on history from the "bottom up,"[10] along with ethnohistory's interest in analysis of culture and society, invites us to move beyond the study of the external and quantifiable to the more deeply textured and nuanced study of *mentalités*, perceptions in encounter and conflict, strategies for adjustment or persistence in relation to the changing real condition of being immigrant and for coping with a changing personal or group sense of ethnos. The task of ethnohistory should be the difficult one suggested in the phrase of Jacobo Timmerman, "to penetrate the affective world of the other." To do that, we need to look at the immigrant and ethnic neighbourhoods of the city without assuming we comprehend the intent of each person's migration project, the intensity of their ethnic networks or of their loyalties to ethnoculture.

To understand the linkage among identity, cognitive maps, psychic worlds,[11] commitment to family and friends, and then to understand how these individual commitments paralleled a continuum of place, family, work site, church, association, street-corner life, we need also to comprehend the immigrants' sense of space. We can do this by simply changing our frame of reference. The great anthropologist Oscar Lewis once lamented that anthropologists who became ethnohistorians spent most of their time talking to old Amerindians and practising a methodology they called participant observation, but rarely bothered to look at the sources of the United States Bureau of Indian Affairs or the Canadian government, since they believed that the written word represented only the view of an arrogant and ignorant conqueror of the indigenous people.[12] Historians of the city have tended to the opposite sin by thinking that they can reconstruct the reality of urban immigrant life from the writings and documents of the caretakers of the host society. Such sources leave the historian on the edge of the city's ethnocultural reality. Recreating the past from them is a bit like writing the history of British Africa or French Indo-China from the memoirs of soldiers and missionaries alone.

Few of Toronto's ethnic neighbourhoods could qualify in the Marxist sense as "internal colonies," societies "within a society based on racial, linguistic and marked cultural differences of social class," and subject to control by "the dominant classes and institutions of the metropolis."[13] Yet the concept of internal colonies is at least as useful a model for prewar Toronto as images of homogeneity or rapid assimilation. It reminds us to look at the ethnic community as a separate place, to think of its interior life and not just its boundaries. It reminds us of what Walter Firey observed studying Boston's neighbourhoods many years ago: a neighbourhood is at one and the same time part of the city hierarchy and system and a "little homeland," a spatial corollary to a set of values, of networks, of ways of thinking and being, of ethnos.[14] In Toronto some groups obviously required a "little homeland" more than others, and the result was immigrant neighbourhoods. English, Scots and Irish, except for concentrations in Cabbagetown, were not confined in enclaves. Despite tell-tale accents, they did not encounter systematic discrimination. They did, as Mackenzie King noted, form associations, from the St. George Society to the Dewi Sant and the Orange Lodge, and they did encounter enough hostility that some concepts of ethnic neighbourhood or enclave apply to them as well. Peoples' ways were shaped by living in neighbourhoods, around them, among a majority group, or indeed even by escaping from them and practising that most common third- or fourth-generation phenomenon, "weekend ethnicity": returning to the immigrant areas for religious services, food supply, haircut, or family visits only on the weekend.

Ethnic neighbourhoods can be studied as concentrated universes in two quite different ways. One is accessible to plotting by analysing factual sources, especially written city records, and by forms of social scientific measurement. Another is more notional. It is about the *mentalités* of immigrants and about the psychic worlds they inhabit.

This more complex and notional sense of the neighbourhood then as an ambience, a psychic world for the immigrants and their children and perhaps their children's children, with its moving mix of ethnoculture, part-cultures and pressures to change the mores and folkways, produced by encounter with the North American situation, is a world we must come to know. If we allow ourselves just for a moment "to surrender," in Vladimir Nabokov's words, "to a sort of retrospective imagination which feeds analytical faculty with boundless alternatives," every usage and event in the enclave becomes an intricate key for studying attitudes and identities.

Borrowing from social anthropology, we can begin to understand the value of extending and deepening our moment of observation of the immigrants and their children in their neighbourhoods.[15] Freed of the retrospective falsification that comes from fervent but anachronistic multiculturalism, and equally free from an historicism that sees all immigrants pausing only momentarily on the threshold to the house of Canadian ways, we have an opportunity to fill in the blank spots on our map of the city. We can find ways to comprehend the group's sense of group, not just the intensity and frequency of the use of neighbourhood or ethnic networks, but the changing significance, for the immigrant and each succeeding generation, of various community institutions, such as a home town club, a nationalist association, or a parish.

By learning more about the role of mutual aid societies, the ethnic press, church, drama and leisure clubs, the importance of islands of acquaintanceship within the community and the ethnolinguistic psychology which made people choose one language over another, as well as about changing symbols and emblematics of the group, we may arrive at a demotic intellectual history, a history of how the people think. If we can begin to know their attitudes about settling, or merely sojourning, about upward mobility, about social class, about other ethnic groups in Toronto, if we can learn more of the dreams they held for their children, the strategies they chose either to persist in their own culture or acculturate in Canada, we will be on the verge of being able to write a whole social and cultural history of the city.

Information and insight into all these ideas are accessible to us if we combine the little used sources generated from inside the community, such as club and church records and ethnic newspaper and print ephemera, with a more extensive and systematic use of oral testimony. The city might then have the sort of history Lawrence Levine describes as "the attempt to present and understand the thought of people who though quite articulate in their own lifetimes have been rendered inarticulate by scholars who devoted too much of their attention to less recalcitrant subjects."[16] Levine's thought parallels almost exactly that of the social anthropologist Clifford Geertz who writes, "at base, thinking is a public activity. Its natural habitat is the house yard, the market place and the town square."[17]

The convergence of the two disciplines holds special possibilities for urban and immigrant studies. Although declining and increasingly fragile, the necessary sources for the study of Italians, Jews, Chinese, Greeks, Macedonians and the many peoples and neighbourhoods of Toronto in the late nineteenth and twentieth century are still available. The equivalent of Geertz's house yard, marketplace and town square existed in each one of Toronto's ethnic neighbourhoods. Throughout Toronto there were such house yards, behind boardinghouses or roughcast cottages in the alleys of the Ward, Kensington or the East End. They were places where kin, friends from home towns in the old country and neighbours gathered. They were also places where small-scale agriculture, commerce, industry and a bit of animal husbandry went on. There people foregathered for seasonal food processing—pickling, butchering, sausage making and wine making—for impromptu picnics and communal meals. They gathered to exchange collective wisdom about important decisions—sending for relatives from the old country, following work opportunities out of the city, moving out of the neighbourhood, improving a house or selling it, allowing a child to continue his or her education. The house yard was place where hundreds of the small human decisions, which affected the city's economy, appearance and culture, were made.

The equivalent of the marketplace in Geertz's analysis were the corner stores, the factories and life on the work gangs. For the children, it was the schoolyards, playgrounds and settlement houses. Each was in a different spatial and psychic relationship to the "little homeland," the ethnic neighbourhood and the ethnic group. They were places where men and women had to negotiate their ethnicity, make those constant adjustments of style and thinking which were the milestones in the process of learning to live within the larger North American urban setting. They learned when one could trust someone from outside the ethnic group. They learned the more difficult lesson of not trusting some even within their own regional group. They had opportunity to study what was threatening and what was useful about municipal politics and city government. In this way, Toronto's ethnic groups thought, reacted and became actors in the city's history.

In the little corner stores, cafés and social clubs, animated and informed debate took place on the politics of the old country and the problems of the new. A participant observer might have seen something of ethnicity as process if he could have recorded the changing ratio of old-world talk to Toronto talk, as well as the levels of intensity accompanying each subject. Surrogate for that field work which was not done is the local ethnic press. Concordances on topics covered and on their placement in the paper give some sense of the changing concerns of the ethnic communities. In the work gangs and factories immigrants had opportunities to understand the advantages and disadvantages of ethnic cohesion in the face of an exploitive capitalist system or other ethnic groups. Encountering workers of other ethnic origins in the factories, they discovered their commonalities and differences. All of these "marketplaces" were the scenes of public discourse and decision making which affected the city itself.

Finally, central to the neighbourhood was what Geertz refers to as the "town square." In many of the city's ethnic neighbourhoods one could reconstruct the neighbourhood outward from the church or *shul*. For usually a religious building, occasionally a secular hall, just as in the villages of origin, defined the geographic and psychic core of the immigrant neighbourhoods. That core affected even those within the ethnic group who chose to go their own way towards secularism, or who joined one of the North American evangelical faiths beckoning them toward rapid acculturation. Whether seen as friend or enemy, the church or the local hall was a part of an immigrant's map and a gathering place. It was in front of the church on Sundays, in the associational hall or home town clubs, or waiting for an ethnic newspaper to appear on a corner stand, in the streets watching children play, or shopping that the ethnic nodal point—no matter what its spatial contours—took on the context of a "town square." Corners in the Ward, in the Italian neighbourhoods to the west, in front of *shuls* or Orthodox churches, on Maria Street in the Junction, served as forums for the evolution of ethnic group thought. It was there that the reinforcing sense of the neighbourhood as ethnic enclave, as well as a sometimes irritating sense of its role as a *villagio pettegolo*, a gossipy village, emerged. Since most such neighbourhoods served as a base camp for those of the immigrant groups who dared to go outside to work in the Ontario north on construction sites, to peddle, or to run fruit stores, confectioneries, dry goods shops and restaurants, the "town square," especially on the weekend, had a special role in both spreading news and reaffirming the coherence of the ethnic group.

We can come much closer to understanding how currents of thought within the ethnic group affected the enclave, its culture and identity. Not understanding these things, it seems unlikely that an urban historian can paint a fair or accurate picture of the immigrant as participant in the larger city. For if we do not know, for example, whether a Catholic priest in a certain parish supported a strike action in a nearby factory, or whether immigrants from a small Balkan country were more preoccupied with the nationalist struggle at home than with their social struggle on a work site, while other immigrants from eastern Europe wrote and performed plays with titles like *Unemployed on Spadina* in order to denounce the Canadian system, we can hardly measure the impact of immigrants on the city's workforce, life and politics, or the impact of the city upon them.

Being part of an immigrant group and living in an ethnic enclave meant hearing and reading both more and less information on various subjects than those in the larger host society did. It meant receiving news with a different emphasis on almost every matter of politics and culture. What was transmitted once in the "town square" and through the ethnic press now reaches people via cable television. Toronto is a city whose populace has always been fractured, in its receipt of information, into ethnocultural groups. To take an example from outside our period, the front page of a Hungarian Marxist newspaper printed in the city in 1950 contained a picture of Ho Chi Minh and a discussion of the Vietnamese problem at a time when Ho Chi Minh was largely unknown to English-speaking Toronto and the tragedy of Indochina remote. It is remarkable that no historian of the city has studied how this multiplicity of overlapping "communication systems" in Toronto affects our political life and intergroup understanding.

In the same way that the fracturing of information is a consequence of being a polyethnic city, so too each ethnic group or immigrant cohort had a different spatial definition of the city itself. Both in the geographical sense of an enclave and in the more notional sense of ambience, the neighbourhood as a combination of individual cognitive maps and psychic worlds for immigrants and their children provided their focus and anchor in the city.

Each sojourner or settler possessed, as well as a detailed cognitive map of his world, a sense of where his fellows were in Toronto and of what parts of the city mattered to him. The immigrant's alternative atlas, of course, could not be confined to Toronto. It included key points such as his town of origin, the routes and stops on his crossing, as well as locations where his extended kin were throughout the world. The historian who tries to fit the ethnic group too neatly, geographically and psychically, into the city does damage both to urban history and to the study of migration and ethnicity itself. For example, Toronto's Ward in the 1900s served both Italians and Jews throughout the province. From it, men who went to work seasonally on the labour intensive northern frontiers of Ontario, or peddled through the lonely countryside, drew supplies and cultural sustenance. Through the neighbourhood they kept in touch with other colonies of their own kind, their home town and fellow townsmen throughout the diaspora. Through the neighbourhood passed cash remittances, ethnic goods—from tomato paste to talissim—brides, returnees and intelligence reports about travel routes, work, housing and reception newcomers could expect in other parts of the country. In this manner the neighbourhood as an ambience was always larger than the actual enclave. On the other hand, many of the immigrants who settled or sojourned in the Ward had very little knowledge or contact with other nearby Toronto neighbourhoods. Toronto was then an urban space which, in semiotic terms, spoke to each immigrant group differently and spoke to all of them. Since their settled British and acculturated neighbours saw the city differently, they misunderstood newcomers' behaviour.

Foreign immigrants and their children rarely developed a balanced map of the whole city. An understanding of its other people, the use of its other spaces, or its history developed slowly. The first *Bulgaro-English Dictionary* included phrases on how to take the streetcar to King Street East "where the Macedonians live," side by side with how to find the Wabash ticket agent for trains to other Macedonian settlements near Chicago or St. Louis. It had no phrases about the Ward or Rosedale.[18] A place of work, or housing, or leisure for one group was a place seen as an unfriendly environment or simply unknown to another group. Thus Macedonians knew there was no work for them at Gooderham's even though that distillery was in the middle of their settlement. Italians knew that one needed to change one's name and hide one's origin to clerk in the big department stores, and all foreigners knew that the Hydro Commission hired only workers of British descent under the pretext, or on the grounds, that communication in English was necessary. Lithuanian men on their way from boardinghouses on Queen Street West to factories in the East End picked up box lunches paid for on a weekly basis from Chinese lunch grills near their boardinghouses. Yet they never ventured into Chinatown for a Chinese meal even though that neighbourhood lay between them and work.

For most groups, picnics and outings, even a visit to the graves of loved ones in Mount Hope Cemetery, required a trek across unfamiliar and threatening space. Leisure itself was a segregated activity for the immigrant generation, and the pattern followed them out of the city. Property owned by members of the ethnic group, by benevolent associations or parishes, usually on the outskirts of Toronto, were safe sites for planned leisure, picnics, or ethnic outings. Pontypool, east of the city, and Belle Ewart, near Lake Simcoe, were such locations for the Jews. Nearby farms served Italians, Macedonians, Chinese and Poles in the same way. In the neighbourhood, men and women built systems and networks that enabled them to survive as Torontonians and, in most instances, made it possible for their children to sally forth into the larger city to work, and to share public leisure places such as the CNE and Sunnyside. Many of the immigrants probably understood their neighbourhood and the city much in the way that Italo Calvino suggests in *Invisible Cities*. There he describes the mythical city of Vasilia—Toronto's real Junction, Cabbagetown, Ward, or Kensington Market would do just as well:

> In a city, to establish the relations to sustain the city's life, the inhabitants stretched strings from the corners of the houses, white

> or black or grey, or black and white, according to whether they mark a relationship of blood or trade, authority, agency. When the strings become so numerous that you can no longer pass among them, the inhabitants leave, the houses are dismantled. Only their strings and their supports remain.[19]

Good urban historians will learn how to read a narrative in those strings and their supports. It will not be easy, for a few locations in the city were the exclusive neighbourhood of a single ethnic group. Kensington Market, once called the *mercato giudeo* by Italian immigrants, had by the twenties and thirties lost is exclusively Jewish character and become polyethnic. The Junction, the city's premier candidate as an ethnic industrial working-class neighbourhood, now boasts a Polish hall, an Albanian hall, a Maltese parish, a little synagogue on Maria Street, A Croatian club, an Irish club and had at one time an Italian pasta factory. The neighbourhood seems always to have been truly polyethnic.

Stores in the Junction that served Canadian Pacific Railway workers in the daytime became Macedonian hangouts at night. Separate and public schools brought children of many backgrounds together. In the battle for control of the young, it was in the playgrounds and schoolyards throughout the city where the guardians of the host society effectively took children away from the streets and from their parents' culture. In fact, if studied closely enough the surface of neighbourhoods like the Junction give way to deeper patterns of sub-neighbourhoods. In the Junction, some streets served the workers in the stockyards, mainly Macedonians, while nearby streets housed artisans, mainly German and Jewish, from the Heinzmann piano factory, once the largest employer in the neighbourhood. Yet other streets housed mostly families which worked for the CPR, mainly Anglo-Celtic. So the ethno-histories of Maria, Mulock and Glendenan streets in the Junction diverge over time almost as much as the histories of the Junction and Kensington Market. In the East End, Cabbagetown, Corktown and the Macedonian's cognitive map of their East-End neighbourhood blurred and shared much the same space. In the same manner the Ward itself, the city's chief Jewish ghetto at the turn of the century, was also the city's Chinatown and its chief Little Italy.

If nothing else, this intimate sharing of areas by immigrant groups suggests that the usual frame of study—immigrants *vis-à-vis* a WASP or Anglo-Celtic dominant society—misses the real dynamic of encounter, exchange and competition among newcomers from many lands. The polyethnic reality reconfirms the view that the history of a great North American city can rarely be properly written unless it is also ethnic and immigration history. Unfortunately for Toronto, the history of the Junction area, the history of the Ward and the history of Kensington Market, just as the history of several ethnic groups not dealt with who lived with high levels of residential segregation in the city before the Second World War—Lithuanians, Maltese and Hungarians, for example—have yet to be done.

Many of Toronto's newcomers had been cultural or religious minorities in their land of origin. Jews, Macedonians, Galicians, even the Catholic Irish and south Italians had had some experience in having to create and sustain their own ethnocultural institutions against regimes that were hostile or remote. Few, however, had experienced the uprooting or, conversely, the freedom to speculate about and alter identity. Although concern about a homeland or about the diaspora of one's people throughout the world persisted, such concerns themselves became elements in the forging of a new sense of group for which the neighbourhood was the territorial base. Karl Deutsch had observed that, "an isolated minority in a strange new country might increase its efforts to recall its past and to standardize its behaviour so as to erase again and again the eroding effects of the new environment on its traditional culture."[20] In such circumstances, the role of leaders and the nature of their status and appeal obviously calls for analysis. Reflective and ideological efforts at maintaining folkways, values and language, although themselves a long step away from primordial ethnicity, especially for those groups from the tsarist borderlands, came in logical sequence for the immigrant in North America. Each ethnoculture seemed to hold differing attitudes on the importance of group coherence. Ethnic leaders and intelligentsia encouraged different strategies for group survival, which posited roles for church, language and nationalist political party in group life.

Some of the political left in each group looked beyond ethnic persistence to a world of contact with the working class of other ethnic groups. As with those who joined North American evangelical churches, the rates of acculturation of those on the left were often more rapid, either because they came to know the larger city more quickly or found the ethnic enclave less nurturing and its leaders—priests, businessmen, foreign consuls—less acceptable. Historians have not reconstructed the degree to which, over two or three generations, ethnicity was the continuing organizer of existence in the city for many people. Some immigrants may have seen their ethnicity as simply an epiphenomenon of immigration—something of value for themselves but not their children or their children's children. Some tried to keep their ethnoculture in the form in which they brought it from the old country; others negotiated their ethnicity, altering its content or displaying ethnocultural ways selectively where they were acceptable to the host society, or when they brought them comfort or seemed right. Ethnic identity, even national feeling for the homeland, remained for most of the first two Canadian generations of any immigrant group a latent value which arose in times of crises—such as an earthquake in the old country, an encounter with prejudice in the new, a measurement for choosing a certain politician in the city for whom to vote.

Whether experience with maintaining minority institutions in a hostile environment was long and deep, as with the Jews, or a relatively new phenomenon of national revival, as with the Galicians and Macedonians, none of the immigrant groups had faced the need to create entirely new institutions. The need to do so, in fact, was a central aspect of ethnicity as North American process. For example, when the Macedonians in Toronto decided to organize their own church in 1911, it lead them into what most Torontonians saw as visibly Macedonian national politics. On the other hand, what they did was almost entirely neoteric for them as Macedonians. People, accustomed to a village church, used to a community of elders who were just that, older and wiser, used to a priest leading them, found themselves gathering in private homes in Macedonian neighbourhoods of the city. They created a slate of immigrant delegates from thirty-one different villages of origin for the purpose of tithing one another to build a single church, not a number of village churches. Reflecting the youth of the immigrant population, only four out of the twenty elected as village elders in Toronto were over thirty years old.[21] The condition of being Macedonian in Toronto, of being ethnic in a Canadian city, did not then replicate the old country any more than it was simply a stage towards acculturation and an Anglo-Canadian lifestyle.

This same irony existed in the creation of an Italian parish or a Polish parish. Although such parishes might appear ethnic to the larger Toronto society, or to the Irish Catholic hierarchy, they were not the "old-world transplanted." At Our Lady of Mt. Carmel, Barese, Sicilian and Venetian patron saints rubbed shoulders in a way that they would not have done in Italy. The "very Italian" feast of San Rocco seemed a mélange of Canadianisms to the immigrants. The mass had an Irish Celebrant, a Jewish boy from the Ward was the solo instrumentalist and "God Save the King" was played.[22] In fact, such churches were a totally new phenomenon for the people in the parish on several levels. Worshipping with co-nationals not from their home town, they encountered identities, accents and folkways they did not know. Often they developed Polish or Italian national identity together in the new world almost coincident with becoming Polish or Italian Torontonians. Moreover, Roman Catholic immigrants had to question, often for the first time, the authority and power of the church in order to gain their separate parish. Though usually viewed by the host society as an import from the old country, the national clubs, parishes and benevolent associations, which transcended home town and *landsleit* loyalties, were essentially a Toronto phenomenon and seen as such by the immigrants.

Ethnoculture is not a thing apart, merely something to which "social events, behaviour, institutions, or processes can be constantly attributed," but is rather a context within which such things can be intelligibly described. Once we see the immigrants as serious actors in the city's history, then the need to know more about their associational life, the intensity and variety of networks of acquaintanceship, the sub-economies which they created in various neighbourhoods and throughout the city, their emblems, folkways and ethnicism (ethnonationalism) becomes obvious. One of the best ways to do this is to learn how to apply the ethnographer's technique of reading "a narrative into cultural artifacts." The goal is not the rediscovery of Toronto's ethnic past, but the discovery of ways to read the significance of ethnicity in the lives of individuals, ethnic groups and city itself.

To practise such retrospective ethnography on immigrant groups in Toronto before 1940, we need to find those "artifacts" such as cultural events through which we can read such a narrative. In special issues of *Polyphony* on the study of the immigrant press, ethnocultural theatre and religious institutions, I have suggested some ways in which sources, related to those institutions interior to the ethnocommunities, could be used to develop a more richly textured history of groups in the city.[23] Oral testimony, used more systematically, could help make the authentic voice of the immigrant in the city heard. If certain sub-groups or generational cohorts were interviewed in conjunction with a larger effort to use the census, city directories or church and school records to build a prosopographic base, then oral history would take on new value and reliability as a source. For example, one could attempt to interview and follow the lives of a single prewar class from St. Agnes school in the heart of Little Italy, or trace the careers and networks of sets of godparents from one year in the church records, or trustees from an orthodox church, or the executive from an ethnocultural association. Done well, such studies would move beyond impression and biography to become the basis of a social history, more intricate and truer than that based on quantifying gross numerical patterns in the census.

Picnics, dances, strikes, sermons, events in an association or benevolent hall, church organizations and enterprises, evenings in a café, saloon or political club are settings which provide a chance to move away from the "thin description" of mobility studies toward the "thick description" possible about the changing mores, emblems and folkways and the constant decision making which is the process of ethnicity in a North American city and the route to understanding the many paths to being a Torontonian. A picnic organized by a *paese* club from Italy or a Macedonian village association, a dance sponsored by a socialist club among Finns or Lithuanians in the city was surrounded by emblems, organizations and sub-events susceptible to analysis. Moreover, such events had different symbolic meaning for different participants. For the immigrant generation such affairs, with their intensity of fellow-feeling, often took priority over all other social activities in their lives. For their children and perhaps even for the immigrants as they grew longer in the land, the annual associational dance or picnic had to compete with a minor league baseball game at Stanley Park or a hockey match at Maple Leaf Gardens. Analysis of the celebration of a saint's feast day, a Ward political outing, or an ethnic pamphlet brings us closer to the real sentiments and real networks of each group in the city at any given time.

For example, the organizing of an annual picnic, beyond being simply a festive event, provided a ceremonial occasion for the playing out and affirming of various obligations, networks and commitments. It was a chance to affirm membership in the ethnoculture and loyalty to group language, traditions, or liturgy. It was the occasion for the healing or confirmation of political or parochial schisms within an ethnic community. It provides us, through its changing emblems, with data which can be finely calibrated for observing ethnoculture as process. In the decision about whether the main motifs of a spring pageant will be drawn from old-country sources or highlight the new Canadian tradition of a group, of how themes of homeland and of new country are mixed, can be read the history of identity. Through such descriptions we might discover real rather than stereotyped differences in predisposition among groups. For example, one benevolent society might respond to labour problems by raising money for strike funds, another might censor members for speaking back to a foreman in a factory and thus threatening the reputation and well-being of the whole ethnic group.

Materials as apparently neutral as those about the running of a credit union can be used to reconstruct the associative, coercive and moral commitments which held an ethnic group together. For example, by studying patterns of those granted loans in a Slavic credit union, dominated by a clergyman, we might discover subtle efforts to impose endogamy on the group by denying loans to those who marry out. Such credit unions could use the need to enforce political orthodoxy, denying, as they did in some instances, credit to those who did not pay lip service to ethnic associations or practise the predominant religion of the ethnic group; or denying it to those who were too far to the political left in the eyes of the mainstream ethnic leadership. Institutions continually redefined the boundaries and values of the group, yet they have not been the subject of serious socio-economic or political analysis.

Recently the good urban historian's task has been likened to that of a traffic cop standing at a busy intersection where two main avenues, one the history of the nation and the other the history of migration processes and of the various groups entering the city, meet.[24] There are also side streets into the intersection which carry the traffic of labour history, women's history, ecclesiastical history. In Toronto not just the streets of the grid, but even more the sidewalks, the blind alleys and the side streets were crowded, before World War Two, with people of many backgrounds about to become actors, or launch their children as actors, in the drama of the city.

In the future, studies of ethnic groups must show a sense of urban space and understand that there was an intricate relationship between the reasons why people migrated to a city, where and how they settled in the city and how they were received. In turn, these studies must show that the patterns of ethnic settlement reflect not just ethnicity but also the reality of the ethnic neighbourhoods as "little homelands," ambiences which were neither simply fossils of the old country nor fully of the new. Such little homelands were the settings for evolving identities, for subeconomies and ethnocultures constantly in process. No one who knows the city's ethnic history should ever again be content with monochromatic histories of city politics and politicians or class analyses of our urban past that lack comprehension of the city's ethnocultural variety.

# Notes

1. Italo Calvino, *Invisible Cities* (New York, 1972), 30.

2. W.L. Mackenzie King, "Foreigners Who Live in Toronto," in *The Daily Mail and Empire*, 25 September 1897.

3. *Missionary Outlook* XXX, 12 (Toronto, December 1910): 267, a special issue on the Fred Victor and other city missions. For secular views of the immigrant quarter as an urban pathology, see *What Is the 'Ward' Going to Do with Toronto* (Toronto: Bureau of Municipal Research, 1918) and Margaret Bell, "Toronto's Melting Pot," *Canadian Magazine* XXXVII, 8 (July 1913): 234–42.

4. James Scobie, *Buenos Aires. Plaza to Suburb, 1870–1910* (New York, 1974), viii.

5. J.M.S. Careless, *Toronto to 1918. An Illustrated History* (Toronto, 1984), effectively incorporates the lives of the Anglo-Celtic common people in his history of the city. On the non-British, see R.F. Harney and H. Troper, *Immigrants: A Portrait of the Urban Experience 1890–1930* (Toronto, 1976) and S. Speisman, *The Jews of Toronto. A History until 1937* (Toronto, 1979).

6. An attempt to apply behaviouralist and mobility measurements to a Canadian city is M. Katz, *The People of Hamilton, Canada West. Family and Class in a Mid-Nineteenth Century City* (Cambridge, Mass., 1975). Studies which use mobility rates analysis specifically to understand ethnic differences are Stephan Thernstrom, "Immigrants and Wasps: Ethnic Differences in Occupational Mobility in Boston, 1880–1940," in *Nineteenth Century Cities: Essays in the New Urban History*, ed. S. Thernstrom and R. Sennett (New Haven, 1969) and T. Kessner, *The Golden Door, Italian and Jewish Immigrant Mobility in New York City, 1880–1915* (New York, 1977). A good critique of the methodology is James Henretta, "Study of Social Mobility—Ideological Assumptions and Conceptual Bias," in *Labour History* 18, 2 (1977): 165–78.

7. Finley Peter Dunne, *Mr. Dooley on Ivrything and Ivrybody* (New York, 1963), 207.

8. See Fredrik Barth, *Ethnic Groups and Boundaries* (Boston, 1969).

9. William Butler Yeats, "Village Ghosts," in *Mythologies* (New York, 1978), 15.

10. The first historian to develop the idea of "history from the bottom up" is Jesse Lemisch. See his "The American Revolution Seen from the Bottom Up," in *Towards a New Past: Dissenting Essays in American History*, ed. B.J. Bernstein (New York, 1968), 3–45. The idea is attributed to B.A. Botkin's *Lay My Burden Down. A Folk History of Slavery* (Chicago, 1945); C. Joyner, "Oral History as Communicative Event: A Folkloristic Perspective," *The Oral History Review* (1979), 47–52.

11. For the concept of cognitive maps, see Kevin Lynch, *The Image of the City* (Cambridge, Mass., 1960).

12. Oscar Lewis, "The Effects of White Contact on Blackfoot Culture," in *Anthropological Essays* (New York, 1970), 138–39.

13. M. LeGuerre, "Internal Dependency: The Structural Position of the Black Ghetto in American Society," *Journal of Ethnic Studies* 6, 4 (1978): 29–44.

14. Walter Firey, "Sentiment and Symbolism as Ecological Variable," *American Sociological Review* 10 (1945), reprinted in *Neighbourhood and Ghetto. The Local Area in Large-Scale Society*, ed. Scott and Ann Greer (New York, 1974).

15. A good sample of this literature can be found in James L. Watson, ed., *Between Two Cultures. Migrants and Minorities in Britain* (Oxford, 1977).

16. Lawrence Levine, *Black Culture and Black Consciousness. Afro-American Folkthought from Slavery to Freedom* (New York, 1977), ix.

17. C. Geertz, "Thick Description: Toward and Interpretive Theory of Culture," and for specific reference to the "social nature of thought," see "Person, Time and Conduct in Bali," in *The Interpretation of Cultures. Selected Essays* by C. Geertz (New York, 1973), 3–32 and 360–61:

> A cultural artifact—whether suttee among Balinese or baseball in America—is analogous to a dream or Freudian slip. While it may have material cause and practical ends, the artifact is ultimately a nexus of significance, a potential narrative which the anthropologist is called on to decipher. If properly addressed, it will tell an important story about the collective mental life of the people among whom it is found.

With the appropriate changes of detail this description of Geertz's idea of a cultural artifact can be applied to ethnohistory or retrospective ethnography in a city like Toronto. The description appears in P. Robinson's review of C. Geertz, *Local Knowledge. Further Essays in Interpretive Anthropology* (New York, 1983), in the *New York Times Book Review* (25 September 1983), 11.

18. D. Malincheff and J. Theophilact, *The First Bulgarian-English Pocket Dictionary* (Toronto, 1913).

19. Calvino, *Invisible Cities*, 76.

20. K. Deutsch, *Nationalism and Social Communication. An Inquiry into the Foundation of Nationality* (Cambridge, Mass., 1966), 121.

21. *50th Anniversary SS. Cyril and Methody Macedonian-Bulgarian Orthodox Cathedral, 1910–1960* (Toronto, 1960).

22. *The Ward Graphic* (Toronto, n.d.), 14. An occasional publication of Central Neighbourhood House, copy in the Multicultural History Society of Ontario collection.

23. *Polyphony: The Bulletin of the Multicultural History Society* 1, 2 (Summer 1978), religion and ethnocultural communities; *Polyphony* 2, 2 (Winter 1979), benevolent and mutual aid societies in Ontario; *Polyphony* 4, 1 (Spring/Summer 1982), the ethnic press in Ontario; and *Polyphony* 5, 2 (Fall/Winter 1983), immigrant theatre.

24. The image is borrowed from Arthur Goren's appreciation of Moses Rischin's study of New York's Lower East Side. See A. Goren, "The Promise of the Promised City: Moses Rischin, American History and the Jews," in *American Jewish History* LXXIII, 2 (December 1983): 173.

# EXPLORING THE NORTH AMERICAN WEST: A COMPARATIVE URBAN PERSPECTIVE*

ALAN F.J. ARTIBISE

A recent conference held at the University of Guelph, Ontario, in August 1982, had as one of its main goals redirecting the field of urban history in the 1980s.[1] The Canadian-American Urban Development Conference was planned by an international organizing committee on the premise that a comparative framework, based on the divergent urban experiences of Canada and the United States, should be adopted by at least North American scholars as an essential part of their research agendas. To this end, participants were invited to explore the related themes of power and decision making in the development of North American cities in an effort to answer the question—to what extent does the border make a difference? At one level, the conference was a success since many of the participants' papers displayed a diversity and vitality that indicated a healthy intellectual state for urban history.[2] At another level, however, it is fair to say that many left Guelph in a state of frustration. A closing panel on "The Future of Urban History," with commentaries by such luminaries as Eric Lampard, Michael Frisch, Anthony Sutcliffe, James Vance, and Gilbert Stelter, was unable to claim that the conference had really come to terms with the comparative approach or even that there was much indication that scholars were moving in that direction.

There are several reasons why the admittedly exalted aims of the conference organizers were not realized. It was evident, first of all, that few of the American participants knew much about the Canadian urban experience and, moreover—apart from a passing interest in the "success" of

**American Review of Canadian Studies* 14, 1 (Spring 1984): 20–44. This article is a revised version of a paper presented at the Annual Meeting of the Pacific Coast Branch of the American Historical Association held at San Diego University in August 1983. I wish to acknowledge that research for this paper was supported by a grant from the Social Sciences and Humanities Research Council of Canada.

Toronto—could care less. This is hardly surprising since very few of the numerous studies of Canadian urban development have found their way across the border. Few American booksellers stock Canadian titles, few libraries systematically acquire Canadian publications, and American journals rarely review volumes published in Canada. There are, of course, exceptions but the general proposition holds.[3] As a result, the pervasive supposition that Canada is very much like the United States—although slightly quaint and romantic—leads to the assumption that Americans have little to learn from the Canadian experience.

In contrast, Canadians know far more about American urban development and, indeed, have acknowledged a major debt to their colleagues in the development of urban history in Canada.[4] Yet few Canadians have put this knowledge to good use in the context of comparative studies, and Canada has yet to produce any historian who has even attempted to interpret the American experience from a Canadian perspective, let alone offer a considered view on America for Americans. At the same time, Canadians are convinced that there are major and enduring differences between the two countries, but very few have attempted to provide solid, empirical evidence of such distinctions.[5]

Equally important in explaining the lack of progress in comparative studies in urban history, however, is the fact that the historiographical and methodological traditions of Canadian and American urban historians are very different. In the United States, historians have been grappling with urban topics since at least 1940 and by the mid-1960s urban history was a rapidly developing field. The "urban crisis," the rapid adoption of quantitative methods, and a widespread concern for "history from the bottom up" all contributed to the expansion of the field. But this growth was so rapid and, some would argue, so tied to a reaction to current fashions that "it raised inevitable questions about how deep the historiographical current really ran."[6] Numerous commentators noted "strong dissatisfaction" with urban history in the 1970s by both practitioners and critics largely as a result of a lack of a consistent focus.[7] Only in recent years has this "urban history crisis" moved toward resolution and, interestingly, the Guelph conference played a role in this development.

The pattern urban history followed was very different in Canada. Urban history developed later in Canada—in the early 1970s—and benefitted from the experiences of both British and American practitioners. Second, rather than concerning themselves unduly with social mobility studies, Canadians escaped the ultimate frustration of the "new urban history" by concentrating on the "city-building process." The main issues examined to date have to do with such themes as power and decision making in such contexts as economic development, urban form, politics and government, and urban culture. In short, Canadians (perhaps naïvely) have not been plagued by self-doubt in recent years and have, instead, been getting on with the task of coming to grips not only with cities and urban life, but with the place of the elusive term "urban" in the larger society.[8]

What is important here and what became apparent at Guelph is that the growing confidence of Canadian urban historians—defined as a sense that they have something to contribute on the larger stage in terms of understanding cities—and the new-found confidence of American urban historians have the potential to develop a new frontier in urban history. This frontier will almost certainly give far stronger influence to what some would call neo-Marxist analysis but which most Canadian urban historians would prefer to label simply a political-economic approach.

Far from being disappointed, then, most participants came away from the Guelph conference with the belief that it was a small but important step in the development of the field. For as scholars in both countries attempt to come to grips with the city—both as a dependent variable (urban as entity) and an independent variable (urban as process)[9]—there will be a growing appreciation not only of what Canadians and Americans can learn from each other but also of the value of adopting a comparative approach. As well, there is in North American urban history a new-found sense of direction based on accepting as essential a framework of interdisciplinary urban history that includes politics, broadly defined. This framework accepts as given the inherently political nature of urban development in North America and moves on to discuss such crucial issues as power, domination, and inequality.[10]

The goal of this paper is to contribute to this laudable process, at least in a modest way. I hasten to add that I have few illusions about any person's ability to redirect the pace and direction of scholarly research. Most scholars already have investments in one or another line of work and these commitments are not easily changed. Still, an interchange may result in some new directions in research. This requires, however, a clear sense of where we want to go and, if nothing else, this paper will suggest some fruitful research agendas.

The comparative method, as it is used in this paper, is defined as a broad gauge, general approach, not a narrow specialized technique. It is a basic research strategy as opposed to a tactical aid to research. The goal is to generate, as a second stage in research, major hypotheses based on the first-stage research already completed. Once generated, these hypotheses can be tested through further case or thematic studies and be followed by a fourth stage of generalization. The goal in this fourth stage is to discover and articulate the meaning of urban both as a dependent and independent variable. This means sorting out—at the local, subregional, regional, national, and international levels—what is unique and what is commonplace; or, to put it another way, since urbanization is a process that is at once universal and particular, it is the task of the urban historian to locate the one within the other.[11] And, it can be suggested, this process can best be done by breaking out of our regional and national boundaries and by examining a variety of issues and themes in a comparative context. Building on the enormous body of historical information that now exists, it is possible to move to a new level in the utilization of these data.

Based on my knowledge of western Canadian urban history and my far more limited knowledge of western American urban history, I will examine several themes that would be better understood if approached from a comparative perspective. There are undoubtedly many other themes that could be examined, but this paper will concentrate on three: the role of boosterism in western urban development; the concept of urbanization as a nationalizing force; and the role of the public sector in shaping western North American cities. In a sense, all these topics are variants on the larger theme of political economy, an exploration of the related themes of power and decision making.

Before turning to an examination of these themes, however, it is important to set the stage by briefly examining the Canadian west and the American west as regions. It is essential to note at the outset that regions within nation-states tend to be extremely flexible and that regional boundaries will vary depending on particular eras or issues. Also, regions may often be subdivided into several subregions or functional regions. Nonetheless, the Canadian and American west share enough geography and history, and have been sufficiently unified in action at times, to possess a sense of distinction from other parts of their respective countries. Most important, both regions were settled during the nineteenth century as part of a process of western expansion and they shared similar technologies, economic bases, and political relationships to the older regions of the country. In any case, the regional approach in terms of western North America offers the possibility of examining the question of power in society from a spatial perspective, utilizing concepts such as core-periphery and metropolis-hinterland.[12]

The theme of boosterism and urban rivalry is persistent in both American and Canadian western urban history. In the United States, Richard Wade's seminal volume, *The Urban Frontier*, examined the role and stressed the importance of boosterism both in promoting urban growth and in building a pride in community accomplishment.[13] Many other American historians have also examined this theme and a vast accumulation of literature on the topic now exists.[14] In Canada, there are fewer studies but the theme of boosterism has also received a good deal of attention.[15] What has not been produced in either country, however, is any detailed study of this theme at a general level.[16] A review of the literature reveals that a general theory of the role of boosterism in determining "winners and losers" and in influencing urban growth rates has been put forward only very recently, and for western Canada only.[17] General surveys of urbanization still stress macro-economic trends and location with respect to resources, transportation and markets as determining forces, while case studies still tend to emphasize the particular actions of key local leaders or groups and their unique circumstances, often disregarding the comparable experience of other cities.

In this context, it is difficult to measure the role of local subjective and volitional forces against the strength of broader ones. It is possible to suggest, however, that a general hypothesis regarding the role of boosterism in the growth of western cities can be formulated: a hypothesis that allows for local variations but which still explains a significant stage in the urbanization of the North American west. The claim so frequently made by the citizens of western towns and cities that their community was self-made—that collective determination could either compensate for a lack of natural advantages or exploit advantages that potentially existed—deserves further examination. The subjective aspects in urban development that can be called boosterism may be considered as an interrelated framework in which community leaders "made decisions and took actions to build up their communities according to their perceptions of the opportunities permitted by the economic, technological and political circumstances.[18]

In the hypothesis suggested for consideration, boosterism takes on an importance that extends far beyond super salesmanship and mindless rhetoric and becomes a key factor in explaining a particular stage in urban development. The success of one western city relative to another was not determined only by a convenient location or by broad, impersonal forces. For, even if all the ingredients for urban growth were present, and even if they pointed toward a particular pattern, it was, in the final analysis, only the skill and initiative of individuals and groups that translated opportunity into reality. The residents of western settlements interacted with their political, economic and technological environment and their hopes, beliefs, energy, community spirit, initiative, and adaptability influenced the rate and pattern of urbanization. And while the role of local governments, business organizations, and individuals was limited in some respects by outside forces, those limitations were for a time minimal.

In an initial stage of citybuilding—which lasted, roughly until World War One—western communities faced very limited constraints on their growth possibilities. City building in western North America in the nineteenth century took place in the midst of several other important developments: notably, the expansion of national economies, the settlement of low-density areas, and the initial utilization of resources in newly settled areas. As well, this was an era when civic élites and municipal governments could wield a great deal of power. Senior governments—whether state, provincial, or federal—were generally non-interventionist and, hence, local communities were left alone to evolve and implement their own policies.[19] It is also important to note that community leaders confronted a major portion of the economic landscape that could be developed relatively free of the residue of earlier decision makers. While older, established cities in the east had the major concentrations of population and dominated the distribution of capital and technology, the newer western cities were relatively unobstructed by earlier commitments and could implement recent improvements immediately and quickly adjust the local economy to the national market structure.

This formative stage was more or less complete by 1920, and boosterism declined rapidly as an explanatory force in western urban development. New forces came into play that sharply limited the impact of internal attempts by civic or business leaders to promote or sustain growth, or to prevent decline. One of these forces was the fact that western cities now had a past that influenced the behaviour of individuals and institutions in the community and a physical infrastructure that could not be adjusted rapidly or easily to respond to new opportunities. As well, three other major forces came into play in both Canada and the United States that also restricted the impact of local initiative. In both countries, there was a rapid decline in local autonomy as state/provincial and federal governments expanded their statutory control over local government, instituted a wide range of administrative and regulatory controls, decreased local powers of taxation, and instituted systems of conditional grants. Coupled with these changes were new patterns of municipal politics that led to a much wider dispersal of local power.[20] As well, certain groups in the private sector were also forcing cities to conform to uniform policies and procedures, including national fire insurance companies and financial institutions headquartered in eastern metropolitan centres. The combined result of these developments was that western cities found it increasingly difficult to adopt and maintain distinct approaches to problems or opportunities that would give them an advantage over their rivals either in the region or elsewhere. Even if the will remained to react creatively to new challenges, western communities by the 1920s no longer had the means to respond.

Local initiative was further weakened as an important variable by the rapid rise of corporate capitalism. The corporation emerged in the late nineteenth century as a means of consolidating huge capital resources and a variety of related economic activities under a single, overall authority.[21] Corporate mergers and the formation of large holding companies became even more pronounced after 1920 as

> corporate giants altered the skylines of the largest cities...; provided a rich lode for urban banks, investment companies, tax lawyers, advertising agencies, communications media, and consulting firms; and created unprecedented networks of interurban communication by shifting their employees from one area to another. Their power and interests extended well beyond the local area...and their direct or indirect participation in local, state and national politics was sometimes massive...When allied with major city banks, some corporations had more authority over the shape and health of the metropolis...than any local elected body.[22]

Cities in the western hinterland or periphery[23] were particularly vulnerable to corporatism; to the fact that "corporations are merely in cities, they are not of cities."[24] In the booster era, the era of the commercial and early industrial city, there was an identification by the booster élites of their fortunes with the fortunes of a specific community. Corporations, however, had no special loyalty to place and increasingly business leaders saw their interests in regional, national, or even international terms. Thus during this second, corporate phase, which lasted through to the 1950s, cities in western North America grew or declined according to circumstances largely beyond their control.[25]

There has been, of course, a third phase in the development of western cities that began in the 1950s and has continued to the present. Resource wealth has fostered sustained hinterland development and created regional metropolitan centres which directly influence the nations' economic, political, and social lives. The western regions which had previously served as a vast economic hinterland of the industrial core began in the twentieth century to siphon people, resources and economic activity away from older, declining regions. The process was by no means uniform—it was especially pronounced in the so-called "Sunbelt" in the United States and in Alberta and British Columbia in Canada—but there was little doubt by the 1970s that the North American west, or at least a substantial portion of the region, had crossed a new threshold.[26]

The broad overview of western urban development, stretching from boosterism to corporatism to regional succession, needs considerable refinement before a more rigorous model can be produced. But once informed by more refined analyses it can improve our understanding of the process of urbanization since it should be apparent that despite differences in scale and in political systems, urban development in the American and Canadian wests followed a remarkably similar evolutionary framework. And, it can be argued, these experiences distinguish western North American urban growth from urban development elsewhere. Furthermore, the concepts outlined here in an attempt to hypothesize orderly patterns for institutions and human activities in western city building link urban history with the more general issue of political economy.

A second theme that is ripe for comparative examination is the widespread belief that urbanization was a nationalizing force in the sense that it reproduced familiar urban patterns and fostered a uniform urban culture. This proposition was put forward by Louis Wirth in the 1930s in his seminal essay, "Urbanism as a Way of Life."[27] Wirth's contention was that cities were distinctive environments that set their inhabitants apart from the surrounding countryside. Since the 1930s, virtually all urban historians have accepted the view that urbanization mutes regional distinctions. Lawrence Larsen, for example, in his recent study of *The Urban West at the End of the Frontier*, notes that "city building in the Americans West...was not a response to geographic or climatic conditions. It was the result of a process perfected earlier...The result was the establishment of a society that mirrored and made the same mistakes as those made earlier in the rest of the country."[28] Similarly, Bradford Luckingham in a review of western urban historiography notes that "from the earliest days western urban dwellers...wished to emulate the great cities of the east. They sought to impose established ways, and culture was considered a key part of the image." In addition to fostering similar cultural traits, urbanization also meant that "the physical characteristics of western urban centers differed little from their eastern counterparts...Western settlers, drawing on their previous experience, carried the accepted eastern norms throughout the American West."[29] Gunter Barth makes similar arguments in his study of San Francisco and Denver. In his view "modes of class distinction and norms of cultural excellence standardized in the older cities to the east were imposed by the young western élites as they sought to transplant stereotypes of American society."[30]

This assertion that western urbanization produced an urban form and an urban culture that closely resembled that of the east has also been put forward in Canada. J.M.S. Careless, for example, argues that by 1913 "life-styles in the western cities had...become largely a counterpart of eastern. This simply indicated the common conditions of modern urban living...In the Canadian West—where indeed, the railway instrument of eastern metropolitanism and industrialism often preceded the settlement of land frontiers—society would be especially likely to exhibit not only the forms but also much of the content of eastern institutions, including the municipal."[31] In another important article, Careless has also argued that "regions usually centre on metropolitan communities, which largely organize them, focus their views and deal with outside metropolitan forces on their behalf."[32] Another major Canadian historian, W.L. Morton, in a comparative article entitled "The Significance of Site in the Settlement of the American and Canadian Wests," argued "that the frontier as a conditioning process...was of doubtful effect after 1870, when modern technology, in the form of the railway, brought the frontier within a day or two of old settled regions...The metropolitan controls, which were political, social, religious, educational, and aesthetic as well as economic, were always particularly strong on the successful frontier."[33]

In recent years, however, the view that urbanization mutes regional distinctions has begun to be challenged by scholars who find the proposition "time and culture bound." The fact is that despite the supposed nationalizing force of urbanization, regions persist in both Canada and the United States and, indeed, there is evidence to suggest that regionalism is increasing in intensity.[35] New questions are thus being asked about the reciprocal relationship between cities and regions. While granting that western cities shared many characteristics with their eastern counterparts—at least in the commercial and industrial eras—it is not necessary to go so far as to argue either that cities, regardless of region, were more like each other than like their non-urban surroundings or that regional metropolitan centres moulded their hinterlands according to an eastern model. As David Goldfield has argued for the American South, "regional elements persist and have collectively produced a particular and limited urbanization that exists in the region to this day."[36]

Several recent publications support this more complex view. In the United States, Robert Fogelson's excellent study of Los Angeles asserts that the city was a departure from familiar patterns, not only because of vast urban sprawl but also because the West Coast metropolis had more single-family and fewer multi-family dwellings than any comparable city in the east. Indeed, rather than reproducing the high-density forms of eastern cities, California's cities became low-density, streetcar- or automobile-connected environments.[37] Interestingly, similar patterns have been identified in Vancouver and Victoria where, it is claimed, individual home ownership rates ran as high as eighty per cent and the landscape was decidedly suburban. "Rather than a dense concentration of workers' housing, as a Pittsburgh or Hamilton might present, potential Vancouver homeowners had access to a wide range of residential locations all within a thirty minute streetcar ride to central city employment." There was, as well, in British Columbia as in California, a "search for the ideal" that was reflected in city building. The importance of southern rather than eastern models for "the way British Columbians live" is apparent in the residential landscape. Styles of housing familiar from California mix with architectural modes of British and Eastern origins...The widespread popularity of Californian styles underlines the ambiguity of British Columbia on the North American west coast—part British, part Canadian, but also part Californian. At the very least, this evidence suggests "that there is and always has been a filtered border at the 49th parallel, which may indeed be weaker than the border between British Columbia and the rest of Canada."[38]

These brief examples put into sharp relief the examples given earlier about imitation being stronger than innovation in western city building. It is apparent that the thesis of western cities replicating familiar eastern urban patterns needs to be cast in a framework that includes a clear sense of time and place. There was a stage in western city building—in the commercial and industrial eras—when imitation outpaced innovation, but new, western patterns of development also began to emerge in the twentieth century. Similarly, while it is clear that most western cities replicated eastern patterns, all of them did not. There is, in other words, a complexity to the thesis that needs to be recognized.[39] It can be argued, for example, that not only are there cases of innovative patterns of city building in the west, there are cities within western North America that have more in common with each other than with cities elsewhere in Canada or the United States. In addition to the west coast "ecotopian" zone stretching from Santa Barbara to Prince George that Joel Garreau's recent reformulation of North American regions identifies,[40] there is the equally notable functional zone related to the urban-centred economies based on energy resources in such areas as Alberta and in portions of the American Sunbelt. Harold Platt, for example, in a study of Houston's emergence as the urban centre of the Southwest, argues that an investigation of the economic, demographic, and political bonds of the city and the countryside reveal reciprocal interactions that "molded a characteristic pattern of development...and stamped a unique imprint of regional culture" on both town and country.[41] Similarly, in a study of Alberta's cities, Peter Smith has identified a distinct urban system with a coherent form and culture that not only distinguishes Alberta from other prairie provinces and from central Canada, but reveals many similarities with urban patterns in Texas.[42] Unfortunately, comparative work on the American Southwest and Alberta has not been undertaken to the same extent as has been the case for California and British Columbia, but it appears that such research will reveal that the two sub-regions share many common patterns of urban development. Certainly it is clear that the east-west imitation thesis needs considerable refinement if a hypothesis that is not narrowly bounded by time and place is to be produced.

Related to this key theme is the issue of the reciprocal relationship of cities and regions. The proposition that "metropolitan centres significantly mould their regions" needs to be carefully assessed in terms of defining the extent to which cities actively create or passively reflect their surrounding hinterlands. The answer to this question will help to isolate factors of regional and national distinction and lead to a clearer understanding of the universal process of urbanization. Finally, a research agenda that focusses on the relationships between cities and regions and that has a North American context promises to revise the traditional metropolitan interpretation of western development, with its connotations of tributary status, economic dependency, and a steep cultural gradient. The rapid growth of cities in both the American and the Canadian West has altered the national locus of economic power and begun to revise the historic divisions between heartland and hinterland. In neither country is the simple dichotomy of metropolis and hinterland valid, at least after 1950.

A third theme within the broad area of political economy is the question of the importance of the public sector in shaping the cities of western North America. For some, this may seem like a rather obvious theme that hardly deserves special mention in an overview such as this since the general patterns of government involvement in economic development in Canada and the United States are well known. In Canada, one of the most honoured themes of scholars is that the state has played an important role in promoting and shaping both economic development generally and urban development particularly.[43] In this literature, the thesis is advanced that Canadians—in contrast with most industrial nations in the western world—place great trust in government and accept with great willingness government involvement in their lives. This thesis is supported by a good deal of empirical evidence, evidence that includes examples from across the country but which also usually stresses the activities of government enterprise in the four western provinces. Indeed, one recent study of supposedly "free enterprise" Alberta stresses the emergence of the provincial government as a business entrepreneur.[44] The deferential character of the Canadian public to government controls and public enterprise has been particularly difficult for Americans to understand, given the widely acknowledged stress placed in the United States on individualism and on resistance to government intervention, especially in many western states.[45]

Closer examination of these generalizations reveals that while there are some differences, government in the United States has been just as important as government in Canada in terms of city building, a fact that is slowly but surely being recognized both in case studies and in surveys.[46] Gerald Nash, for example, in his survey of western development in the twentieth century, devotes a good deal of attention to the role of the federal government in recent western urban growth.[47] And other studies notably by Daniel Elazar and Mark Gelfrand, have provided further convincing evidence that the public sector has played a major and often crucial role in American city building.[48] Similar general and particular studies exist for Canada.[49] What is missing, however, is any attempt to compare the experiences either of the two countries or of regions within the countries. Yet comparison in this case immediately reveals very interesting distinctions, for while the magnitude of public sector involvement—especially in the west—appears to be quite similar, the involvement has taken quite different forms. An examination of these different forms can teach scholars a good deal about the western North American city. A continentalist view, vigorously asserted by neo-Marxist writers, stresses that cities and city systems in advanced capitalist countries reveal similarities in urban form and in the underlying process of urbanization and, while some differences are conceded, these are viewed as superficial. A more rigorous political-economy approach not only will allow scholars to test the presupposition that cities in both countries have a homogeneous set of characteristics, but will also explain why they are similar or substantially and importantly different.[50]

The key distinction in terms of public sector involvement is jurisdictional. In the United States, the federal government has played the key role in urban affairs, while in Canada public sector activity stems largely from municipal and provincial governments. This striking difference between federalism in the two countries is not quickly explained, but one view is that the belief in the "American way of life" is so pervasive "that the American character has tended to coalesce about" an almost unitary form of government; a form that "almost obviates the federal nature of the American state, since regional and/or state concerns appear to be truly overwhelmed by the sense of nationhood."[51] In Canada, by contrast, one of the few unifying symbols—particularly in the western provinces—is "Ottawa bashing"; there is a perennial clash between federal and provincial governments. It can be argued, then, that the U.S. federation is far more static in the sense that the respective roles of the states and the federal government have long since been decided with the federal government in the ascendancy (the current administration notwithstanding). The Canadian confederation is far more dynamic and fluid, with power shifting among the various governments over time and space.

How do these statements relate to urban policy and the nature and shape of western North American cities? A detailed answer is beyond the scope of this paper, but several examples can indicate the richness of this area for comparative research. The American federal government has played a major role in the redistribution of population spatially through highway spending, aerospace and defense expenditures, water resource development, and the subsidization of new house building. Through a range of devices, the American federal government has influenced the pattern and system of urban development much more significantly than the supposedly more interventionist Canadian federal government. Moreover, there have been significant sectional differences in federal–city relations with, for example, western cities benefitting more from federal expenditures than cities in other regions.[52] Recent articles on urbanization in California and on the role of the federal government in the development of Portland have begun to investigate this phenomenon,[53] but far more research needs to be completed.

In Canada, by contrast, the role of the federal government in urban affairs is quite different. All Canadian provinces—and especially western provinces—jealously guard their constitutional authority over municipalities against intrusion by Ottawa. In 1977, for example, the province of Alberta asserted its authority by refusing to allow the city of Calgary to accept funds from the federal government.[54] This weakness on the part of the federal government in urban affairs was reflected two years later in the disbanding of the federal Ministry of State for Urban Affairs, created in 1971.[55] At the same time, the public sector does dramatically influence the shape and character of western Canadian cities. Municipalities exercise a high degree of planning control and local governments are often active market participants in land development, as in the case in Red Deer, Alberta; Prince George, British Columbia; and Saskatoon, Saskatchewan.[56] Similarly, western cities have developed public transit systems with no federal aid and modest provincial assistance (in Edmonton and Calgary, for example). Municipalities and provinces in western Canada also own railroads, telephone systems, power companies, and airlines. In short, direct government intervention through public ownership is vast; the level of control and the range of controls are far-reaching.[57]

Given these sharp distinctions, what conclusions can be drawn? At this point, it is necessary to be modest and simply note that the locus of public sector intervention in the city-building process is very different in the two countries. Knowing this, however, begs the far more important question of the impact of the public sector on urban development. Are our respective cities monuments to our differences or to our similarities? Without giving a direct answer, one research agenda can be suggested that might enable both Americans and Canadians to look at the development of their cities in a more revealing way.

The rapid rise of the Canadian west, and especially Alberta, in the 1970s is a close parallel to the emergence of the American Sunbelt, and the relative economic decline of the central Canadian heartland approximates the decline of the American northeast.[58] The causes of regional decline are very similar and include not only changing energy costs, stagnating manufacturing industries, and the outflow of professionals and skilled labour, but an important transfer of wealth and income via government policies—federal defense policies in the United States and provincial resource policies in Canada. A sharper focus is possible by concentrating on urban development in Texas and Alberta. In Texas, Harold Platt has argued that Houston and Galveston shared a similar context for development for over sixty years, including similar populations, economic functions, pace of city building, and tone of society.[59] The same can be said of Calgary and Edmonton in Alberta. Interestingly, however, the previously balanced configuration of local forces was upset by the oil boom; in Texas, a relatively free market economy allowed Houston to pull ahead sharply and to quickly become the premier city of the Southwest. But the public sector—in the form of federal expenditures on slum clearance, parks, buildings, transportation facilities, and defense—also played a key role in the growth of Houston.[60] A similar pattern might well have emerged in Alberta, with Calgary assuming primary status, were it not for government intervention. There, the provincial government intervened to divide the spoils of the oil industry and to maintain a remarkable parity between Edmonton and Calgary.[61]

Despite the differences in growth patterns between Houston and Calgary, and the different forms of public sector involvement in city building, recent biographies of the two cities offer an intriguing focus for more detailed comparisons.[62] The common cattle ranching and oil based economies of their respective hinterlands have, for example, shaped the development of both cities. As well, the international oil business has meant much direct interchange between the two communities. At the same time key structural differences are apparent. In contrast to mineral title resting originally with the individual surface title holder in Texas, all rights in Alberta reside with the Crown. This, combined with Canada's centralized and eastern-dominated banking system, assured a less prominent role for the local entrepreneurial élite and a larger role for the "province as entrepreneur." Yet McComb's chapter on "Conservatism and Culture" in Houston is of particular interest, for Calgary as much as Houston is the most conservative city within its national orbit.[63] Such parallels and contrasts call for further study and a detailed examination of the development of the two cities, one as a measure of the other, promises to be very rewarding.

The goal of this article was to make a modest contribution to North American comparative urban research by examining several themes that were considered to be especially open to such analysis. It was also noted that many other themes could and should be opened to international scrutiny. Certainly I realize how myopic, vulnerable and short-lived explanations and interpretations can be, particularly ones that attempt even in a rudimentary way to deal with a vast body of complex data that require multiple skills to interpret. In these circumstances, generalizations, at best, are tentative, contingent upon partial evidence, and subject to refinement or even replacement. Still, articles such as this are fuel empowering the continuous reworking of history, and the more scholars are able to break out of specific cocoons, the richer are the potentials for more satisfying and enduring theories. I am reminded here of a recent conference on ''Urbanization in the Americas'' held at the University of British Columbia in 1979 in conjunction with the Forty-Third International Congress of Americanists.[64] This ambitious gathering attempted to place Latin American cities in perspective alongside those of the United States and Canada, thus fulfilling the hemispheric aims of the Congress. Like the Guelph conference, this gathering failed to produce any explicit comparisons that were rooted in a firm understanding of the urban experience in Latin America, the United States, and Canada. But the conference did prove to be a rewarding experience; it resulted, in Canada at least, in an enriched perspective on urban development.

All this is not to say that this paper proposes comparative research as an alternative to more traditional approaches; indeed, comparative research can proceed only if the basic building blocks are in place. Comparative research is, rather, another string in the bow of the urban historian. But it is an extremely important string, as H.J. Dyos noted, since it recognizes the need to connect and relate both the micro and macro aspects of that most complex of processes—urbanization.[65]

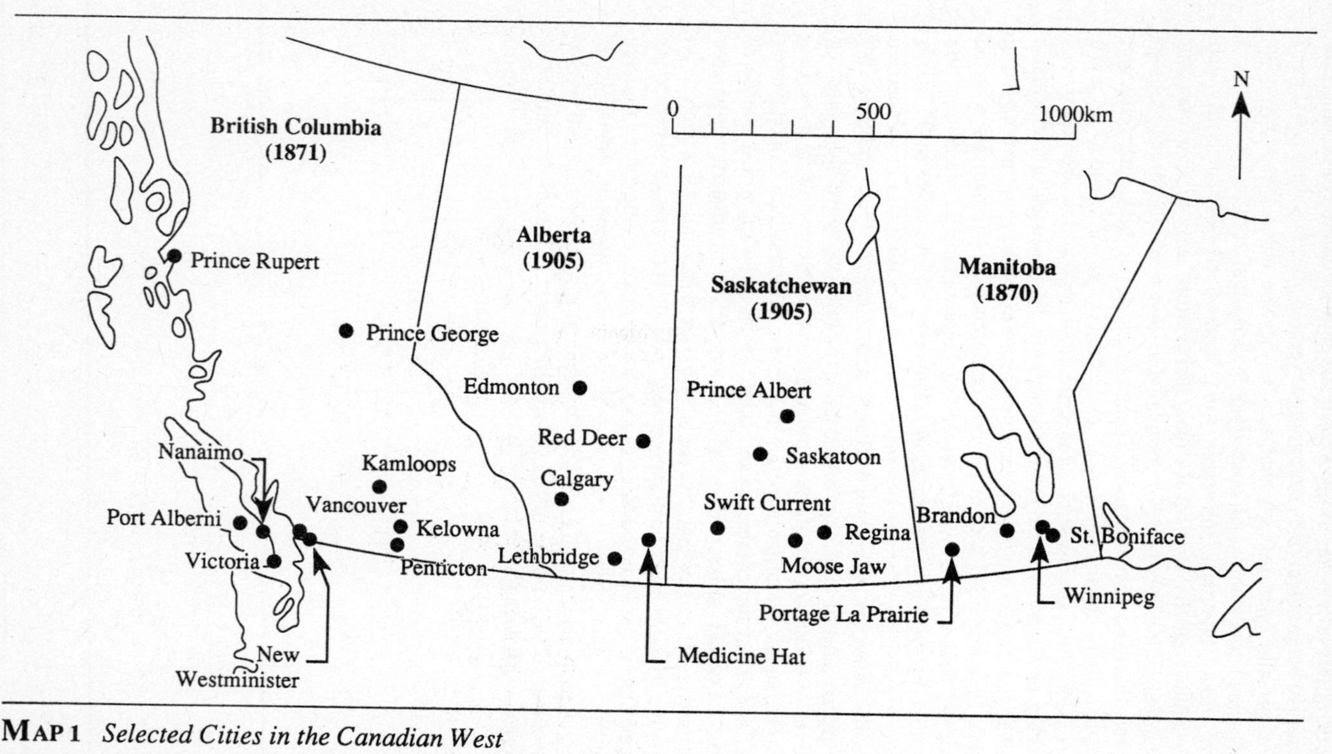


**MAP 1** *Selected Cities in the Canadian West*

NOTE: Date indicates year that territory joined the Dominion of Canada as a province.

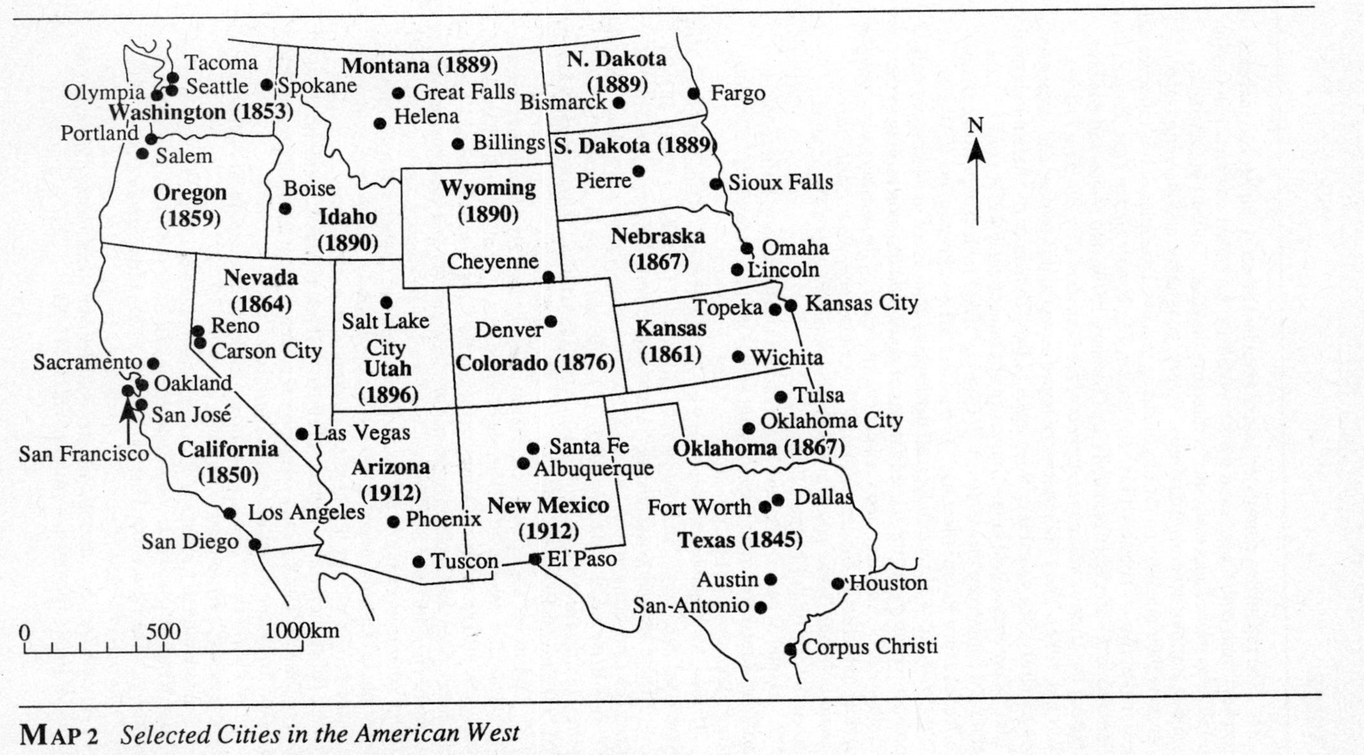


MAP 2 *Selected Cities in the American West*

NOTE: Date indicates year that territory was admitted to the Union as a state.

# Notes

1. The organizing committee was chaired by Gilbert A. Stelter and included members from both Canada and the United States. An earlier conference in Guelph in 1977 has proved successful in "redirecting the field," at least in Canada, by bringing together several disciplines—history, geography, and planning—and focussing their attention on the city-building process. Examples of this influence can be found in two volumes: Artibise and Stelter, *The Usable Urban Past: Politics and Planning in the Modern Canadian City* (Toronto, 1979), and Stelter and Artibise, *Shaping the Urban Landscape: Aspects of the Canadian City-Building Process* (Toronto, 1982). The 1982 conference hoped to repeat this process and, moreover, was mindful of the valuable critique made of the "Dynamics of Modern Industrial Cities" Conference held at the University of Connecticut in 1979, especially the need for a conference theme. James E. Cronin, "The Problem with Urban History: Reflections on a Recent Meeting," *Urbanism Past and Present*, no. 9 (Winter, 1979–1980), 40–43. Accordingly, all participants were asked to address not only comparative issues but the related themes of power and decision making in the development of American and Canadian cities. Many of these essays were brought together in Gilbert A. Stelter and Alan F.J. Artibise, eds., *Power and Place: Canadian Urban Development in the North American Context* (Vancouver, University of British Columbia Press, 1986).

2. Daniel Schaffer, "A New Threshold for Urban History: Reflections on Canadian-American Urban Development at the Guelph Conference," *Planning History Bulletin* 4, 3 (1982): 1–10.

3. See, for example, a review essay by John G. Corbett, "Canadian Cities: How 'American' Are They?" in *Urban Affairs Quarterly* 13, 3 (March 1978): 383–94.

4. There are many examples of "acknowledgement." For two, see Bruce M. Stave, "A Conversation with Gilbert A. Stelter: Urban History in Canada," *Journal of Urban History* 6, 2 (February 1980): 177–210; and Bruce M. Stave, "Urban History in Canada: A Conversation with Alan F.J. Artibise," *Urban History Review* VIII, 3 (February 1980): 110–43.

5. One recent attempt is Pierre Berton, *Why We Act Like Canadians* (Toronto, 1982). This slim volume is "A Personal Exploration of Our National Character" and is presented as a series of letters written to Berton's American friend "Sam." Berton describes the Canadian emphasis on "peace, order and good government," the paternalistic Mountie as a national hero, the Loyalist legacy, the significance of Canada's ethnic mosaic, and the formative influence of climate and wilderness landscape. In Berton's judgement, these forces of history, culture, and geography produced people who are law-abiding, deferential toward authority, cautious, prudent, élitist, moralistic, tolerant (of ethnic differences), cool, unemotional, and solemn. But he offers virtually no empirical evidence and it is fair to say that few Canadian historians would accept his arguments.

6. Michael Frisch, "American Urban History as an Example of Recent Historiography," *History and Theory* 18, 3 (1979): 350–77.

7. In addition to Cronin and Frisch, see John Sharpless and John Bass Warner, "Urban History," *American Behavioural Scientist* 21, 2 (1977): 221–44; Theodore Hershberg, "The New Urban History: Toward an Interdisciplinary History of the City." *Journal of Urban History* 5, 1 (November 1978): 3–40; and the "Special Book Review Section" dealing with the Philadelphia Social History Project in the *Journal of Urban History* 8, 4 (August 1982): 447–84.

8. See, for example, the introductory essay in Alan F.J. Artibise and Gilbert A. Stelter, *Canada's Urban Past: A Bibliography to 1980 and Guide to Canadian Urban Studies* (Vancouver, 1981), xiii–xxxii.

9. Ibid for discussion of these terms, and Hershberg, "The New Urban History."

10. See, for example, the comments of T.J. McDonald in the *Journal of Urban History* 8, 4 (August 1982): 454–62.

11. For a good discussion of the relationship between local history and urban history see Bruce M. Stave, "A Conversation with H.J. Dyos: Urban History in Great Britain," *Journal of Urban History* 5, 4 (August 1979): 469–500. As Dyos notes on p. 498, "one big challenge confronting young historians is this need to search for a means of connecting and relating both the macro and the micro aspects, the process of subtending everything and the place in which it is to be found operating." There have, of course, been many efforts devoted to comparative urban history, but very few that compare the Canadian and American experiences. See, for example, the special issue of the *Urban Affairs Quarterly* 11, 1 (September 1975) devoted to "The City in Comparative Perspective," and Lloyd Rodwin, *Nations and Cities: A Comparison of Strategies for Urban Growth* (Boston, 1970).

12. See Gilbert A. Stelter, "A Regional Framework for Urban History," *Urban History Review* 13 (February, 1985): 193–204. A useful discussion of Canadian regionalism is Raymond Breton, "Regionalism in Canada," in *Regionalism and Supranationalism: Challenges and Alternatives to the Nation-State in Canada and Europe*, ed. D. M. Cameron (Montreal, 1981), 57–80.

13. Richard C. Wade, *The Urban Frontier: The Rise of Western Cities, 1790–1830* (Cambridge, 1959).

14. Including, for example, Daniel J. Boorstin, *The Americans: The National Experience* (New York, 1965), 113–68; J. Christopher Schnell and Patrick E. McLear, "Why the Cities Grew: An Historiographical Essay on Western Urban Growth, 1850–1880," Missouri Historical Society Bulletin 28 (1972): 162–77; Charles N. Glaab, "Visions of Metropolis: William Gilpin and Theories of City Growth in the American West," *Wisconsin Magazine of History* 65 (1961): 21–31; Gilbert A. Stelter, "The City and Westward Expansion: A Western Case Study," *The Western Historical Quarterly* 4 (1973): 187–202; and Kenneth W. Wheeler, *To Wear A City's Crown: The Beginnings of Urban Growth in Texas* (Cambridge, 1968). See also the articles and books cited in Bradford Luckingham, "The City in Westward Movement: A Bibliographical Note," *The Western Historical Quarterly* 5 (1974): 295–306; and Bradford Luckingham, "The American West: An Urban Perspective," *Journal of Urban History* 8,1 (November, 1981): 99–106.

15. Several articles on boosterism can be found in Alan F.J. Artibise, *Town and City. Aspects of Western Canadian Urban Development* (Regina, 1981). They include: Artibise, "Boosterism and the Development of Prairie Cities, 1871–1913"; John Gilpin, "Failed Metropolis, The City of Strathcona, 1891–1912"; Max Foran, "The Making of a Booster: W.F. Orr and Nineteenth-Century Calgary"; L.H. Thomas, "Saskatoon, 1883–1920: The Formative Years"; B. Potyondi, "In Quest of Limited Urban Status: The Town-Building Process in Minnedosa, 1870–1904"; and Paul Voisey, "Boosting the Small Prairie Town, 1904–1931; An Example from Southern Alberta." Other articles that deal with aspects of boosterism include Robert A.J. McDonald, "City Building in the Canadian West: A Case Study of Economic Growth in Early Vancouver, 1886–1893," *BC Studies* 43 (1979): 3–28; J.M.S. Careless, "The Business Community in the Early Development of Victoria, B.C." in *Canadian Business History*, ed. D.S. Macmillan (Toronto, 1972), 104–23; A.B. Kilpatrick, "A Lesson in Boosterism: The Contest for the Alberta Provincial

Capital, 1904–1906," *Urban History Review* VIII, 3 (February, 1980): 47–190; and J.C. Weaver, "Elitism and the Corporate Ideal: Businessmen and Boosters in Canadian Civic Reform, 1890–1920," in *Cities in the West*, ed. A.R. McCormack and I. MacPherson (Ottawa, 1975), 48–73.

16. The best studies to date deal with one region—the American South—in a particular time period, while the other is a historiographical review of existing literature. See Blaine A. Brownell, *The Urban Ethos in the South, 1920–1930* (Baton Rouge, 1975), and Elizabeth Bloomfield, "Community, Ethos and Local Initiative in Urban Economic Growth: Review of a Theme in Canadian Urban History," *Urban History Yearbook* (forthcoming).

17. Alan F.J. Artibise, "City Building in the Canadian West: From Boosterism to Corporatism," *Journal of Canadian Studies* 17, 3 (Fall 1982): 35–44.

18. Bloomfield, "Community, Ethos and Local Initiative," 1.

19. Jon C. Teaford, "The Evolution of Municipal Autonomy in the United States" and John H. Taylor, "The Evolution and Decline of Canadian Urban Autonomy," (Papers presented at the Canadian–American Urban Development Conference, Guelph, August 1982).

20. For a review of this theme in the United States, see David C. Hammack, "Problems in the Historical Study of Power in the Cities and Towns of the United States, 1800–1960," *American Historical Review* 83, 2 (April 1978): 323–49. In Canada, see the material cited in Artibise, "City Building in the Canadian West."

21. In the U.S., see David R. Goldfield and Blaine A. Brownell, *Urban America: From Downtown to No Town* (Boston, 1979), chap.12. In Canada, see L. Gertler and R. Crowley, *Changing Canadian Cities* (Toronto, 1967).

22. Goldfield and Brownell, *Urban America*, 333–34.

23. These terms are used in both Canada and the United States, but especially in Canada. See, for example, J.M.S. Careless, "Metropolis and Region: The Interplay Between City and Region in Canadian History," *Urban History Review*, no. 3–78 (February 1979), 99–112; L.D. McCann, "The Myth of the Metropolis: The Role of the City in Canadian Regionalism," *Urban History Review* IX, 3 (February 1981): 52–58; and McCann, ed., *Heartland and Hinterland: A Geography of Canada* (Scarborough, 1982).

24. Taylor, "Canadian Urban Autonomy."

25. A discussion of one aspect of corporatism is David A. Heenan, "The Search for Regional Headquarters Cities: A Comparative View," *Urbanism Past and Present* 7, 2 (1982): 17–72.

26. The process of regional succession is discussed in a variety of sources. For examples, see Gertler and Crowley, *Changing Canadian Cities*; P.J. Smith, "Alberta Since 1945: The Maturing Settlement System," in *Hinterland and Heartland: A Geography of Canada*, ed. L.D. McCann (Scarborough, 1982), 295–337; James Simmons, "The Evolution of the Canadian Urban System," in *The Usable Urban Past: Planning and Politics in the Modern Canadian City*, ed. Alan F.J. Artibise and Gilbert A. Stelter (Toronto, 1979), 9–34; Beverly Duncan and Stanley Lieberson, *Metropolis and Region in Transition* (Beverly Hills, 1970); Carl Abbott, "The American Sunbelt: Idea and Region," *Journal of the West* 18, 3 (July 1979): 5–18; and George Sternlieb and James W. Hughes, "New Regional and Metropolitan Realities of America," *Journal of the American Institute of Planners* 43, 3 (July 1977): 227–40.

27. Louis Wirth, "Urbanism as a Way of Life," *American Journal of Sociology* 44 (1938): 1–24.

28. Lawrence H. Larsen, *The Urban West at the End of the Frontier* (Lawrence, 1978), 19.
29. Luckingham, "The City in Westward Movement," 297–98.
30. Ibid., 302; Gunter Barth, "Metropolitanism and Urban Élites in the Far West: San Francisco and Denver," in *The Age of Industrialism in America: Essays in Social Structure and Cultural Values,* ed. F.C. Faber (New York, 1968), 158–87; and Barth, *Instant Cities: Urbanization and the Rise of San Francisco and Denver* (New York, 1975). See also Lawrence H. Larsen and Robert L. Branyan, "The Development of an Urban Civilization on the Frontier of the American West," *Societas* 1 (1971): 33–50.
31. J.M.S. Careless, "Aspects of Urban Life in the West, 1870–1914," in *The Canadian City: Essays in Urban History,* ed. Gilbert A. Stelter and Alan F.J. Artibise (Toronto, 1977), 125–41.
32. J.M.S. Careless, "Metropolis and Region: The Interplay Between City and Region in Canadian History Before 1914," *Urban History Review,* no. 3–78 (February, 1979), 99–118.
33. *Agricultural History* 25 (1951): 97–104.
34. See, for example, Brian J.C. Berry and John D. Kasarda, *Contemporary Urban Ecology* (New York, 1977), 377.
35. Breton, "Regionalism in Canada."
36. David R. Galdfield, "The Urban South: A Regional Framework," *American Historical Review* 86, 5 (1981): 1009–1034.
37. Robert M. Fogelson, *The Fragmented Metropolis: Los Angeles, 1850–1930* (Cambridge, 1967).
38. Deryck W. Holdsworth, "House and Home in Vancouver: Images of West Coast Urbanism, 1886–1929," in *The Canadian City,* ed. Stelter and Artibise, 186–211; and Holdsworth, "Regional Distinctiveness in an Industrial Age: Some California Influences on British Columbia Housing," *The American Review of Canadian Studies* XII, 2 (1982): 64–81. See also Barry Gough, "Canadian and American Frontiers: Some Comments, Comparisons and a Case Study (British Columbia and California)," in *The Bellingham Collection of Geographical Studies,* ed. M.C. Brown and Graeme Wynn, B.C. Geographical Series, no. 27 (Vancouver, 1979), 7–18. A good comparative study of population characteristics is Norbert Macdonald, "Population Growth and Change in Seattle and Vancouver, 1880–1960," *Pacific Historical Review* 39 (August 1970): 297–321.
39. Recent reviews of John S. Reps, *Cities of the American West: A History of Frontier Urban Planning* (Princeton, 1979) have recognized this complexity. Howard Rabinowitz has stated that "we will never get at the real nature of western urbanization if we simply look at western cities as imitations of the large eastern and midwestern cities whose development continues to shape the way we look at American urban history." See "Reps on the Range: An Anti-Turnerian Framework for the Urban West," *Journal of Urban History* 8, 1 (November 1981): 91–97. And Pierce Lewis notes that Reps' comparisons of eastern and western cities—that they differed little—will "cause discomfort" to historians. See "The Urban Idea on America's Western Frontier," *Journal of Historical Geography* 7, 1 (1981): 95–100.
40. Joel Garreau, *The Nine Nations of North America* (Boston, 1981), 245–86.
41. Harold L. Platt, "Houston at the Crossroads: The Emergence of the Urban Center of the Southwest," *Journal of the West* XVIII, 3 (July 1979): 51–61.
42. Peter J. Smith and Denis B. Johnson, *The Edmonton–Calgary Corridor* (Edmonton, 1978); and Smith, "Alberta Since 1945: The Maturing Settlement

System," in *Heartland and Hinterland*, ed. McCann, 295–337.

43. See, for example, W.L. Easterbrook and M.H. Watkins, "Introduction," in *Approaches to Canadian Economic History* (Toronto, 1967), XIV; and James W. Simmons, "The Impact of the Public Sector on the Canadian Urban System," in *Power and Place*, ed. Stelter and Artibise.

44. John Richards and Larry Pratt, *Prairie Capitalism: Power and Influence in the New West* (Toronto, 1979).

45. John Mercer and Michael A. Goldberg, "Value Differences and Their Meaning for Urban Development in Canada and the U.S.A.," in *Power and Place*, ed. Stelter and Artibise.

46. See, for example, Goldfield and Brownell, *Urban America*, who wrote that "beginning with the New Deal, the neglect of local affairs by Washington officials and agencies ended forever. Since that time, the ties between federal and local governments have been extensive" (p. 366). It should be noted, however, that dating this "new" relationship from 1933 is questionable. See Daniel Elazar, "Urban Problems and the Federal Government: A Historical Inquiry," *Political Science Quarterly* LXXXII (1969): 505–25. Elazar argues that while "recent federal responses to urban problems have been of unprecedented scope and magnitude ... there is considerable evidence that they are not unprecedented in their roots and may not even be unprecedented in their impact."

47. Gerald D. Nash, *The American West in the Twentieth Century: A Short History of an Urban Oasis* (Englewood Cliffs, 1973).

48. Elazar, "Urban Problems and the Federal Government," and Mark Gelfand, *A Nation of Cities: The Federal Government and Urban America, 1933–1965* (New York, 1975).

49. See, for example, Simmons, "The Impact of the Public Sector on the Canadian Urban System"; Gertler and Crowley, *Changing Canadian Cities*; Mercer and Goldberg, "Urban Development in Canada and the U.S.A."; David G. Bettison, *The Politics of Canadian Urban Development* (Edmonton, 1975); and David G. Bettison, John K. Kenward, and Carrie Taylor, *Urban Affairs in Alberta* (Edmonton, 1975).

50. These arguments are developed in terms of "urban culture" by Mercer and Goldberg, "Urban Development in Canada and the U.S.A."

51. Ibid. See also the analysis of federalism and regionalism in Canada and the United States in Roger Gibbins, *Regionalism: Territorial Politics in Canada and the United States* (Toronto, 1982).

52. Elazar, "Urban Problems and the Federal Government."

53. Robert W. Lotchin, "The City and the Sword in Metropolitan California, 1919–1941," *Urbanism Past and Present* 7 (Summer/Fall, 1982): 1–16; and Carl Abbott, "Portland in the Pacific War: Planning from 1940 to 1945," *Urbanism Past and Present* 6 (Winter/Spring, 1981): 12–24.

54. Lionel D. Feldman and Katharine A. Graham, "Intergovernmental Relations and Urban Growth: A Canadian View," *Local Government Studies* 5, 1 (1979): 69–84.

55. Elliott J. Feldman and Jerome Milch, "Coordination or Control? The Life and Death of the Ministry of State for Urban Affairs," in *Politics and Government of Urban Canada*, 4th ed., ed. L.D. Feldman (Toronto, 1981), 246–64.

56. See, for example, J. David Hulchanski, "The Origin of Land Use Planning in Alberta, 1900–1945," Research Paper no. 119, Centre for Urban and Community Studies, University of Toronto (1981); Don Davis, *Advanced Land Acquisition by Local Government: The Saskatoon Experience* (Saskatoon, 1972); and Mercer and Goldberg, "Urban Development in Canada and the U.S.A."

57. For one discussion, see Eric Hanson, "The Future of Western Canada: Economic, Social, Political," *Canadian Public Administration* 18, 1 (1975): 104–20.
58. See Richards and Pratt, *Prairie Capitalism*, 174; and Sternlieb and Hughes, "New Regional and Metropolitan Realities of America."
59. Platt, "Houston at the Crossroads."
60. David G. McComb, *Houston: The Bayon City* (Austin, 1969), especially chapter 6. McComb notes that in the early 1930s Houston received federal loans and grants totalling $3 878 162, leading the state, with Fort Worth second at $1 148 977.
61. Smith, "Alberta Scince 1945." See also B.M. Barr, ed., *Calgary: Metropolitan Structure and Influence* (Victoria, 1975); and P.J. Smith, ed., *Edmonton: The Emerging Metropolitan Pattern* (Victoria, 1978).
62. McComb, *Houston*; and Max Foran, *Calgary: An Illustrated History* (Toronto, 1979).
63. See, for example, R.W. Wright, "Free Enterprise in Alberta," Discussion Paper no. 78, Department of Economics, University of Calgary (1982); and J.D. House, *The Last of the Free Enterprisers: The Oilmen of Calgary* (Toronto, 1980). House refers to Calgary as the "Houston of the North."
64. Several of the papers presented at the conference were published in *Urbanization in the Americas: The Background in Comparative Perspective*, ed. Woodrow Borah, Jorge Hardoy, and Gilbert A. Stelter (Ottawa, 1980).
65. Bruce Stave, "A Conversation with H.J. Dyos: Urban History in Great Britain," *Journal of Urban History* 5, 4 (August 1979): 469–500.

# FURTHER READING

## Bibliographies

Most of the books and articles listed here were published during the 1980s. For earlier work, see the book-length bibliography, Alan F.J. Artibise and Gilbert A. Stelter, *Canada's Urban Past* (Vancouver: University of British Columbia Press, 1981), which is organized by regions and individual cities.

Annual updates during the 1980s can be found in the *Urban History Review*, the major Canadian publication in the field of urban history. Also useful are the annual bibliographies in the *Canadian Historical Review* and in regionally oriented periodicals such as *Acadiensis*, *Revue d'histoire de l'Amérique française*, and *B.C. Studies*.

Canadian materials are also regularly listed in several international urban history publications. These include the British *Urban History Yearbook* and the American *Urban History Newsletter*, which are described in more detail below.

## Journals and Newsletters

The three major journals in the field were all begun during a tremendous burst of interest in urban history in the early 1970s.

The *Urban History Review*, currently published by the City of Toronto Archives for the Canadian Urban History Association, is edited by John Weaver. It specializes in Canadian articles and book reviews of a more general character. It also acts as a newsletter, announcing conferences, major publications, and current research projects.

The *Urban History Yearbook*, published by Leicester University Press in Great Britain, was founded by the legendary H.J. Dyos, the intellectual pioneer of modern urban history; it is now edited by Richard Rodger. Its articles, reviews, and bibliographies are international in scope.

The *Journal of Urban History*, published by Gage in the United States, also is international in coverage. It has been edited for many years by Blaine Brownell; David Goldfield is the new editor. In addition to articles, this journal specializes in major review essays and includes an interview with an urban historian on a regular basis.

Two newsletters founded recently reflect a resurgence of interest and activity in the field. These provide up-to-date information on conferences, research, and recent publications. Canadian information is usually included. Unfortunately, both newsletters have the same name which may be confusing.

The *Urban History Newsletter* from the United States is published for the newly formed American Urban History Association. Its annual bibliography contains a Canadian section provided by Mark Cortiula of the University of Guelph.

The *Urban History Newsletter* from Great Britain is sponsored by the Centre for Urban History. Its editor, Peter Clark, provides especially good coverage of international conferences.

## The Study of Urban History

### *International*

Kathleen Neils Conzen, "Community Studies, Urban History, and American Local History," in *The Past Before Us*, ed. Michael Kammen (Ithaca: Cornell University Press, 1980).

H.J. Dyos, "Urbanity and Suburbanity," in *Exploring the Urban Past, Essays in Urban History by H.J. Dyos,* ed. David Cannadine and David Reeder (Cambridge: Cambridge University Press, 1982).

Michael Ebner, "Urban History: Retrospect and Prospect," *Journal of American History* 68 (June 1981): 69–84.

Howard Gillette, and Zane Miller, eds., *American Urbanism: A Historiographical Review* (New York: Greenwood Press, 1987).

Seymour Mendelbaum, "Thinking about Cities as Systems: Reflections on the History of an Idea," *Journal of Urban History* 11 (1985): 139–50.

Raymond A. Mohl, "New Perspectives on American Urban History," in *The Making of Urban America,* ed. Mohl (Wilmington, Delaware: Scholarly Resources Imprint, 1988).

Dennis Smith, "In Pursuit of the Urban Variable," *Journal of Urban History* 14 (May 1988): 399–405.

Bruce Stave, "A Conversation with Sam Bass Warner, Jr.: Ten Years Later," *Journal of Urban History* 11 (November 1984): 83–113.

Paul Wheatley, "European Urbanization: Origins and Consummation," *Journal of Interdisciplinary History* 17 (1986): 415–30.

### *Canada*

Alan F.J. Artibise, and Paul-André Linteau, *Evolution of Urban Canada: An Analysis of Approaches and Interpretations* Report No. 4 (Winnipeg: Institute of Urban Studies, 1984).

Donald Davis, " 'The Metropolitan Thesis' and the Writing of Canadian Urban History," *Urban History Review* 14 (October 1985): 95–113.

Chad Gaffield, "Social Structure and the Urbanization Process: Perspectives on Nineteenth Century Research," in *The Canadian City: Essays in Urban and Social History*, ed. Gilbert A. Stelter and Alan F.J. Artibise (Ottawa: Carleton University Press, 1984), 262–81.

Gilbert A. Stelter, "A Regional Framework for Urban History, *Urban History Review* 13 (February, 1985): 193–206.

Gilbert A. Stelter, "A Sense of Time and Place: The Historian's Approach to Canada's Urban Past," in *Contemporary Approaches to Canadian History*, ed. Carl Berger (Toronto: Copp Clark Pitman, 1987), 165–80.

Gilbert A. Stelter, "Urban History," in *A Reader's Guide to Canadian History* 2, ed. J.L. Granatstein and Paul Stevens (Toronto: University of Toronto Press, 1982): 96–113.

## General Trends in Urban Development

### *International*

Paul Bairoch, *Cities and Economic Development, From the Dawn of History to the Present* (Chicago: University of Chicago Press, 1988).

Brian J.L. Berry, *Comparative Urbanization: Divergent Paths in the Twentieth Century* (New York: St. Martin's Press, 1981).

Woodrow Borah, Jorge Hardoy, and Gilbert Stelter, eds., *Urbanization in the Americas: The Background in Historical Perspective* (Ottawa: National Museum of Man, 1980).

Gordon Cherry, ed., *Cities and Plans: The Shaping of Urban Britain in the Nineteenth and Twentieth Centuries* (London: Edward Arnold, 1988).

Georges Duby, gen. ed., *Histoire de la France urbaine* (Paris: Seuil, 1980–85), 5 vols.

James Elliot, *The City in Maps: Urban Mapping to 1900* (London: The British Library, 1987).

Derek Fraser, and Anthony Sutcliffe, eds., *The Pursuit of Urban History* (London: Arnold, 1983).

David R. Goldfield, "The Urban South: A Regional Framework," *American Historical Review* 86 (December 1981): 1009–34.

David R. Goldfield, and Blaine Brownell, *Urban America: From Downtown to No Town* (Boston: Houghton Mifflin, 1979).

Alan Gowans, *The Comfortable House. North American Suburban Architecture, 1890–1930* (Cambridge, Mass.: MIT Press, 1986).

Mark Girouard, *Cities & People: A Social and Architectural History* (New Haven: Yale University Press, 1985).

Jorge E. Hardoy, ed., *Urbanization in Latin America: Approaches and Issues* (New York: Anchor Books, 1975).

Paul Hohenberg, and Lynn H. Lees. *The Making of Urban Europe, 1000–1950* (Cambridge, Mass.: Harvard University Press, 1985).

Kenneth T. Jackson, *Crabgrass Frontier: The Suburbanization of the United States* (New York: Oxford University Press, 1985).

Jane Jacobs, *Cities and the Wealth of Nations* (New York: Random House, 1984).
Josef W. Konvitz, *The Urban Millenium: The City-Building Process from the Early Middle Ages to the Present* (Carbondale, Ill: Southern Illinois University Press, 1985).
Kevin Lynch, *A Theory of Good City Form* (Cambridge, Mass.: MIT Press, 1981).
Blake McKelvey, *American Urbanization: A Comparative History* (Glenview, Illinois: Scott, Foresman and Company, 1973).
Zane L. Miller, *The Urbanization of Modern America: A Brief History* 2d ed. (San Diego: Harcourt Brace Jovanovich, 1987).
Eric Monkonen, *America Becomes Urban: The Development of U.S. Cities & Towns, 1780–1980* (Berkeley: University of California Press, 1988).
A.E.J. Morris, *History of Urban Form: Before the Industrial Revolutions* 2d ed. (Harlow, Eng.: Longman's Scientific and Technical, 1988).
R.J. Morris, ed., *Class, Power and Social Structure in British Nineteenth-Century Towns* (Leicester: Leicester University Press, 1986).
Richard Morse, " 'Peripheral' Cities as Cultural Arenas (Russia, Austria, Latin America)," *Journal of Urban History* 10 (August, 1984): 423–52.
Paul Oliver, *Dwellings: The House Across the World* (Austin: University of Texas Press, 1987).
Frans van Poppel, "Urban-rural Differences in Demographic Behaviour: The Netherlands, 1850–1960," *Journal of Urban History* 15 (August, 1989): 363–98.
S.K. Schultz, *Constructing Urban Culture: American Cities and City Planning, 1800–1920* (Philadelphia: Temple University Press, 1988).
Gilbert A. Stelter, "The Classical Ideal: Cultural and Urban Form in Eighteenth-Century Britain and America," *Journal of Urban History* 10 (August, 1984).
Anthony Sutcliffe, ed., *Metropolis, 1890–1940* (London: Mansell, 1984).
James E. Vance Jr., *This Scene of Man: The Role and Structure of the City in the Geography of Western Civilization* (New York: Harper's College Press, 1977).
Jan de Vries, *European Urbanization, 1500–1800* (Cambridge, Mass.: Harvard University Press, 1984).
M.A. Weiss, *The Rise of the Community Builders: The American Real Estate Industry and Urban Planning* (New York: Columbia University Press, 1987).

*Canada*

Christopher Armstrong, and H.V. Nelles, *Monopoly's Moment: The Organization and Regulation of Canadian Utilities, 1830–1930* (Philadelphia: Temple University Press, 1986).
Alan F.J. Artibise, "Canada as an Urban Nation," *Daedalus* 117 (Fall 1988): 237–64.

Alan F.J. Artibise, ed., *Town and City: Aspects of Western Canadian Urban Development* (Regina: Canadian Plains Research Center, 1981).
Alan F.J. Artibise, and Gilbert A. Stelter, eds., *The Usable Urban Past: Planning and Politics in the Modern Canadian City* (Toronto: Macmillan, 1979).
Norman R. Ball, ed., *Building Canada: A History of Public Works* (Toronto: University of Toronto Press, 1988).
J.M.S. Careless, *Frontier and Metropolis: Regions, Cities and Identities in Canada before 1914* (Toronto: University of Toronto Press, 1989).
Jon Caulfield, "Canadian Urban 'Reform' and Local Conditions: An Alternative to Harris's 'Reinterpretation'," *International Journal of Urban and Regional Research* 12 (September 1988): 477–84.
Frederic A. Dahms, *The Heart of the Country: From the Great Lakes to the Atlantic Coast—Rediscovering the Towns and Countryside of Canada* (Toronto: Deneau, 1988).
Stephen Davies, "Reckless Walking Must Be Discouraged: The Automobile Revolution and the Shaping of Modern Urban Canada to 1930," *Urban History Review* 18 (October 1989): 123–38.
Donald Davis, "Competition's Moment: The Jitney-Bus and Corporate Capitalism in the Canadian City, 1914–29," *Urban History Review* 18 (October 1989): 103–22.
Neil Field, "Migration Through the Rural-Urban Hierarchy: Canadian Patterns," *Canadian Journal of Regional Science* 11 (Spring 1988): 33–56.
Lorraine Gaboury, Yves Landry and Hubert Charbonneau, "Démographic différentielle en Nouvelle-France: villes et compagnes," *Revue d'histoire de l'Amérique française* 38 (Winter 1985): 357–78.
Michael A. Goldberg, and John Mercer, *The Myth of the North American City: Continentalism Challenged* (Vancouver: University of British Columbia Press, 1986).
Leonard O. Gertler, and Ronald W. Crowley, *Changing Canadian Cities: The Next 25 Years* (Toronto: McClelland and Stewart, 1977).
Robert F. Harney, "The Immigrant City," *Vice Versa*, no. 24 (June 1988): 4–6. (Part of a total issue on Canadian urban questions.)
Richard Harris, "The Interpretation of Canadian Urban Reform: A Reply to Caulfield," *International Journal of Urban and Regional Research* 12 (September 1988): 485–90.
Gerald Hodge, *Planning Canadian Communities* (Toronto: Methuen, 1986).
Gerald Hodge, and Mohammed Qadeer, *Towns and Villages in Canada: The Importance of Being Unimportant* (Toronto: Butterworths, 1983).
John N. Jackson, *The Canadian City: Space, Form, Quality* (Toronto: McGraw-Hill Ryerson, 1973).
André Lachance, *La vie urbaine en Nouvelle-France* (Montreal: Boréal Express, 1987).
David C. Lai, *Chinatowns: Towns within Cities in Canada* (Vancouver: University of British Columbia Press, 1988).

Joann Latremouille, *Pride of Home: The Working Class Housing Tradition in Nova Scotia, 1749–1949* (Hantsport, Nova Scotia: Lancelot, 1986).
Réjean Legault, "Architecture et forme urbaine: L'example du triplex à Montréal de 1870 à 1914," *Urban History Review* 18 (June 1989): 1–10.
Paul-André Linteau, "Urbanization—Planning and Management of Urban Space," *Forces,* no. 78 (Summer 1987), 49–52.
Warren Magnusson, and Andrew Sancton, eds., *City Politics in Canada* (Toronto: University of Toronto Press, 1983).
Greg Marquis, "The Contours of Canadian Urban Justice, 1830–1875," *Urban History Review* 15 (February 1987): 269–73.
L.D. McCann, ed., *Heartland and Hinterland: A Geography of Canada* (Scarborough, ON: Prentice-Hall, 1982).
L.D. McCann, ed. *People and Place: Studies of Small Town Life in the Maritimes* (Fredericton: Acadiensis Press, 1987).
Robert J. Morris, "The Reproduction of Labour and Capital: British and Canadian Cities during Industrialization," *Urban History Review* 18 (June 1989): 49–62.
George Nader, *Cities of Canada* 2 vols. (Toronto: Macmillan, 1975 and 1977).
Shane O'Dea, "The Built Environment and the Shaped Landscape," *Canadian Review of American Studies* 18, 1 (1987): 93–100.
Sherry Olson, "Paternalism and Urban Reform," *Urban History Review* 17 (February 1989): 143–47.
Robert Robson, *Canadian Single Industry Communities: A Literature Review and Annotated Bibliography* (Sackville, New Brunswick: Rural and Small Town Research and Studies Programme, Mount Allison University, 1986).
L.H. Russwurm, and C.R. Bryant, *The City's Countryside: Land and its Management in the Rural-Urban Fringe* (London: Longmans, 1984).
Gilbert A. Stelter, and Alan F.J. Artibise, eds., *The Canadian City: Essays in Urban and Social History* (Ottawa: Carleton University Press, 1984).
Gilbert A. Stelter, and Alan F.J. Artibise, eds., *Power and Place: Canadian Urban Development in the North American Context* (Vancouver: University of British Columbia Press, 1986).
Gilbert A. Stelter, and Alan F.J. Artibise, eds., *Shaping the Urban Landscape: Aspects of the Canadian City-Building Process* (Ottawa: Carleton University Press, 1982).
John C. Weaver, *Shaping the Canadian City: Essays on Urban Politics and Policy, 1890–1920* (Toronto: Institute of Public Administration of Canada, 1977).

## Selected Biographies of Canadian Cities

T.W. Acheson, *Saint John, The Making of a Colonial Urban Community* (Toronto: University of Toronto Press, 1985).

Frederick H. Armstrong, *A City in the Making: Progress, People & Perils in Victorian Toronto* (Toronto: Dundurn Press, 1988).

Frederick H. Armstrong, *The Forest City, An Illustrated History of London, Canada* (Windsor Publications, 1986).

Eric Arthur, *Toronto, No Mean City* 3d ed., revised by Stephen Otto (Toronto: University of Toronto Press, 1986).

Alan F.J. Artibise, *Winnipeg: An Illustrated History* (Toronto: Lorimer, 1977).

Douglas Baldwin, and Thomas Spira, *Gaslights, Epidemics and Vagabond Cows: Charlottetown in the Victorian Era* (Charlottetown: Ragweed Press, 1988).

Peter A. Baskerville, *Beyond the Island, An Illustrated History of Victoria* (Windsor Publications, 1986).

J. William Brennan, *Regina: An Illustrated History* (Toronto: Lorimer, 1989).

J.M.S. Careless, *Toronto to 1918: An Illustrated History* (Toronto: Lorimer, 1984).

André Charbonneau, Yvon Desloges, and Marc Lafrance, *Québec. The Fortified City: From the 17th to the 19th Century* (Ottawa: Parks Canada, 1982).

William Dendy, and William Kilbourn, *Toronto Observed: Its Architecture, Patrons and History* (Toronto: Oxford University Press, 1986).

John English, and Kenneth McLaughlin, *Kitchener: An Illustrated History* (Waterloo: Wilfrid Laurier University Press, 1983).

Max Foran, *Calgary: An Illustrated History* (Toronto: Lorimer, 1978).

John Gilpin, *Edmonton, Gateway to the North* (Windsor Publications, 1984).

Benjamin Higgins, *The Rise—and Fall? of Montreal* (Moncton Canadian Institute for Research on Regional Development, 1986).

James T. Lemon, *Toronto since 1918: An Illustrated History* (Toronto: Lorimer, 1985).

Paul-André Linteau, *The Promoters' City: Building the Industrial Town of Maisonneuve, 1883–1918* (Toronto: Lorimer, 1985).

Robert A.J. McDonald, and Jean Barman, eds., *Vancouver Past: Essays in Social History* (Vancouver: University of British Columbia Press, 1986).

Kenneth McLaughlin, *Cambridge, The Making of a Canadian City* (Windsor Publications, 1987).

Brian S. Osborne, and Donald Swainson, *Kingston, Building on the Past* (Westport, ON: Butternut Press, 1988).

Elizabeth Pacey, *Georgian Halifax* (Hantsport, Nova Scotia: Lancelot Press, 1987).

A.J.H. Richardson, Geneviève Bastien, Doris Dubé, and Marthe Lacombe, *Quebec City: Architects, Artisans, and Builders* (Ottawa: National Museum of Canada, 1984).

Patricia Roy, *Vancouver: An Illustrated History* (Toronto: Lorimer, 1980).

David T. Ruddell, *Québec City, 1765–1832: The Evolution of a Colonial Town* (Ottawa: Canadian Museum of Civilization, History Division, 1986).

Victor Russell, ed., *Forging a Consensus: Historical Essays on Toronto* (Toronto: University of Toronto Press, 1984).
W. Austin Squires, *History of Fredericton* (Fredericton: City of Fredericton, 1984).
Gilbert A. Stelter, ''Studying the Region,'' in *Guelph and Wellington County: A Bibliography of Settlement and Development since 1800* by
Elizabeth Bloomfield and Stelter (Guelph: Guelph Regional Project, University of Guelph, 1988), 1–13.
Nancy Tausky, and L.D. DiStefano, *Victorian Architecture in London and Southwestern Ontario* (Toronto: University of Toronto Press, 1986).
John H. Taylor, *Ottawa: An Illustrated History* (Toronto: Lorimer, 1985).
John Weaver, *Hamilton: An Illustrated History* (Toronto: Lorimer, 1982).
Brian Young, *In Its Corporate Capacity, The Seminary of Montreal as a Business Institution, 1816–76* (Montreal: McGill-Queen's University Press, 1986).

An honest attempt has been made to secure permission for all material used, and if there are errors or omissions, these are wholly unintentional and the publisher will be grateful to learn of them.

David B. Hanna, "Creation of an Early Victorian Suburb in Montreal," *Urban History Review* IX, 2 (October 1980): 38–64.

Peter G. Goheen, "Communications and Urban Systems in Mid-Nineteenth Century Canada," *Urban History Review* XIV, 3 (February 1986): 235–45. Reprinted with permission of the Canadian Urban History Association, City of Toronto Archives.

F.A. Dahms, "The Evolution of Settlement Systems: A Canadian Example, 1851–1970" *Journal of Urban History* 7, 2 (February 1981): 169–204; Paul-André Linteau, "Canadian Suburbanization in a North American Context—Does the Border Make a Difference?" *Journal of Urban History* 13, 3 (May 1987): 252–74.

Michael Doucet and John Weaver, "The North American Shelter Business, 1860–1920," *Business History Review* 58 (Summer 1984): 234–62. Copyright © 1984 by the President and Fellows of Harvard College. Reprinted by permission of Harvard Business School.

Bettina Bradbury, "The Family Economy and Work in an Industrializing City" CHA, *Historical Papers* (1979), 71–96. Reprinted by permission of the Canadian Historical Association and the author.

Robert R. Harney, "Ethnicity and Neighbourhoods" in *Gathering Place: Peoples and Neighbourhoods of Toronto, 1834–1945* (Toronto: Multicultural History Society of Ontario, 1985), 1–24. Reprinted with permission of the Multicultural History Society.

L.D. McCann, "The Mercantile–Industrial Transition in the Metals Towns of Pictou County 1857–1931," *Acadiensis* 10 (Spring 1981): 29–64. Reprinted with permission of *Acadiensis*.

Alan F.J. Artibise, "Exploring the North American West: A Comparative Urban Perspective," *American Review of Canadian Studies* 14, 1 (Spring 1984): 20–44. Reprinted with permission of *American Review of Canadian Studies*.

1 2 3 4 5 4764-6 94 93 92 91 90